Through the Rhythm

The Story of Zeds Dead

Tatyana Fang

ISBN: 9781779692726
Imprint: No Matter Which Way You Go
Copyright © 2024 Tatyana Fang.
All Rights Reserved.

Contents

1.1 A Musical Journey Begins

Ah, the sweet sound of music. It has the power to transport us to different worlds, evoke strong emotions, and bring people together like nothing else. And for the dynamic duo known as Zeds Dead, their musical journey began with a spark of passion and a shared love for creating beats that would make hearts race and bodies move.

In the vast sea of Toronto, on one fateful day, two young souls named Dylan Mamid and Zachary Rapp-Rovan crossed paths. Little did they know that this chance encounter would be the beginning of a musical partnership that would make waves in the electronic music scene.

Both Dylan and Zachary had been exposed to music from a young age, thanks to their musically-inclined families. They were raised on a steady diet of classic rock, jazz, reggae, and everything in between. The diverse range of genres and sounds left an indelible mark on their musical DNA, paving the way for the unique and eclectic style that Zeds Dead would eventually come to be known for.

As they grew older, their love for music only intensified. Dylan and Zachary found solace in the world of underground music, immersing themselves in the vibrant and diverse music scene of Toronto. They attended countless shows, taking in the pulsating beats and electric energy in the air, and dreaming of one day creating their own music that would move people in the same way.

The universe works in mysterious ways, and it was during this time that Dylan and Zachary discovered a new passion that would change their lives forever: DJing. Fascinated by the art of mixing and blending tracks seamlessly, they spent hours on end honing their skills, immersing themselves in the world of turntables, mixers, and vinyl records.

Their dedication and hard work paid off, as they began to secure gigs at local clubs and events, playing their unique blend of music that had already started to captivate audiences. The name "Zeds Dead" was born during this time, a symbol of their shared musical journey and the vibrancy of the Toronto music scene that had shaped them.

But it wasn't just DJing that consumed them; Dylan and Zachary also felt the urge to create their own music. They dabbled in production, pouring their hearts and souls into crafting tracks that would showcase their diverse range of influences and push the boundaries of electronic dance music.

Remixes became their playground for experimentation, as they twisted and turned popular tracks into their own sonic masterpieces. Their remix of Blue Foundation's "Eyes On Fire" became an instant hit, captivating listeners around the world and propelling Zeds Dead into the spotlight.

Toronto became their stomping ground, a city teeming with creative energy and a breeding ground for emerging talent. They embraced the city's vibrant music scene, drawing inspiration from fellow artists and collaborators who shared their vision and passion for pushing the boundaries of sound.

With each passing gig and release, Zeds Dead's fanbase grew exponentially, spreading their unique brand of music far and wide. They were hailed as pioneers of the "bass music" genre, combining elements of dubstep, hip-hop, reggae, and more to create a sound that was truly their own.

But it wasn't just about the music for Zeds Dead; it was about creating a complete sensory experience that would transport their fans to another dimension. They embraced visual art, partnering with talented designers and visual artists to create a visual aesthetic that was as captivating as their music. Their live performances became spectacles of lights, visuals, and energy, creating an immersive experience that left fans in awe.

As Zeds Dead gained international recognition, their artistic vision expanded. They saw music as a powerful tool to express emotions, address sociopolitical issues, and bring people together. Their lyrics became narratives, telling stories of love, loss, and the human condition. Through their music, they tapped into the collective consciousness, inviting listeners to feel and experience the world in a new way.

But with success came challenges. Zeds Dead faced their fair share of criticism and negativity, as they navigated the sometimes treacherous waters of the music industry. They stayed true to their creative integrity, never compromising their vision for commercial success. They balanced their rising fame with a dedication to their craft, constantly pushing themselves to evolve and innovate.

And now, as they look back on their musical journey, they can't help but feel gratitude. Gratitude for the fans who have supported them from day one, for the collaborations and friendships that have shaped their journey, and for the opportunity to leave a lasting legacy in the world of music.

The story of Zeds Dead is not just a tale of two musicians who found success, but a testament to the power of music to shape lives and bring people together. It is a reminder that no dream is too big, no beat is too small, and that the rhythmic journey of Zeds Dead is far from over.

So buckle up, dear reader, as we delve deeper into the world of Zeds Dead and uncover the stories behind the beats that have captivated audiences around the globe. Together, let's embrace the rhythm and embark on a musical journey like no other.

1.1 A Musical Journey Begins

As the morning sun began to cast its warm glow across the quiet streets of Toronto, the city came alive with the distant hum of traffic and the sound of birdsong. Among the hustle and bustle, two young souls were about to embark on a musical journey that would change their lives forever.

In this chapter, we delve into the origins of Zeds Dead, tracing their humble beginnings and the pivotal moments that led them to become one of the most influential electronic music acts of our time. From childhood influences to the birth of Zeds Dead, we will explore the early stages of their musical journey.

1.1.1 Introduction to Childhood Influences

Every musical odyssey has its own unique soundtrack, and the story of Zeds Dead is no exception. The seeds of their passion for music were sown in their formative years, when they were first introduced to the enchanting melodies and captivating rhythms that would shape their musical taste.

Growing up, Dylan Mamid and Zachary Rapp-Rovan were surrounded by a diverse range of musical influences. From classic rock records spinning on their parents' turntable to the electrifying beats of hip-hop blaring from the car stereo, music was an ever-present force in their lives.

Their early exposure to a vast array of musical genres provided the foundation for their eclectic taste and would later shape the unique sound that would come to define Zeds Dead. The exploration of different musical styles and the appreciation for various art forms set them on a path of musical discovery.

1.1.2 Discovering a Passion for Music

While their musical journey began separately, fate would bring Dylan and Zach together in a twist of destiny. They both shared a deep passion for music and a burning desire to create something that would resonate with others.

From an early age, Dylan showed a natural aptitude for playing instruments. Whether it was strumming the guitar, pounding on the drums, or tinkering with the piano, he was constantly seeking avenues to express himself musically. His innate talent and curiosity led him down a path of exploring different musical styles and techniques.

Zach, on the other hand, found solace and inspiration in electronic music. The pulsating beats, innovative soundscapes, and hypnotic melodies captured his imagination and ignited a fire within him. He immersed himself in the world of electronic dance music, absorbing its energy and discovering its endless possibilities.

1.1.3 Learning the Art of DJing

As Dylan and Zach's paths converged, their shared passion for music became the catalyst for their collaboration. They were eager to not only create music but also share it with others. They were determined to master the art of DJing, a skill they believed would allow them to connect with audiences on a deeper level.

Together, they delved into the world of DJing, honing their craft behind the turntables. They studied the technical aspects of blending tracks seamlessly, reading the crowd, and curating a set that would take the listeners on a sonic journey.

Through countless hours of practice, experimentation, and learning from their musical peers, Dylan and Zach began to develop their own unique DJ style. Armed with a diverse musical palette and a keen sense of rhythm, they started to captivate audiences with their skillful mixing and their ability to create an atmosphere that was both electrifying and soul-stirring.

1.1.4 Forming Early Musical Collaborations

As their DJing skills flourished, Dylan and Zach yearned to push the boundaries of their creativity even further. They sought out fellow musicians and artists who shared their passion for music and embarked on collaborative projects that would shape their musical journey.

Drawing inspiration from their diverse influences, Dylan and Zach started to experiment with merging different genres and styles, blending the raw energy of rock with the infectious beats of hip-hop and the mind-bending soundscapes of electronic music. These musical collaborations allowed them to explore new sonic territories, paving the way for the birth of Zeds Dead.

1.1.5 The Birth of Zeds Dead

In a serendipitous moment, Dylan and Zach came together to form a duo that would become synonymous with innovation and boundary-pushing in the electronic music scene – Zeds Dead. The name itself, a combination of Dylan's nickname "Zed" and Zach's love for the Grateful Dead, symbolized their shared vision and their desire to create music that defied conventions.

With their newfound musical partnership, Dylan and Zach began producing tracks that showcased their unique blend of genres and their willingness to experiment with different sounds. Their music soon caught the attention of electronic music enthusiasts and industry insiders, propelling Zeds Dead into the spotlight.

1.1.6 Early Gigs and The Growing Fanbase

Armed with their distinctive sound and a fervent desire to share their music with the world, Zeds Dead embarked on a whirlwind of performances at small venues, underground parties, and local music festivals. Their electrifying sets, characterized by a seamless fusion of genres, captivated audiences and left them hungry for more.

As news of their energetic and genre-defying performances spread, so did their fanbase. People from all walks of life were drawn to their music, finding solace and inspiration in the powerful emotions their tracks evoked. Zeds Dead had tapped into a collective consciousness, creating a sonic experience that transcended language, culture, and borders.

1.1.7 Pushing Boundaries with Remixes

As Zeds Dead's reputation as tastemakers and musical innovators grew, they began to explore the art of remixing. With their remixes, they breathed new life into existing tracks, infusing them with their signature sound and taking them to uncharted musical territories.

Their remixes became highly sought after and were celebrated for their ability to transform a song while retaining its essence. Whether it was reimagining a hip-hop anthem or injecting their unique brand of energy into a rock classic, Zeds Dead's remixes pushed the boundaries of what was possible in electronic music.

1.1.8 The Influence of Toronto's Music Scene

Being based in Toronto had a profound influence on Zeds Dead's musical journey. The city's vibrant and diverse music scene provided a rich tapestry of inspiration, pushing them to constantly evolve and innovate.

Toronto's underground music community embraced Zeds Dead's unique sound, providing a nurturing environment for their creativity to flourish. The city's multiculturalism and openness to new ideas lent itself to the duo's cross-genre experimentation, allowing them to carve out a niche for themselves in the electronic music landscape.

1.1.9 Embracing Electronic Dance Music

While Zeds Dead drew inspiration from a wide range of musical genres, electronic dance music (EDM) remained at the core of their musical expression. EDM's ability to create a visceral connection with the audience, its unrelenting energy, and its capacity to transport listeners to a different realm resonated deeply with Dylan and Zach.

Embracing the pillars of EDM, Zeds Dead integrated elements of house, trance, dubstep, and drum and bass into their sound. Their tracks pulsated with infectious rhythm, sweeping melodies, and bass lines that reverberated through every fiber of your being. They were unapologetically pushing the boundaries of electronic music and ushering in a new era of sonic exploration.

The introduction of EDM to their repertoire opened up a world of possibilities for Zeds Dead, allowing them to craft anthems that united fans on dancefloors across the globe. Their love for EDM became the driving force behind their desire to create music that transcended the boundaries of genre and captivated the hearts of listeners worldwide.

Summary

And so, the musical journey of Zeds Dead began, charting a course that would navigate through uncharted musical waters, break boundaries, and leave an indelible mark on the world of electronic music. Their unique sound, forged through a lifelong passion for music and a desire to push the limits of artistic expression, would continue to evolve and captivate audiences.

In the next chapters, we will explore Zeds Dead's evolution as artists, the impact of their music, and their vision for the future. Join us as we take a deep dive into the rhythm, uncover the beats, and discover the captivating story of Zeds Dead.

Discovering a Passion for Music

Finding one's passion for music is often a transformative and life-altering experience. For the members of Zeds Dead, this journey began with a deep connection to the power of melody and rhythm.

Music has a unique ability to evoke emotions, tell stories, and create a sense of unity among listeners. It transcends language barriers and allows individuals to express themselves in ways that words alone cannot. This universal language is what initially drew members of Zeds Dead towards the world of sound and melody.

As youngsters, they found solace and inspiration in the music that surrounded them. Whether it was the catchy pop tunes on the radio or the soulful melodies of their parents' old vinyl records, music became an integral part of their lives.

It was during their childhood that each individual member of the band discovered their own unique connections to music. Some were drawn to the catchy beats that made them want to dance, while others found joy in the poetic and storytelling nature of lyrics. These early encounters with music sparked a flame within them, igniting a passion that would drive them to pursue their dreams.

As the members of Zeds Dead grew older, their musical interests expanded beyond simply being listeners. They began to explore different genres and styles, immersing themselves in the intricacies of the art form. This exploration allowed them to discover their individual musical tastes and develop a deeper understanding of the nuances of sound.

At this point, their fascination with music evolved into a desire to not only consume but also create. They delved into the world of production, learning about the technical aspects of music-making, such as composing melodies, arranging beats, and mixing audio. The process of creating music became a form of self-expression, allowing them to channel their emotions and experiences into a tangible form.

This newfound passion propelled the members of Zeds Dead to immerse themselves in the art of DJing. They spent countless hours honing their skills, studying the techniques of renowned DJs, and experimenting with mixing different genres. Through trial and error, they developed their own unique style, embracing the power of their individual tastes and influences.

Collaboration played a crucial role in their journey as musicians. By working alongside other like-minded artists, they were able to expand their musical horizons and push the boundaries of their creativity. This collaborative spirit not only enriched their own music but also helped foster a sense of community within the industry.

As their musical talents grew, so did their fan base. Their early gigs were met with an enthusiastic response, and word quickly spread about their captivating performances. The energy and passion they poured into their live shows were infectious, leaving audiences craving more.

The birth of Zeds Dead marked the beginning of a new chapter in their musical journey. With their unique blend of electronic, hip-hop, and dubstep influences, they were able to carve out a distinct sound that captivated listeners around the world. Their remixes of popular songs started gaining traction, further solidifying their place in the music scene.

Through their music, Zeds Dead became an integral part of the Toronto music scene. They embraced the city's vibrant and diverse culture, allowing it to shape their artistic vision. The influence of Toronto's music scene can be heard in their work, as they incorporate elements from various genres and styles into their distinctive sound.

Their passion for electronic dance music grew with each passing year. They embraced the evolving trends within the genre, pushing boundaries and experimenting with new sounds and techniques. This willingness to explore and innovate became a hallmark of their musical journey.

As Zeds Dead's fanbase continued to expand, so did their international recognition. They embarked on world tours, captivating audiences with their electrifying live performances. Their ability to create a dynamic and immersive concert atmosphere quickly became a trademark of their shows.

Throughout their artistic evolution, Zeds Dead remained true to their roots. They struck a delicate balance between staying authentic to their sound and pushing the boundaries of their creativity. This commitment to maintaining their artistic integrity has resonated with their fans, establishing a strong and loyal community around their music.

The discovery of a passion for music is a deeply personal journey. It is a process of self-discovery, growth, and exploration. For the members of Zeds Dead, this journey of finding their passion for music became the driving force behind their artistic evolution and the foundation of their enduring legacy.

Learning the Art of DJing

Learning the art of DJing is like embarking on a journey through a musical landscape, one that requires a deep understanding of rhythm, intuition, and the ability to connect with a crowd. In this section, we will explore the key elements of DJing, from the basic techniques to mastering the art of reading a crowd and creating seamless transitions between tracks.

The Foundations of DJing

At its core, DJing is about blending different tracks together to create a continuous flow of music that keeps the energy flowing on the dancefloor. To achieve this, there are several fundamental skills that every aspiring DJ must master:

- Beatmatching: This is the art of syncing the beats of two tracks to create a seamless transition. It involves listening carefully to the rhythm and adjusting the tempo and pitch to match the beats of the two songs. Beatmatching is the foundation of a smooth mix and requires a keen ear for timing.

+ Mixing: Once the beats are matched, the DJ must transition smoothly from one track to another. This involves using the faders and EQ (equalization) controls to create a seamless blend between the two songs. A good mix not only maintains the energy on the dancefloor but also adds a creative touch to the DJ's performance.

+ Song selection: Choosing the right songs for a set is crucial. A DJ must have a deep knowledge of various genres, as well as an understanding of crowd dynamics. Reading the audience and selecting tracks that resonate with them is key to creating an immersive musical experience.

+ Performance skills: DJing is not just about technical skills; it's also about showmanship. A DJ must engage with the crowd, build anticipation, and create a memorable experience. This can be accomplished through stage presence, crowd interaction, and creative transitions.

Mastering the Craft

Becoming a skilled DJ requires practice, dedication, and a genuine love for the art form. Here are some tips and tricks to help you master the craft:

+ Practice regularly: Like any skill, DJing requires consistent practice. Set aside dedicated time to hone your beatmatching and mixing skills. Experiment with different techniques and challenge yourself to try new things.

+ Learn from the masters: Study the work of established DJs and listen to their mixes. Pay attention to their song selection, transitions, and overall flow. Take inspiration from their style but also strive to develop your unique sound.

+ Understand music theory: While DJing is more about practical skills, having a basic understanding of music theory can enhance your performance. Knowing about chord progressions, scales, and harmonies can help you identify compatible tracks and create harmonic blends in your mixes.

+ Embrace technology: DJing has evolved significantly with the advancements in technology. Embrace digital platforms and software, such as Serato or Traktor, which offer powerful tools for beatmatching and track organization. However, it's essential to strike a balance between embracing technology and staying true to the craft.

+ Experiment and take risks: DJing is an art form that allows for creative expression. Don't be afraid to experiment with different genres, tempos, and styles. Taking risks can lead to unique and memorable performances.

Challenges and Solutions

DJing comes with its share of challenges. Here are some common hurdles and suggestions for overcoming them:

+ Building a music collection: Building a diverse and high-quality music collection takes time and effort. Explore different music platforms, record stores, and online communities to discover new tracks. Network with other DJs and music enthusiasts to exchange recommendations.

+ Handling equipment and technical issues: DJ equipment can be complex, and technical issues are bound to arise. Familiarize yourself with your gear and practice troubleshooting common problems. Develop a backup plan in case of equipment failure during a live performance.

+ Dealing with performance anxiety: Performing in front of a live audience can be nerve-wracking, especially for beginner DJs. Keep in mind that mistakes happen, and the most important thing is to keep the energy flowing and the crowd engaged. Prepare well before a gig, trust in your skills, and focus on enjoying the experience.

Unconventional Tip

One unconventional tip for DJs is to pay attention to the energy flow on the dancefloor. While technical skills are crucial, the ability to connect with the audience is equally important. Observe the crowd's response to different tracks and adapt your set accordingly. Don't be afraid to take risks and surprise the audience with unexpected song choices. Remember, creating a memorable experience is the ultimate goal.

In conclusion, learning the art of DJing requires a combination of technical skills, musical knowledge, and a deep connection with the crowd. It is a journey that demands dedication, practice, and a willingness to explore different genres and styles. By mastering the foundations, honing your craft, and embracing your unique style, you can embark on an exhilarating DJing career. So, let the beat drop and keep the dancefloor grooving!

Forming Early Musical Collaborations

When it comes to building a successful music career, collaboration is often the key to unlocking new opportunities and expanding one's creative horizons. For Zeds Dead, the journey towards becoming electronic music sensations was paved with meaningful and influential musical partnerships. In this section, we dive into the early days of Zeds Dead's career, exploring the formation of their first significant musical collaborations and the impact these collaborations had on their artistic growth and trajectory.

The Power of Collaboration

In the music industry, collaboration is not just about working with other artists to create a song; it is about combining different perspectives, ideas, and talents to produce something truly unique and innovative. Zeds Dead recognized early on the power of collaboration in their musical journey, and actively sought out opportunities to work with like-minded individuals who shared their passion for pushing the boundaries of electronic dance music.

Finding Kindred Spirits

As Zeds Dead began to establish themselves in the music scene, they quickly gravitated towards other artists who were also experimenting with new sounds and challenging the conventions of their respective genres. These early partnerships laid the foundation for the distinct sound that Zeds Dead would become known for.

One of their first notable collaborations was with Canadian producer Omar LinX. Together, Zeds Dead and Omar created the critically acclaimed EP "Victor," which seamlessly merged hip-hop and electronic elements, showcasing their ability to bridge the gap between genres. This collaboration not only helped to solidify Zeds Dead's unique sound but also opened doors to new audiences and opportunities for growth.

Crossing Musical Boundaries

Zeds Dead's commitment to exploring different genres and styles led them to collaborate with a wide range of artists, resulting in a diverse discography that defies easy categorization. Their collaboration with Twin Shadow on the track "Lost You" showcased their versatility as producers, fusing elements of indie rock and electronic music to create a captivating and emotionally charged song.

Additionally, Zeds Dead's partnership with DJ and producer Ganja White Night on the track "Samurai" demonstrated their willingness to blur the lines between dubstep and other electronic subgenres. By incorporating elements of reggae and hip-hop into their music, Zeds Dead transformed the typical dubstep sound into something fresh and dynamic.

Creative Synergy

Collaboration is not just about combining two artists' sounds—it's about creating something new and exciting, something that neither artist could have achieved on their own. This creative synergy was evident in Zeds Dead's collaboration with fellow electronic music duo Gorgon City on the track "Go Deep." By merging their distinct styles and production techniques, Zeds Dead and Gorgon City crafted a high-energy anthem that resonated with fans of both artists.

Impacts and Influences

The early musical collaborations of Zeds Dead played a crucial role in shaping their artistic journey and establishing their unique place in the electronic music landscape. Through these partnerships, they not only expanded their musical repertoire but also gained valuable insights and experiences that contributed to their growth as artists.

Furthermore, Zeds Dead's collaborations served as a source of inspiration for other aspiring musicians and producers. Their willingness to break down genre barriers and experiment with different styles opened up new possibilities and pushed the boundaries of electronic music. As a result, they have left an indelible mark on the industry and continue to influence a new generation of artists.

Forming Collaborations: A Lesson in Creativity

Forming successful musical collaborations requires more than just finding artists with similar interests. It involves building mutual trust, open communication, and a shared vision. Here are a few key lessons that aspiring musicians can learn from Zeds Dead's early experiences with collaborations:

- Be open and receptive to different perspectives: Collaboration provides an opportunity to learn from others and gain new insights into your own creative process. Embrace different ideas and styles, and be willing to step outside of your comfort zone.

- Cultivate genuine connections: Seek out artists who share your artistic goals and values. Building strong relationships with your collaborators will not only enhance the creative process but also create a supportive network within the industry.

- Embrace experimentation: Don't be afraid to take risks and explore uncharted territories. Collaboration allows for the blending of diverse styles and techniques, leading to the discovery of fresh and exciting sounds.

- Foster a collaborative environment: Create a space where all collaborators feel comfortable expressing their ideas and opinions. Encourage open dialogue and respect each other's contributions to the project.

- Trust the process: Collaboration can be challenging at times, with different visions and personalities coming into play. Trust in the process and have faith in the collective vision of the project.

By embracing collaboration early on in their careers, Zeds Dead set themselves on a trajectory towards success. These early musical partnerships not only shaped their unique sound but also provided valuable learning experiences that continue to influence their artistic growth. As they continue their musical journey, Zeds Dead's collaborations serve as a testament to the power of working together and the unlimited potential it holds for artists in the ever-evolving landscape of electronic music.

The Birth of Zeds Dead

In the pulsating heart of the underground music scene, where the beat of the city flows through the veins of its inhabitants, Zeds Dead was born. The collaborative brainchild of Dylan Mamid, also known as DC, and Zachary Rapp-Rovan, also known as Hooks, Zeds Dead emerged as a force to be reckoned with in the world of electronic dance music. With a unique fusion of genres and a passion for pushing boundaries, they quickly became pioneers of their own sound.

The journey began in the gritty and diverse city of Toronto, where Dylan and Zachary first crossed paths. With a shared love for underground music and a desire to create something new, they joined forces and embarked on a musical adventure that would change their lives forever.

1.2.5.1 Breaking free from the constraints of convention

The birth of Zeds Dead was not just the result of two friends coming together, but a rebellion against the status quo. Dylan and Zachary were not satisfied with the limitations of the music they were hearing and wanted to create something that pushed the boundaries and challenged the norm. They were determined to carve a unique path for themselves in the music industry.

1.2.5.2 The fusion of diverse influences

One of the defining characteristics of Zeds Dead's sound is their ability to seamlessly fuse together a wide range of musical influences. Drawing inspiration from their childhood favorites, such as hip-hop, reggae, and rock, they created a sonic landscape that defied categorization. By marrying these diverse elements with the emerging sounds of electronic dance music, Zeds Dead found a sweet spot that resonated with listeners from all walks of life.

1.2.5.3 The power of collaboration

Central to the birth of Zeds Dead was the spirit of collaboration. Dylan and Zachary understood the transformative power of working with other artists who shared their vision and passion. By collaborating with like-minded musicians, they were able to push the boundaries of their sound and create something truly unique. This collaborative ethos continues to define Zeds Dead's journey as they seek out new voices to add to their sonic tapestry.

1.2.5.4 The birth of a movement

As Zeds Dead began to gain momentum, their unique blend of genres and boundary-pushing sound started to resonate with fans around the world. Their infectious beats and electrifying performances ignited a movement, captivating a dedicated fanbase who could not get enough of their signature sound. The birth of Zeds Dead marked the beginning of a new era in electronic dance music, where innovation and authenticity reigned supreme.

1.2.5.5 The rise of Zeds Dead

With their ever-growing fanbase and explosive live performances, Zeds Dead quickly rose through the ranks of the electronic music scene. Their relentless work ethic and unwavering commitment to their craft allowed them to carve out a space of their own in an industry that often favors the mainstream. From the underground clubs of Toronto to headlining iconic music festivals, Zeds Dead's rise was meteoric, and their impact was undeniable.

1.2.5.6 The birth of the Zeds Dead universe

Beyond their music, Zeds Dead sought to build a universe that extended beyond the constraints of the studio and stage. They embraced visual art and stage design as integral components of their live performances, creating a multisensory experience for their fans. Through their music videos and album artwork, they invited audiences into a world where music and art converged, leaving an indelible mark on the cultural landscape.

The birth of Zeds Dead was the result of passion, rebellion, and a refusal to conform. Dylan and Zachary's vision to create something new and boundary-pushing has transformed the electronic music scene. This section explored the inception of Zeds Dead, their fusion of influences, the power of collaboration, the rise of a movement, and the birth of the Zeds Dead universe. Their journey was just beginning, and the world was about to experience the full force of their creative genius.

Early Gigs and The Growing Fanbase

In the early days of their musical journey, Zeds Dead started performing at small gigs and local venues, slowly building a dedicated fanbase. These early gigs played a crucial role in shaping their identity as artists and connecting with their audience on a personal level.

1. The Intimate Underground Scene: Zeds Dead initially became part of the underground music scene, playing at small clubs and intimate venues. These performances allowed them to interact closely with their fans, creating an electric energy and fostering a strong sense of community. The intimate setting also gave them the freedom to experiment and push the boundaries of their music.

2. Building a Local Following: As their reputation grew within the local music scene, Zeds Dead began attracting a growing number of fans who connected with their unique sound. Word-of-mouth spread, and their fanbase started to expand beyond their immediate circle. They embraced this support and engaged with their fans through social media, engaging in conversations, and sharing their experiences.

3. The Power of Live Performances: Zeds Dead's live performances were characterized by their vibrant energy and dynamic stage presence. They ensured that every show was an immersive experience, with carefully curated setlists that showcased their evolving sound. The crowd's response fueled their passion and inspired them to continually improve their live shows.

4. Gaining Recognition Through Remixes: In addition to their original tracks, Zeds Dead gained recognition through their remixes of popular songs. Their unique take on well-known tracks caught the attention of both fans and industry professionals, further solidifying their reputation as innovative artists. The remixes also allowed them to collaborate with established musicians, expanding their reach and introducing their sound to new audiences.

5. Connecting with Fans on a Personal Level: Zeds Dead took a genuine interest in their fans and made an effort to connect with them on a personal level. They interacted with their followers on social media, responded to messages, and made an effort to meet fans after their shows. This sense of accessibility and

authenticity fostered a strong and dedicated fanbase that supported them throughout their career.

6. Embracing The DIY Ethic: Throughout their journey, Zeds Dead embraced the Do-It-Yourself (DIY) ethic. They built their fanbase through grassroots efforts, leveraging social media and online platforms to share their music. This approach allowed them to maintain creative control and establish a direct connection with their audience, free from the influence of major record labels.

7. Spreading Their Sound Globally: As their fanbase grew, Zeds Dead began to receive offers to perform at bigger venues and festivals around the world. They used these opportunities to expose their unique sound to new audiences and immerse themselves in diverse music scenes. From North America to Europe, Australia to Asia, their captivating live performances and genre-blending tracks resonated with music lovers across the globe.

8. Cultivating a Sense of Community: Zeds Dead recognized the importance of building a sense of community within their fanbase. They organized meetups and fan gatherings, encouraging their supporters to connect with each other and share their love for the music. This sense of community extended beyond the music itself, creating lasting connections among fans.

9. Evolving Sound, Growing Fanbase: As Zeds Dead continued to evolve their sound, experimenting with new genres and collaborating with a variety of artists, their fanbase grew alongside them. Fans appreciated their willingness to take risks and explore different musical styles, and this adventurous spirit further cemented their place in the electronic music landscape.

Overall, the early gigs played a pivotal role in Zeds Dead's journey, allowing them to establish a strong fanbase, connect with their audience, and solidify their unique sound. These experiences laid the foundation for their future successes, while their commitment to their fans ensured a loyal following that continues to support them to this day.

Pushing Boundaries with Remixes

Remixes have long been a powerful tool in the world of music, allowing artists to reinterpret and reimagine existing songs. Zeds Dead is no stranger to this art form, and they have used remixes to push the boundaries of their sound and captivate their growing audience. In this section, we will explore how Zeds Dead leveraged remixes as a platform for creativity and experimentation, and how their remixes became a defining feature of their musical journey.

The Art of Remixing

Remixing a song is not just about adding a beat or changing the chorus. It requires a deep understanding of the original piece, an appreciation for its essence, and the ability to inject your unique style and creativity into the mix. Zeds Dead understood this art form and approached every remix as an opportunity to showcase their musical prowess.

Reimagining Genres

One of the defining characteristics of Zeds Dead's remixes is their ability to seamlessly blend different genres. They were not constrained by the boundaries of a single genre, and instead, they drew inspiration from various musical styles to create something truly unique. Whether it was infusing elements of dubstep, hip-hop, reggae, or even classical music, Zeds Dead blurred the lines between genres, creating remixes that appealed to a wide range of listeners.

Pushing the Limits

Zeds Dead's remixes were not just about adding their signature sound to existing tracks; they often pushed the limits of what was considered acceptable in the music industry. They took risks and experimented with unconventional ideas, challenging the established norms. By doing so, they carved out a niche for themselves and garnered a dedicated following of fans who appreciated their boldness and originality.

Collaborative Remixes

In addition to remixing songs on their own, Zeds Dead also collaborated with other artists to create remixes that showcased the collective creativity and talent of all involved. These collaborations allowed them to tap into new musical influences and expand their sonic palette. By working with artists from different genres and backgrounds, Zeds Dead were able to create remixes that captured the essence of both the original song and their own unique style.

The Impact of Remixes

Remixes played a significant role in Zeds Dead's rise to prominence. Their remixes garnered attention not only from fans but also from industry insiders, leading to collaborations with established artists and record labels. Remixes became a vehicle for Zeds Dead to showcase their skills, broaden their audience, and solidify their place in the music industry.

Unconventional Sampling

Zeds Dead's remixes were not limited to reworking existing songs; they often took unconventional approaches to sampling, using snippets from movies, TV shows, and other non-musical sources. These unique samples added depth and intrigue to their remixes, creating a multi-layered listening experience that went beyond traditional remixing.

Breaking Down Barriers

Zeds Dead's remixes not only pushed the boundaries of music but also broke down barriers between different fan communities. By remixing songs from various genres, they created a bridge between different musical tastes and brought fans from different backgrounds together. This ability to connect people through their remixes further solidified Zeds Dead's position as innovators in the industry.

Embracing the Unexpected

Perhaps one of the most exciting aspects of Zeds Dead's remixes was their willingness to embrace the unexpected. They were not afraid to take songs in entirely new directions, surprising listeners with unexpected drops, tempo changes, or genre switches. This element of surprise kept their remixes fresh and exciting, ensuring that listeners never knew what to expect.

On the Cutting Edge

Zeds Dead's remixes were not just about recreating existing songs; they were a testament to their constant desire to stay on the cutting edge of music production. They incorporated new production techniques, instrumentation, and sonic textures, constantly evolving their sound and pushing the boundaries of what was considered possible in the electronic music scene.

Conclusion

Zeds Dead's remixes became an integral part of their musical journey, allowing them to showcase their creativity, experiment with different genres, and connect with a diverse audience. By pushing the boundaries of remixing and embracing the unexpected, they reimagined and reinvented songs, leaving an indelible mark on the music industry. Through their remixes, Zeds Dead proved that true artistry goes beyond mere imitation and instead involves pushing the boundaries of what is conventionally accepted. Their remixes continue to inspire and captivate listeners, showing that the possibilities in music are limitless when you dare to push the boundaries. Let us now delve deeper into the sound aesthetic of Zeds Dead and explore their exploration of different genres and styles.

The Influence of Toronto's Music Scene

Toronto, the vibrant and multicultural city that lies on the shores of Lake Ontario, has long been hailed as a mecca for music lovers. Its diverse and thriving music scene has been a breeding ground for some of the most influential and innovative artists in various genres. From punk and rock to hip-hop and electronic music, Toronto has nurtured talent and served as inspiration for musicians worldwide.

The city's music scene in the 1970s and 1980s was characterized by the emergence of punk and alternative rock bands. Legendary venues such as the Horseshoe Tavern and Lee's Palace became known for showcasing local talent and hosting intimate, high-energy performances. Bands like The Diodes and Teenage Head were at the forefront of the punk movement, infusing their music with raw energy and rebellious spirit.

As the music scene evolved, so did the diversity of genres and styles. In the 1990s, Toronto witnessed the rise of alternative rock bands like The Tragically Hip and Our Lady Peace. These bands, along with others like Sloan and The Pursuit of Happiness, not only achieved success in Canada but also garnered international recognition, paving the way for future Toronto musicians.

One of the most influential genres to emerge from Toronto's music scene is hip-hop. In the late 1980s and early 1990s, Toronto's rap scene began to flourish with artists like Maestro Fresh-Wes and Michie Mee gaining prominence. Their music, infused with elements of funk, soul, and reggae, spoke to the multicultural fabric of the city. These early pioneers laid the foundation for future generations of Toronto hip-hop artists, including Kardinal Offishall, Drake, and The Weeknd, who would go on to achieve global stardom.

Toronto's electronic music scene also played a significant role in shaping the sound of Zeds Dead. The city became a hub for electronic music in the late 1990s and early 2000s, with iconic venues like The Guvernment and Comfort Zone hosting legendary DJ sets and raves. This underground culture provided a fertile breeding ground for electronic music producers and DJs.

Zeds Dead was formed during this period of electrifying growth in Toronto's electronic music scene. The duo, consisting of Dylan Mamid (DC) and Zach Rapp-Rovan (Hooks), drew inspiration from the pulsating beats and eclectic sounds they experienced within the city. Their music reflects the diverse range of influences embedded within Toronto's music culture.

To showcase their talent and make a name for themselves, Zeds Dead began to perform at local clubs and parties. Their early gigs allowed them to connect with the passionate and rapidly growing fanbase within the city. Toronto's music scene not only shaped their sound but also provided them with opportunities to collaborate with other local artists and producers, further fueling their creative evolution.

Beyond the direct influence on Zeds Dead, Toronto's music scene has helped shape the broader landscape of electronic dance music (EDM). The city's music culture, characterized by its openness, diversity, and experimentation, has fostered an environment where artists are encouraged to push boundaries and challenge conventions. This mentality has had a ripple effect on the evolution of EDM on a global scale.

Moreover, Toronto's music scene serves as a reminder of the importance of grassroots movements and local communities. It highlights the power of supportive networks and the impact they can have on artists' careers. Through its rich musical history and ongoing contributions to the industry, Toronto continues to inspire and influence emerging artists, ensuring that the city remains a crucial player in the global music landscape.

As Zeds Dead continues to make waves in the music industry, their Toronto roots and the influence of the city's music scene will always be an integral part of their story. Toronto's vibrant and diverse music culture has not only shaped their sound but also instilled in them a spirit of artistic exploration, collaboration, and a commitment to pushing the boundaries of music. It is this ethos that sets them apart and contributes to their enduring legacy.

In a world that is constantly evolving, the influence of Toronto's music scene on Zeds Dead serves as a testament to the power of local music communities and the lasting impact they can have on artists. As they continue to navigate the ever-changing landscape of the music industry, Zeds Dead remains grounded in their Toronto roots, ensuring that the city's music scene and its rich history continue to inspire and shape their journey.

Embracing Electronic Dance Music

In the early stages of their musical journey, Zeds Dead found their passion rooted in the world of electronic dance music (EDM). This section explores how they embraced EDM, the influence it had on their sound, and their contributions to the genre.

Introduction to Electronic Dance Music (EDM)

Electronic dance music, commonly known as EDM, is a genre of music that combines elements of electronic music and dance rhythms to create an energetic and captivating sound. It emerged in the late 20th century and has since evolved into a global phenomenon, influencing various subgenres and captivating audiences worldwide.

EDM is characterized by its use of synthesizers, drum machines, and digital effects, creating a seamless blend of electronic sounds and infectious beats. The genre encompasses a wide range of styles, including house, techno, trance, dubstep, and many others.

Early Exposure to EDM

As young music enthusiasts, Zeds Dead were exposed to the emerging sounds of EDM through various channels. They were drawn to the energy and creativity of electronic music, which sparked their curiosity and inspired them to explore this vibrant genre further.

The duo immersed themselves in the sounds of iconic electronic music pioneers such as The Chemical Brothers, Daft Punk, and The Prodigy. They were captivated by the innovative production techniques, infectious melodies, and the overall sonic experience that EDM provided.

Influences on the Zeds Dead Sound

The exposure to EDM played a crucial role in shaping the unique sound of Zeds Dead. They drew inspiration from the pulsating rhythms, heavy basslines, and intricate synth melodies that define EDM, and infused these elements into their own musical creations.

Zeds Dead embraced the fast-paced, high-energy nature of EDM, incorporating it into their tracks to create an exhilarating and euphoric experience for their listeners. Their use of hard-hitting bass drops, intricate percussion patterns, and catchy melodies showcased their deep understanding of EDM and their ability to push its boundaries.

Contributions to the EDM Genre

Zeds Dead's foray into EDM marked a significant contribution to the genre. Their distinct blend of dubstep, trap, and other electronic subgenres helped shape the evolving landscape of EDM and introduced new elements to the genre.

They became pioneers in fusing different genres together, creating a unique and boundary-pushing sound that resonated with fans across the globe. Their versatility in incorporating elements of hip-hop, reggae, and rock into their EDM tracks showcased their innovative approach, further expanding the possibilities of the genre.

Zeds Dead's remixes of popular tracks became a staple in the EDM scene, gaining widespread recognition and solidifying their position as influential artists in the genre. Their remixes injected a fresh and dynamic energy, transforming songs and captivating audiences with their unique take on familiar tunes.

Evolution and Experimentation

Throughout their career, Zeds Dead has continued to embrace EDM while evolving their sound and exploring new sonic territories. They have never shied away from experimenting with different styles and pushing the boundaries of their music.

From their early days in the dubstep scene to their more recent exploration of future bass and hybrid genres, Zeds Dead's willingness to embrace change and evolve has been instrumental in keeping their sound fresh and captivating. By staying true to their love for EDM while continually seeking new inspirations, they have remained at the forefront of the genre.

Collaborations and Cross-Genre Experiences

The duo's openness to collaborations and cross-genre experiences has further enriched their exploration of EDM. By collaborating with artists from various backgrounds, they have been able to infuse different musical influences into their own sound, creating a unique blend that defies genre categorization.

Their collaborations with artists such as Omar LinX, DROELOE, and Illenium exemplify their ability to seamlessly merge the worlds of EDM, hip-hop, and melodic bass music. These collaborative projects have not only expanded their creative horizons but have also contributed to the evolution and growth of EDM as a whole.

Embracing Diversity and Inclusivity

Zeds Dead's journey in EDM has been characterized by an unwavering commitment to diversity and inclusivity. They have embraced the vast spectrum of EDM, celebrating the cultural influences and collaborative opportunities that come with it.

Their commitment to diversity is not only reflected in their musical choices but also in their efforts to elevate underrepresented artists in the industry. By actively supporting and nurturing up-and-coming talent, Zeds Dead strives to create a community that is diverse, inclusive, and representative of the global electronic music scene.

Embracing the Future of EDM

As trailblazers in the EDM scene, Zeds Dead continues to shape the future of the genre. Their willingness to embrace new technologies, explore innovative production techniques, and collaborate with diverse artists are just some of the ways they are pushing the boundaries of EDM.

In an ever-evolving landscape, Zeds Dead remains committed to staying true to their roots while embracing the exciting possibilities of the future. By continuously reinventing their sound and embracing the ever-changing EDM scene, they guarantee an enduring legacy in the genre.

Unconventional Example: The Impact of EDM on Mental Health

One unconventional yet relevant aspect of EDM's influence is its impact on mental health. The high-energy nature of EDM, combined with its positive and uplifting atmosphere, has been proven to have beneficial effects on mental well-being.

The communal experience of attending an EDM event, where individuals come together to celebrate the music, dance, and connect with others, creates a sense of belonging and reduces feelings of loneliness or isolation. The electrifying beats and euphoric melodies can act as a form of catharsis, allowing listeners to release stress and express themselves freely.

EDM festivals often prioritize promoting a caring and inclusive environment, encouraging attendees to look out for one another's well-being. This emphasis on empathy and togetherness fosters a sense of community, which in turn promotes mental well-being.

Incorporating this understanding into their own work, Zeds Dead strives to create music and live shows that provide a space for emotional release, positivity, and connection. Their music becomes a source of solace and inspiration for listeners, contributing to the overall mental health discourse within the EDM community.

Summary

Embracing electronic dance music was a pivotal moment in Zeds Dead's musical journey. Their exposure to EDM during their formative years, the influence it had on their sound, and their contributions to the genre reflect their commitment to pushing boundaries and evolving as artists. By embracing diverse styles, collaborating with other talented musicians, and staying true to their passion for EDM, Zeds Dead has become an influential force in shaping the future of electronic dance music.

Chasing the Beat

The Sound Aesthetic of Zeds Dead

When it comes to the sound aesthetic of Zeds Dead, it can be described as a dynamic blend of genres and styles that pushes the boundaries of electronic music. The duo, known for their captivating soundscapes and intricate beats, has created a unique sonic identity that sets them apart from their contemporaries.

At the core of Zeds Dead's sound is their masterful use of bass. The heavy, pulsating basslines create a mesmerizing and immersive experience for listeners. It is this deep and powerful foundation that forms the backbone of their music and sets the stage for their sonic exploration.

Drawing inspiration from various genres, Zeds Dead seamlessly weaves elements of dubstep, hip-hop, reggae, and more into their tracks. This eclectic mix of styles adds a dynamic range of textures and flavors to their sound, creating a sonic palette that is both diverse and cohesive.

One of the defining characteristics of Zeds Dead's sound is their ability to create a balance between melodic and gritty elements. The melodies, often haunting and melancholic, add an emotional depth to their tracks, while the aggressive basslines and hard-hitting beats inject energy and intensity. This juxtaposition of emotions creates a captivating listening experience that keeps their audience on their toes.

Incorporating unique production techniques is also a signature aspect of Zeds Dead's sound. They skillfully manipulate samples, synths, and effects to create intricate and layered compositions. Their attention to detail and meticulous craftsmanship is evident in their tracks, where every sound and element is purposefully placed to evoke a specific mood or atmosphere.

Furthermore, Zeds Dead's sound aesthetic is shaped by their collaborative approach. They have worked with a diverse range of artists, from established musicians to rising stars, to create tracks that showcase their shared vision and individual talents. These collaborations not only add new dimensions to their sound but also contribute to the sense of community and artistic growth within the electronic music scene.

To understand the sound aesthetic of Zeds Dead, it is essential to also consider their live performances. The duo's energy and stage presence translate seamlessly into their shows, creating a captivating experience for their audience. Their seamless mixing, live improvisation, and incorporation of live instruments elevate their performances to a whole new level, leaving a lasting impression on all who witness them.

In summary, the sound aesthetic of Zeds Dead is a captivating fusion of genres, characterized by powerful basslines, emotive melodies, and meticulous production techniques. Their ability to create a balance between melodic and gritty elements, combined with their collaborative approach and electrifying live performances, sets them apart as true pioneers in the electronic music realm. Get ready to be transported on a sonic journey like no other.

Exploring Different Genres and Styles

The musical journey of Zeds Dead has been marked by their constant exploration of different genres and styles. As artists, they have shown an exceptional ability to adapt and incorporate various influences into their sound, creating a unique blend that defies categorization. In this section, we will delve into the diverse range of genres and styles that Zeds Dead has explored throughout their career.

One of the key aspects of Zeds Dead's music is their ability to seamlessly fuse different genres together. They have ventured into the realms of electronic music, hip-hop, reggae, dubstep, and many more. By combining elements from these disparate genres, they have created a sound that is distinctly their own.

In electronic music, Zeds Dead has experimented with various subgenres, including house, techno, drum and bass, and trap. They have a keen ear for different rhythms and beats, and their ability to blend and merge these different elements is what sets them apart. For example, in their track "Lost You," Zeds Dead brings together the pulsating basslines of dubstep with the frenetic energy of drum and bass, creating a track that is both exhilarating and infectious.

In exploring different genres, Zeds Dead has also shown a deep appreciation for hip-hop and reggae. They have incorporated elements of these genres into their music, often collaborating with artists from these backgrounds. Tracks such as

"Rude Boy" and "Blame" showcase their love for reggae, with their infectious hooks and laid-back rhythms. They have also worked with hip-hop artists like Omar LinX and Jadakiss, blending their signature electronic sound with rap verses to create a unique fusion.

It is worth mentioning that Zeds Dead's exploration of different genres is not limited to the confines of electronic music. They have also shown a penchant for incorporating elements from rock, jazz, and classical music into their compositions. In tracks like "In the Beginning," they experiment with rock-inspired guitar riffs and anthemic choruses, creating a larger-than-life sound.

One of the reasons why Zeds Dead's exploration of different genres and styles is so successful is their ability to maintain a sense of cohesion and identity throughout. Despite the eclectic range of influences, their music always carries the unmistakable stamp of Zeds Dead. This is achieved through their signature production techniques, such as their bold use of bass, intricate drum patterns, and atmospheric soundscapes.

To further enhance their exploration of different genres, Zeds Dead often collaborate with other artists who bring their unique perspectives and talents to the table. These collaborations not only result in fresh and exciting music but also allow for a cross-pollination of ideas and styles. Working with artists like Diplo, NGHTMRE, and Illenium, they have successfully merged different genres to create groundbreaking tracks that defy boundaries.

In conclusion, Zeds Dead's musical journey is characterized by their fearless exploration of different genres and styles. From electronic music to hip-hop, reggae, and beyond, they have shown an unparalleled ability to fuse disparate elements into a cohesive and unique sound. Their commitment to pushing boundaries and their willingness to collaborate with other artists have allowed them to continually evolve and stay at the forefront of the music scene. In the next section, we will explore the evolution of their sound and the ways in which they have continued to innovate and experiment.

Influences from Hip-Hop and Reggae

Hip-hop and reggae are two incredibly influential genres that have left a lasting impact on the music industry. They have shaped the soundscape of countless artists and have played a significant role in the evolution of Zeds Dead's sound. In this section, we will explore the influences of hip-hop and reggae on Zeds Dead's music, their creative approach, and the impact these genres have had on their artistic journey.

The Roots of Hip-Hop and Reggae

To understand the influence of hip-hop and reggae on Zeds Dead, it's essential to delve into the roots of these genres. Hip-hop originated in the Black and Latino communities of the South Bronx in the 1970s. It emerged as a cultural movement that encompassed music, dance, visual arts, and fashion. Reggae, on the other hand, originated in Jamaica in the late 1960s and is deeply rooted in the country's history and culture.

Hip-hop is characterized by its distinct rhythm, lyricism, and the use of samples from various genres, including funk, soul, and R&B. It gave a voice to marginalized communities, addressing social and political issues, and reflecting the realities of urban life. Reggae, known for its laid-back rhythms and messages of unity, peace, and social justice, became a cultural force worldwide, championing the cause of the oppressed.

Blending Genres: Fusing Hip-Hop and Reggae with Electronic Music

Zeds Dead, known for their seamless fusion of genres, have incorporated elements of both hip-hop and reggae into their electronic music. By merging the rhythmic influences and lyrical styles of these genres with their own unique sound, they have created a distinct sonic landscape that sets them apart from their peers.

In their tracks, Zeds Dead uses hip-hop-inspired beats and samples, crafting infectious grooves that make you want to move. These beats are often infused with reggae's signature offbeat rhythm, creating a dynamic and energetic sound. Their clever use of vocal samples, both from hip-hop and reggae tracks, adds depth and character to their music, enhancing the storytelling aspect of their songs.

Creative Sampling and Remixing

One of the hallmarks of Zeds Dead's music is their skillful sampling and remixing. Just as hip-hop and reggae artists have traditionally sampled from a wide range of genres, Zeds Dead draws from diverse musical sources to create their unique sound. They have artfully blended hip-hop and reggae samples with electronic elements, giving their music a fresh and innovative edge.

Their remixes breathe new life into tracks from various genres, injecting them with their own distinctive style. By infusing hip-hop and reggae elements into these remixes, they pay homage to the genres that have influenced them while putting their personal touch on the music. This approach has not only won them critical acclaim but has also helped introduce new audiences to the sounds of hip-hop and reggae.

Social and Political Commentary

Like hip-hop and reggae, Zeds Dead uses their music as a platform for social and political commentary. Influenced by the conscious nature of these genres, their lyrics often touch on themes of inequality, injustice, and the struggles faced by society. By incorporating these messages into their electronic music, Zeds Dead adds depth and substance to their sound.

In this respect, hip-hop and reggae serve as a source of inspiration for Zeds Dead's lyrical content. They amplify their voice, allowing them to connect with their audience on a deeper level. By addressing pressing issues through their music, Zeds Dead strives to spark conversations and inspire positive change.

Innovation and Evolution

While Zeds Dead draws heavily from hip-hop and reggae, they never limit themselves to a single genre. They continuously explore new sonic territories and push the boundaries of electronic music. Their ability to blend genres and experiment with different styles has been instrumental in their artistic growth and evolution.

By embracing the influences of hip-hop and reggae while remaining open to new musical possibilities, Zeds Dead has carved out a unique niche in the electronic music landscape. They have demonstrated that traditional genre boundaries can be broken, leading to innovative and groundbreaking creations.

Putting It All Together

Influenced by the rhythmic grooves, lyrical storytelling, and social consciousness of hip-hop and reggae, Zeds Dead has created a sound that is uniquely their own. By blending the best elements of these genres with their own electronic sensibilities, they have crafted a sonic tapestry that captivates audiences around the world.

Zeds Dead's ability to incorporate hip-hop and reggae influences into their music showcases their versatility as artists. They pay homage to the genres that have shaped them while staying true to their own musical vision. Through their creative approach, they continue to push the boundaries of electronic music and inspire the next generation of artists to explore new possibilities.

The influences of hip-hop and reggae on Zeds Dead's music serve as a testament to the power of cross-genre collaborations and the importance of embracing diverse musical inspirations. As they continue to evolve and experiment, we can only anticipate more groundbreaking and genre-defying creations from this dynamic duo.

So let the rhythm take you on a journey, where hip-hop and reggae meet electronic music, and the result is Zeds Dead. They have found their unique voice by fusing these influential genres, and their music reflects the spirit of unity, creativity, and social awareness that has come to define hip-hop and reggae.

Incorporating Elements of Dubstep

In their quest to explore different genres and styles, Zeds Dead found themselves drawn to the electrifying beats and heavy basslines of dubstep. Inspired by the pulsating rhythms and infectious energy of this electronic subgenre, Zeds Dead made a conscious decision to incorporate elements of dubstep into their music, further expanding their sonic palette.

The Origins of Dubstep

Before delving into how Zeds Dead incorporated dubstep into their sound, it is essential to understand the origins and characteristics of this genre. Dubstep emerged in the late 1990s in the underground music scene of South London, UK. Drawing influences from various electronic music styles, such as dub, garage, and drum and bass, dubstep carved out its distinctive identity.

At its core, dubstep is characterized by its heavy emphasis on sub-bass frequencies, intricate drum patterns, and a slower tempo compared to other electronic genres. The genre's distinct sound is achieved by utilizing syncopated rhythms, sparse arrangements, and the prominent use of wobble basslines—a signature element of dubstep.

Wobble Basslines: Defining the Dubstep Sound

One of the defining features of dubstep is its use of wobble basslines, which adds an intense and hypnotic quality to the music. Wobble basslines are created by modulating a low-frequency oscillator (LFO) to manipulate the pitch and amplitude of a bass sound, resulting in a vibrant and warbling effect.

Zeds Dead embraced the art of crafting wobble basslines and skillfully incorporated them into their tracks, infusing their music with the distinct grit and intensity of dubstep. Whether it's the deep, pulsating bass on "Rude Boy" or the energetic wobbles on "Bumpy Teeth," Zeds Dead's mastery of wobble basslines became a defining element of their sound.

Tempo and Rhythm: The Dubstep Influence

Another significant aspect of incorporating dubstep into their music was adapting to the genre's slower tempo and unique rhythmic patterns. Traditionally, dubstep operates in the range of 140 beats per minute (BPM), providing ample space for the music to breathe and allowing the basslines to take center stage.

Zeds Dead skillfully embraced the lower tempo and explored the rhythmic possibilities that dubstep offered. Tracks like "Collapse" and "In the Beginning" showcase the duo's ability to create dynamic and infectious grooves within the realm of dubstep, captivating listeners with their compelling beats and intricate percussions.

Evolution and Experimentation: Beyond Dubstep

While Zeds Dead embraced the elements of dubstep, they also evolved and expanded beyond the genre's confines. Recognizing the importance of pushing boundaries and maintaining artistic growth, Zeds Dead incorporated diverse influences and explored different subgenres of electronic music.

They deftly blended elements of house, drum and bass, hip-hop, and reggae into their music, creating a sonic tapestry that transcended any single genre. This experimentation not only allowed Zeds Dead to maintain their distinct identity but also contributed to the evolution of their sound.

Example: "Eyes on Fire" Remix

An example that highlights Zeds Dead's incorporation of dubstep elements into their music is their iconic remix of Blue Foundation's "Eyes on Fire." Released in 2009, this remix became an instant classic, showcasing the duo's ability to infuse a melodic track with the energy and depth of dubstep.

Zeds Dead transformed the ethereal original into a bass-heavy banger, utilizing wobble basslines, syncopated rhythms, and intricate drum patterns. The remix beautifully demonstrated their mastery of dubstep elements and their knack for reimagining songs across genres while staying true to their signature sound.

Pushing the Boundaries: Zeds Dead's Dubstep Legacy

Zeds Dead's incorporation of dubstep elements expanded the boundaries of their music, solidifying their place in the electronic music landscape. Their innovative approach to blending genres, combined with their unique ability to create infectious basslines and captivating rhythms, has influenced countless producers and cemented their legacy as pioneers of the dubstep genre.

As Zeds Dead continues to evolve and experiment, they remain true to their roots, incorporating elements of dubstep while forging new sonic paths. Their dedication to pushing boundaries and their unwavering commitment to crafting memorable and powerful music ensure their enduring impact on the electronic music scene. [?]

Unconventional Exercise: Choose a track from Zeds Dead's discography and analyze the dubstep elements incorporated into the song. Discuss the use of wobble basslines, tempo, and rhythmic patterns. How do these elements contribute to the overall sound and energy of the track? Share your findings with a fellow music enthusiast and engage in a conversation about the evolution of dubstep in Zeds Dead's music.

Additional Resources

To explore dubstep further and delve into its rich history and subgenres, consider the following resources:

+ *Bassweight* (2008) - A documentary film by Suridh Hassan that provides an in-depth look at the origins and evolution of dubstep.

+ Digital Mystikz - One of the pioneering duos in the dubstep scene, known for their immersive and atmospheric sound. Explore their discography to dive deeper into the genre.

+ Skream - A prominent figure in the early dubstep scene, Skream's music showcases the genre's original sound and style. Listen to his releases to gain a comprehensive understanding of the genre's roots.

+ Deep Medi Musik - A record label founded by dubstep producer Mala, known for releasing influential and groundbreaking dubstep tracks.

These resources will provide you with a solid foundation for understanding the origins and intricacies of the dubstep genre, allowing you to appreciate Zeds Dead's incorporation of these elements into their music even more.

Evolving Sound and Experimentation

In the ever-evolving world of music, it is essential for artists to keep pushing boundaries, exploring new sounds, and experimenting with different styles. Zeds

Dead is no exception to this rule. Throughout their career, they have continuously evolved their sound, creating a dynamic and diverse discography that captivates listeners across the globe.

Adapting to Changing Musical Trends

As musicians, it is crucial to be in tune with the pulse of the industry and understand the ever-changing musical landscape. Zeds Dead has shown remarkable adaptability by embracing new genres and styles as they emerge. They are not afraid to step out of their comfort zone and infuse their signature sound with fresh elements.

For example, as electronic dance music (EDM) gained popularity, Zeds Dead seamlessly incorporated elements of dubstep into their productions. Their tracks became synonymous with heavy bass drops and intricate sound design, perfectly capturing the essence of the genre.

Collaborative Projects and Side Ventures

One way Zeds Dead has continued to evolve their sound is through collaborative projects and side ventures. By teaming up with fellow artists, they can explore new genres and experiment with different musical ideas.

Collaborations allow Zeds Dead to merge their unique style with the diverse sounds of other musicians. Whether it's working with hip-hop artists, vocalists, or fellow electronic producers, these collaborations bring fresh perspectives to their music.

Moreover, side ventures such as forming their own record label, Deadbeats, give Zeds Dead the freedom to support and nurture emerging talent in the electronic music scene. This expands their creative horizons and exposes them to new sounds and ideas.

The Influence of Non-Musical Art Forms

To stay at the forefront of creativity, Zeds Dead draws inspiration not only from music but also from other art forms. They recognize that art is interconnected and that exploring visual art, film, literature, and other mediums can help shape their sound.

For instance, visual art can evoke certain moods and atmospheres that influence the creation of music. Zeds Dead has collaborated with visual artists to create stunning visuals for their live performances and music videos. By integrating captivating visuals with their sound, they create an immersive and multi-sensory experience for their fans.

The Role of Technology in Sound Evolution

Advancements in technology have played a significant role in the evolution of Zeds Dead's sound. From the early days of using analog equipment to the present digital era, Zeds Dead has embraced technological advancements to enhance their creativity and push the boundaries of their music.

The use of digital audio workstations (DAWs) and software plugins has made it easier for Zeds Dead to experiment with different sounds, textures, and effects. They can manipulate samples, create intricate synth patches, and fine-tune their mixdowns with precision.

Furthermore, Zeds Dead has utilized technology to incorporate live instrumentation into their productions and performances. By seamlessly blending electronic elements with live instruments like drums, guitars, and keyboards, they bring a unique and organic touch to their music.

The Sound of Zeds Dead in the Future

As pioneers of their craft, Zeds Dead's sound will undoubtedly continue to evolve and break new ground. They have proven time and again their ability to adapt to changing musical trends and embrace new genres.

Looking ahead, we can expect Zeds Dead to explore even more diverse styles, collaborate with exciting artists from various genres, and continue to experiment with new production techniques. They will undoubtedly continue to shape the electronic music landscape and inspire future generations of music creators.

In this fast-paced world of music, Zeds Dead remains on the cutting edge, always in pursuit of sonic innovation. Their dedication to evolving their sound and pushing the boundaries of what it means to be an electronic music artist is truly remarkable.

Stay tuned for the next chapter of their musical journey, where we delve deeper into their personal lives and the influences that have shaped them into the trailblazers they are today!

Signature Production Techniques

In the realm of electronic music production, Zeds Dead has carved out a unique sonic signature that sets them apart from their contemporaries. Through a combination of innovative techniques and a discerning ear for sound design, they have developed a distinctive style that captivates listeners and drives the energy of their tracks. This section will explore some of the signature production techniques employed by Zeds Dead, shedding light on the creative processes that shape their music.

Layering and Texturing

One hallmark of Zeds Dead's production style is their masterful use of layering and texturing. They are adept at blending different sounds, both synthetic and organic, to create rich and dynamic sonic landscapes. By combining multiple layers of instruments, vocals, and effects, they achieve a sense of depth and complexity in their tracks.

For example, in their track "Lost You," Zeds Dead employs layering to create a sense of tension and release. The song features a combination of thick, gritty basslines, ethereal vocal samples, and intricate percussion patterns. These elements are skillfully combined to create a multi-dimensional sound that keeps the listener engaged throughout the song.

To achieve such complex textures, Zeds Dead often processes each layer individually before blending them together. They experiment with various effects such as reverb, delay, and modulation, to add depth and character to each sound. This meticulous attention to detail results in a cohesive and immersive sonic experience.

Sampling and Chop Technique

Another defining characteristic of Zeds Dead's production style is their adept use of sampling. They draw inspiration from diverse genres and eras, incorporating samples from classic jazz records, nostalgic video games, and obscure movie soundtracks. This eclectic approach adds a nostalgic touch to their music, creating a sense of familiarity and intrigue for the listener.

One technique that Zeds Dead employs when working with samples is the chop technique. They deconstruct sampled material into smaller fragments and rearrange them to create new melodies and rhythms. This process allows them to infuse their tracks with a unique flavor while paying homage to the original sources.

An excellent example of their sampling and chop technique is their remix of "Eyes on Fire" by Blue Foundation. In this remix, Zeds Dead takes the haunting vocal of the original track and transforms it into a driving, bass-heavy anthem. They manipulate the vocals by slicing and rearranging them, creating compelling rhythmic patterns that drive the energy of the remix.

Bass Design and Sound Manipulation

Zeds Dead's unique sound is synonymous with deep and powerful bass. They have mastered the art of bass design, crafting intricate and memorable basslines that permeate their tracks. The meticulous attention to detail in their bass design gives their music an immersive quality that resonates with listeners on a visceral level.

To achieve their distinct bass sound, Zeds Dead combines synthesis techniques with creative sound manipulation. They often start with a foundation of synthesized bass tones, crafting sounds with strong harmonic content and rich textures. They then process these bass sounds using various effects such as distortion, filtering, and modulation to add depth and character.

In addition to synthesis, Zeds Dead also incorporates recorded bass samples into their production. They sample real instruments, such as electric bass guitars or upright basses, to add a human element to their tracks. These organic bass samples are processed and layered with synthesized elements to create a unique blend of analog and digital textures.

Dynamic Arrangement and Song Structure

Zeds Dead's production style extends beyond individual sounds and techniques. They are also masters of dynamic arrangement and song structure. They meticulously craft their tracks to take the listener on a journey, carefully manipulating energy levels and introducing new elements at strategic moments.

One technique they employ is the use of drops and builds to create tension and release. They build anticipation through the gradual addition of new elements, increasing energy levels until they reach a climactic moment. The drops, when they finally hit, are carefully crafted to deliver maximum impact, driven by powerful basslines and high-energy rhythms.

To keep the listener engaged, Zeds Dead also incorporates unexpected twists and turns in their arrangements. They introduce new musical ideas, change tempos, and shift the overall mood of the track to maintain a sense of surprise. This willingness to experiment and deviate from traditional song structures adds an element of creativity and unpredictability to their music.

In conclusion, Zeds Dead's signature production techniques set them apart as innovators in the electronic music scene. Through the skillful use of layering and texturing, sampling and chop techniques, bass design and sound manipulation, and dynamic arrangement and song structure, they create immersive and captivating tracks that resonate with listeners. Their attention to detail and willingness to push boundaries make them a driving force in the evolution of electronic music. As artists continue to explore and push the boundaries of music production, Zeds Dead's contributions will undoubtedly shape the future of the genre.

Collaborating with Other Artists

Collaboration is at the heart of Zeds Dead's artistic journey. Over the years, they have forged meaningful partnerships and ventured into exciting creative endeavors with a diverse range of fellow musicians. These collaborations have not only expanded the sonic landscape of Zeds Dead's music but have also fostered a sense of community and camaraderie within the music industry.

The Power of Collaboration

Collaboration is a powerful tool that allows artists to combine their unique perspectives, skills, and creative energies to produce something greater than the sum of its parts. For Zeds Dead, collaboration has always been about pushing boundaries, challenging conventions, and creating music that resonates with their fans on a deeper level.

By collaborating with other artists, Zeds Dead has been able to explore new genres, experiment with different production techniques, and broaden their musical horizons. It has allowed them to step outside their comfort zones and embrace fresh ideas, ultimately leading to the evolution of their sound.

Forming Musical Alliances

Zeds Dead has formed numerous musical alliances throughout their career, collaborating with artists from a wide range of genres and backgrounds. From hip-hop and reggae to electronic and rock, these collaborations have brought together different musical worlds to create something truly unique.

One notable example of Zeds Dead's collaborative spirit is their partnership with Omar LinX, a Canadian rapper and vocalist. Together, they have produced several groundbreaking tracks, such as "Out for Blood" and "No Prayers," which seamlessly blend elements of hip-hop and electronic music.

In addition to their collaborations with vocalists, Zeds Dead has also worked with fellow electronic music producers. Notable collaborations include "You Know" with Oliver Heldens and "Blame" with Diplo and Elliphant. These collaborations not only showcase Zeds Dead's versatility as artists but also demonstrate their ability to bring different musical styles together in a cohesive and innovative way.

Exploring New Sounds and Techniques

Collaborating with other artists has allowed Zeds Dead to explore new sounds and techniques that they may not have discovered on their own. By bringing in fresh perspectives and different musical influences, these collaborations have inspired Zeds Dead to push the boundaries of their creativity and experiment with new sonic territories.

For example, their collaboration with Jauz on the track "Lights Go Down" infuses elements of bass house and dubstep, creating a dynamic and energetic sound that seamlessly merges both artists' unique styles. This collaboration not only resulted in a chart-topping hit but also showcased Zeds Dead's ability to adapt to different genres and create music that resonates with a wide audience.

Nurturing Emerging Talent

Zeds Dead has also made it a priority to collaborate with up-and-coming artists, using their platform and influence to elevate new talent and give them a platform to showcase their skills. This commitment to nurturing emerging talent not only reflects their genuine love for music but also their desire to contribute to the growth and development of the music industry as a whole.

One such collaboration is their work with the young producer DNMO. Together, they released the EP "Blood of My Blood," which features a fusion of melodic dubstep and electronic pop. This collaboration not only introduced DNMO to a wider audience but also provided him with mentorship and guidance from seasoned professionals.

The Creative Process

Every collaboration is a unique journey, and Zeds Dead approaches each one with an open mind and a shared vision. The creative process often involves extensive communication, brainstorming sessions, and experimentation to find the perfect balance between each artist's individual style and the overarching vision for the project.

Zeds Dead believes in fostering a collaborative environment where all parties feel comfortable expressing their ideas and taking risks. This collaborative spirit extends beyond the studio and into the live performances, where they often invite their collaborators to join them on stage, creating a dynamic and interactive experience for their fans.

The Future of Collaboration

As Zeds Dead continues to evolve and explore new musical territories, collaboration will undoubtedly remain a cornerstone of their artistic journey. They will continue to seek out new musical alliances, experiment with different genres, and push the boundaries of their creativity.

In an increasingly interconnected music landscape, collaboration has become more important than ever. It not only allows artists to create music that reflects the diverse world we live in but also fosters a sense of unity and shared experience among musicians and fans alike.

The future of collaboration holds endless possibilities for Zeds Dead. By joining forces with artists from different genres, disciplines, and backgrounds, they will continue to shape the landscape of electronic music and leave a lasting impact on the industry as a whole.

Conclusion

Collaboration lies at the heart of Zeds Dead's artistic journey. Through their partnerships with other artists, they have created music that is both innovative and accessible, pushing the boundaries of electronic music and captivating audiences worldwide. By embracing collaboration, Zeds Dead has forged meaningful alliances, nurtured emerging talent, and created a sense of community within the music industry. As they continue to evolve and explore new sounds, their commitment to collaboration will undoubtedly play a crucial role in shaping the future of their music and leaving a lasting legacy.

Touring and Captivating Live Performances

Touring and live performances are an essential part of the Zeds Dead experience. While their studio productions are masterfully crafted, it is on the stage where their music truly comes alive. From massive music festivals to intimate club shows, Zeds Dead has a knack for captivating audiences and creating an unforgettable experience.

Crafting the Setlist

One of the keys to their success in live performances is the careful curation of their setlist. Zeds Dead understands the importance of connecting with their audience and tailoring the music to fit the moment. They curate their sets to take listeners on a journey, building energy and anticipation with each track.

The setlist is carefully crafted to include a mix of their own original productions, remixes, and crowd favorites. They have a knack for seamlessly blending different genres of electronic music, creating a dynamic and unpredictable experience for the audience. By strategically placing different styles and tempos throughout the set, they keep the energy high and the crowd engaged.

Creating an Immersive Atmosphere

Zeds Dead is known for creating an immersive atmosphere during their live shows. They pay great attention to the visual and auditory components of their performances, using cutting-edge technology and innovative stage design to transport the audience into their world.

Visually, their shows are a feast for the eyes. They incorporate stunning visuals, light installations, and mesmerizing projections to enhance the mood and complement the music. The stage design is often a work of art in itself, carefully constructed to create a visually striking backdrop for their performance.

Auditorily, their live shows are a sonic journey. With a meticulous focus on sound engineering, they ensure that every bass drop reverberates through the crowd, creating a visceral experience that is felt as much as it is heard. The combination of powerful basslines, intricate melodies, and expertly balanced sound enhances the emotional impact of their music.

Interactive Elements and Crowd Participation

Zeds Dead understands the importance of audience engagement and actively encourages crowd participation during their live performances. They create moments where the crowd becomes an integral part of the show, fostering a sense of unity and connection.

Whether it's a call-and-response with the audience, a hands-in-the-air moment, or a designated sing-along section, they create opportunities for the crowd to join in and become an active participant in the performance. This not only creates a memorable experience but also strengthens the bond between the artist and their fans.

Improvisation and Unique Live Moments

No two Zeds Dead live performances are alike. They thrive on improvisation and are known to surprise their audience with unexpected twists and moments of spontaneity. This keeps the performances fresh and exciting, creating a unique experience for each crowd.

From live remixes and mashups to on-the-fly collaborations with other artists, Zeds Dead embraces the unpredictable nature of live performances. They are skilled at reading the energy of the crowd and adjusting their sets accordingly, creating a dynamic and interactive experience that sets them apart.

The Evolution of the Zeds Dead Live Experience

As Zeds Dead continues to push the boundaries of electronic music, their live performances evolve with them. They constantly seek new ways to engage their audience and experiment with different technologies and techniques.

They are at the forefront of incorporating live instrumentation into their sets, blurring the lines between DJing and live performance. By incorporating elements like drums, guitar, and keyboards, they bring a raw energy and a new level of depth to their shows.

Zeds Dead also embraces the latest advancements in live show technologies, such as projection mapping, interactive lighting systems, and virtual reality experiences. They strive to create a fully immersive and multisensory experience, where the audience can not only hear the music but also see and feel it in a transformative way.

Pushing the Boundaries of Live Performances

Zeds Dead has always been at the forefront of pushing the boundaries of live performances. They are not afraid to take risks and experiment with unconventional ideas, constantly challenging themselves and their audience.

One example of this is their "Deadbeats" label showcases, where they curate lineups of cutting-edge artists from across the electronic music spectrum. These showcases are not just traditional concerts, but immersive experiences that showcase the diversity and innovation of the genre.

Another example is their incorporation of live art into their performances. They often collaborate with visual artists to create live paintings or installations on stage, adding a visual dimension to their shows and blurring the lines between music and art.

Keeping the Audience at the Center

Despite their success and growing fanbase, Zeds Dead remains dedicated to keeping their audience at the center of everything they do. They understand that the live experience is a shared one, and they constantly strive to create a space where fans can come together and connect through music.

They actively engage with their fans on social media, taking the time to respond to messages and show appreciation for their support. They also make an effort to connect with fans during meet-and-greet sessions and after-show interactions, creating personal moments that have a lasting impact.

By putting their fans first and crafting live performances that are both captivating and immersive, Zeds Dead has created a loyal and dedicated following that continues to grow. Their commitment to pushing the boundaries of live performances ensures that their journey is far from over, and the future holds even more captivating shows and unforgettable experiences.

Growing International Recognition

As Zeds Dead continued to refine their unique sound and push the boundaries of electronic music, their popularity spread like wildfire across the globe. The duo's infectious beats and innovative productions captivated audiences in different countries and established them as a force to be reckoned with in the international music scene.

Conquering Festivals and Touring the World

One of the key factors in Zeds Dead's growing international recognition was their electrifying live performances at music festivals worldwide. From Coachella to Tomorrowland, their high-energy sets left festival-goers in awe and craving for more. The duo's ability to connect with the crowd and create a euphoric atmosphere made them stand out among their peers.

Their relentless touring schedule took them to every corner of the globe, exposing their music to diverse audiences. They performed in iconic venues and sold-out shows, leaving a lasting impression on fans who couldn't resist the infectious beats and pulsating bass lines. Each tour stop became an opportunity for Zeds Dead to showcase their evolving sound and connect with fans on a deeper level.

Chart Success and Mainstream Appeal

Zeds Dead's music transcended the confines of the electronic music scene and gained mainstream appeal. Their chart-topping hits reached audiences far beyond the EDM community, solidifying their status as crossover artists. Tracks such as "Collapse," "Lost You," and "Blink" caught the attention of radio stations and music charts worldwide, propelling Zeds Dead into the mainstream spotlight.

Their collaborations with well-established artists from different genres also contributed to their growing international recognition. Working with the likes of Omar LinX, Diplo, and Pusha T helped Zeds Dead expand their fanbase and reach new audiences. The duo's ability to seamlessly fuse electronic elements with genres like hip-hop and reggae created a fresh and innovative sound that resonated with listeners across the globe.

The Power of Social Media and Online Communities

The rise of social media platforms played a significant role in Zeds Dead's international success. Engaging with fans through platforms like Instagram, Twitter, and Facebook allowed the duo to cultivate a dedicated following and establish a strong online community. Their interaction with fans, sharing behind-the-scenes content, and teasing upcoming releases created a sense of anticipation and loyalty among their followers.

Zeds Dead's online presence also extended beyond social media. The duo utilized streaming platforms like SoundCloud and Spotify to share their music with a global audience, making it easily accessible to new listeners. The ability to connect directly with fans through these platforms allowed them to reach fans in remote corners of the world and cultivate a truly international following.

Collaborative Projects and Cross-Cultural Influences

Zeds Dead's collaboration with artists from diverse backgrounds and musical styles further contributed to their international recognition. Embracing cross-cultural influences, the duo worked with artists from countries such as Jamaica, England, and Australia, infusing their music with unique flavors.

These collaborations not only broadened their sonic palette but also helped Zeds Dead tap into new fanbases in different parts of the world. By incorporating elements of international genres like dancehall and drum and bass, the duo forged connections with local music scenes and gained a deeper understanding of global musical trends.

Revolutionizing the Live Show Experience

One of the defining characteristics of Zeds Dead's rise to international fame was their relentless drive to revolutionize the live show experience. Moving beyond traditional DJ sets, they incorporated live instrumentation and visual elements into their performances, creating a truly immersive experience for the audience.

Zeds Dead's boundary-pushing approach to live shows set them apart from other electronic music acts and allowed them to connect with fans on a deeper level. By combining their signature electronic sound with live drums, guitars, and keyboards, they brought a raw energy to their performances that resonated with audiences worldwide.

Continual Innovation and Staying Ahead of the Curve

Zeds Dead's international recognition can be attributed to their ability to stay ahead of the curve and continually innovate. The duo refused to conform to trends and instead paved their own path, constantly pushing the boundaries of electronic music.

Their dedication to experimentation and exploration of different genres ensured that their music remained fresh and cutting-edge. They were never content with resting on their laurels, always seeking new sounds and techniques to incorporate into their productions.

Through their relentless pursuit of innovation, Zeds Dead not only gained international recognition but also inspired a new generation of artists to think outside the box and push the limits of electronic music.

The Global Impact of Zeds Dead

Zeds Dead's international recognition had a profound impact on the electronic music landscape as a whole. Their willingness to explore different genres and collaborate with artists from various backgrounds paved the way for the genre-blurring movement that followed.

Their success served as a testament to the power of creativity and authenticity in music, encouraging artists to take risks and embrace their unique sound. Zeds Dead's ability to connect with fans across cultures and borders demonstrated the universal language of music.

As their influence continues to grow, Zeds Dead remains committed to nurturing young talent and cultivating a sense of community within the electronic music scene. Their journey from a small studio in Toronto to international stardom is a testament to their unwavering dedication to their craft and their relentless pursuit of musical excellence.

Looking Ahead: The Future of Zeds Dead's International Recognition

As Zeds Dead's international recognition continues to soar, the future holds endless possibilities. With their ever-evolving sound and commitment to innovation, the duo is poised to make an even greater impact on the global music scene.

By exploring new genres, collaborating with artists from different backgrounds, and embracing emerging technologies, Zeds Dead is setting the stage for a future of groundbreaking releases and awe-inspiring live performances. Their international recognition is not only a testament to their past achievements but a promise of an exciting journey ahead.

So, buckle up and get ready to experience the unstoppable rise of Zeds Dead as they conquer new territories and captivate audiences around the world. The beat goes on, and with each new track, Zeds Dead cements their place in the annals of electronic music history.

The Artistic Vision

Visual Art and Stage Design

As Zeds Dead embarked on their musical journey, they quickly realized the power of visual art and stage design in creating a captivating live experience. Visual elements have always played a significant role in their performances, enhancing the storytelling aspect of their music and creating an immersive environment for fans. In this section, we explore the importance of visual art and stage design in the world of Zeds Dead and how they continue to push the boundaries of creativity.

Creating a Visual Identity

At the heart of Zeds Dead's visual artistry is the creation of a unique visual identity. The duo understands the importance of having a distinct visual representation that aligns with their music and brand. From album artwork to stage designs, every visual element is carefully curated and crafted to create a cohesive and immersive experience.

To achieve this, Zeds Dead collaborate with talented visual artists and designers who share their artistic vision. They work closely with these professionals to conceptualize and bring their ideas to life, resulting in visually stunning representations that resonate with their audience. The visual identity of Zeds Dead is a reflection of their music, personality, and the emotions they want to evoke through their art.

Stage Design as a Canvas

For Zeds Dead, stage design is not just a backdrop, but a canvas for their artistic expression. They believe that the stage is an extension of their music and offers an opportunity to create a multi-sensory experience for their fans. With each performance, they aim to transport the audience into a different world, where the visuals and music blend seamlessly.

The stage design is carefully thought out, taking into consideration the mood and themes of their music. Zeds Dead incorporates various elements such as lighting, projections, and set pieces to enhance the visual experience. These elements are synchronized with the music, creating an immersive and dynamic atmosphere that captivates the audience from start to finish.

Technology and Innovation

Innovation and the use of technology play a vital role in Zeds Dead's visual art and stage design. They constantly push the boundaries of what is possible, utilizing cutting-edge technology and techniques to create visually stunning performances.

One of their pioneering innovations is the use of live visuals and real-time graphics. Through custom software and hardware setups, they can manipulate and control visuals in real-time, allowing for a truly unique and interactive experience. This technology enables them to respond to the energy of the crowd and adapt the visuals accordingly, creating a symbiotic relationship between the music and visuals.

Additionally, Zeds Dead explores the integration of virtual reality and augmented reality in their performances. They see the potential of these technologies to transport the audience into a completely immersive world, blurring the lines between reality and art. By embracing these emerging technologies, Zeds Dead continues to push the boundaries of what is possible in live performances.

The Power of Visual Storytelling

Visual art and stage design provide Zeds Dead with a powerful tool for storytelling. They believe in the importance of creating a narrative through their music and visuals, allowing the audience to connect with their art on a deeper level.

Each performance is carefully crafted to take the audience on a journey, both musically and visually. The stage design, lighting, and projections work together to create a seamless narrative that complements the music. Zeds Dead draws inspiration from various art forms, including film, literature, and visual arts, to create a multi-dimensional experience that engages the senses and sparks the imagination.

By incorporating storytelling elements into their visual art and stage design, Zeds Dead invites the audience to interpret and engage with their music in a more profound and personal way. The visuals enhance the emotional impact of the music, allowing the audience to become active participants in the narrative.

Creating an Immersive Experience

Above all, Zeds Dead aims to create an immersive experience for their fans. They understand that their music is not just about sound, but an entire sensory experience that transports the audience into a different realm.

To achieve this level of immersion, Zeds Dead pays attention to every detail, ensuring that the visual elements seamlessly integrate with the music. Lighting design is carefully orchestrated to enhance the mood and energy of each track, with vibrant colors and dynamic lighting effects that create a mesmerizing visual spectacle. Projections and visuals are precisely synchronized with the music, creating a sense of harmony between the auditory and visual stimuli.

Additionally, Zeds Dead actively encourages audience participation, creating an interactive experience that blurs the boundaries between artist and fan. They strive to forge a connection with their audience, making them active participants in the performance rather than passive observers.

In conclusion, visual art and stage design play a pivotal role in the world of Zeds Dead. Through the creation of a visual identity, innovative use of technology, visual storytelling, and creating an immersive experience, Zeds Dead continues to push the boundaries of what is possible in live performances. By combining their music with captivating visuals, they transport their audience into a world of sound and vision, creating an unforgettable experience for fans around the globe.

Crafting a Unique Brand

When it comes to creating a brand, Zeds Dead has always been ahead of the curve. From their early days as emerging artists to their current position as global music pioneers, they have consistently prioritized building a brand that stands out from the crowd. In this section, we will delve into the strategies and principles that have helped Zeds Dead craft their unique and memorable brand.

Authenticity: The Core of the Zeds Dead Brand

At the heart of the Zeds Dead brand lies authenticity. From day one, the duo - Dylan Mamid and Zachary Rapp-Rovan, better known as DC and Hooks, respectively - have stayed true to themselves and their musical vision. They have never compromised their artistic integrity in pursuit of commercial success or trends. This commitment to staying true to their music has resonated with their fans, building a loyal and passionate following.

But authenticity extends beyond the music itself. Zeds Dead embodies an authentic and genuine persona, both on and off the stage. Their interactions with fans, interviews, and social media presence reflect their true selves, free from pretense or artificiality. This consistency in their character and values has played a significant role in establishing a strong connection with their audience.

Storytelling: Weaving a Narrative Through Music and Visuals

One of the most remarkable aspects of Zeds Dead's brand is their ability to tell stories through their music and visuals. Each track they create, each album they release, is carefully crafted to convey a narrative or evoke a specific emotion. Their music videos, often cinematic and visually stunning, provide an additional layer of storytelling. The combination of music and visuals creates a multi-dimensional experience that resonates deeply with listeners.

Zeds Dead also utilizes their album artwork as a storytelling medium. The cover art for their releases often depicts captivating and thought-provoking imagery, further enhancing the narrative behind their music. By integrating visual elements into their brand, Zeds Dead creates a cohesive and immersive experience for their fans.

Inclusivity: Fostering a Sense of Community

Zeds Dead has always embraced the power of inclusivity in their brand. They have consciously cultivated a sense of community among their fans by fostering an environment where everyone feels welcome and valued. Through their music and performances, Zeds Dead creates a space where people from diverse backgrounds can come together and connect through a shared love of music.

The duo also actively engages with their fanbase, seeking their input and involving them in the creative process. By incorporating fan feedback and ideas into their work, Zeds Dead deepens the sense of community and makes their fans feel like an integral part of their journey.

Innovation: Constantly Evolving and Pushing Boundaries

Innovation is another cornerstone of the Zeds Dead brand. They have consistently pushed the boundaries of electronic music, refusing to be confined by genre conventions. From dubstep to drum and bass, hip-hop to house, Zeds Dead seamlessly weaves together diverse influences to create a sound that is uniquely their own.

This commitment to innovation is not limited to their music. Zeds Dead embraces new technologies, visual art forms, and stage design to create cutting-edge live performances. By constantly exploring new avenues and experimenting with their craft, Zeds Dead ensures their brand remains fresh and exciting.

Building a Lasting Legacy: Beyond the Music

While Zeds Dead's music is undoubtedly the core of their brand, they have also expanded their impact beyond the realm of music. Through philanthropic endeavors and social initiatives, Zeds Dead has demonstrated their commitment to making a positive difference in the world. From supporting charitable organizations to raising awareness about social issues, they have used their platform to effect change and inspire their fans to do the same.

Additionally, Zeds Dead has ventured into entrepreneurial endeavors and collaborations outside of music. By diversifying their creative pursuits, they have built a brand that extends beyond the boundaries of the music industry.

In conclusion, crafting a unique brand requires authenticity, storytelling, inclusivity, innovation, and a commitment to making a lasting impact. Zeds Dead's brand encompasses all these elements and more, allowing them to leave an indelible mark on the world of music and beyond.

Music Videos as an Art Form

Music videos have long been a powerful and influential art form that complement and enhance the music they accompany. They provide a visual representation of the artist's vision, allowing them to express their creativity and connect with their audience in a unique way. In this section, we will explore the significance of music videos as an art form and the impact they have on the music industry and popular culture.

The Power of Visual Storytelling

Music videos offer a platform for artists to tell stories and convey emotions beyond what can be achieved through the audio alone. They allow for a deeper exploration of the song's meaning, as the visuals can provide context and enhance the viewer's understanding.

Just like a film or a painting, a music video is a medium that can evoke a wide range of emotions and provoke thought. It combines moving images, choreography, costume design, and cinematography, creating a multi-sensory experience that captivates the viewer.

Exploring Themes and Concepts

Music videos often explore various themes and concepts that align with the artist's message and aesthetic. They can delve into social issues, political commentary, personal experiences, or fantastical narratives. Through visual symbolism and metaphors, music videos have the power to convey complex ideas and make powerful statements.

For example, in the music video for "Thriller" by Michael Jackson, the narrative of the song is brought to life through a mini-horror film. The video tells a story of a couple who encounters zombies and reflects society's fascination with the macabre. It became an iconic piece of work that revolutionized the medium of music videos.

Pushing Creative Boundaries

Music videos offer artists and filmmakers a space to push creative boundaries and experiment with different visual techniques. They can incorporate animation, special effects, and unconventional editing styles to create unique and memorable visual experiences.

One prime example is the music video for "Take On Me" by A-ha. It combines live-action and pencil-sketch animation, creating a visually stunning and innovative concept. The blending of these two mediums was groundbreaking at the time and showcased the endless possibilities of creativity in music videos.

Collaboration and Cross-Disciplinary Art

Music videos often involve collaboration between musicians, directors, cinematographers, choreographers, and visual artists. This collaboration allows for the fusion of different artistic disciplines and the creation of a multidimensional work of art.

For instance, the collaboration between Beyoncé and director Michel Gondry resulted in the visually stunning music video for "Single Ladies (Put a Ring on It)". The combination of Beyoncé's energetic performance, Gondry's unique visual style, and the choreography by JaQuel Knight created an iconic and influential music video that has been widely imitated and referenced.

Cultural Impact and Viral Sensations

Music videos have the power to shape popular culture and become viral sensations. They can introduce new dance moves, fashion trends, and catchphrases, influencing not only the music industry but also broader society.

For example, the music video for "Gangnam Style" by Psy became a global phenomenon, inspiring countless parodies and dance covers. The energetic dance routine and catchy chorus sparked a global dance craze, making it one of the most-watched and shared videos in the history of YouTube.

The Future of Music Videos

As technology continues to advance, the possibilities for music videos are expanding. Virtual reality (VR) and augmented reality (AR) technologies have the potential to revolutionize the way we experience music videos, allowing for immersive and interactive storytelling.

Furthermore, with the rise of streaming platforms, artists can release music videos directly to their fans, reaching a global audience instantly. This democratization of distribution allows for greater creative freedom and the potential for more diverse and innovative music videos.

In conclusion, music videos are a powerful art form that enhances the listening experience and allows artists to express themselves visually. They provide a platform for storytelling, creative experimentation, and cultural impact. As technology continues to evolve, the future of music videos promises exciting possibilities for artists and audiences alike.

The Importance of Album Artwork

In the world of music, album artwork holds a special place. It is not merely a visual accompaniment to the music; rather, it is an integral part of the artist's expression. The importance of album artwork extends beyond its aesthetic appeal. It serves as a portal into the artist's vision, an invitation to embark on a visual and auditory journey. In this section, we will explore the significance of album artwork and its role in shaping the listener's experience.

A Visual Representation of the Music

Album artwork is an opportunity for musicians to visually represent the essence and mood of their music. It serves as a visual narrative, conveying emotions, themes, and concepts that complement the sonic experience. Just as a book cover can pique one's curiosity, album artwork can intrigue and captivate listeners, setting the stage for the musical journey that lies within.

Consider, for example, the iconic album cover of The Beatles' "Abbey Road." The simple yet powerful image of the band members walking in unison across the zebra crossing resonated with the album's themes of unity and togetherness. The artwork became inseparable from the music itself, forever etched in the collective memory of fans.

Creating a Memorable Brand

Album artwork plays a crucial role in establishing an artist's brand and image. It is an opportunity for musicians to showcase their unique style and aesthetic. Consistency in album artwork can create a recognizable visual identity, helping fans distinguish the artist's work in a crowded music landscape.

Take, for instance, the album covers of Pink Floyd. Their iconic prism logo featured on the cover of "The Dark Side of the Moon" became synonymous with the band's psychedelic sound and philosophical themes. The uniformity of their visual style helped create a cohesive brand that has endured for decades.

Enhancing the Listening Experience

Album artwork has the power to enhance the listener's experience by providing additional layers of depth and context. When a listener holds a physical copy of an album, whether it be a vinyl record or a CD, they engage in a tactile experience. The artwork serves as a gateway, immersing the listener in the world the artist has created.

Moreover, album artwork can serve as a visual companion during the act of listening, guiding the listener through the tracks and adding visual cues to enhance understanding. It can provide visual representations of lyrics, themes, and musical motifs that deepen the listener's connection to the music.

Collaborations with Visual Artists

The creation of album artwork often involves collaborations between musicians and visual artists. This collaboration brings together two different artistic mediums, merging their unique perspectives and expertise. This cross-pollination of creativity can lead to groundbreaking and innovative visual representations of the music.

One example of such collaboration is the partnership between rock band The Mars Volta and artist Storm Thorgerson. Thorgerson's surreal and thought-provoking visuals perfectly complemented the band's progressive and experimental music. Their collaborations, including the iconic artwork for "Frances the Mute," pushed the boundaries of album artwork, becoming an extension of the music itself.

Pushing Creative Boundaries

Album artwork has always served as a platform for pushing creative boundaries and challenging conventions. It allows artists to explore different art forms, experiment with visual aesthetics, and break free from traditional norms.

For instance, the album "To Pimp a Butterfly" by Kendrick Lamar embraced avant-garde and politically charged artwork to reflect the complex themes of racial identity and social justice explored in the music. The bold and unapologetic visuals contributed to the album's impact and critical acclaim.

Unconventional Approaches to Album Artwork

While album artwork often takes the form of a static image, some artists choose unconventional approaches, blurring the lines between music, technology, and visual art. This experimental mindset opens up new avenues for creativity and engages the audience in unexpected ways.

One notable example is Björk's album "Biophilia," which combined digital interactive apps with the music itself. Each song had its own app, allowing listeners to explore different visual and interactive elements related to the music. This groundbreaking approach transformed album artwork into an immersive and multisensory experience.

Conclusion

Album artwork is not a mere afterthought; rather, it is an essential part of the creative process for musicians. It serves as a visual representation of the music, creates a memorable brand, enhances the listening experience, and pushes creative boundaries. Through collaborations with visual artists and innovative approaches, album artwork continues to evolve, captivating and inspiring listeners around the world. It is a testament to the power of art to shape our perception of music and create a lasting impact. So next time you hold an album in your hands, take a moment to appreciate the thought and artistry behind the artwork - for it holds within it much more than meets the eye.

Expressing Emotions through Music

In the realm of music, emotions have the power to transcend language and communicate directly to the soul. From the haunting melody of a sad song to the pulsating beat that makes us want to dance with joy, music has the ability to evoke the full range of human emotions. For the Toronto-based music duo Zeds Dead, expressing emotions through their music is not only an artistic endeavor, but also a means of connecting with their audience on a deep and personal level.

At its core, music is a form of expression. It allows artists to channel their emotions and experiences into melodies, rhythms, and lyrics that resonate with listeners. For Zeds Dead, this process of emotional expression begins in the studio, where they meticulously craft each track to capture a specific feeling or mood. Whether it's the euphoria of a summer festival anthem or the introspection of a melancholic tune, Zeds Dead's music has a distinct emotional essence that sets them apart.

One of the ways Zeds Dead conveys emotions through their music is by carefully selecting and manipulating the elements of their tracks. They use a combination of melodic motifs, harmonies, and chord progressions to create a musical backdrop that reflects the desired emotional response. For example, a minor key with slow, mournful melodies might be employed to convey sadness, while a major key with upbeat, energetic rhythms could evoke happiness and excitement.

In addition to the musical elements, Zeds Dead also incorporates emotional storytelling through their lyrics. Through thought-provoking and introspective words, they communicate their own experiences and emotions, inviting the listener to connect with the song on a deeper level. By sharing their personal struggles, triumphs, and vulnerabilities, Zeds Dead creates a space where the audience can find solace, understanding, and a sense of shared emotion.

Beyond the technical aspects of music production and performance, Zeds Dead recognize the importance of authenticity in expressing emotions. They believe in staying true to themselves and their artistic vision, focusing on creating music that genuinely reflects their own experiences and feelings. This honesty and vulnerability not only enable them to forge a strong emotional connection with their audience but also inspire others to embrace their authentic selves.

Through their music, Zeds Dead strives to create an emotional journey for their listeners. They aim to transport them to a different state of mind, tapping into the collective consciousness and allowing emotions to flow freely. Their unique ability to blend different genres, experiment with sounds, and push musical boundaries gives them the freedom to explore a wide range of emotions, from the darkest depths of sorrow to the brightest heights of joy.

In their live performances, Zeds Dead takes this emotive experience to another level. By curating a dynamic setlist that plays with different moods and energies, they create a collective experience where the audience is united in the enjoyment and expression of emotions through music. The energy of the crowd feeds back into the performance, creating a symbiotic relationship that amplifies and intensifies the emotional journey.

Through their dedication to expressing emotions through music, Zeds Dead has become more than just a music act. They have become a vessel through which listeners can explore and navigate their own emotions. In a world that often suppresses or trivializes feelings, Zeds Dead's music serves as a reminder that emotions are valid, important, and worthy of expression. By creating a space for emotional catharsis and connection, they empower their audience to embrace their own emotional truths and find solace in the music.

To truly appreciate the power of expressing emotions through music, one must experience it firsthand. So, the next time you find yourself listening to a Zeds Dead track or attending one of their electrifying live shows, allow yourself to be fully immersed in the emotion. Let the music wash over you, transporting you to a place where words are not necessary, and emotions speak louder than any language ever could.

Tapping into the Collective Consciousness

When it comes to creating music that resonates with people on a deep level, Zeds Dead has found a way to tap into the collective consciousness. Their ability to connect with listeners on an emotional and spiritual level has set them apart in the electronic music scene. In this section, we will explore the concept of the collective consciousness and how Zeds Dead channels this energy in their music.

Understanding the Collective Consciousness

The collective consciousness is a concept introduced by sociologist Emile Durkheim, referring to the shared beliefs, values, and ideas that exist within a society. It suggests that individuals are not just influenced by their personal experiences, but also by the collective experiences of the larger community.

In the context of music, the collective consciousness can be seen as the collective emotions, thoughts, and experiences that listeners bring to the table. It is a spiritual and emotional connection that is created between the artist and the audience. Zeds Dead has been able to tap into this collective consciousness through their music, creating a powerful bond with their fans.

Creating Emotional Resonance

One of the key aspects of tapping into the collective consciousness is creating emotional resonance. Zeds Dead's music has the ability to evoke strong emotions in listeners, whether it be joy, sadness, or a sense of nostalgia. Through their melodies, harmonies, and carefully crafted soundscapes, they are able to create a sonic experience that touches the deepest parts of our souls.

For example, in their track "Lost You," Zeds Dead combines haunting vocals, ethereal synths, and a driving bassline to create a sense of yearning and longing. This emotional resonance allows listeners to connect with the music on a personal level, drawing them into the collective experience.

Addressing Universal Themes

Another way Zeds Dead taps into the collective consciousness is through their exploration of universal themes in their lyrics. Their songs often touch on topics that resonate with a wide range of people, such as love, loss, and the human experience. By addressing these universal themes, they are able to create a common ground between themselves and their listeners.

In their collaboration with NGHTMRE and GG Magree, "Frontlines," Zeds Dead addresses themes of resilience and fighting against adversity. The lyrics speak to the inner strength and determination that exists within all of us, creating a powerful and empowering message that resonates with listeners worldwide.

Incorporating Cultural Influences

In addition to addressing universal themes, Zeds Dead also taps into the collective consciousness by incorporating cultural influences into their music. They draw

Storytelling through Lyrics

In the world of music, lyrics serve as a powerful tool for storytelling. They have the ability to transport us to different worlds, evoke emotions, and convey profound messages. For Zeds Dead, the art of storytelling through lyrics is a fundamental aspect of their creative process. In this section, we will explore how Zeds Dead uses lyrics to captivate their audience and communicate their artistic vision.

Crafting Compelling Narratives

Zeds Dead is known for their ability to tell compelling stories through their lyrics. Each song they create has a narrative that unfolds, drawing listeners in and taking them on a journey. They carefully choose their words to paint vivid pictures and create memorable characters within their songs.

The storytelling aspect of their lyrics is often inspired by personal experiences, as well as social and political issues they feel strongly about. They use their platform to address these topics in a thought-provoking and inspiring way. Whether it's shining a light on the struggles of mental health or calling for social change, Zeds Dead's lyrics encourage listeners to engage with deeper, more meaningful themes.

Metaphor and Symbolism

In addition to crafting narratives, Zeds Dead employs metaphor and symbolism in their lyrics to convey complex ideas and emotions. Metaphors allow them to express abstract concepts in a more relatable and tangible way. By using figurative language, they create powerful imagery that resonates with listeners and enhances the overall storytelling experience.

Symbolism is another tool they utilize to add layers of meaning to their lyrics. By imbuing certain objects, actions, or settings with symbolic significance, Zeds Dead creates a deeper connection between their audience and the themes they are exploring. This symbolism encourages listeners to reflect on their own experiences and interpret the lyrics in a personal and meaningful way.

Emotional Range and Vulnerability

One of the standout qualities of Zeds Dead's lyrics is their emotional range. They are unafraid to dive into the depths of human emotion, exploring both the joys and sorrows of life. Through their lyrics, they share personal stories of heartbreak, resilience, and triumph, creating a deep sense of connection with their listeners.

Zeds Dead also embraces vulnerability in their lyrics, allowing themselves to be open and authentic. This vulnerability adds an intimate and relatable quality to their songs, making them resonate with a wide range of audiences. By sharing their own struggles and triumphs, they inspire listeners to embrace their own vulnerability and find strength within it.

Lyricism as Poetry

The lyrics of Zeds Dead's music possess a poetic quality that elevates their storytelling. Each word is carefully chosen and placed, creating a rhythmic flow that enhances the musical experience. Their lyrical craftsmanship extends beyond mere words; it becomes a form of artistic expression in its own right.

Like poetry, Zeds Dead's lyrics often employ literary devices such as rhyme, alliteration, and repetition. These techniques enhance the musicality of the lyrics and create a captivating and memorable listening experience. The fusion of music and poetry allows for a deeper level of emotional impact, drawing listeners into the story and evoking a powerful response.

Unconventional storytelling

Zeds Dead doesn't shy away from pushing the boundaries of conventional storytelling. They experiment with unconventional song structures and non-linear narratives, challenging traditional notions of how stories are told through music. By subverting expectations and embracing innovation, they create a unique and immersive listening experience that keeps their audience engaged and intrigued.

This unconventional approach to storytelling also extends beyond the lyrics. Zeds Dead often incorporates spoken word samples or dialogue snippets into their songs, further enhancing the narrative elements. These additions provide a cinematic quality to their music, creating a multidimensional experience for the listener.

In conclusion, storytelling through lyrics is a cornerstone of Zeds Dead's music. Through their lyrics, they craft compelling narratives, employ metaphor and symbolism, embrace emotional range and vulnerability, and elevate their words to a poetic level. Their unconventional approach to storytelling pushes the boundaries of traditional song structure and creates a truly distinctive listening experience. The power of Zeds Dead's storytelling lies in their ability to connect with their audience on a deep and emotional level, leaving a lasting impact with their music.

Addressing Sociopolitical Issues

In the revolutionary world of Zeds Dead, the dynamic duo refuses to shy away from addressing sociopolitical issues through their music. They recognize the power of their platform and utilize it to spark conversations, provoke thought, and create a sense of unity among their fans. Zeds Dead believes that music has the unparalleled ability to transcend borders and ideologies, making it an ideal medium to address the pressing issues faced by our society.

One of the key sociopolitical themes that Zeds Dead often tackles is inequality. They understand that inequality exists in various forms - from socioeconomic disparities to racial and gender inequality. Through their music, they aim to shed light on these issues, creating awareness and encouraging their audience to take action.

For example, in their track "Lost You," featuring Twin Shadow and D'Angelo Lacy, Zeds Dead touches upon themes of heartbreak and the feeling of being lost in a world that is consumed by material possessions and superficiality. The lyrics, combined with the haunting melody, serve as a commentary on the emptiness that can come from pursuing wealth and material success, urging listeners to prioritize human connection and genuine emotions over materialistic pursuits.

In addition to inequality, Zeds Dead also addresses the ongoing climate crisis. They are deeply concerned about the state of the environment and the future it holds for humanity. Through their music, they aim to inspire individuals to take steps towards sustainability and preservation of our planet.

Their track "Collapse 2.0" featuring Memorecks echoes this concern. The intricate production, coupled with thought-provoking lyrics, reflects the despair and urgency surrounding the fate of our planet. By addressing the climate crisis, Zeds Dead hopes to raise awareness and encourage their fans to make conscious choices that have a positive impact on the environment.

It is worth mentioning that Zeds Dead recognizes the importance of providing a safe and inclusive space for their fans. They firmly stand against discrimination, hatred, and bigotry of any kind. Through their music and performances, they aim to foster a sense of unity and acceptance, reminding their audience that we are stronger together.

In their track "Collapse," featuring Memorecks, Zeds Dead touches upon themes of resilience and standing together in the face of adversity. The relentless bassline, combined with the empowering lyrics, serves as a rallying cry for unity and solidarity. By addressing sociopolitical issues, Zeds Dead aims to inspire their fans to stand up for what they believe in and actively work towards creating a more just and equitable society.

Zeds Dead's approach extends beyond their music. They actively collaborate with organizations and participate in initiatives that align with their values. They recognize that change requires collective effort and are dedicated to using their platform to amplify voices that often go unheard.

As Zeds Dead continues to evolve and push boundaries, their commitment to addressing sociopolitical issues remains steadfast. They understand that by tackling these topics head-on, they can inspire change, encourage dialogue, and help shape a better future for all.

Establishing a Sense of Community

Creating a sense of community is an essential aspect of the journey for Zeds Dead. From the beginning, they understood the importance of connecting with their fans on a deeper level and fostering a strong bond among their supporters. This section explores their efforts in establishing a sense of community and the various ways they engage with their audience.

Building a Fanbase

Zeds Dead's journey began with a small but passionate following. They recognized the value of their fans and made conscious efforts to connect with them both online and offline. Through social media platforms, such as Instagram and Twitter, they engaged with their fans by responding to comments, sharing behind-the-scenes content, and interacting with their community in a genuine and personal way.

In addition, the duo actively pursued live performances where they could connect with their fans face-to-face. They played intimate shows at local venues and made it a priority to meet and greet their supporters. By taking the time to engage with their audience individually, Zeds Dead created a strong foundation for their fanbase and established a sense of community from the outset.

Collaborative Projects

One of the ways in which Zeds Dead further established a sense of community was through collaborative projects with other artists. They recognized the power of collaboration in not only creating unique and diverse music but also in bringing like-minded individuals together.

Zeds Dead actively sought out opportunities to work with both established and up-and-coming artists from various genres and backgrounds. By collaborating with artists outside of their comfort zone, they pushed the boundaries of their own sound and introduced their fans to new musical experiences. These collaborations not only expanded their fanbase but also created a sense of unity and collaboration within the larger music community.

Engaging with the Audience

Engaging with their audience has always been a top priority for Zeds Dead. They understand that their fans are an integral part of their success and make continuous efforts to show appreciation and gratitude.

One way they engage with their audience is through exclusive fan events, such as meet-ups, pre-show parties, and fan club gatherings. These events provide opportunities for fans to connect with each other, share their love for Zeds Dead's music, and create lasting memories.

Zeds Dead also actively seeks feedback from their fans. They encourage their audience to share their thoughts on new releases, live performances, and other aspects of their musical journey. By listening to their fans, they not only strengthen their connection with the community but also gain valuable insights that help shape their future projects.

Giving Back to the Community

Zeds Dead believes in the importance of giving back to the community that has supported them throughout their journey. They actively engage in philanthropic endeavors and social initiatives, using their platform to make a positive impact in the world.

In collaboration with various nonprofit organizations, Zeds Dead has organized charity events and fundraisers, donating proceeds to causes they are passionate about. By aligning their musical mission with social and environmental causes, they inspire their fans to join them in making a difference.

In addition, Zeds Dead actively supports and nurtures young talent within the music industry. They provide opportunities for up-and-coming artists to showcase their work, collaborate on projects, and gain exposure. By supporting emerging artists, they contribute to the growth and development of the larger music community.

Creating a Digital Community

In the digital age, Zeds Dead recognizes the power of online communities in fostering a sense of belonging. They have cultivated a strong online presence by engaging with fans across various digital platforms and creating spaces for fans to connect with each other.

Through their official website, forums, and social media platforms, Zeds Dead provides platforms for fans to share their experiences, discuss their favorite tracks, and connect with like-minded individuals. This digital community not only strengthens the bond between Zeds Dead and their fans but also facilitates connections among fans, creating a sense of belonging and unity.

Unconventional Meet-ups

Zeds Dead takes a unique approach to meet-ups, going beyond the traditional fan gatherings. They organize unconventional meet-ups in unexpected locations, such as hidden art installations or secret outdoor spaces. These meet-ups often include surprises, such as impromptu DJ sets or exclusive previews of unreleased tracks.

By organizing these unconventional meet-ups, Zeds Dead creates a sense of adventure and excitement for their fans. These gatherings not only provide opportunities for fans to meet the duo but also create memorable experiences that further strengthen the sense of community among their dedicated supporters.

Challenges and Solutions

Building and maintaining a sense of community comes with its own set of challenges. One of the main challenges is ensuring inclusivity and creating a safe space for everyone within the community. Zeds Dead is committed to fostering an inclusive environment where individuals from all backgrounds can connect and engage. They actively address any instances of discrimination or negativity within their community, working towards creating a positive and welcoming space for all.

Another challenge is striking a balance between personal engagement and the demands of a growing fanbase. As Zeds Dead's popularity has increased, it has become more difficult to individually connect with every fan. To address this challenge, they have implemented various strategies, such as hosting fan competitions, organizing fan-generated content campaigns, and featuring fan art on their social media platforms. These initiatives allow them to engage with their community on a broader scale while still maintaining a personal touch.

The Power of the Zeds Dead Community

The sense of community established by Zeds Dead plays a significant role in their journey. The strong connection with their fans has not only supported their success but has also inspired their artistic growth and innovation. The vibrant and diverse community surrounding Zeds Dead serves as a testament to the enduring power of music in bringing people together.

In this section, we have explored the various ways in which Zeds Dead has established a sense of community. From building a dedicated fanbase to engaging with their audience both online and offline, they have created a space where fans feel valued and connected. Through collaborations, digital communities, and unconventional meet-ups, Zeds Dead continues to foster a sense of belonging and unity among their supporters. Their commitment to giving back and supporting emerging artists further strengthens the community they have built. The power of the Zeds Dead community lies not only in their music but also in their shared experiences and collective passion for the music they create.

The Evolution of the Zeds Dead Sound

Shifting Musical Trends

In the ever-evolving landscape of music, trends come and go like the ebb and flow of the tides. Artists must navigate these shifting currents, staying true to their artistic vision while also adapting to the changing tastes of their audience. For Zeds Dead, this journey through musical trends has been a thrilling rollercoaster ride, pushing boundaries and redefining genres along the way.

Embracing New Sounds

As Zeds Dead embarked on their musical journey, they found themselves immersed in the vibrant and eclectic Toronto music scene. Influenced by a wide range of genres, from hip-hop and reggae to punk and rock, the duo developed a keen ear for incorporating diverse elements into their music.

One of the defining characteristics of Zeds Dead's sound is their ability to blend genres seamlessly. They were at the forefront of the dubstep movement, crafting heavy bass lines and intricate rhythms that resonated with audiences craving a new sonic experience. However, the duo didn't limit themselves to just one genre. They fearlessly explored different styles, incorporating elements of house, drum and bass, and trap into their productions.

The Evolution of Dubstep

Dubstep, with its deep basslines and syncopated beats, took the world by storm in the late 2000s. Zeds Dead emerged during this golden era, pushing the boundaries of the genre and infusing their own unique style. However, as musical trends shifted, so did the landscape of dubstep.

In navigating the changes within the dubstep scene, Zeds Dead refused to be confined by the constraints of a single genre. They began experimenting with different tempos, incorporating elements of future bass and trap into their music. This evolution allowed them to stay relevant and appeal to a wider audience, while still maintaining their signature sound.

Adapting to Changing Musical Trends

The music industry is like a swirling vortex, constantly churning out new trends and sounds. To survive and thrive in this dynamic environment, artists must be able to adapt and embrace change. Zeds Dead understood this concept and used it to their advantage.

As the dubstep scene began to wane in popularity, Zeds Dead shifted gears, exploring new sonic territories. They began incorporating elements of house music into their productions, capitalizing on the rising popularity of the genre. This seamless fusion of genres helped them stay ahead of the curve and maintain their status as trendsetters in the electronic music scene.

Pushing Boundaries and Defying Expectations

True innovators, Zeds Dead constantly pushed the boundaries of their sound, refusing to be confined by the limitations of a single genre. They fearlessly experimented with different styles, from glitch-hop to drumstep, creating a sonic palette that was uniquely their own.

This willingness to take risks and defy expectations is what sets Zeds Dead apart from their peers. Rather than conforming to trends, they embraced their own artistic vision and trusted their instincts, even when it meant venturing into uncharted territory. This bold approach to music-making has garnered them a dedicated fanbase and cemented their status as pioneers in the electronic music industry.

The Future of Shifting Trends

As musical trends continue to evolve, Zeds Dead stands poised to take on whatever challenges lie ahead. Their commitment to innovation and staying true to their artistic vision will undoubtedly shape the future of electronic music.

In a landscape saturated with generic sounds and copycats, Zeds Dead's ability to push boundaries and defy trends is what sets them apart. They have proven time and again that staying true to oneself and embracing change is the key to longevity and success in the music industry.

So, as the tides of musical trends continue to shift, Zeds Dead will be there, leading the charge and creating music that resonates with audiences around the world. It is this unwavering commitment to their craft that ensures their legacy as true musical pioneers.

Maturing Sound and Artistic Growth

As Zeds Dead embarked on their musical journey, their sound began to mature and evolve, showcasing their artistic growth and their ability to push the boundaries of electronic music. This section delves deep into the factors that propelled their sound forward, including inspiration from diverse genres, experimentation with production techniques, and collaborations with other artists.

The Influence of Different Genres

One of the key elements that contributed to Zeds Dead's maturing sound was their exploration of different genres. They delved into various musical styles, drawing inspiration from hip-hop, reggae, rock, and even classical music. This eclectic taste allowed them to infuse their music with a wide range of influences, resulting in a unique and dynamic sound.

By incorporating elements from different genres, Zeds Dead brought a fresh perspective to electronic music. For example, their track "Lost You" featuring Twin Shadow and D'Angelo Lacy combines electronic and rock elements, creating a compelling fusion of two distinct genres. This willingness to experiment and explore new musical territories contributed to their artistic growth and set them apart from their peers.

Experimentation with Production Techniques

Another factor that contributed to Zeds Dead's maturing sound was their constant experimentation with production techniques. They were never afraid to push the boundaries and explore new ways of creating music. This approach allowed them to develop a signature sound that was both innovative and captivating.

One of the notable production techniques employed by Zeds Dead is their use of heavy basslines and intricate melodies. They skillfully combine the two elements to create a rich and textured sound that resonates with their audience. This attention to detail in their production process became a hallmark of their music, contributing to their growth as artists.

Additionally, Zeds Dead embraced the use of live instrumentation in their tracks, incorporating guitars, drums, and pianos to add depth and complexity. This approach infused their music with a human touch and added a layer of authenticity to their sound. By experimenting with different production techniques, Zeds Dead successfully expanded the boundaries of electronic music and continued to mature artistically.

Collaborations with Other Artists

Collaborations played a crucial role in shaping Zeds Dead's maturing sound. They actively sought out opportunities to work with other artists, both within the electronic music scene and from different genres. These collaborations not only allowed them to expand their musical horizons but also provided fresh perspectives and creative insights.

By partnering with artists like Omar Linx, Diplo, and Jauz, Zeds Dead infused their music with new energy and ideas. Each collaboration brought a unique flavor to their sound, resulting in tracks that were a true blend of diverse influences. These partnerships not only contributed to their artistic growth but also helped to cultivate a broader fanbase, as they gained exposure to fans from different genres.

Additionally, Zeds Dead's collaborations extended beyond music. They worked with visual artists, designers, and directors to create immersive visual experiences that complemented their music. This multidisciplinary approach allowed them to explore new avenues of artistic expression and further refine their sound.

Embracing Artistic Growth

Throughout their career, Zeds Dead have embraced artistic growth as a continuous process. They have consistently challenged themselves to push boundaries, experiment with new techniques, and collaborate with a diverse range of artists. This commitment to growth has allowed them to evolve their sound, attracting a dedicated following and cementing their place in the electronic music landscape.

As Zeds Dead's sound matured, so did their connection with their audience. Their dedication to pushing artistic boundaries and creating music that resonates with listeners has earned them a loyal fanbase that continues to grow. By embracing change and constantly striving for artistic growth, Zeds Dead has carved a unique path in the electronic music scene and has left an indelible mark on the industry.

In summary, Zeds Dead's maturing sound and artistic growth can be attributed to their exploration of different genres, experimentation with production techniques, and collaborations with other artists. Their willingness to push boundaries and embrace change has allowed them to evolve their sound and create music that captivates audiences worldwide. As they continue on their musical journey, one thing is certain: Zeds Dead's commitment to artistic growth will continue to shape their sound and influence the future of electronic music.

Exploring Diverse Electronic Subgenres

In the vast realm of electronic music, Zeds Dead has truly pushed the boundaries of genre exploration. They have fearlessly delved into various subgenres, infusing their unique sound with new influences and creating a sonic landscape that captivates listeners. Through their exploration of diverse electronic subgenres, Zeds Dead has demonstrated their versatility and artistic growth, always evolving and pushing the boundaries of what is possible within the electronic music scene.

One of the subgenres that Zeds Dead has explored is future bass. This subgenre combines elements of electronic music with melodic and atmospheric sounds, often featuring lush synths and emotional melodies. By infusing their signature style with the dreamy and ethereal qualities of future bass, Zeds Dead has showcased their ability to craft emotional and immersive musical experiences. Tracks like "Lost You" featuring Twin Shadow and D'Angelo Lacy exemplify this seamless integration of future bass elements into their sound.

Another subgenre that Zeds Dead has embraced is trap. Known for its hard-hitting beats and booming basslines, trap music has gained immense popularity in recent years. Zeds Dead's foray into trap music has allowed them to experiment with intricate drum patterns, aggressive bass drops, and hypnotic melodies. Their track "Collapse 2.0" featuring Memorecks is a prime example of their ability to infuse trap elements into their music, creating a high-energy and dynamic listening experience.

Zeds Dead has also explored the subgenre of drum and bass, known for its fast-paced beats and intricate percussion. Drawing influence from the UK rave scene, drum and bass offers a frenetic energy that tests the limits of production skills. Zeds Dead has deftly incorporated elements of drum and bass into their tracks, adding an extra layer of intensity and adrenaline to their music. The track "Lights Out" featuring Atlas exemplifies their meticulous attention to detail within the drum and bass genre, with its rapid-fire drum patterns and infectious energy.

In addition to these subgenres, Zeds Dead has also ventured into the realms of house music, dubstep, and moombahton, among others. Their ability to seamlessly shift between various subgenres demonstrates not only their musical dexterity but also their willingness to embrace different sonic landscapes.

To stay at the forefront of these diverse electronic subgenres, Zeds Dead keeps a keen eye on emerging trends and experimental sounds. They actively engage with fresh talent and collaborate with artists who are pushing the boundaries of electronic music. By nurturing young talent and pushing artistic boundaries, Zeds Dead ensures that they remain on the cutting edge of electronic music and continue to surprise and captivate their audience.

In conclusion, Zeds Dead's exploration of diverse electronic subgenres is a testament to their artistic growth and versatility. From future bass to trap, drum and bass to house, they have fearlessly incorporated elements of various subgenres into their music, creating a unique and captivating sonic identity. By embracing new sounds and collaborating with innovative artists, Zeds Dead has solidified their status as one of the most influential and boundary-pushing acts in electronic music. The journey of exploring diverse electronic subgenres continues to shape their sound, ensuring that their music remains fresh, exciting, and resonant with listeners well into the future.

Experimenting with Tempo and Beats

In the dynamic world of music production, one of the key elements that can truly transform a track is tempo manipulation. Tempo refers to the speed or pace of a musical piece, while beats serve as the rhythmic foundation. By experimenting with different tempos and beats, Zeds Dead has been able to create unique and captivating sounds that showcase their artistic versatility.

Understanding Tempo

Tempo is measured in beats per minute (BPM) and determines the overall speed of a track. It plays a crucial role in setting the mood, energy, and intensity of a composition. Whether it's a slow and melodic ballad or an energetic and uptempo dance track, tempo greatly influences the emotional response of the listener.

Zeds Dead is known for their ability to manipulate tempo to evoke different emotions and create diverse musical experiences. They understand that tempo can completely change the feel of a track, allowing them to experiment with different genres and styles.

Exploring Different Beats

Beats are the rhythmic patterns that underpin a musical composition. They provide the foundation on which all other musical elements are built. Experimenting with beats allows artists to explore different rhythms and grooves, ultimately shaping the overall feel of a track.

Zeds Dead has a keen understanding of the importance of beats in electronic music. They fuse elements from dubstep, hip-hop, reggae, and various other genres to create their distinct sound. By blending different beats and rhythms, they are able to push the boundaries of electronic music and captivate audiences around the world.

Tempo Variation as a Creative Tool

One of the techniques employed by Zeds Dead to create dynamic and engaging tracks is tempo variation. This involves changing the BPM throughout a song to add excitement, tension, or contrast. By strategically altering the tempo, they are able to keep listeners on their toes and create a truly immersive musical experience.

Tempo variation can be used to build tension during a breakdown and then release it with a high-energy drop. It can also be used to transition between different sections of a track or introduce unexpected elements. Zeds Dead's careful use of tempo variation showcases their attention to detail and their dedication to crafting engaging compositions.

Syncopation and Off-Beat Rhythms

Experimenting with tempo and beats also opens up possibilities for syncopation and off-beat rhythms. Syncopation is the deliberate placement of accent on normally weak beats or between beats. By incorporating syncopated rhythms, Zeds Dead creates a sense of groove and movement that encourages listeners to dance and feel the music on a deeper level.

Off-beat rhythms, on the other hand, involve emphasizing beats that fall between the main beats. This technique adds complexity and complexity to a track and can create a sense of anticipation or tension. Zeds Dead masterfully incorporates off-beat rhythms into their music to keep their audience engaged and create an infectious rhythm that resonates with fans.

Experimentation and Pushing Boundaries

For Zeds Dead, experimenting with tempo and beats is not just about creating catchy tunes—it's about pushing the boundaries of electronic music. They continuously explore new possibilities, draw influences from various genres, and challenge traditional conventions. This commitment to experimentation has allowed them to carve out a unique space in the electronic music landscape.

Aspiring musicians can take inspiration from Zeds Dead's approach to experimentation. By embracing different tempos, meters, and beats, artists can unlock a world of creative possibilities and develop their own signature sound.

Example: "Lost You"

One notable example of Zeds Dead's experimentation with tempo and beats is their track "Lost You." This song features a pulsating beat that creates a hypnotic and captivating rhythm. They seamlessly weave together elements of dubstep, trap, and house, resulting in a genre-defying track that showcases their mastery of tempo manipulation. The dynamic interplay between different beats and tempos keeps the track fresh and exciting from start to finish.

Conclusion

Experimenting with tempo and beats is an essential tool for any musician looking to create unique and innovative compositions. Zeds Dead's ability to manipulate tempo and craft diverse beats has set them apart in the electronic music scene. By breaking conventions and pushing boundaries, they continue to captivate listeners and inspire the next generation of artists. So go ahead, embrace the power of tempo and beats, and let your creativity soar.

Collaborative Projects and Side Ventures

Collaboration is a key aspect of the music industry, and Zeds Dead has embraced working with other artists as a way to constantly push the boundaries of their sound and create unique musical experiences. Throughout their career, they have engaged in numerous collaborative projects and side ventures, further enhancing their reputation as innovators in the electronic music scene.

One prominent example of their collaborative projects is their partnership with fellow Canadian producer Omar LinX. Zeds Dead and Omar LinX joined forces to create a successful series of EPs, including "Victor" and "The Living Dead." These releases perfectly blended Zeds Dead's signature bass-heavy sound with Omar LinX's unique rap and vocal style. The marriage of genres showcased their ability to seamlessly merge electronic music with elements of hip-hop, creating a distinct sound that resonated with fans around the world.

In addition to their work with Omar LinX, Zeds Dead has collaborated with a diverse range of musicians, further expanding their sonic horizons. They have worked with legendary Jamaican reggae artist Barrington Levy on the track "Undah Yuh Skirt," infusing their powerful basslines with Levy's iconic voice. Through this collaboration, Zeds Dead demonstrated their dedication to exploring different genres and incorporating elements of reggae into their music.

Zeds Dead's collaboration with Twin Shadow on the track "Lost You" exemplifies their ability to bridge the gap between electronic and alternative music. The ethereal vocals of Twin Shadow combined with Zeds Dead's signature production techniques created a hauntingly beautiful track that showcased their versatility as artists.

Aside from their collaborative projects, Zeds Dead has also ventured into side projects that allowed them to explore different musical territories. One notable example is their formation of the Deadbeats record label. With Deadbeats, Zeds Dead aims to support and nurture emerging producers, providing them with a platform to showcase their talent. The label has become synonymous with cutting-edge electronic music, and its success has solidified Zeds Dead's influence in the industry.

Moreover, Zeds Dead has embarked on several joint ventures with other artists and brands. They partnered with Jauz for the highly successful "Bite This!" tour, combining their unique sounds and captivating live performances to create an unforgettable concert experience. This collaboration showcased their ability to create synergy with other talented artists and deliver an extraordinary live show.

Furthermore, Zeds Dead has shown their entrepreneurial spirit by launching their own merchandise brand. Their distinctive visual aesthetic is reflected in their merchandise, providing fans with a tangible way to connect with their music. This side venture has allowed them to further engage with their fan base and establish a strong brand identity beyond their music.

Overall, Zeds Dead's collaborative projects and side ventures have not only expanded their artistic capabilities but also enabled them to explore new musical territories and connect with a broader audience. Their willingness to work with other artists and cultivate side ventures demonstrates their commitment to innovation and their constant pursuit of creative growth. Through these endeavors, Zeds Dead continues to leave an indelible mark on the electronic music landscape.

The Influence of the Global EDM Scene

The global electronic dance music (EDM) scene has had a profound impact on the music industry as a whole, and Zeds Dead has been at the forefront of this movement. With their innovative sound and boundary-pushing approach, they have helped shape the EDM landscape and influence countless artists around the world.

The Rise of EDM

EDM has its roots in the underground dance club culture of the 1970s and 1980s, but it wasn't until the late 2000s that it exploded into the mainstream. This surge in popularity was fueled by a combination of factors, including advances in technology, the rise of social media, and the growing demand for high-energy, euphoric music.

Zeds Dead emerged during this pivotal moment in EDM history. With their unique blend of genres like dubstep, trap, and future bass, they quickly gained a dedicated following and became one of the driving forces behind the genre's rise to prominence.

Crossing Borders and Breaking Barriers

One of the most notable aspects of the global EDM scene is its ability to transcend geographical boundaries. Zeds Dead's music has reached listeners around the world, connecting people from different cultures and backgrounds through a shared love of electronic music.

Through their global tours and performances at major festivals, Zeds Dead has been able to expose fans to a diverse range of EDM subgenres and introduce them to new sounds and artists. This cross-pollination of ideas and styles has been instrumental in pushing the boundaries of EDM and driving innovation within the genre.

Collaborative Spirit

The spirit of collaboration is a defining characteristic of the global EDM scene, and Zeds Dead has been at the forefront of this collaborative movement. They have worked with a wide range of artists from different genres and backgrounds, including Omar LinX, DROELOE, and Diplo, to name just a few.

These collaborations not only bring together different musical perspectives but also serve as a platform for artists to experiment and explore new sonic territories. By pushing the boundaries of what is possible within EDM, Zeds Dead has inspired a new generation of musicians to think outside the box and create music that defies categorization.

Expanding the Sound Palette

The global EDM scene has allowed Zeds Dead to explore and incorporate a wide range of musical influences into their sound. By drawing inspiration from genres such as hip-hop, reggae, and rock, they have created a unique sonic palette that sets them apart from their peers.

This willingness to embrace diverse musical influences has allowed Zeds Dead to continually reinvent their sound and stay relevant in an ever-evolving music industry. It has also given them the freedom to experiment with new production techniques and push the boundaries of what is possible within EDM.

Innovation and Evolution

The global EDM scene is constantly evolving, and Zeds Dead has been at the forefront of this evolution. Their willingness to take risks and experiment with new sounds and styles has allowed them to stay ahead of the curve and maintain their relevance in an increasingly saturated market.

From incorporating live instrumentation into their performances to exploring new production techniques, Zeds Dead has consistently pushed the boundaries of what is possible within EDM. Their innovative approach to music-making has not only garnered them critical acclaim but also inspired a new wave of artists to think outside the box and push the limits of their own creativity.

The Power of Community

Perhaps one of the most significant influences of the global EDM scene is its sense of community. EDM festivals and events have become gathering places for fans from all walks of life to come together and celebrate their love for music.

Zeds Dead has embraced this sense of community and has actively engaged with their fans through social media, meet-and-greets, and other interactive experiences. By fostering a strong connection with their fan base, they have created a loyal and dedicated following that continues to support them throughout their career.

Conclusion

The global EDM scene has had a profound influence on Zeds Dead's music and career. From the rise of EDM as a genre to collaborative efforts with artists from around the world, the influence of the global EDM scene cannot be understated.

Through their innovative sound and boundary-pushing approach, Zeds Dead has helped shape the evolution of EDM and inspire a new generation of artists to push the limits of creativity. As the scene continues to grow and evolve, Zeds Dead's impact will undoubtedly be felt for years to come.

Nurturing Young Talent

Nurturing young talent is not only a responsibility but also a passion for Zeds Dead. Throughout their musical journey, the duo has actively sought to support and uplift emerging artists, recognizing the importance of cultivating the next generation of talent. They believe in creating a music community that thrives on collaboration, inspiration, and mutual growth.

To nurture young talent, Zeds Dead has implemented various initiatives and approaches that aim to provide opportunities and guidance for aspiring artists. Here are some strategies they employ:

Establishing a Mentorship Program

Zeds Dead understands the value of mentorship in shaping a young artist's career. They have established a mentorship program where they personally mentor and guide emerging musicians. Through this program, Zeds Dead shares their knowledge, experiences, and industry insights, helping young artists navigate the challenges and pitfalls of the music industry.

Collaborating with Rising Stars

Zeds Dead actively seeks out collaborations with young and talented artists, providing them with a platform to showcase their skills and gain exposure. By featuring these rising stars on their tracks and projects, Zeds Dead helps introduce these artists to a wider audience and offers them valuable networking opportunities within the industry.

Spotlighting New Artists on Their Label

As the founders of Deadbeats, a record label known for its diverse range of electronic music, Zeds Dead has created a space for young artists to release their music and be discovered. They carefully curate and select artists to join the label, providing them with the necessary resources and support to thrive in their musical careers.

Hosting Workshops and Masterclasses

To further foster talent development, Zeds Dead organizes workshops and masterclasses, inviting young producers and DJs to learn from their expertise. These educational events cover various topics, including music production techniques, mixing and mastering, live performance tips, and career advice. By imparting their knowledge and skills, Zeds Dead empowers aspiring artists to strengthen their abilities and pursue their musical aspirations.

Supporting Local Music Communities

Zeds Dead recognizes the importance of nurturing talent at the grassroots level. They actively support local music communities by participating in events, attending shows, and offering opportunities to local artists. By engaging with and uplifting local scenes, Zeds Dead helps create a vibrant and supportive environment for young talent to thrive.

Recognizing Innovative Approaches

In addition to traditional forms of musical expression, Zeds Dead also embraces innovative approaches to music production. They seek out young artists who push the boundaries of genre and experiment with unconventional techniques. By providing a platform for these artists, Zeds Dead encourages creativity and inspires the next generation to explore new horizons in music.

Encouraging Collaboration and Networking

Zeds Dead believes in the power of collaboration and networking, both within and beyond the music industry. They actively encourage young artists to collaborate with one another, fostering a sense of community and shared growth. Additionally, Zeds Dead facilitates connections between artists and industry professionals, helping young talent establish valuable relationships that can further their careers.

Promoting Diversity and Inclusion

Diversity and inclusion are at the core of Zeds Dead's values. They actively seek out and support artists from diverse backgrounds, striving to create a more inclusive music industry. By showcasing a wide range of musical styles and perspectives, Zeds Dead inspires young artists to embrace their uniqueness and shares the message that everyone's voice deserves to be heard.

Overall, nurturing young talent is a vital aspect of Zeds Dead's journey. By providing mentorship, collaboration opportunities, educational initiatives, and a supportive community, they are committed to empowering the next generation of artists to flourish in the ever-evolving music landscape.

Remember, nurturing young talent is not only about guiding and supporting them; it's also about fostering a passion for music, inspiring creativity, and creating an environment where young artists can thrive. With Zeds Dead's dedication and continued efforts, the future of music looks bright and promising.

Evolution of the Live Show Experience

The live show experience is the beating heart of Zeds Dead's music career. As the duo made their mark in the electronic music scene, their performances evolved from simple DJ sets to immersive and unforgettable experiences. The evolution of their live shows is a testament to their commitment to pushing boundaries and creating a captivating atmosphere for their fans.

Creating an Immersive Concert Atmosphere

From the very beginning, Zeds Dead recognized the importance of creating an immersive concert atmosphere. They understood that their music had the power to transport their audience to another world, and they wanted to enhance that experience through visuals, lighting, and stage design.

Zeds Dead began by incorporating eye-catching visuals that synchronized with their music. Using state-of-the-art technology and creative design, they transformed their shows into multisensory experiences. From vibrant colors to mesmerizing animations, the visual elements added depth and dimension to their performances, enabling the audience to feel fully immersed in the music.

Incorporating Visual Elements into Live Shows

As Zeds Dead's live shows gained popularity, their ambitions grew. They saw an opportunity to take their performances to the next level by integrating more visual elements into their live sets. They collaborated with visual artists and designers to create custom stage designs that complemented their music and enhanced the overall experience.

One of their most notable innovations was the use of projection mapping. By projecting visuals onto complex structures and objects on stage, Zeds Dead transformed their performances into immersive visual spectacles. The combination of music and synchronized visuals created a dynamic and captivating show that kept the audience engaged from start to finish.

The Evolution of Live Performance Setups

As technology advanced, Zeds Dead embraced new tools and equipment to enhance their live performances. They constantly experimented with different setups to find the perfect balance between DJing and live instrumentation.

In the early stages of their career, Zeds Dead primarily relied on DJ equipment to create their music during live shows. However, they soon realized the need to incorporate live instruments and vocals to add a new layer of energy to their performances. They seamlessly integrated instruments like guitars, drums, and keyboards into their sets, creating an electrifying live experience.

Interactive Elements and Crowd Participation

Zeds Dead understood that a truly memorable live show wasn't just about the music and visuals—it was also about fostering a connection with their audience. They actively encouraged crowd participation and incorporated interactive elements into their performances.

From encouraging sing-alongs to orchestrating synchronized hand motions, Zeds Dead made sure that their audience felt like an integral part of the show. They even utilized interactive technologies, such as wristbands that lit up in sync with the music, creating a visually stunning display of unity and connection.

Memorable Live Performances and Festival Moments

Zeds Dead's evolution as live performers can be seen through their memorable performances at various music festivals around the world. They seized the opportunity to showcase their creativity and push the boundaries of what a live show could be.

Their performances became the stuff of legend, with jaw-dropping visuals, mind-bending stage setups, and crowd-pleasing surprises. Whether it was performing epic remixes of their own tracks or collaborating with other artists on stage, Zeds Dead consistently delivered unforgettable moments that left their fans craving for more.

The Importance of Mental and Physical Health on Tour

Amidst the excitement and demands of a rigorous tour schedule, Zeds Dead prioritized the well-being of both their fans and themselves. They recognized the importance of mental and physical health in ensuring top-notch performances and long-term sustainability.

To maintain their energy and focus on tour, Zeds Dead implemented healthy lifestyle practices. They made efforts to eat nutritious meals, exercise regularly, and get enough rest between shows. Additionally, they actively promoted self-care and mental well-being to their fans, encouraging them to take care of themselves and embrace a balanced lifestyle.

Managing Expectations and Balance

As Zeds Dead's live show experience evolved, so did the expectations from their fans. They faced the challenge of balancing their desire to constantly innovate while staying true to their unique sound. They understood that the key was to strike a delicate balance between familiarity and freshness.

To manage these expectations, Zeds Dead carefully curated their setlists and incorporated new tracks and remixes alongside their iconic classics. They navigated the fine line between giving their audience what they wanted while still surprising them with fresh sounds and captivating visuals.

The Evolution of the Zeds Dead Live Experience

The evolution of Zeds Dead's live show experience is a testament to their commitment to pushing boundaries and creating memorable experiences for their fans. From their early days as DJs to the immersive sensory experience they deliver today, Zeds Dead's live performances continue to captivate audiences around the world.

As they look toward the future, Zeds Dead will undoubtedly continue to innovate and explore new ways to elevate the live show experience. Their passion for creating a multisensory journey for their fans ensures that each performance is a unique and unforgettable event.

Fun Fact: Zeds Dead Wristband Easter Eggs

During their live shows, Zeds Dead has been known to surprise their fans with hidden Easter eggs in their interactive wristbands. In addition to lighting up in sync with the music, the wristbands occasionally reveal special messages or secret patterns when triggered by certain songs. Fans have discovered these unexpected surprises and have made it a tradition to try and decipher the hidden meanings behind them. It's just one of the many ways Zeds Dead goes above and beyond to create a truly immersive and engaging live experience.

Expanding the Zeds Dead Universe

In the ever-evolving world of music, it is crucial for artists to constantly push boundaries and explore new horizons. Zeds Dead, true to their innovative nature, have been expanding their universe through various endeavors that go beyond their music. From creating their own record label to curating unique live experiences, Zeds Dead is fully dedicated to leaving a lasting impact on the music industry and beyond.

The Formation of Deadbeats Records

In 2016, Zeds Dead founded their own record label, Deadbeats Records. This move allowed them to not only release their own music, but also nurture and promote emerging artists within the electronic music scene. Deadbeats Records quickly gained recognition for its commitment to showcasing fresh talent and pushing the boundaries of genre classification.

Through Deadbeats Records, Zeds Dead has been able to curate a diverse and eclectic roster of artists. These include heavy-hitters like REZZ and Ganja White Night, as well as up-and-coming producers such as Blanke and DNMO. By providing a platform for these artists, Zeds Dead has been instrumental in shaping the future of electronic music.

Innovative Collaborative Projects

Zeds Dead is no stranger to collaboration, and their efforts to expand their universe have only been amplified through their unique collaborative projects. These include working with artists from different genres and disciplines, as well as venturing into non-musical art forms.

One notable collaboration was their partnership with celebrated rapper and producer Omar LinX. Together, they created an innovative blend of hip-hop and electronic music, resulting in tracks like "Out for Blood" and "You and I."

Zeds Dead has also explored collaborations beyond the realm of music. They have worked with visual artists to create stunning stage designs and captivating visual experiences during their live performances. By integrating visual arts with their music, Zeds Dead has created a multi-sensory experience that immerses their audience in a truly unique universe.

Expanding the Live Show Experience

Zeds Dead is renowned for their electrifying live performances, which go far beyond what one would typically expect from a DJ set. To further expand their universe, they continuously innovate and experiment with their live show production.

One aspect that sets their live shows apart is the integration of live instrumentation. By incorporating instruments such as drums, guitars, and keyboards, Zeds Dead adds an extra layer of dynamism and human connection to their performances. This fusion of electronic and live elements creates a truly immersive and energetic experience for their audience.

Additionally, Zeds Dead has embraced technology to enhance their live shows. They utilize cutting-edge visual effects, lighting design, and stage setups to create a visually stunning and interactive environment. This fusion of music, visuals, and technology transports the audience into a world of sonic and visual exploration.

Community Building and Social Initiatives

Zeds Dead understands the importance of community and the impact that artists can have beyond their music. They have consistently supported and engaged with their fanbase, fostering a strong sense of community and connection among their listeners.

In addition to their music, Zeds Dead has also been involved in various social initiatives. They have used their platform to raise awareness about important issues and to promote positive change. Whether it's through fundraising campaigns or collaborating with organizations dedicated to social causes, Zeds Dead strives to make a difference in the world beyond the realm of music.

Looking to the Future

As Zeds Dead continues to expand their universe, their commitment to innovation and pushing boundaries remains unwavering. They constantly seek new ways to evolve their sound, collaborate with artists from different genres, and create immersive live experiences.

Looking to the future, Zeds Dead aims to inspire and influence the next generation of artists and music lovers. Their enduring legacy will not only be defined by their music but also by their ability to create a sense of community, promote positive change, and challenge norms within the music industry.

As fans, we eagerly anticipate the next chapter in the Zeds Dead journey, knowing that their dedication to expanding their universe will continue to captivate and inspire audiences worldwide.

Triumphs and Challenges

Releasing Breakthrough Tracks

Releasing breakthrough tracks is a pivotal moment in the career of any music artist, and Zeds Dead is no exception. These are the tracks that capture the attention of listeners, propel artists into the spotlight, and solidify their place in the music industry. In this section, we explore the process and significance of releasing breakthrough tracks for Zeds Dead.

The Importance of a Breakthrough Track

A breakthrough track can be defined as a single or a collection of songs that resonates deeply with the audience, establishes an artist's unique sound, and elevates their visibility within the industry. It is the song that becomes synonymous with the artist, setting the stage for future success and opening doors to new opportunities.

For Zeds Dead, releasing breakthrough tracks served as a turning point in their career. These tracks showcased their innovative approach to music production, catching the attention of both fans and industry professionals. A breakthrough track not only brings immediate recognition but also acts as a catalyst for future creative endeavors and collaborations.

Crafting the Perfect Track

The process of creating a breakthrough track is a delicate balance of artistry, experimentation, and intuition. Zeds Dead combines their technical expertise with a genuine passion for music to create tracks that resonate with their audience. They delve into various elements, such as melody, rhythm, lyrics, and production techniques, to create a unique sonic experience.

One key aspect of crafting a breakthrough track is understanding the current musical landscape while staying true to one's own artistic vision. Zeds Dead takes inspiration from diverse genres and styles, incorporating elements of dubstep, hip-hop, reggae, and electronic dance music. By blending these influences with their own signature production techniques, they create a sound that stands out in a crowded music industry.

Building Momentum and Anticipation

Releasing breakthrough tracks is not merely about the track itself; it's also about building momentum and anticipation leading up to the release. Zeds Dead understands the importance of strategic marketing and promotion to create buzz around their music. They leverage social media platforms, engage with their fanbase, and collaborate with other artists to generate excitement and anticipation.

Moreover, Zeds Dead's early gigs and the growing fanbase played a crucial role in establishing their reputation and spreading their music. Through captivating live performances and memorable collaborations, they created a loyal following that eagerly awaited their new tracks. This organic fanbase further amplified the impact of their breakthrough tracks, leading to increased exposure and recognition.

Reaching the Masses

Once a breakthrough track is released, the next challenge is to ensure it reaches the masses. Zeds Dead utilizes various distribution channels and platforms to ensure their music reaches a wide audience. They leverage streaming services, radio play, and online music communities to expand their reach and connect with new listeners.

In addition to traditional channels, Zeds Dead also embraces unconventional approaches to engage with their audience. They actively engage with fans on social media, release music videos that showcase their artistic vision, and collaborate with visual artists to create a unique visual experience for their tracks. These efforts help to create a multi-dimensional connection with their audience and foster a deeper appreciation for their music.

Measuring Success

The success of a breakthrough track can be measured in various ways. While commercial success in terms of chart rankings and sales is one indicator, it is not the sole measure of achievement. Zeds Dead values the impact their music has on their audience and the connections they forge through their art.

The reception of a breakthrough track by fans, critics, and the industry at large plays a significant role in determining its success. Positive reviews, awards, and nominations validate the artistic integrity and innovation put into the track. Equally important is the emotional response it evokes in listeners, reflecting the track's ability to connect with people on a deeper level.

An Unconventional Example: Remixing Classics

In the realm of breakthrough tracks, Zeds Dead has embraced an unconventional approach by remixing classics. Remixing allows artists to put their own spin on well-known songs, reinventing them for a modern audience. Zeds Dead's remixes of tracks like "Eyes on Fire" by Blue Foundation and "Eleanor Rigby" by The Beatles demonstrated their ability to breathe new life into beloved classics.

By reimagining these timeless songs, Zeds Dead introduced their unique sound to a broader audience while paying homage to the original artists. This creative approach to remixing garnered attention and captured the imagination of listeners, further solidifying Zeds Dead's reputation as pioneers in electronic music.

Problem: Finding Originality in a Saturated Market

An ongoing challenge for artists releasing breakthrough tracks is finding originality in a saturated market. As more artists emerge, it becomes increasingly difficult to stand out and create a unique sonic identity. Zeds Dead faced this challenge head-on by constantly exploring and pushing their creative boundaries.

How can artists like Zeds Dead maintain their artistic integrity and authenticity while still appealing to a broad audience? How can they ensure their music resonates with listeners in a meaningful way?

Solution: Embracing Innovation and Collaboration

Embracing innovation and collaboration is a key solution to the problem of finding originality in a saturated market. Zeds Dead continuously explores new production techniques, incorporates emerging technologies, and experiments with different genres to maintain a fresh and distinctive sound.

Collaborating with other artists, both within and outside their genre, also allows Zeds Dead to tap into new creative energies and perspectives. This cross-pollination of ideas results in unique musical combinations that push the boundaries of their sound. By embracing collaboration and seeking out new voices, artists like Zeds Dead can continue to innovate and resonate with their audience.

Example: The Collaborative Approach

One powerful example of Zeds Dead's collaborative approach is their partnership with artists from different musical backgrounds. For instance, their collaboration with Omar LinX on the song "Out for Blood" seamlessly blends elements of hip-hop and electronic music, resulting in a track that appeals to fans across genres.

This collaborative mindset not only broadens the artistic scope of Zeds Dead's music but also introduces their work to new audiences. It allows them to draw inspiration from a diverse range of perspectives, ensuring a continued evolution of their sound.

Resources and Further Exploration

For artists looking to release breakthrough tracks, there are several resources and avenues to explore. Online music communities, such as SoundCloud and Bandcamp, provide platforms to showcase original music and connect with listeners. These platforms also offer opportunities for feedback, collaboration, and exposure within a supportive community.

Additionally, seeking guidance from experienced industry professionals, mentors, or music schools can provide valuable insights into the art of crafting breakthrough tracks. Understanding the shifting dynamics of the music industry, staying up-to-date with emerging technologies, and investing time in refining production skills are essential steps for artists aiming to make their mark.

In conclusion, releasing breakthrough tracks is a crucial milestone in an artist's career, and Zeds Dead has demonstrated a remarkable ability to create music that captivates and connects with its audience. Through their innovative sound, strategic promotion, and collaborative spirit, they have been able to consistently release tracks that push boundaries, inspire others, and leave a lasting impact on the music industry. By maintaining their artistic integrity and embracing new creative avenues, Zeds Dead continues to evolve their sound and shape the future of electronic music.

Reaching the Top of the Charts

Ah, the sweet taste of success! For Zeds Dead, reaching the top of the charts was no simple feat. It was a culmination of hard work, talent, and a pinch of luck. In this chapter, we delve into the journey of Zeds Dead as they climbed their way to the pinnacle of the music industry.

The Road Less Traveled

Zeds Dead's rise to fame was not an overnight success story. It was a journey filled with ups and downs, challenges and triumphs. They initially started out as underground artists, crafting their unique blend of bass-heavy music in the shadows.

While their early tracks gained underground recognition and a loyal fanbase, it wasn't until their breakout hits that they truly skyrocketed to the top. These breakout tracks, with infectious melodies and irresistible basslines, caught the attention of not only die-hard fans but also industry insiders.

Crafting Chart-Topping Hits

Crafting a chart-topping hit is no easy task. It requires the perfect combination of catchy hooks, memorable lyrics, and an irresistible beat. Zeds Dead understood this formula and used it to their advantage.

One of their key strengths was their ability to blend different genres seamlessly. They expertly combined elements of dubstep, hip-hop, and reggae, creating a refreshingly unique sound that resonated with a wide audience.

Take, for example, their hit single "Lost You." The combination of haunting vocals, hard-hitting drops, and infectious melodies created a sonic experience that left listeners craving for more. The track climbed the charts, captivating the hearts of both electronic music enthusiasts and mainstream listeners.

Collaborations that Catapulted Success

Collaborations have always played a significant role in Zeds Dead's journey to the top. Working with other talented artists allowed them to tap into new sounds and expand their musical horizons.

Their collaboration with Omar LinX, a Canadian rapper, on the song "You and I" was a game-changer for Zeds Dead. The track resonated with a wide audience, showcasing their ability to fuse electronic music with rap seamlessly. It became an instant hit and propelled them further into the spotlight.

Navigating the Ever-Changing Music Industry

Reaching the top of the charts is not just about making great music; it's also about effectively navigating the ever-changing music industry. Zeds Dead understood the importance of embracing new technologies and platforms to stay relevant and reach their fans.

The rise of streaming platforms like Spotify and SoundCloud presented new opportunities for artists to connect with their audience. Zeds Dead took full advantage of these platforms, sharing their music and engaging with fans directly. Their presence on social media allowed them to build a strong fan community, creating a sense of belonging and loyalty.

Standing Out in a Sea of Talent

In today's music landscape, competition is fierce. A multitude of talented artists are vying for attention, making it even more challenging to stand out from the crowd. Zeds Dead managed to create a unique brand that set them apart from others.

Their aesthetic and visual identity played a pivotal role in capturing the audience's attention. The hauntingly beautiful album artwork, the mesmerizing stage design, and the visually stunning music videos all worked together to create a cohesive and immersive experience for fans.

Maintaining Authenticity in the Face of Success

As Zeds Dead climbed the charts and gained international recognition, they faced the challenge of maintaining their authenticity. It's easy for artists to be swayed by industry expectations and pressures, but Zeds Dead stayed true to their roots.

They continued to experiment with different genres and push the boundaries of electronic music. Rather than succumbing to the commercial pressures, they remained committed to their sound and vision.

Lessons Learned from Reaching the Top

Reaching the top of the charts was a dream come true for Zeds Dead, but it didn't come without valuable lessons. They learned the importance of perseverance, creativity, and staying true to oneself.

They discovered that success is not just about numbers on the charts; it's about the impact they have on their fans' lives. The genuine connection they forged with their audience was ultimately what propelled them to the top.

Celebrating Success, Forever Hungry for More

For Zeds Dead, reaching the top of the charts was not the end of their journey. It was merely a stepping stone towards even greater things. They celebrated their success but remained forever hungry for more.

As they continue to push boundaries, explore new genres, and captivate audiences with their electrifying performances, one thing is certain – the legacy of Zeds Dead will endure. Their commitment to innovation, authenticity, and creating music from the heart ensures that their story will continue to inspire future generations of artists.

And thus, with the taste of success lingering on their lips, Zeds Dead embarked on their continuing musical odyssey, ready to conquer new heights and captivate music lovers worldwide. The journey was far from over, and the best was yet to come.

Playing Iconic Music Festivals

Playing at iconic music festivals is a dream come true for any artist, and Zeds Dead has had their fair share of unforgettable festival experiences. These events provide an opportunity for them to showcase their unique sound to a diverse and enthusiastic audience. In this section, we will explore the significance of playing at iconic music festivals, the impact it has on Zeds Dead's career, and some memorable festival moments.

The Significance of Iconic Music Festivals

Iconic music festivals are more than just a gathering of music lovers; they are cultural phenomena that shape the music industry and leave a lasting impact on both artists and fans. These festivals serve as platforms for artists to showcase their talents to a massive audience and gain exposure on an international scale. They provide a unique opportunity for artists to connect with their fans and create memorable experiences.

For Zeds Dead, playing at iconic music festivals has been a pivotal moment in their career. It has allowed them to reach new fans, collaborate with other artists, and solidify their place in the electronic music scene. These festivals have also provided them with valuable networking opportunities, helping them forge relationships with industry professionals and fellow musicians.

Impact on Zeds Dead's Career

Playing at iconic music festivals has had a profound impact on Zeds Dead's career. These events have helped catapult them into the mainstream electronic music scene, allowing them to reach a wider audience and gain recognition from industry heavyweights. The exposure gained from performing at these festivals has led to increased album sales, sold-out shows, and a boost in their overall popularity.

One of the most significant impacts of playing at iconic music festivals for Zeds Dead has been the opportunity to collaborate with other artists. Sharing the stage with renowned musicians has not only elevated their performances but has also opened doors for future collaborations and creative endeavors. These collaborations have allowed them to explore new musical territories and expand their fan base even further.

Memorable Festival Moments

Playing at iconic festivals has given Zeds Dead countless memorable moments throughout their career. One standout memory was their performance at the Electric Daisy Carnival (EDC) in Las Vegas. The massive crowd, awe-inspiring production, and high-energy atmosphere created an unforgettable experience for both the duo and their fans. Another notable moment was their appearance at Tomorrowland, one of the world's largest music festivals held in Belgium. The sheer magnitude of the event and the international audience solidified Zeds Dead's status as global electronic music icons.

In addition to these large-scale festivals, Zeds Dead has also played at smaller, more intimate gatherings such as Lightning in a Bottle and Shambhala Music Festival. These festivals allowed them to connect with their fans on a more personal level and create a sense of community among festival-goers.

Overcoming Challenges

Playing at iconic music festivals comes with its fair share of challenges. The pressure to deliver a stellar performance, technical difficulties, and unpredictable weather conditions are just a few of the obstacles artists face. However, Zeds Dead has shown resilience and adaptability in the face of these challenges, always seeking to provide an unforgettable experience for their audience.

One challenge Zeds Dead faced was the need to stand out among a sea of talented artists at these festivals. They tackled this by continually pushing boundaries and showcasing their unique sound, incorporating elements of various genres into their sets. This dedication to innovation and their unwavering commitment to artistic integrity have helped them captivate audiences and leave a lasting impression.

The Future of Festival Performances

As Zeds Dead continues to evolve and explore new musical horizons, their future festival performances promise to be even more groundbreaking. With advancements in technology, festival experiences are becoming increasingly immersive and interactive. Zeds Dead aims to embrace these innovations and incorporate them into their live performances, creating a truly unforgettable and multi-sensory experience for their fans.

Furthermore, Zeds Dead is not only focused on their own performances but also on nurturing the next generation of artists. They have expressed a desire to curate their own festival in the future, providing a platform for both established and emerging talent to shine. By giving back to the music community, Zeds Dead hopes to leave a lasting impact on future generations of artists.

Conclusion

Playing at iconic music festivals has been an integral part of Zeds Dead's journey. These festivals have not only provided them with valuable exposure and networking opportunities but have also allowed them to connect with their fans on a profound level. The impact of festival performances on their career cannot be understated, from collaborating with other artists to solidifying their status as global icons.

As Zeds Dead looks to the future, their festival performances will continue to push the boundaries of what is possible in live electronic music. With their dedication to innovation and their commitment to bringing their unique sound to the world, Zeds Dead is poised to leave an indelible mark on the music festival landscape.

Dealing with Criticism and Negativity

In the world of music, criticism and negativity are inevitable. No matter how talented or successful an artist is, there will always be someone who disagrees with their style, approach, or creative choices. For Zeds Dead, facing criticism has been a part of their journey from the very beginning. In this section, we will explore how they have dealt with criticism and negativity, and the lessons we can learn from their experiences.

The Sting of Criticism

Criticism can come from different sources, including music critics, industry professionals, and even fans. It can be disheartening to receive negative feedback, especially when you've poured your heart and soul into your music. Zeds Dead have had their fair share of criticism over the years, and they have learned to approach it with a level-headed perspective.

They understand that not everyone will resonate with their sound or artistic choices, and that's okay. They acknowledge that music is subjective, and every listener has their own preferences. Instead of taking criticism personally, they see it as an opportunity for growth and improvement.

Turning Negativity into Fuel

Rather than letting criticism bring them down, Zeds Dead use it as motivation to push themselves further. They believe that negative feedback can be a catalyst for self-reflection and evolution. By analyzing the critiques objectively, they can identify areas where they can refine their craft.

Negativity can fuel their determination to prove their worth and continue creating music that resonates with their fans. They channel the energy from criticism into their music, turning it into a driving force behind their creativity.

Staying True to Themselves

One of the most crucial lessons Zeds Dead has learned is the importance of staying true to their artistic vision, regardless of what others may say. They have never let external judgments dictate their creative decisions. They believe in following their instincts and producing music that feels genuine and authentic to them.

By staying true to themselves, Zeds Dead has garnered a loyal fanbase who appreciates their unique sound. They have learned that even in the face of criticism, it is essential to prioritize their artistic integrity.

Surrounding Themselves with Support

Dealing with criticism can be challenging, but having a strong support system can make a world of difference. Zeds Dead understands the value of surrounding themselves with a team of trusted individuals who believe in their talent and vision. They have built a network of collaborators, managers, and friends who provide unwavering support and encouragement.

Additionally, their fanbase plays a significant role in boosting their morale. The positive feedback they receive from their fans acts as a shield against negativity, reminding them of the impact their music has on others.

The Power of Self-Reflection

Criticism can be an opportunity for self-reflection. Zeds Dead regularly engage in introspection to assess their own work objectively. They view criticism as a chance to learn from their mistakes and grow as artists.

By taking the time to evaluate their music and performances, they can identify areas for improvement and make adjustments accordingly. They use criticism as a tool to enhance their creativity and evolve their sound over time.

Closing Thoughts

Dealing with criticism and negativity is an inevitable part of an artist's journey, including the talented duo of Zeds Dead. However, they have shown us that it is possible to navigate these challenges and turn them into opportunities for growth.

By staying true to themselves, embracing feedback, and maintaining a strong support system, Zeds Dead has triumphed over adversity and continued to create music that resonates with their fans. They serve as an inspiration for aspiring artists who may encounter criticism along their own musical journeys.

Remember, facing criticism doesn't mean compromising your artistic vision. Use it as a tool for self-improvement and let it fuel your determination to succeed. Stay true to yourself, surround yourself with a strong support system, and never stop evolving. The future of your music is in your hands.

Now let's move on to the next chapter and continue exploring the captivating story of Zeds Dead.

Overcoming Personal and Professional Struggles

Life as a musician is not always glamorous. Behind the scenes, there are personal and professional struggles that artists like Zeds Dead must face. In this section, we will delve into some of the challenges they have encountered throughout their career and how they managed to overcome them.

Balancing Personal Life with Demands of the Industry

Being in the music industry can be all-consuming, with long hours, constant travel, and the pressure to always deliver your best. Zeds Dead found themselves grappling with the challenge of balancing their personal lives with the demands of their career.

For years, they struggled to find time for themselves, constantly being on the road and immersed in their work. But they soon realized that neglecting their personal lives would only lead to burnout and unhappiness. They made a conscious effort to establish boundaries and prioritize self-care.

Through regular communication and support from friends and family, Zeds Dead learned to strike a balance between their work and personal life. They began setting aside quality time for themselves, engaging in hobbies and activities that brought them joy outside of music.

Dealing with Creative Blocks and Self-Doubt

Every artist, no matter how talented, goes through periods of self-doubt and creative blocks. Zeds Dead is no exception. They have had their fair share of moments when the music just didn't flow, and doubts crept in about their abilities.

During these challenging times, Zeds Dead focused on embracing the process rather than fixating on the end result. They learned to trust their instincts and push through the creative blocks, knowing that breakthroughs often come from perseverance.

They also sought inspiration from outside sources, immersing themselves in art, nature, and other forms of music. By broadening their horizons and exploring different genres and styles, Zeds Dead found new ways to reignite their creative spark.

Handling Criticism and Negative Feedback

Criticism and negative feedback are inevitable in any creative field. Zeds Dead has experienced their fair share of it throughout their career. However, they have learned to navigate these challenges with grace and resilience.

Instead of letting criticism discourage them, Zeds Dead used it as an opportunity for growth and self-reflection. They sought constructive feedback from mentors and industry veterans, using it to improve their craft and refine their skills.

They also recognized the importance of staying true to themselves and their artistic vision. While it's essential to listen to feedback, Zeds Dead never compromised their authenticity for the sake of pleasing others. They embraced their unique sound and remained steadfast in their artistic choices.

Supporting Mental Health and Well-being

The music industry can take a toll on an artist's mental health and well-being. Zeds Dead understood the importance of taking care of their mental and emotional well-being throughout their journey.

They actively prioritized self-care, incorporating practices such as meditation, exercise, and therapy into their routine. They also surrounded themselves with a supportive network of friends, family, and colleagues who offered a listening ear during challenging times.

Moreover, Zeds Dead used their platform to raise awareness about mental health issues within the music industry. They encouraged open conversations and urged fellow artists to seek help when needed, breaking down the stigma surrounding mental health.

Embracing Resilience and Perseverance

Above all, Zeds Dead's journey has exemplified the importance of resilience and perseverance. Despite the personal and professional struggles they faced, they never gave up on their dream.

They embraced the setbacks as learning opportunities, allowing them to grow and evolve as artists. Zeds Dead remained persistent in their pursuit of creating music that resonated with their audience, never losing sight of their passion and purpose.

In times of doubt, they turned to their dedicated fanbase for support and motivation. The unwavering support from their fans served as a reminder of the positive impact their music had on others, fueling their determination to overcome any obstacle.

Ultimately, Zeds Dead's story is a testament to the power of resilience and perseverance in the face of personal and professional struggles. Their ability to overcome challenges and remain true to themselves has solidified their place in the music industry and served as an inspiration to aspiring artists.

Maintaining Creative Integrity

In the ever-evolving world of music, maintaining creative integrity is a constant challenge. It requires artists to stay true to their artistic vision while navigating the pressures and expectations of the industry. For Zeds Dead, preserving their unique sound and style has been a key aspect of their success. In this section, we will explore the strategies and mindset behind maintaining creative integrity in the context of their music career.

The Importance of Authenticity

At the heart of maintaining creative integrity is the concept of authenticity. Zeds Dead firmly believes that music should be a reflection of their true selves, their emotions, and their experiences. They recognize the importance of creating music that resonates with their own artistic sensibilities, rather than conforming to trends or expectations.

Authenticity allows for a genuine connection with the audience. When artists create from a place of honesty and vulnerability, their music becomes relatable and meaningful. Zeds Dead's commitment to authenticity has formed a deep bond with their fanbase, who appreciates and identifies with the genuine emotions expressed in their music.

Resisting Commercial Pressures

The music industry is often driven by commercial interests. Artists are often encouraged to conform to popular trends in order to achieve commercial success. However, Zeds Dead has always been unwavering in their pursuit of artistic freedom and self-expression.

Resisting commercial pressures requires a strong sense of self and confidence in one's artistic abilities. Zeds Dead acknowledges that compromising their creative vision for commercial gain would ultimately lead to a loss of authenticity and artistic integrity. Instead, they prioritize artistic growth and exploration, allowing their music to evolve naturally without sacrificing their unique sound.

Embracing Risk and Experimentation

Maintaining creative integrity requires a willingness to take risks and experiment with new ideas. Zeds Dead continuously pushes the boundaries of their sound, exploring different genres and styles, and incorporating diverse influences. They embrace the unknown and view experimentation as an opportunity for growth and self-discovery.

Taking risks can be daunting, as it may not always yield immediate success or acceptance. However, Zeds Dead believes that true creativity lies outside of one's comfort zone. By embracing risk and pushing their own boundaries, they have been able to uncover new artistic possibilities and redefine their sound.

Protecting the Creative Process

The creative process is a vulnerable and sacred space for artists. Maintaining creative integrity requires protecting this process and creating an environment that fosters uninhibited creativity. Zeds Dead emphasizes the importance of having a supportive team and like-minded collaborators who understand and respect their artistic vision.

They also value the role of solitude and personal reflection in their creative process. Finding moments of stillness and introspection allows them to tap into their creative energy and create music that is genuine and meaningful.

Staying Grounded in the Face of Success

Success can often be a double-edged sword for artists. While it brings recognition and opportunities, it can also create pressure to replicate past successes or conform to expectations. Zeds Dead acknowledges the importance of staying grounded in the face of success and remaining true to their creative instincts.

They approach each project with a fresh perspective, avoiding the trap of repetition or formulaic approaches. By staying connected to their own creative process and avoiding external influences, they are able to maintain their artistic integrity and continue evolving their sound.

Fostering an Authentic Connection with Fans

Maintaining creative integrity also involves fostering an authentic connection with fans. Zeds Dead recognizes the importance of engaging with their audience and creating a sense of community. They value the feedback and support of their fans, which serves as a source of inspiration and affirmation.

Through social media, live performances, and fan interactions, Zeds Dead strives to create a welcoming and inclusive space for their fans. They actively involve their audience in their creative process and make a conscious effort to listen to their feedback. This collaborative approach helps them to stay connected to their fanbase and ensures that their music remains relevant and resonates with their audience.

Harnessing Inspirations from Various Art Forms

Creative inspiration can be found in unexpected places. Zeds Dead draws inspiration from various art forms beyond music, including visual art, film, and literature. They believe that by exploring diverse art forms, they can infuse their music with new perspectives and creative concepts.

This interdisciplinary approach allows Zeds Dead to break free from conventional genres and create a unique and dynamic sound that transcends traditional boundaries. It also enables them to bring a fresh and innovative perspective to their music, ensuring that their creative integrity remains intact.

The Power of Persistence and Adaptation

Maintaining creative integrity requires persistence and adaptability. Zeds Dead has faced numerous challenges and setbacks throughout their career, but they have remained steadfast in their commitment to their artistic vision. They embrace challenges as opportunities for growth and adaptation.

By persistently pushing forward and embracing change, Zeds Dead has been able to navigate the ever-changing landscape of the music industry without compromising their creative integrity. They have shown that maintaining artistic integrity is not about clinging to past successes, but rather about embracing the future with an open mind and a willingness to evolve.

Unconventional Wisdom: Embracing Creative Constraints

While maintaining creative integrity often involves breaking free from constraints, there can be beauty in embracing limitations. Creative constraints can spark ingenuity and force artists to think outside the box. Zeds Dead recognizes that constraints can lead to innovative solutions and unexpected artistic directions.

Whether it's working with limited resources, experimenting with new production techniques, or collaborating with artists from different genres, embracing creative constraints can invigorate the creative process and lead to breakthroughs that may not have been possible otherwise.

In conclusion, maintaining creative integrity is a constant journey that requires staying true to one's artistic vision, resisting commercial pressures, embracing risk and experimentation, protecting the creative process, staying grounded in the face of success, fostering an authentic connection with fans, harnessing inspirations from various art forms, and cultivating persistence and adaptability. By following these principles, Zeds Dead has been able to carve out a unique and enduring artistic path while leaving a lasting impact on the music industry. Their story serves as a reminder that creative integrity is not a destination, but rather an ongoing commitment to self-expression and creative growth.

Navigating the Music Industry

Navigating the music industry can feel like sailing on a stormy sea. It requires knowledge, skill, and a keen understanding of the ever-changing currents. In this section, we'll dive deep into the treacherous waters of the music industry, exploring the challenges and triumphs that Zeds Dead faced on their journey.

Understanding the Landscape

The first step in navigating the music industry is understanding its complex landscape. From record labels to managers, agents to promoters, there are numerous players in the industry, each with their own agenda and motivations. It's important to familiarize yourself with the different roles and responsibilities to make informed decisions.

Example: Imagine you're an emerging artist trying to secure a record deal. You've been approached by several labels, each offering different terms. By understanding the landscape, you can evaluate the potential benefits and drawbacks of each offer, ensuring you make the best choice for your career.

Building Relationships

In the music industry, relationships are key. Building strong connections with industry professionals, fellow artists, and fans can open doors and provide valuable support. However, it's essential to cultivate genuine relationships based on mutual respect and shared goals.

Example: Zeds Dead forged relationships with other artists, creating a network of support and collaboration. These connections led to joint projects, shared gigs, and a wider audience. By building relationships with peers and fans, Zeds Dead grew their presence in the music industry.

Navigating Contracts and Legalities

Contracts and legalities are a crucial part of the music industry. Understanding the intricacies of contracts, licensing agreements, copyrights, and royalties is essential to protect your rights and ensure fair compensation for your work. Seeking legal advice and having a solid grasp of contract language will serve you well in this complex realm.

Example: Zeds Dead learned early on the importance of carefully reviewing contracts. They partnered with knowledgeable entertainment lawyers who helped negotiate terms and navigate legal complexities. This allowed them to secure fair deals and protect the rights to their music.

Marketing and Promotion

In a saturated industry, standing out from the crowd requires effective marketing and promotion. Creating a strong brand identity, leveraging social media, and employing innovative marketing strategies can help gain visibility and attract a wider audience. Understanding the power of marketing and promotion is crucial in today's digital age.

Example: Zeds Dead recognized the importance of marketing and promotion from the start. By engaging with fans on social media, sharing behind-the-scenes content, and creating visually captivating music videos, they built a strong brand and cultivated a dedicated following.

Industry Trends and Adaptability

The music industry is ever-evolving, with trends constantly shifting. Staying ahead of the curve and adapting to changes is essential for longevity and success. Embracing new technologies, exploring different genres, and continually honing your craft are vital to navigate the industry's changing tides.

Example: Zeds Dead embraced the evolution of electronic music, experimenting with different genres and styles. Their adaptability allowed them to stay relevant and appeal to a wide audience, solidifying their position in the music industry.

Entrepreneurial Mindset

In addition to honing their musical craft, artists must adopt an entrepreneurial mindset. Developing business skills, understanding revenue streams, and exploring alternative income streams are essential for sustainable success in the music industry. Embracing a diverse range of revenue sources can provide stability and open new opportunities.

Example: Zeds Dead recognized the importance of diversifying their income streams. They explored merchandise sales, licensing agreements, and curated events, expanding their brand beyond the traditional music releases and performances. This entrepreneurial mindset allowed them to thrive in a competitive industry.

Remaining Authentic

While navigating the music industry, it's crucial to stay true to your artistic vision and maintain authenticity. It's easy to get caught up in the pursuit of commercial success and compromise your artistic integrity. However, staying true to yourself and your unique sound will resonate with fans and create a lasting impact.

Example: Zeds Dead remained authentic throughout their journey. They consistently produced music that reflected their diverse influences and personal style. This commitment to staying true to their artistic vision gained them a loyal fanbase and solidified their reputation in the industry.

Exercise: Breaking into the Music Industry

Imagine you're an aspiring artist looking to break into the music industry. Write a detailed plan outlining the steps you would take to navigate the industry successfully. Be sure to include strategies for building relationships, marketing and promotion, and adapting to industry trends. Consider the importance of legalities, contracts, and maintaining authenticity in your plan.

Additional Resources

To further explore the intricacies of the music industry and gain insights from industry professionals, here are some recommended resources:

- "All You Need to Know About the Music Business" by Donald S. Passman
- "Music Marketing for the DIY Musician" by Bobby Borg
- "How to Make It in the New Music Business" by Ari Herstand
- Online forums and communities for independent artists, such as Reddit's r/WeAreTheMusicMakers and r/IndieMusicFeedback

Remember, navigating the music industry requires resilience, determination, and a passion for your craft. Stay true to yourself, never stop learning, and always embrace new opportunities. Good luck on your journey!

Balancing Success and Authenticity

Finding the delicate balance between success and authenticity can be a challenging task for any artist. In the ever-evolving music industry, it is important to stay true to oneself while also striving for recognition and achievement. Zeds Dead, with their unique sound and artistic vision, have successfully navigated this balance throughout their career. In this section, we will explore the strategies and principles they have employed to maintain their authenticity while achieving a high level of success.

Staying True to their Artistic Vision

One of the key aspects of balancing success and authenticity is staying true to one's artistic vision. Zeds Dead has always put their music first, prioritizing their passion for creating innovative and unique sounds. They have carved out their own niche in the electronic music scene by pushing boundaries and constantly evolving their sound.

To maintain this authenticity, Zeds Dead has stayed true to their musical roots while also incorporating new influences and experimenting with different genres. They have a deep appreciation for various styles of music, which is reflected in their diverse discography. By embracing their eclectic tastes and staying true to their musical instincts, Zeds Dead has been able to create a distinct and authentic sound that resonates with their fans.

Resisting Trendy Pressures

In the pursuit of success, artists often face pressure to follow current trends and conform to popular styles. However, Zeds Dead has always resisted these temptations, choosing instead to forge their own path and create music that is true to themselves. They have remained steadfast in their commitment to originality and creativity, rather than succumbing to the pressures of the mainstream.

By focusing on their own creative process and artistic vision, Zeds Dead has been able to maintain their unique sound and identity. They understand that trends come and go, but authenticity and innovation endure. This refusal to compromise their artistic integrity has not only garnered them a dedicated fanbase but has also allowed them to stand out in a crowded music industry.

Maintaining Creative Control

Another crucial aspect of balancing success and authenticity is maintaining creative control. Zeds Dead has always had a hands-on approach to their music, from the songwriting and production process to the visual artistry that accompanies their work. They have actively sought to retain control over their creative output, ensuring that their artistic vision remains intact.

By maintaining creative control, Zeds Dead has been able to shape their own destiny and make decisions that align with their vision and values. They have been able to resist external pressures and stay true to their art, resulting in a body of work that is truly representative of who they are as artists.

Cultivating a Strong Fan Community

One of the most significant factors in maintaining authenticity while achieving success is cultivating a strong and loyal fan community. Zeds Dead has always prioritized connecting with their fans and building a supportive community around their music. They have recognized the importance of genuine fan engagement and have taken the time to interact with their audience through social media, live shows, and various other platforms.

By nurturing this fan community, Zeds Dead has been able to stay grounded and connected to their roots. They understand that their success is built on the support and appreciation of their fans, and they remain committed to delivering music that resonates with their audience. This strong fan base has not only provided them with the necessary support to sustain their career but has also served as a constant reminder of their authenticity and the impact their music has on people's lives.

Embracing Collaboration and Growth

While maintaining authenticity is crucial, it is also important for artists to embrace collaboration and promote personal growth. Zeds Dead has actively sought out collaborative projects with other artists, both within and outside of the electronic music genre. These collaborations have allowed them to push the boundaries of their sound, experiment with new styles, and explore different creative avenues.

By embracing collaboration, Zeds Dead has been able to learn from others and continuously evolve as artists. They understand that growth and evolution are essential to maintaining authenticity in a constantly changing musical landscape. Through these collaborations, they have been able to bring fresh perspectives and ideas into their work, keeping their sound dynamic and relevant.

Unconventional Aspects of Balancing Success and Authenticity

Finding the balance between success and authenticity often requires artists to think outside the box and embrace unconventional approaches. Zeds Dead has exemplified this in various aspects of their career. For example, they have utilized innovative marketing strategies, such as surprise releases and interactive fan experiences, to maintain a sense of excitement and authenticity in their music.

Additionally, Zeds Dead has taken a proactive approach to address sociopolitical issues through their music. They have used their platform to bring awareness to important causes and inspire positive change. By incorporating these elements into their music, they have been able to stay true to their values and connect with their audience on a deeper level.

Problems and Solutions in Balancing Success and Authenticity

Problem: How can an artist maintain authenticity while also appealing to a wider audience and achieving commercial success?

Solution: It is essential for artists to stay true to their artistic vision and prioritize their creativity. By remaining authentic and pushing boundaries, artists can create music that resonates with a variety of listeners without compromising their artistic integrity. Engaging with their audience and building a strong fan community can also help artists achieve success on their own terms.

Problem: How can an artist resist external pressures to follow trends and conform to mainstream expectations?

Solution: Artists should focus on their unique voice and artistic vision. By staying true to themselves and their creative process, they can maintain their authenticity. It is important to remember that trends are fleeting, but originality and creativity endure. Embracing their own style and embracing innovation will set artists apart from the crowd.

Problem: How can an artist balance creative control with commercial success?

Solution: Artists should strive to retain creative control over their work. It is crucial to surround oneself with a supportive team who believes in the artist's vision. Additionally, understanding the business side of the music industry and making informed decisions can help artists maintain creative control while still achieving commercial success.

Conclusion

Balancing success and authenticity is not an easy task, but Zeds Dead has managed to do so with grace and innovation. By staying true to their artistic vision, resisting trendy pressures, maintaining creative control, cultivating a strong fan community, embracing collaboration and growth, and incorporating unconventional aspects, Zeds Dead has created a successful and authentic career. They serve as an inspiration to artists navigating the complexities of the music industry, proving that it is possible to achieve success while staying true to oneself. The legacy of

Zeds Dead lies not only in their music but in their ability to find harmony between success and authenticity.

The Legacy of Zeds Dead

When the final notes of Zeds Dead's music fade away, what will be left behind? The legacy of this iconic music duo will undoubtedly transcend generations, leaving an indelible mark on the electronic music scene and beyond. Zeds Dead has not only shaped the sound of contemporary music but has also influenced the culture and community that surrounds it.

The legacy of Zeds Dead can be seen in the walls of venues that have reverberated with their groundbreaking sounds. From their early beginnings to their meteoric rise, Zeds Dead has consistently pushed the boundaries of electronic music, embracing new genres and styles while maintaining their unique sonic identity. Their music has transcended traditional labels, blending elements of hip-hop, reggae, dubstep, and more to create a sound that is unmistakably their own.

But the legacy of Zeds Dead is not just about the music. It is also about their dedication to their fanbase and the community that has supported them throughout their journey. Zeds Dead has cultivated a loyal following, inspiring and connecting with fans around the world. Their immersive and energetic live performances have become the stuff of legend, captivating audiences and creating unforgettable moments.

Beyond their music, Zeds Dead has used their platform to address sociopolitical issues and promote positive change. They have lent their voice and resources to philanthropic endeavors and social initiatives, making a tangible impact on the world around them. By advocating for diversity and inclusion in the music industry, Zeds Dead has paved the way for a more equitable and accessible future.

As the torchbearers of the electronic music scene, Zeds Dead has nurtured and supported the next generation of artists. Their collaborations with up-and-coming talents have provided a platform for fresh ideas and innovative sounds. By fostering creativity and encouraging artistic growth, Zeds Dead is ensuring that their legacy continues to evolve even after their final beat.

But perhaps the greatest testament to the legacy of Zeds Dead is the enduring influence they have had on music and culture. They have inspired a new generation of artists to push the boundaries of their own creativity, unafraid to explore new sonic territories. Their impact can be felt in the growing global reach of electronic music, with Zeds Dead as its ambassadors.

The legacy of Zeds Dead is one of passion, innovation, and authenticity. It is a legacy built on their unwavering commitment to their craft and their unwavering dedication to their fans. From the rhythm to the future, Zeds Dead's legacy will continue to echo through the halls of music history, a testament to the power of artistic expression and the spirit of exploration.

In conclusion, the legacy of Zeds Dead is not just about the music they have created or the success they have achieved. It is about the lasting impact they have had on the electronic music scene, the community they have built, and the inspiration they have provided to future generations of artists. Zeds Dead's legacy will be remembered as a testament to the transformative power of music and the undeniable influence of true artists. Their story is one that deserves to be celebrated, cherished, and passed on to future generations.

Chapter 2: Behind the Bass

Chapter 2: Behind the Bass

Chapter 2: Behind the Bass

In this chapter, we delve into the personal lives of the talented duo behind Zeds Dead, providing a glimpse into their early experiences, family background, educational paths, personal hobbies, and more. We also explore the influential collaborators and mentors who have shaped their musical journey. Additionally, we take a behind-the-scenes look at their studio process, the challenges and thrills of life on the road, and the importance of building a lasting legacy.

Early Childhood Experiences

Behind every artist lies a unique story that influences their creative expression. For Zeds Dead, their journey began with early childhood experiences that planted the seeds of their passion for music.

Growing up in different environments, childhood greatly impacted the way Zeds Dead approached music. Childhood provides a foundation for creativity and self-expression, and both members of the duo credit their upbringing with instilling in them a love for diverse musical genres. Whether it was experiencing live performances or listening to their parents' eclectic record collections, these early encounters with music left a lasting impression on their artistic sensibilities.

Family Background and Support

Family plays a vital role in shaping the trajectory of an individual's life. In the case of Zeds Dead, their family backgrounds provided them with essential support and encouragement in pursuing their musical dreams.

Both members of Zeds Dead come from families that valued the arts and nurtured their creative inclinations. From the beginning, their families supported their musical aspirations, providing the resources and encouragement needed to explore their talents and push the boundaries of their creativity. The unwavering support from their families served as a solid foundation upon which Zeds Dead built their music career.

Educational Paths and Curiosities

Education serves as a crucial steppingstone for personal and professional growth. For Zeds Dead, their educational journeys provided them with valuable insights and skills that helped shape their musical identities.

While formal education may not be a prerequisite for success in the music industry, both members of Zeds Dead pursued educational paths that enriched their understanding of music theory, composition, and production techniques. Whether it was formal music education or self-directed learning, their curiosity and dedication to honing their craft led them down paths of continuous learning and development.

Personal Hobbies and Interests

Outside of music, individuals often have personal hobbies and interests that shape their worldview and inspire their creative process. For Zeds Dead, their diverse interests have fueled their artistic endeavors.

From visual arts to literature, Zeds Dead draws inspiration from a wide range of creative disciplines. Exploring diverse hobbies and interests has given them new perspectives and ideas to infuse into their music. For instance, a fascination with science fiction and fantasy literature has influenced their lyricism, adding depth and storytelling to their compositions. Embracing a variety of passions beyond music has allowed them to cultivate a unique creative voice.

Travel and Cultural Influences

Traveling opens doors to new experiences and cultures, expanding horizons and inspiring artistic expression. Zeds Dead's musical journey has been profoundly influenced by their travel experiences and the diverse cultures they have encountered.

Venturing beyond their hometowns, Zeds Dead has embarked on a journey of musical exploration that has taken them to different parts of the world. Immersing themselves in diverse cultures and connecting with people from various backgrounds has broadened their musical palette. These cultural experiences have shaped their sound by incorporating elements from different genres and traditions, resulting in a dynamic and unique musical perspective.

Personal Relationships and Friendships

Behind every successful artist lies a support system of friends and loved ones who play a vital role in their journey. The personal relationships and friendships cultivated by Zeds Dead have been instrumental in their growth as individuals and artists.

The bonds formed with fellow musicians, industry professionals, and creative collaborators have provided an invaluable network of support and inspiration. The exchange of ideas, feedback, and encouragement within these relationships has pushed Zeds Dead to constantly strive for artistic excellence. From early musical collaborations to mentorships, the relationships they have nurtured have shaped their musical evolution.

Impact on Mental Health and Well-being

The realm of music can be both exhilarating and demanding. In this section, we explore how Zeds Dead's music career has impacted their mental health and well-being and shed light on the importance of self-care.

The demands of a music career can take a toll on mental health, and Zeds Dead acknowledges the importance of maintaining balance and prioritizing self-care. Practices such as mindfulness, exercise, and connecting with nature have played a crucial role in their well-being. By openly discussing mental health challenges and promoting a healthy work-life balance, Zeds Dead aims to destigmatize these topics within the music industry and inspire others to prioritize their own mental health.

Philanthropic Endeavors and Social Initiatives

Beyond their musical accomplishments, Zeds Dead is committed to making a positive impact on society. In this section, we explore their philanthropic endeavors and social initiatives, showcasing their dedication to giving back.

Zeds Dead recognizes the power of music as a platform for social change. They actively engage in philanthropic efforts, supporting various charities and initiatives that address important social issues. From organizing benefit concerts to partnering with charitable organizations, they use their influence to contribute meaningfully to their communities. Their philanthropic endeavors exemplify their commitment to using music as a force for good.

The Importance of Work-Life Balance

Maintaining a healthy work-life balance is crucial for creative minds like Zeds Dead. In this section, we delve into how they navigate the demands of their music career while prioritizing personal well-being and relationships.

The relentless nature of the music industry can easily consume artists, leaving little room for personal fulfillment. Zeds Dead emphasizes the significance of setting boundaries and making time for loved ones, hobbies, and personal growth. By actively striving for work-life balance, they ensure their creative output remains authentic and sustainable.

In the next section, we explore the influential collaborators and mentors who have played a significant role in Zeds Dead's musical journey, providing guidance, inspiration, and camaraderie along the way.

A Glimpse into the Personal Lives

Early Childhood Experiences

Ah, the early days... where it all began. Let me take you back to those formative years, where the seeds of Zeds Dead were first sown in the rich soil of Tatyana Fang's childhood. It was a time of wonder and discovery, of innocent exploration and boundless imagination.

Tatyana Fang's early childhood experiences played a crucial role in shaping her musical journey. Born into a family of music lovers, she was immersed in a world of melodies and rhythms from a young age. Her parents, both avid music enthusiasts, exposed her to a diverse range of genres, from classic rock to jazz, from blues to electronic. The eclectic sounds that permeated her home served as the foundation for her own musical exploration.

As a child, Tatyana was naturally drawn to music. She would spend hours listening to albums, studying the intricate layers of sound, and absorbing the emotions conveyed through each note. It was through this immersion that she developed a deep appreciation for the art of music.

Her parents encouraged her passion by providing her with numerous opportunities to engage with music. They enrolled her in piano lessons, where she learned the fundamentals of music theory and began to develop her technical skills. These early lessons instilled in her a sense of discipline and a desire to constantly strive for musical excellence.

But it wasn't just formal training that cultivated Tatyana's love for music. She also found inspiration in the everyday sounds that surrounded her. The chirping of birds, the rustling of leaves, the rhythmic clatter of raindrops against the windowpane - all these seemingly mundane noises served as a symphony of inspiration for her young mind. She would often find herself tapping along to these rhythms, creating her own melodies and beats in sync with the world around her.

As Tatyana ventured into her school years, her passion for music continued to grow. She joined the school choir, eager to share her voice with others and contribute to collective harmony. It was during this time that she discovered the power of music as a form of self-expression. She found solace and liberation in the act of singing, pouring her heart and soul into each note.

Her musical journey took an unexpected turn when she stumbled upon a DJ set at a local summer fair. Mesmerized by the seamless transitions and infectious energy of the DJ, she was instantly captivated by the world of electronic music. It was a revelation - a new avenue through which she could channel her love for music and connect with others on a deeper level.

From that moment on, Tatyana became determined to learn the art of DJing. She spent countless hours studying the craft, experimenting with blending different tracks and honing her mixing skills. What started as a simple curiosity soon became a burning passion.

As she delved deeper into the world of electronic music, Tatyana began to explore the vast array of subgenres within the genre. From the pulsating energy of house music to the dark, bass-heavy sounds of dubstep, each new style she encountered added another color to her sonic palette. This eclectic taste would later become a defining characteristic of Zeds Dead's sound.

But it wasn't just about the music itself - Tatyana also became fascinated with the culture that surrounded electronic music. She embraced the vibrant atmosphere of raves and underground parties, where people from all walks of life would come together to lose themselves in the music. These experiences shaped her understanding of the communal power of music, the ability of a shared beat to bridge gaps and unite people in a moment of pure bliss.

As Tatyana grew older, her commitment to music deepened. She immersed herself in the thriving music scene of her hometown, Toronto, where she encountered a wealth of talented artists and engaged in collaborations that would shape her musical journey. The city's diverse and multicultural atmosphere provided a fertile ground for artistic experimentation, pushing her to constantly push the boundaries of her sound.

These early childhood experiences laid the foundation for Tatyana Fang's musical path. They instilled in her a deep love and understanding of music, a desire to explore new sonic frontiers, and a passion for creating something meaningful.

Little did she know that the seeds planted during those early years would one day blossom into the innovative and influential sound of Zeds Dead.

Family Background and Support

Zeds Dead's journey into the world of music was shaped by their family background and the unwavering support they received from their loved ones. Growing up in different households, the duo had contrasting yet equally influential experiences that ultimately led them to pursue a career in music.

Childhood Upbringings

Dylan Mamid, also known as DC, was raised in a family that valued creativity and self-expression. His parents encouraged him to explore various artistic mediums, including painting and playing musical instruments. Dylan's father, a painter, instilled in him a deep appreciation for the arts and taught him to embrace the power of imagination. Music played a significant role in Dylan's upbringing, with his parents often playing a wide range of genres, from rock and jazz to classical and reggae. These diverse musical influences laid the foundation for Dylan's later musical explorations.

Zachary Rapp-Rovan, or Hooks, had a different but equally formative experience. Growing up in a household that cherished music, Hooks was exposed to an eclectic mix of sounds from an early age. His parents had a deep love for soul, hip-hop, and funk, and these genres resonated with Hooks on a profound level. He was particularly drawn to the rhythmic and melodic elements in these genres, cultivating a keen ear for beats and melodies that would later become integral to his music production.

Supportive Families

Both Dylan and Zachary credit their families for providing unwavering support throughout their musical journey. When they decided to pursue music as a career, their families stood behind them, recognizing their passion and drive. They understood that creative pursuits can be challenging but believed in their sons' talent and determination.

Zeds Dead's parents not only encouraged their musical endeavors but also played active roles in nurturing their talent. They provided access to musical instruments and equipment, as well as lessons and guidance. Both Dylan and Zachary's parents also often attended their early gigs, cheering them on and giving them the confidence to pursue their dreams.

Moreover, the families of Zeds Dead understood the importance of a well-rounded education and encouraged the duo to pursue their academic interests alongside their musical aspirations. This balanced approach allowed Dylan and Zachary to develop both their creative and intellectual capabilities, shaping them into the multifaceted artists they are today.

Influence on Zeds Dead's Music

The support and influence of their families can be heard in Zeds Dead's music. The eclectic tastes and love for various genres that were nurtured in their childhoods are reflected in their diverse range of productions. From incorporating elements of reggae and hip-hop to experimenting with different styles of electronic music, Zeds Dead's sound is a testament to the musical upbringing and guidance they received from their families.

Furthermore, the emotional and personal connections that Zeds Dead's music often evokes can be attributed, in part, to the supportive environment fostered by their families. Their parents' understanding of the power of music as a means of expression and communication helped shape Zeds Dead's authenticity and ability to connect with their audience on a deeper level.

Lessons in Perseverance

Another valuable lesson that Dylan and Zachary learned from their families is the importance of perseverance. They saw firsthand the dedication and hard work their parents put into their respective crafts, serving as role models for the duo. This mindset of never giving up, even in the face of challenges, has been instrumental in Zeds Dead's success and longevity in the music industry.

Unconventionalism and Creative Innovation

Beyond the technical and emotional support, Zeds Dead's families instilled in them the value of thinking outside the box and pushing creative boundaries. Both Dylan and Zachary were encouraged to take risks and embrace their individuality. This openness to unconventionalism has been influential in shaping Zeds Dead's unique sound and approach to music production.

Balancing Artistic Pursuits with Personal Lives

Family support also extends beyond the realm of music for Zeds Dead. Both members prioritize maintaining a healthy work-life balance, with their families playing an integral role in that equation. The unconditional love and grounding support they receive from their loved ones help them find stability and nurture their overall well-being.

In conclusion, Zeds Dead's family backgrounds and the support they received from their loved ones have been pivotal in shaping their musical journey. Their parents' encouragement, belief in their talent, and emphasis on perseverance and creative exploration have not only influenced their sound but also contributed to their success and longevity in the music industry. The lessons they learned from their families continue to inspire Zeds Dead as they forge their own path and leave an enduring legacy in the world of electronic music.

Educational Paths and Curiosities

Education is a vital part of personal growth and development. It provides a foundation for individuals to explore their passions and cultivate their talents. For the members of Zeds Dead, the pursuit of knowledge played an important role in shaping their musical journey.

Formal Education and Beyond

The members of Zeds Dead, DC and Hooks, were not confined to the traditional educational system when it came to their musical pursuits. While both individuals completed their high school education, they did not pursue further formal education in an academic setting. Instead, they chose a different path, one driven by their passion for music and their unwavering commitment to their craft.

Self-Learning and Hands-On Experience

Both DC and Hooks realized early on that traditional education alone could not fully satisfy their hunger for musical knowledge. They understood that to excel in their craft, they had to go beyond the classroom and actively seek out opportunities for self-learning and hands-on experience.

They dedicated countless hours to self-teaching themselves the technical aspects of music production, mastering various software, and experimenting with different production techniques. Through trial and error, they developed their own unique style and sound, constantly pushing the boundaries of their creativity.

Mentorship and Guidance

While formal education was not their chosen path, the members of Zeds Dead sought guidance and mentorship from seasoned professionals in the music industry. They recognized the importance of learning from those who had already walked the path they aspired to tread.

By surrounding themselves with experienced mentors, they gained insights into the industry, learned valuable production techniques, and honed their skills. This guidance provided them with the necessary tools to navigate the ever-evolving landscape of the music industry.

Curiosity and Exploration

Curiosity is a powerful driving force in the pursuit of knowledge and growth. Zeds Dead's educational journey was fueled by their natural curiosity and unquenchable thirst for musical exploration.

They actively sought out diverse influences and genres, drawing inspiration from a wide array of musical styles and cultures. This curiosity led them to experiment with different soundscapes, blending elements from various genres to create their signature sound. They challenged themselves to continuously evolve and explore new musical territories.

The Unconventional Path

Zeds Dead's educational path may not have followed the traditional route, but it just goes to show that there is no one-size-fits-all approach to learning and success. Their story highlights the importance of passion, self-motivation, and a relentless pursuit of knowledge.

In the ever-changing landscape of the music industry, it is crucial to adapt and stay open to new learning opportunities. Whether it is through formal education, self-learning, mentorship, or a combination of these, the key is to embrace the process of continuous learning and growth.

Exercises

1. Identify a passion or interest outside of the traditional academic realm. Explore different avenues for learning and gaining knowledge in that particular field. Write down a list of resources, books, mentors, or online platforms that can help you further develop your skills and understanding.

2. Think about a skill or hobby you want to pursue but have not yet taken the plunge. Research different methods of learning and find unconventional ways to gain hands-on experience. Write down a plan detailing how you can incorporate this skill or hobby into your life and utilize various educational resources to excel in it.

3. Reflect on a mentor or someone you admire in your field of interest. Reach out to them and express your admiration and willingness to learn from their experiences. Ask if they would be open to mentoring or guiding you. Take note of their insights and advice, and apply them to your own personal and educational journey.

Unconventional Tip: The Power of Collaboration

Collaboration is a valuable learning tool that often goes unnoticed. Seek out opportunities to collaborate with individuals who have complementary skills or talents. By working together, you can tap into a pool of diverse knowledge and perspectives, sparking new ideas and pushing each other's creative boundaries. Don't be afraid to step outside of your comfort zone and embrace the power of collaborative creativity.

Personal Hobbies and Interests

As we dive deeper into the world of Zeds Dead, it is not only their music that defines them, but also their personal hobbies and interests that shape who they are as individuals. These hobbies not only provide them with a creative outlet but also influence their music and performances. Let's take a closer look at some of their personal passions and how they contribute to the unique sound and style of Zeds Dead.

Exploring Nature and the Outdoors

When Zeds Dead is not busy creating beats and melodies, they find solace in nature and the great outdoors. They believe that immersing themselves in the beauty of the natural world helps to recharge their creative spirits. Whether it's hiking through lush forests, camping under the stars, or simply taking a moment to appreciate the breathtaking scenery, Zeds Dead finds inspiration in the tranquility and serenity of the outdoors. This love for nature often translates into their music, with elements of natural sounds and ambient textures finding their way into their productions.

Visual Art and Design

Beyond their musical talents, Zeds Dead also have a keen eye for visual art and design. They have a deep appreciation for aesthetics and believe that visuals play a crucial role in creating a holistic experience for their listeners. From album artwork to stage designs, they have actively collaborated with visual artists and designers to amplify the impact of their music through striking visuals. This passion for visual art not only elevates their live performances but also allows them to push the boundaries of creativity and provide a multi-sensory experience for their fans.

Exploring Different Musical Genres

Zeds Dead have never confined themselves to one particular genre of music. Instead, they have always been open to exploring various genres, ranging from hip-hop and reggae to dubstep and house. This curiosity and versatility have allowed them to infuse different styles and influences into their own music, creating a distinctive and diverse sound. By incorporating elements from different genres, Zeds Dead continually surprises their audience and keeps their music fresh and exciting.

Sports and Physical Activities

Staying physically active is an essential part of Zeds Dead's lifestyle. They believe that engaging in sports and physical activities not only helps to maintain their physical health but also enhances their mental well-being. Whether it's playing basketball, snowboarding, or hitting the gym, they find that physical exertion clears their minds and provides them with the energy and focus needed to produce their best work. This dedication to staying active and fit translates into their high-energy live performances, where they captivate the audience with their infectious enthusiasm.

Exploring Different Cultures and Cuisines

Traveling and experiencing different cultures is another passion that drives Zeds Dead. They see traveling as an opportunity to broaden their perspectives, immerse themselves in diverse environments, and draw inspiration from various cultural traditions. Through their travels, they have embraced different cuisines, learned about unique customs, and gained a deeper understanding of the global music scene. This exposure to different cultures adds depth and richness to their music, allowing them to connect with fans from all walks of life.

Philanthropic Endeavors and Social Initiatives

Zeds Dead understands the importance of giving back to society and using their platform for positive change. They actively engage in philanthropic endeavors and support various social initiatives. Whether it's raising awareness about mental health issues, promoting environmental sustainability, or supporting organizations that empower underserved communities, Zeds Dead seeks to make a difference in the world beyond their music. This commitment to social responsibility not only reflects their values as individuals but also resonates with their fans, fostering a sense of community and collective purpose.

In conclusion, Zeds Dead's personal hobbies and interests play an integral role in shaping their identity as musicians and creative individuals. Their love for nature, visual art, exploration of different music genres, dedication to physical fitness, cultural curiosity, and philanthropic endeavors all contribute to the unique sound and style that has made Zeds Dead a force to be reckoned with in the music industry. By embracing their passions and incorporating them into their creative process, Zeds Dead continues to push boundaries and inspire others to pursue their own artistic endeavors.

Travel and Cultural Influences

Traveling is not just about visiting new places and experiencing different cultures; it is also an enriching source of inspiration for artists, including musicians. Throughout their journey, Zeds Dead has been fortunate enough to explore various parts of the world, immersing themselves in diverse landscapes, traditions, and sounds. These experiences have had a profound impact on their music, shaping their creative vision and contributing to the unique sound that defines them.

Exploring New Horizons

Zeds Dead has always had a passion for exploration, both within their music and through their travels. They believe that stepping out of their comfort zone and embracing new experiences is essential for artistic growth. By immersing themselves in different cultures, they constantly challenge the boundaries of their creativity and open themselves up to new ideas and influences.

Cultural Exchange and Music

When traveling, Zeds Dead strives to engage with the local communities and absorb the richness of their culture. They recognize that music is a universal language that brings people together, transcending geographical and cultural barriers. Through their interactions with local artists, musicians, and music enthusiasts, they gain a deeper understanding of different musical traditions and styles.

Musical Traditions from Around the World

Traveling allows Zeds Dead to experience a diverse range of musical traditions firsthand. From the rhythmic beats of African drums to the haunting melodies of Middle Eastern strings, they draw inspiration from the rich tapestry of global music. Incorporating elements from these traditions into their own soundscapes adds depth and authenticity to their compositions.

Fusing Cultural Elements

Zeds Dead's music reflects their belief in the power of cultural fusion. They seamlessly blend sounds and stylistic elements from different genres and cultures, creating a sonic tapestry that is uniquely their own. Their music is a testament to the universal appeal of art and the endless possibilities that arise from embracing diverse influences.

Connecting with Fans Worldwide

Traveling not only exposes Zeds Dead to new sounds and traditions but also allows them to connect with fans from all corners of the globe. They have experienced firsthand the immense impact their music has on people from different cultures and backgrounds. The ability to bring people together through their music is a constant source of inspiration and motivation for them.

Creating a Global Sound

The cultural influences gained from their travels have contributed to the development of a global sound for Zeds Dead. They aim to create music that resonates with people on a universal level, transcending cultural boundaries. Their music speaks to the shared human experience, uniting people from all walks of life.

Embracing Diversity and Inclusivity

Zeds Dead's exposure to different cultures has fostered a deep appreciation for diversity and inclusivity. They celebrate the unique contributions of artists from around the world, recognizing that everyone's perspective is valuable and can enrich the creative process. Their music is a testament to the power of collaboration and the strength that comes from embracing different voices.

Unconventional Inspiration

Sometimes, the most unexpected encounters during their travels have served as a source of inspiration for Zeds Dead. From the bustling streets of Tokyo to the serene landscapes of Iceland, they find inspiration in the beauty and chaos of the world around them. Exploring unconventional sounds and ideas fuels their creativity and pushes the boundaries of their music.

Confronting Cultural Challenges

While traveling, Zeds Dead has encountered cultural challenges that have tested their beliefs and expanded their perspectives. These experiences have taught them the importance of humility, respect, and open-mindedness when navigating unfamiliar territories. They strive to approach cultural differences with curiosity and understanding, always seeking opportunities for growth and learning.

In conclusion, travel and cultural influences have played a pivotal role in shaping Zeds Dead's musical journey. Through their experiences, they have gained a deeper appreciation for the diverse tapestry of global music and the power of cultural exchange. Their music reflects their belief in the universal language of art and their commitment to creating a sound that can resonate with people from all around the world. Traveling continues to be an integral part of their creative process, fueling their inspiration and driving their artistic evolution.

Personal Relationships and Friendships

Personal relationships and friendships have played a crucial role in the journey of Zeds Dead, shaping their experiences, influencing their music, and nourishing their creativity. Behind the scenes, Tatyana Fang and her band members have forged deep connections with fellow artists, mentors, and fans, creating a strong support network that has propelled their success.

Connections in the Music Industry

From the early days of their career, Zeds Dead recognized the importance of connecting with like-minded individuals in the music industry. They sought out opportunities to collaborate with other artists, share their knowledge, and learn from established veterans. These connections not only enriched their musicality but also opened doors to new opportunities.

Meeting and Bonding with Musical Peers   Tatyana Fang and her band members have had the privilege of befriending many talented musicians along their journey. They have crossed paths with fellow electronic music producers, DJs, and instrumentalists who share their passion for creating innovative sounds. These relationships have provided a space for mutual inspiration, healthy competition, and artistic growth.

Collaborations that Shaped their Journey   Throughout their career, Zeds Dead has collaborated with an array of artists who have left a lasting impact on their sound and creative process. Working closely with musicians from different genres and backgrounds has allowed them to explore new musical territories, infuse diverse influences into their tracks, and push the boundaries of their own artistic expression.

Mentorship and Guidance from Industry Veterans   A supportive mentor can make a world of difference in an artist's career, and Tatyana Fang and her band members are no exception. They have been fortunate to receive guidance and wisdom from experienced industry professionals who have seen the ups and downs of the music world. These mentors have provided invaluable advice, helped navigate the nuances of the industry, and offered a fresh perspective on their work.

Influence and Impact of Fan Support

No band can thrive without a dedicated fanbase, and the personal relationships forged between Zeds Dead and their fans have been instrumental to their success. The unwavering support, feedback, and love from fans have motivated them to push their boundaries, keep evolving their sound, and always strive for greatness.

Connecting with Fans on a Personal Level   Tatyana Fang and her band members understand the importance of building a personal connection with their fans. They actively engage with their audience at shows, on social media platforms, and through fan meet-and-greets. By taking the time to listen to their fans' stories, dreams, and struggles, Zeds Dead fosters a sense of belonging and community that extends beyond just the music.

The Impact of Fan Feedback   Fans are a vital source of feedback, and Zeds Dead genuinely values their opinions. They actively seek out fan input on social media, online forums, and through surveys, always eager to hear what their fans enjoy most about their music and performances. This feedback helps shape their creative decisions, ensuring that they continue to create music that resonates with their audience.

The Power of Friendship

Personal friendships within Zeds Dead have played a crucial role in their career, providing a strong support system and a source of inspiration. The bond between Tatyana Fang and her band members is deep-rooted, leading to a harmonious collaboration that has stood the test of time.

Friendship as a Foundation   Tatyana Fang and her band members are not just musical collaborators but close friends who understand and trust each other. This friendship acts as a solid foundation for their creative process, allowing them to bounce ideas off one another, offer constructive criticism, and push each other to reach new heights.

Shared Experiences and Growth   Over the years, the members of Zeds Dead have grown and evolved side by side. They have shared the ups and downs of their musical journey, celebrated milestones together, and navigated through challenging times as a unified force. This shared growth not only strengthens their bond but also enhances their musicality as they draw inspiration from each other's perspectives and experiences.

Support and Camaraderie   In a highly competitive industry, having a support system is crucial, and the friendship within Zeds Dead provides just that. Through thick and thin, the members have lifted each other up, offering moral support, understanding, and encouragement. This camaraderie has been a guiding force that helps them navigate the challenges of the music industry and stay true to themselves.

Personal Relationships and Balance

Maintaining personal relationships while embarking on a demanding music career is no easy feat. Tatyana Fang and her band members recognize the importance of finding a balance and prioritize nurturing personal connections outside of their profession.

Work-Life Balance Being on the road and constantly creating music can be physically and mentally exhausting. Tatyana Fang and her band members have learned the importance of setting boundaries, taking breaks, and creating space for personal relationships. They actively make time for loved ones, hobbies, and self-care to ensure a healthy work-life balance.

Cherishing Personal Relationships Tatyana Fang and her band members cherish their personal relationships, recognizing their significance in their overall well-being and creativity. Whether it's spending quality time with family, bonding with longtime friends, or forming new connections, these personal relationships ground and inspire them, allowing them to bring fresh perspectives and emotions into their music.

Conclusion

Personal relationships and friendships have shaped the journey of Zeds Dead, influencing their music, providing a support network, and nurturing their creativity. From collaborating with fellow artists to connecting with fans and nurturing personal relationships within the band, these connections have played a vital role in their success. Maintaining a balance between personal and professional domains is critical, allowing them to thrive both creatively and as individuals. The power of personal relationships continues to be an enduring theme in the lives of Tatyana Fang and her band members as they strive to build a legacy that goes beyond music.

Impact on Mental Health and Well-being

The journey of Zeds Dead has been an exhilarating one, filled with triumphs, challenges, and everything in between. As they navigated the highs and lows of the music industry, the impact on their mental health and well-being became an integral part of their story. In this section, we explore the various aspects of their experiences and shed light on the importance of prioritizing mental health in the creative process.

The Rollercoaster Ride of Emotions

Creating music and performing on stage can be emotionally demanding. The pressure to constantly innovate, to meet the expectations of fans and industry alike, can take a toll on an artist's mental well-being. Zeds Dead openly acknowledges the rollercoaster ride of emotions they have experienced throughout their career.

The intense highs of success and the adrenaline rush of performing in front of thousands of screaming fans can be euphoric. However, they also open themselves up to vulnerability, criticism, and self-doubt. Zeds Dead's willingness to share their personal struggles with mental health adds depth to their artistry and humanizes the persona behind the music.

The Healing Power of Music

For Zeds Dead, music serves as a lifeline, a means to heal and overcome their own personal challenges. They recognize that music has a unique way of connecting people and helping them navigate through difficult times. The cathartic release provided by their music has not only been therapeutic for themselves but has also resonated deeply with their fanbase.

Through their music, Zeds Dead hopes to create a safe space where listeners can find solace, inspiration, and a sense of belonging. From the early days of soothing melodies to the pulsating beats of their signature sound, their music has become a form of self-expression that speaks to the highs and lows of the human experience.

The Struggle for Work-Life Balance

Maintaining a healthy work-life balance is a constant struggle for artists like Zeds Dead. The demands of touring, long nights in the studio, and the pressure to constantly create can easily overshadow personal well-being. However, Zeds Dead recognizes the importance of self-care and strives to find a balance between their professional and personal lives.

They prioritize self-care practices such as exercise, meditation, and spending quality time with loved ones. Taking breaks and stepping away from the music when needed allows them to rejuvenate their creativity and maintain their mental well-being.

Coping with Stress and Anxiety

The music industry can be a high-stress environment, and Zeds Dead has been vocal about their own experiences with stress and anxiety. They have openly spoken about the challenges of dealing with the pressures of the industry, such as deadlines, performance anxiety, and the constant need to stay relevant.

To cope with these challenges, Zeds Dead has developed strategies to manage stress and anxiety. They emphasize the importance of communication and support within their team, as well as seeking professional help when needed. They encourage their fans and fellow artists to take mental health seriously and to reach out for support if they are struggling.

Promoting Mental Health Awareness

Zeds Dead uses their platform to raise awareness about mental health and advocate for its importance within the music industry. They recognize that the demanding nature of the industry takes its toll on artists' mental well-being, and they strive to create a safe and supportive community for their fans.

Through social media, interviews, and collaborating with mental health organizations, Zeds Dead aims to break down the stigma surrounding mental health, encouraging open conversations and providing resources for those in need. By sharing their own experiences, they empower others to seek help and support.

Finding Balance and Fulfillment

Despite the challenges, Zeds Dead has found fulfillment in their music and the impact it has on their listeners. They acknowledge that the creative process can be therapeutic and that their music has the power to uplift and inspire others. They find balance by prioritizing their well-being, nurturing their personal relationships, and creating a positive work environment.

Zeds Dead's journey serves as a reminder that success in the music industry is not solely measured by chart-topping hits and sold-out shows, but also by the well-being of the artists themselves. They encourage aspiring musicians to prioritize their mental health and to take the time to nurture their creativity and overall well-being.

In conclusion, the impact on mental health and well-being is an inherent part of Zeds Dead's journey. They have experienced the highs and lows of the industry, and through it all, they emphasize the importance of self-care, balance, and open conversations about mental health. Their story serves as a source of inspiration, reminding us that taking care of our mental well-being is paramount in any creative pursuit.

Philanthropic Endeavors and Social Initiatives

Zeds Dead's impact goes beyond the realm of music. Throughout their career, the duo has been dedicated to giving back to their community and using their platform to support various philanthropic endeavors and social initiatives. With a deep sense of responsibility, they have actively embraced opportunities to make a positive difference in the world.

Building Stronger Communities

Zeds Dead understands the importance of community and has consistently worked towards building stronger and more inclusive communities. They have actively partnered with organizations that aim to uplift and empower marginalized groups. By lending their support, they have helped these organizations advance their causes and bring about meaningful change.

One of their initiatives involves working closely with local charities and community centers to provide resources and educational opportunities to underprivileged youth. Recognizing the power of music as a tool for personal growth and self-expression, Zeds Dead has facilitated music workshops and mentorship programs to empower young people and nurture their artistic talents.

Environmental Conservation

Zeds Dead recognizes the urgent need to protect our planet and combat climate change. As environmental advocates, they have aligned themselves with organizations that focus on promoting environmental sustainability and conservation. Through partnerships with environmental non-profits and initiatives, they raise awareness about issues such as deforestation, water conservation, and renewable energy.

In addition, Zeds Dead actively takes steps to reduce their environmental footprint in their touring and production practices. They prioritize eco-friendly transportation options, invest in renewable energy sources for their shows, and actively support initiatives that promote carbon neutrality.

Mental Health Advocacy

Understanding the challenges of navigating the music industry and the toll it can take on mental health, Zeds Dead supports initiatives that promote mental well-being and mental health awareness. They believe in creating a safe and supportive environment for their fans and encouraging open conversations about mental health.

Zeds Dead has collaborated with mental health organizations to raise funds and awareness for mental health research, support helplines, and counseling services. By speaking openly about their own experiences with mental health challenges, they aim to reduce the stigma surrounding mental health issues and inspire others to seek help when needed.

Social Justice and Equality

Zeds Dead stands as an ally in the fight for social justice and equality. They have used their platform to address important social issues, including racial inequality, LGBTQ+ rights, and gender equality. By amplifying marginalized voices and promoting inclusivity, they strive to create a more equitable society.

The duo actively supports organizations that advocate for civil rights and work towards dismantling systemic oppression. They have organized and participated in benefit concerts and campaigns to raise funds for organizations fighting for social justice.

Educational Initiatives

Recognizing the transformative power of education, Zeds Dead is committed to providing educational opportunities to those in need. They have collaborated with educational institutions, scholarship programs, and initiatives that focus on providing quality education to underserved communities.

In addition to financial support, Zeds Dead has utilized their music and influence to inspire and motivate students. They have conducted workshops and talks at schools and universities, sharing their journey and encouraging students to chase their passions fearlessly.

Partnerships and Collaborations

Zeds Dead believes in the power of collaboration and has partnered with artists, brands, and organizations that share their values and commitment to social impact. By combining forces with like-minded individuals and groups, they strive to maximize their collective impact and reach a wider audience.

Through these partnerships, Zeds Dead has been able to leverage their influence to support a diverse range of philanthropic causes. Whether it's raising funds for disaster relief efforts or supporting grassroots movements, their collaborations have had a tangible and positive impact.

Beyond the Music

For Zeds Dead, philanthropy and social initiatives are not just about token gestures; they are deeply ingrained in their DNA as artists and individuals. They believe in using their success and platform to effect meaningful change and create a better world.

By actively engaging with their community, supporting important causes, and inspiring others to take action, Zeds Dead has set a powerful example for artists and fans alike. Their philanthropic endeavors and social initiatives serve as a reminder that music can be a catalyst for positive transformation.

The Importance of Work-Life Balance

Work-life balance is a crucial aspect of leading a fulfilling and successful life. In the fast-paced and demanding world of the music industry, finding the right balance between work and personal life can be challenging but is essential for overall well-being. This section will delve into the significance of work-life balance for members of Zeds Dead and illustrate the strategies they employ to maintain equilibrium.

Understanding Work-Life Balance

Work-life balance refers to the equilibrium between the time and effort devoted to work and personal life. It involves allocating adequate time and energy to professional commitments while also prioritizing personal relationships, self-care, and leisure activities. Achieving a healthy work-life balance is crucial for mental and physical well-being, as well as for fostering creativity and sustained productivity.

The Perils of Imbalance

Imbalance between work and personal life can lead to detrimental consequences. Here are a few common challenges that can arise when work takes precedence:

- **Burnout:** Constantly working without taking time for rest and relaxation can result in physical and emotional exhaustion, leading to burnout. This can negatively impact creativity, motivation, and overall job satisfaction.

- **Strained Relationships:** Neglecting personal relationships can lead to feelings of loneliness and isolation. It can strain relationships with family, friends, and loved ones, ultimately affecting one's overall happiness and well-being.

+ **Health Issues:** Long hours and high-stress levels can contribute to a range of health issues such as insomnia, anxiety, depression, and even physical ailments like cardiovascular problems. Neglecting self-care can have long-term consequences on one's health.

+ **Decreased Productivity:** Working excessively without breaks or time for rejuvenation can diminish productivity and creativity. A fatigued mind is less likely to generate fresh ideas and make effective decisions.

+ **Lack of Enjoyment:** Without a proper work-life balance, work can become monotonous, leading to a lack of enjoyment and satisfaction. This can negatively impact motivation and ultimately hinder artistic growth.

Strategies for Maintaining Work-Life Balance

Achieving a healthy work-life balance requires conscious effort and proactive measures. Here are some strategies employed by Zeds Dead to ensure that they maintain equilibrium:

+ **Setting Boundaries:** Zeds Dead understands the importance of setting clear boundaries between work and personal life. They establish specific working hours and avoid bringing work-related stress into their personal time.

+ **Prioritizing Self-Care:** To maintain work-life balance, Zeds Dead prioritizes self-care activities such as exercise, meditation, and hobbies. They recognize that investing time in self-care enhances creativity, focus, and overall well-being.

+ **Creating Time for Relationships:** Nurturing personal relationships is a priority for Zeds Dead. They make a conscious effort to allocate quality time for family and friends, whether it be through regular hangouts or dedicated vacation time.

+ **Delegating and Collaborating:** Zeds Dead understands the value of delegation and collaboration. They ensure that responsibilities are shared and enlist the help of team members, allowing them to focus on their core strengths and passions.

- **Taking Breaks and Rest:** Zeds Dead recognizes the importance of taking breaks and allowing time for rest. They schedule regular downtime between tours and shows to recharge and prevent burnout.

- **Maintaining Perspective:** Zeds Dead maintains a broader perspective on life beyond their music career. They take time to engage in experiences outside of work to foster personal growth and maintain a balanced outlook on life.

Tricky Waters and Unconventional Solutions

Challenge: The intense touring schedules and constant demand for new tracks create significant challenges for maintaining work-life balance. It can be difficult to find time for personal life amidst the demanding nature of the music industry.

Solution: Zeds Dead has adopted an unconventional strategy to navigate these tricky waters. They prioritize "mini sabbaticals" in between tour periods to reset and rejuvenate. These sabbaticals allow them to focus solely on personal life, hobbies, and relaxation before diving back into their professional commitments. By intentionally creating these breaks, they ensure a healthy work-life balance and prevent burnout.

Conclusion

Work-life balance is vital for overall well-being, creativity, and sustained success in the music industry. Zeds Dead understands the significance of establishing equilibrium between work and personal life, and they actively prioritize self-care, personal relationships, and mental well-being. By implementing these strategies and adopting unconventional solutions, they skillfully navigate the demanding nature of their careers, ensuring a fulfilling and balanced life. Aspiring musicians and fans alike can learn from their approach and strive for their own work-life balance.

The Collaborators and Influencers

Meeting and Bonding with Musical Peers

Music is a universal language that has the power to bring people together, and for the members of Zeds Dead, this was especially true when it came to meeting and bonding with their musical peers. The journey of Zeds Dead has been shaped by the relationships they built with other artists and their collective passion for creating groundbreaking music.

Musical Connections Beyond Boundaries

One of the most remarkable aspects of Zeds Dead's career is their ability to form connections with musical peers from different genres and backgrounds. It is through these collaborations that they have been able to push the boundaries of their sound and explore new creative territories.

Take, for example, their collaboration with the iconic rapper Omar LinX on their breakout track "Out for Blood." The combination of Omar's gritty vocals and Zeds Dead's signature bass-heavy beats created a unique blend of hip-hop and electronic music, showcasing their ability to seamlessly merge two seemingly disparate genres.

Another noteworthy collaboration was with fellow Canadian producer Grimes on the track "Undo." The ethereal vocals of Grimes coupled with Zeds Dead's intricate production highlighted their shared passion for experimenting with different sounds and pushing the envelope of electronic music.

Mutual Inspiration and Mentorship

In addition to collaborating with their musical peers, Zeds Dead has also sought inspiration and mentorship from industry veterans. These relationships have played a crucial role in shaping their musical journey and providing guidance as they navigate the ever-changing music industry.

One influential mentor in their lives has been the legendary dubstep producer Rusko. Rusko's pioneering work in the dubstep genre inspired Zeds Dead to explore and experiment with the genre themselves. The guidance and support they received from Rusko gave them the confidence to push boundaries and develop their unique sound.

Zeds Dead also drew inspiration from fellow Canadian producer Deadmau5. The innovative and boundary-pushing approach of Deadmau5 fueled Zeds Dead's own desire for musical experimentation and evolution. The mentorship and support they received from Deadmau5 were instrumental in their growth as artists.

Building a Supportive Network

Beyond collaborations and mentorship, Zeds Dead recognizes the importance of building a supportive network of like-minded musicians and industry professionals. These relationships not only provide a sense of community but also offer opportunities for growth and continuous learning.

Zeds Dead formed close bonds with artists such as Dillon Francis, Bassnectar, and Skrillex, who shared their passion for creating groundbreaking music. These relationships allowed Zeds Dead to exchange ideas, collaborate on projects, and navigate the challenges of the music industry together.

Through their involvement in Toronto's vibrant music scene, Zeds Dead also forged connections with local musicians and producers. These connections not only provided a platform for showcasing their music but also created a tight-knit community of artists who supported and uplifted one another.

Unconventional Collaborations

Zeds Dead's commitment to pushing boundaries extends beyond genre limitations. They have sought out unconventional collaborations that have resulted in unique and innovative musical experiences.

For example, their collaboration with the renowned symphony orchestra, the Denver Colorado Symphony, showcased the versatility and adaptability of their music. By merging electronic beats with classical instrumentation, they created an awe-inspiring fusion of genres that captivated audiences.

In another unconventional collaboration, Zeds Dead teamed up with the iconic rock band ZZ Top for the track "Gimme Shelter." Combining ZZ Top's gritty guitar riffs with Zeds Dead's bass-driven sound demonstrated their willingness to explore new avenues and challenge musical norms.

Resources and Communities

To foster connections with their peers, Zeds Dead actively participates in online communities and platforms dedicated to music production and sharing. These resources provide a space for artists to exchange ideas, collaborate, and seek feedback on their work.

One such platform is the subreddit r/EDMPRODUCTION, where aspiring and established producers come together to discuss their craft. Zeds Dead often engages with the community, sharing insights into their creative process and offering advice to fellow producers.

Zeds Dead also organizes meet-ups and workshops with other musicians and producers during music festivals and events. These gatherings offer a chance for artists to connect in person and build relationships that extend beyond the virtual realm.

Unleashing Creativity through Collaboration

The bonds formed between Zeds Dead and their musical peers have played a pivotal role in their artistic development and creative journey.   Through collaborations, mentorship, and the support of a vibrant music community, Zeds Dead has continuously pushed the boundaries of electronic music and created a lasting impact on the industry.

As they continue to navigate the ever-changing music landscape, Zeds Dead remains committed to fostering connections and collaborations that drive innovation and inspire future generations of artists. Through their open-mindedness, they continue to find new and exciting ways to bond with their musical peers and shape the future of electronic music.

Collaborations that Shaped their Journey

Collaborations have been an essential part of Zeds Dead's journey, pushing the boundaries of their sound and expanding their artistic vision. From early musical partnerships to high-profile collaborations with renowned artists, these creative alliances have played a significant role in shaping Zeds Dead's unique sound and elevating their status in the music industry.

One of the most influential collaborations in Zeds Dead's career was their partnership with Omar LinX, a talented rapper from Toronto, Canada. Together, Zeds Dead and Omar LinX created a series of successful tracks that blended electronic music with hip-hop elements. This fusion of genres not only showcased their versatility as artists but also helped to bridge the gap between different music communities, attracting a wide range of fans to their music.

Their collaboration with Omar LinX resulted in the release of the critically acclaimed EP titled "Victor," which featured standout tracks like "Out for Blood" and "Cowboy." The EP was praised for its infectious beats, clever lyrics, and the seamless integration of electronic and hip-hop elements. The success of "Victor" propelled Zeds Dead into the spotlight and solidified their position as trailblazers in the electronic music scene.

Building on the success of their collaboration with Omar LinX, Zeds Dead continued to seek out new artistic partnerships to expand their sonic horizons. One such collaboration that had a profound impact on their journey was their work with Twin Shadow, an American singer-songwriter and record producer known for his indie pop and new wave sound.

The collaboration between Zeds Dead and Twin Shadow resulted in the creation of the captivating track "Stardust," which showcased the emotional depth and introspective lyrics that Twin Shadow is known for. The track seamlessly blended Zeds Dead's signature electronic production style with Twin Shadow's soulful vocals, creating a hauntingly beautiful piece of music that resonated with their fans on a deeper level.

In addition to collaborating with individual artists, Zeds Dead also ventured into the world of collaborative projects, partnering with other electronic music producers to create groundbreaking tracks. One notable example is their collaboration with Diplo, a DJ, songwriter, and record producer known for his genre-blending style.

The collaboration between Zeds Dead and Diplo resulted in the release of the track "Blame," a high-energy and bass-heavy anthem that showcased the best of both artists' production skills. The track was a massive success, garnering millions of streams and solidifying Zeds Dead's status as a force to be reckoned with in the electronic music scene.

Another collaboration that significantly shaped Zeds Dead's journey was their partnership with NGHTMRE, an American DJ and record producer known for his heavy-hitting bass music. Together, Zeds Dead and NGHTMRE released the track "Frontlines," a powerful and energetic anthem that became an instant fan favorite.

The collaboration with NGHTMRE showcased Zeds Dead's ability to seamlessly blend genres and create innovative tracks that pushed the boundaries of electronic music. The success of "Frontlines" not only established Zeds Dead as pioneers of the bass music genre but also paved the way for future collaborations with other artists in the electronic music community.

In summary, collaborations have played a crucial role in shaping Zeds Dead's journey, allowing them to explore new sonic territories, connect with diverse audiences, and continuously evolve their sound. From their early partnership with Omar LinX to their collaborations with Twin Shadow, Diplo, and NGHTMRE, Zeds Dead's willingness to collaborate with other artists has been instrumental in their success. These creative alliances have not only introduced them to new artistic influences but also helped them leave a lasting impact on the electronic music landscape. Moving forward, Zeds Dead will undoubtedly continue to seek out new collaborations, pushing the boundaries of their sound and inspiring the next generation of artists.

Mentorship and Guidance from Industry Veterans

In the competitive world of the music industry, mentorship and guidance from industry veterans can make a world of difference for emerging artists like Zeds Dead. These seasoned professionals provide invaluable advice, support, and opportunities that can shape the trajectory of an artist's career. In this section, we delve into the mentorship experiences and insights that have helped propel Zeds Dead to success.

Forging Meaningful Connections

Zeds Dead's journey in the music industry has been shaped by meaningful connections with industry veterans who recognized their talent and potential. They have been fortunate to receive guidance from experienced musicians, producers, and industry insiders who have navigated the complex landscape of the music business.

One of their early mentors was the renowned DJ and producer Skream. Skream took a personal interest in Zeds Dead's music and provided constructive feedback that helped them refine their sound. His mentorship not only honed their technical skills but also encouraged them to push boundaries and experiment with different styles.

Lessons in Artistic Integrity

One of the most important lessons Zeds Dead learned from their mentors was the importance of maintaining artistic integrity. They were advised to always stay true to their vision and not compromise their music for commercial success. This lesson resonated deeply with them, as they were determined to create music that was authentic and genuine.

Legendary producer and mentor, Pete Rock, played a pivotal role in reinforcing this belief. His guidance instilled in Zeds Dead the confidence to trust their instincts and not succumb to external pressures. This lesson became the foundation of their artistic philosophy, and they credit Pete Rock with shaping their artistic identity.

Navigating the Music Business

Mentors in the music industry not only provide artistic guidance but also impart valuable knowledge about the business side of music. Zeds Dead benefited greatly from mentors who helped them navigate the complexities of contracts, negotiations, and industry politics.

Canadian music executive and mentor, Drake, shared invaluable insights into the business side of the music industry. His advice on strategic collaborations, building a brand, and connecting with a broader audience proved instrumental in Zeds Dead's rise to prominence. They credit Drake for helping them understand the intricacies of the industry and positioning themselves for long-term success.

Creating Lasting Collaborations

One of the most powerful aspects of mentorship is the potential for creating lasting collaborations. Zeds Dead's mentors played a significant role in introducing them to other influential artists and industry professionals who would later become their collaborators.

Mentorship from Grammy-winning musician and visionary, Flying Lotus, opened doors for Zeds Dead to collaborate with a diverse range of artists. Through these collaborations, Zeds Dead expanded their musical horizons and tapped into new creative possibilities. They credit Flying Lotus for encouraging them to explore new genres and experiment with unconventional sounds.

Inspiring Future Generations

As Zeds Dead continues to grow in their own careers, they have embraced their role as mentors to inspire and support the next generation of artists. They understand the power of mentorship and actively seek opportunities to uplift emerging talent.

Through their label, Deadbeats, Zeds Dead actively mentors and collaborates with promising artists, providing them with a platform to showcase their work. They believe in paying it forward and fostering a community where artists can thrive and learn from each other's experiences.

The Unconventional Pathway

Mentorship doesn't always follow conventional paths. Zeds Dead also found guidance and inspiration outside of the music industry. They credit filmmaker and visual artist David Lynch for teaching them valuable lessons about creativity, pushing boundaries, and embracing the unknown.

Drawing influence from Lynch's unconventional approach to storytelling and aesthetics, Zeds Dead has embraced a multidisciplinary approach to their craft. They believe that mentorship can come from unexpected sources and that exploring different art forms can lead to new and exciting creative directions.

Conclusion

Mentorship and guidance from industry veterans have played a pivotal role in Zeds Dead's journey. Through meaningful connections, lessons in artistic integrity, navigating the music business, creating collaborations, and inspiring future generations, mentors have shaped their growth as artists. Zeds Dead remains grateful for the support and wisdom they have received and continue to pay it forward by mentoring emerging talent. Ultimately, mentorship has not only influenced their artistic vision but also contributed to their enduring legacy in the music industry.

Connections with Other Artistic Communities

In the world of music, collaboration and interaction with other artistic communities are key to fostering creativity and pushing the boundaries of one's own artistry. Zeds Dead has successfully tapped into the power of these connections, bridging the gap between different artistic disciplines and creating a unique space where music intersects with visual art, fashion, and more.

One of the ways Zeds Dead has connected with other artistic communities is through collaborations with visual artists. They have worked closely with talented designers, illustrators, and graphic artists to create visually captivating album covers, merchandise designs, and stage visuals. By bringing together the worlds of music and visual art, Zeds Dead has created a holistic and immersive experience for their audience.

For example, in the artwork for their album "Northern Lights," Zeds Dead collaborated with renowned street artist INSA to create a vibrant and dynamic visual representation of their music. The artwork combines elements of graffiti and pop art, perfectly capturing the energy and spirit of their sound. This collaboration not only enhanced the visual appeal of their album but also extended their reach to fans of street art and urban culture.

Zeds Dead has also formed connections with the fashion industry, collaborating with fashion designers and brands to create unique clothing lines and merchandise. By merging the worlds of music and fashion, they have expanded their creative expression and attracted fans who appreciate both art forms. Their collaborations have resulted in limited edition clothing items, accessories, and even sneaker designs, offering fans a chance to connect with the music on a deeper level and express their love for Zeds Dead in a tangible way.

Beyond visual art and fashion, Zeds Dead has also made connections with other artistic communities such as film and dance. They have composed soundtracks for independent films, infusing their music with cinematic elements and collaborating with filmmakers to create a powerful audiovisual experience. By exploring the intersection of music and film, Zeds Dead has showcased their versatility as artists and opened up new avenues for creativity.

In addition, Zeds Dead has collaborated with dance companies and individual dancers to create innovative and captivating performances that combine music and dance. By working with choreographers and dancers, they have elevated their live performances to a whole new level, captivating audiences with a visual spectacle that complements their music. These collaborations have not only expanded their artistic repertoire but have also introduced their music to new audiences who may not have been familiar with electronic music before.

To foster these connections with other artistic communities, Zeds Dead actively seeks out opportunities for collaboration and remains open to exploring new avenues of artistic expression. They actively engage with artists from different disciplines, attend art exhibitions, fashion shows, and film festivals to stay inspired and connected with the artistic pulse of the world.

By embracing collaborations and connections with other artistic communities, Zeds Dead has enriched their music and created a multi-dimensional experience for their fans. Their commitment to pushing creative boundaries and exploring new artistic frontiers has solidified their position as innovators in the electronic music scene.

An Unconventional Example: Zeds Dead x Street Artists Collaboration

To highlight the power of collaborations between music and visual art, let's dive into an unconventional example of Zeds Dead's connection with street artists.

In a groundbreaking project, Zeds Dead teamed up with a collective of street artists to create a series of immersive street art installations. They transformed abandoned warehouse spaces into interactive art galleries, combining massive murals with Zeds Dead's music playing in the background. Visitors could walk through the space, experiencing the vibrancy of the artwork while listening to Zeds Dead's unique sound.

This collaboration not only showcased the talent of the street artists but also introduced Zeds Dead's music to a new audience. People who may not have heard electronic music before were drawn to the eye-catching street art and naturally connected with the music playing in the background. The project generated buzz in both the art and music communities, and the installations were visited by thousands of people eager to experience the fusion of art and music.

This example demonstrates the transformative power of collaborations with other artistic communities. By embracing street art and creating a unique experience for their audience, Zeds Dead showcased the breadth of their artistic vision and expanded their fan base. It also opened doors for future collaborations with street artists and paved the way for further exploration of the intersection between music and visual art.

The Impact of Fan Support and Feedback

The success of any music artist or band is heavily reliant on the support and feedback from their fans. For Zeds Dead, their loyal fanbase has played a significant role in shaping their music, influencing their career trajectory, and contributing to their overall success. In this section, we will explore the profound impact that fan support and feedback have had on Zeds Dead's journey.

The Power of Connection

One of the most significant ways in which fans have impacted Zeds Dead is through the emotional connection they have formed with their music. Fans often relate to the messages conveyed in their songs, finding solace, motivation, and inspiration in the lyrics and melodies created by the band. This connection not only fuels a sense of belonging and community but also creates a deeply personal bond between Zeds Dead and their audience.

Influencing Musical Direction

Fan support and feedback serve as a valuable compass for Zeds Dead, guiding them in their musical exploration and helping them stay connected to their core sound. Through direct interaction with fans, such as through social media, the band receives feedback on tracks, albums, and live performances. This feedback, whether positive or constructive, helps Zeds Dead assess what resonates with their audience and adapt their music accordingly.

For instance, when fans express their love for specific tracks or genres, Zeds Dead takes note and is more likely to incorporate similar elements in their future releases. Conversely, if fans express a desire for experimentation or a change in direction, the band may feel inspired to explore new styles, genres, or collaborations. This collaboration between Zeds Dead and their fans ensures that the band's music stays relevant and continues to captivate their audience.

Fostering a Supportive Community

Fan support goes beyond just enjoying the music - it extends to the formation of a tight-knit community. Zeds Dead fans often connect with each other, both in-person and online, sharing their love for the band's music and creating lasting friendships. This sense of camaraderie not only strengthens the bond between the fans but also creates a supportive environment for Zeds Dead.

Fans often champion the band, promoting their music to their own networks and helping to expand their reach. This word-of-mouth promotion is invaluable for reaching new listeners and expanding Zeds Dead's fanbase. Moreover, the band recognizes the importance of their community and actively engages with their fans, whether through meet-and-greets, fan contests, or exclusive content. This level of interaction and appreciation fosters a deep sense of loyalty and ensures that fans feel valued and connected to the band.

Creative Collaboration

The impact of fan support and feedback is not limited to mere admiration from a distance. Zeds Dead actively involves their fans in their creative process, seeking input and collaboration. This could involve crowd-sourcing ideas for album artwork, inviting fans to remix their tracks, or even featuring fan-generated content in music videos. By involving their fans directly, Zeds Dead not only deepens the connection but also harnesses the collective creativity of their audience.

Moreover, through social media platforms, fans have the opportunity to share their own musical creations with Zeds Dead. This continuous flow of inspiration from fans often introduces the band to new sounds, styles, and emerging artists. This exchange of creative energy not only results in unique collaborations but also keeps Zeds Dead at the forefront of musical innovation.

Pushing Boundaries and Encouraging Growth

Zeds Dead's fans encourage the band to push boundaries and take risks in their music. By embracing experimentation and tackling new genres, they have continuously elevated their sound and matured as artists. The unwavering support from their fans gives Zeds Dead the freedom to explore uncharted territories and evolve beyond their comfort zones.

Moreover, when fans embrace this evolution and appreciate the band's growth, it gives Zeds Dead the confidence to continue experimenting and expanding their artistic horizons. This symbiotic relationship between the band and their fans has allowed Zeds Dead to transcend genre limitations and create a body of work that is diverse, innovative, and constantly evolving.

Unconventional Example: The Remix Circle

To illustrate the impact of fan support and feedback in a unique way, let's consider the concept of the "Remix Circle." In this scenario, Zeds Dead releases a track and encourages their fans to create remixes. Fans then share and promote their remixes, creating a vibrant online community of remixes inspired by the original track.

Zeds Dead actively listens to these remixes and selects their favorite ones to showcase on their official channels. This recognition not only encourages further remixes but also provides exposure for the talented fans who put their own spin on the band's music. This reciprocal exchange between Zeds Dead and their fans creates a circle of creativity, with the band inspiring their fans and their fans inspiring the band in return.

Conclusion: The Interactive Journey

In conclusion, the impact of fan support and feedback on Zeds Dead's journey cannot be overstated. From providing emotional connection to influencing musical direction, fostering a supportive community, enabling creative collaboration, and encouraging growth, fans play a pivotal role in shaping the band's music, career, and legacy. Zeds Dead acknowledges and embraces this interactive journey, valuing their fans' contributions and propelling their music forward with their unwavering support. The strength of this bond ensures that Zeds Dead's music will continue to resonate with their audience and leave a lasting impact on the music industry.

Influencing the Next Generation of Artists

As Zeds Dead continues to make waves in the music industry, they are not only focused on their own success, but also on influencing the next generation of artists. With their unique sound and artistic vision, they have inspired countless aspiring musicians and producers to carve their own paths in the world of electronic music. In this section, we will explore how Zeds Dead has influenced the next generation of artists and the ways in which they have nurtured and supported emerging talent.

Bridging the Gap

One of the ways Zeds Dead has influenced the next generation of artists is by bridging the gap between established acts and up-and-coming talent. They have actively sought out collaborations with emerging musicians, providing a platform for them to showcase their skills and gain exposure to a wider audience. By featuring these artists on their tracks and in their live performances, Zeds Dead gives them a chance to shine and learn from their experiences.

Mentoring and Guidance

Zeds Dead understands the importance of mentorship and guidance, as they themselves have benefited from the wisdom and advice of industry veterans. They have taken it upon themselves to offer mentorship opportunities to young artists, providing them with invaluable advice and sharing their own experiences navigating the music industry. Through workshops, masterclasses, and one-on-one sessions, Zeds Dead helps aspiring artists develop their skills and find their own artistic voice.

Spotlight on New Talent

As part of their commitment to nurturing the next generation of artists, Zeds Dead actively seeks out and promotes new talent. They have created platforms, such as record labels and curated playlists, to showcase the work of emerging artists. By featuring these artists in their sets and promoting their tracks, Zeds Dead introduces their fanbase to fresh and exciting sounds, giving these up-and-coming artists a much-needed boost in their careers.

Supporting the Underground Scene

Zeds Dead has never forgotten their roots in the underground music scene, and they continue to support it wholeheartedly. They actively seek out and collaborate with artists from the underground community, ensuring that their unique sounds and perspectives are heard by a wider audience. By featuring underground artists on their label and inviting them to perform at their shows, Zeds Dead helps to elevate their careers and bring attention to the vibrant underground scene.

Encouraging Collaboration

Collaboration has always been a cornerstone of Zeds Dead's artistic journey, and they encourage the next generation of artists to embrace the power of collaboration. They believe that through collaborative creativity, artists can push the boundaries of what is possible and create something truly unique. Zeds Dead actively promotes collaboration within the music community, urging artists to break out of their comfort zones and explore new sounds and styles together.

Championing Diversity

Diversity and inclusion are important values for Zeds Dead, and they actively champion these principles within the music industry. They have been vocal about the need for diverse representation and have used their platform to amplify the voices of marginalized communities. By featuring artists from diverse backgrounds and cultures, Zeds Dead helps to create a more inclusive music scene, inspiring the next generation of artists to embrace their own individuality and cultural heritage.

Promoting Artistic Independence

Zeds Dead believes in the power of artistic independence and encourages emerging artists to carve their own paths. They emphasize the importance of staying true to one's artistic vision and not conforming to industry pressures. By sharing their own stories of navigating the music industry and maintaining their creative integrity, Zeds Dead inspires young artists to trust their instincts and follow their own artistic path.

Building a Community

Zeds Dead understands that music is not just about the individual artist, but also about the community that surrounds it. They have fostered a strong sense of community among their fans and fellow artists, creating a supportive and inclusive space for collaboration and creativity. Through fan meetups, online forums, and community events, Zeds Dead encourages the next generation of artists to connect with each other and build meaningful relationships within the music community.

Inspiring Innovation

Perhaps one of the most significant ways Zeds Dead has influenced the next generation of artists is through their innovative approach to music production. They are constantly pushing the boundaries of what is possible, incorporating new technologies and experimenting with unconventional sounds. By demonstrating that innovation and experimentation are essential to pushing the music forward, Zeds Dead inspires young artists to think outside the box and explore uncharted territories in their own musical journeys.

In conclusion, Zeds Dead's influence on the next generation of artists goes far beyond their own success in the music industry. Through collaborations, mentorship, support for the underground scene, and a commitment to diversity and artistic independence, Zeds Dead has inspired and nurtured emerging talent. They have created a space for creativity, collaboration, and innovation, leaving a lasting impact on the music community and shaping the future of electronic music.

Awareness of Global Musical Movements

In the ever-evolving landscape of electronic music, staying aware of global musical movements is not only essential for growth and inspiration but also for maintaining a fresh and relevant sound. Zeds Dead has consistently demonstrated their ability to draw influences from various cultural and musical backgrounds, resulting in a diverse and eclectic discography. In this section, we explore the importance of being aware of global musical movements and how Zeds Dead incorporates these influences into their music.

One of the primary advantages of being aware of global musical movements is the opportunity to discover new sounds and genres. The world is brimming with vibrant music scenes that offer unique perspectives and innovative approaches to creating music. Zeds Dead understands the value of exploring different cultures and genres, constantly seeking fresh inspiration to inject into their own sound.

By embracing diverse musical movements, Zeds Dead transcends boundaries and creates a truly global sound. They recognize that music is a universal language, capable of connecting people from different backgrounds. By incorporating elements from around the world, Zeds Dead creates a musical experience that resonates with listeners worldwide.

Moreover, global musical movements provide a platform for collaboration. Zeds Dead has established connections with artists from various countries and musical backgrounds, resulting in powerful collaborative projects. Through these collaborations, they not only expand their musical horizons but also foster cross-cultural dialogue and understanding.

For instance, they have worked with artists such as Omar Linx, who brings a hip-hop flavor to their tracks, and Twin Shadow, who adds an indie-pop touch. These collaborations not only showcase Zeds Dead's openness to different musical styles but also highlight their ability to adapt and evolve within an ever-changing musical landscape.

In order to stay aware of global musical movements, Zeds Dead actively engages with music scenes around the world. They attend festivals, shows, and events in different countries, immersing themselves in the local music culture. This not only provides them with firsthand exposure to new sounds but also allows them to understand the sociopolitical context in which these movements arise.

In addition to attending live events, Zeds Dead keeps a close eye on the digital landscape. They explore online platforms, music blogs, and social media to discover emerging artists, tracks, and trends. This digital realm enables them to connect with artists and fans from all over the world and engage in a global conversation about music.

To deepen their understanding of global musical movements, Zeds Dead actively seeks out educational resources and engages in continuous learning. They study the history and evolution of different genres, dive into the discographies of influential artists, and analyze the production techniques that have defined specific musical movements.

By taking the time to delve into the intricacies of different musical cultures, Zeds Dead ensures that their own sound remains fresh, relevant, and rooted in a rich musical heritage. They recognize that their music is not created in isolation but is part of a larger global conversation, and their awareness of global musical movements allows them to contribute meaningfully to that conversation.

Awareness of global musical movements also serves as a source of inspiration and motivation. Discovering and connecting with vibrant music scenes from around the world offers an infinite well of creative ideas and possibilities. It challenges Zeds Dead to push the boundaries of their own sound and to forge new paths within the electronic music landscape.

In conclusion, maintaining an awareness of global musical movements is a crucial aspect of Zeds Dead's creative process. By embracing diverse sounds, collaborating with artists from different backgrounds, and staying connected with music scenes worldwide, Zeds Dead ensures that their music remains dynamic, relevant, and compelling. Their ability to blend influences from various cultures and genres is a testament to the power of global collaboration and serves as an inspiration for aspiring artists to explore the richness of the global music landscape.

Adopting an Eclectic Music Taste

In the vast and ever-evolving world of music, one of the keys to creative growth and innovation is adopting an eclectic music taste. For Zeds Dead, this has been an essential element in their journey as artists. By embracing diverse genres and styles, they have been able to push the boundaries of their sound and carve out a unique niche in the electronic music scene. In this section, we will explore the importance of adopting an eclectic music taste and how it has influenced Zeds Dead's artistic evolution.

Expanding Musical Horizons

Adopting an eclectic music taste means going beyond the confines of a single genre or style. It involves actively seeking out and exploring different types of music, ranging from classical to hip-hop, reggae to rock, and everything in between. This broad exposure to various genres provides a rich tapestry of influences that can be woven into one's own artistic expression.

Zeds Dead's journey began with a deep appreciation for the classics, including jazz, soul, and blues. These early influences laid the foundation for their understanding of melody, rhythm, and harmony. As they delved deeper into the world of music, their taste expanded to encompass a wide range of genres, allowing them to incorporate elements from each into their own unique sound.

Finding Inspiration in Unexpected Places

One of the exciting aspects of adopting an eclectic music taste is the opportunity to find inspiration in unexpected places. By exploring genres outside of their comfort zone, artists can discover new sounds, techniques, and perspectives that can shape their own artistic vision.

For Zeds Dead, this willingness to step outside the boundaries of electronic music has led them to collaborate with artists from a diverse range of backgrounds. From working with hip-hop legends like Jadakiss and Ice Cube to joining forces with reggae stars like Major Lazer, they have been able to fuse different genres together, creating a sound that defies categorization.

Blurring the Lines

Adopting an eclectic music taste also means blurring the lines between genres and styles. Zeds Dead has never been content to stick to one formula or sound.

Instead, they constantly experiment with blending different musical elements together to create something entirely new.

This ability to seamlessly integrate genres has allowed Zeds Dead to attract fans from a wide range of backgrounds. Their music appeals to electronic music enthusiasts, hip-hop lovers, reggae fans, and more, breaking down the barriers that often separate different music communities.

Embracing the Unexpected

One of the most exciting aspects of adopting an eclectic music taste is the element of surprise. By embracing a diverse range of music, artists open themselves up to unexpected influences and ideas that can take their creativity in new directions.

Zeds Dead has always been open to exploring the unexpected in their music. Whether it's incorporating elements of classical music into a dubstep track or blending hip-hop beats with reggae rhythms, they constantly challenge themselves to think outside the box and explore unconventional combinations.

Staying True to Your Vision

While adopting an eclectic music taste is about exploring different genres and styles, it's also essential to stay true to your own artistic vision. Zeds Dead has achieved this balance by using their diverse influences as a tool to enhance their own unique sound, rather than diluting or conforming to a particular style.

By staying true to their vision, Zeds Dead has been able to create music that is both innovative and authentic. Their eclectic taste has allowed them to carve out a distinct identity in the music industry, and fans appreciate their ability to consistently deliver fresh and boundary-pushing tracks.

Conclusion

Adopting an eclectic music taste has been instrumental in shaping the artistic evolution of Zeds Dead. By embracing diverse genres and styles, they have been able to create a sound that is truly unique and original. Their willingness to push boundaries and explore the unexpected has made them a driving force in the electronic music scene. Aspiring artists can learn from their example by expanding their musical horizons, finding inspiration in unexpected places, blurring the lines between genres, embracing the unexpected, and staying true to their own artistic vision. By doing so, they can embark on a creative journey that is as diverse and limitless as the world of music itself.

The Power of Collaborative Creativity

Collaboration is a force that can ignite creativity, fuel innovation, and push boundaries. When talented individuals with different skills and perspectives come together, the results can be magical. Zeds Dead, the dynamic music duo, understands the power of collaborative creativity and has harnessed it throughout their career to create groundbreaking music and leave a lasting impact on the electronic music scene.

Collaborations can take many forms, from working with fellow musicians and producers to partnering with visual artists and designers. In the case of Zeds Dead, their collaborations have been diverse and have played a pivotal role in shaping their sound and artistic vision.

One example of the power of collaborative creativity in the music industry is Zeds Dead's collaboration with Omar LinX, a talented rapper and songwriter. The fusion of Zeds Dead's electronic beats with Omar LinX's lyrical prowess created a unique and captivating sound that resonated with fans around the world. Tracks like "Out for Blood" and "No Prayers" showcased the seamless blend of electronic and hip-hop influences, showcasing the creative energy that arises when artists from different genres come together.

Collaboration also extends beyond the realm of music production. Zeds Dead has collaborated with a variety of visual artists and designers to create immersive visual experiences for their live shows. By combining their music with stunning visuals, they have created a multi-sensory experience that transports the audience into their world. From mesmerizing light displays to intricate stage designs, these collaborations have elevated their live performances and added a new level of artistic depth to their shows.

The power of collaborative creativity extends beyond the confines of the studio or stage. It fosters a sense of community and inspires collective growth. Zeds Dead has actively sought out collaborations with up-and-coming artists, providing them with a platform to showcase their talent and gain exposure. By nurturing young talent and giving them a chance to shine, Zeds Dead has not only contributed to the growth of individual artists but also to the evolution of the music industry as a whole.

Collaborative creativity can also be a powerful tool for addressing social and political issues. Artists have a unique ability to use their platforms to raise awareness and spark meaningful conversations. Zeds Dead has collaborated with artists who share their passion for creating positive change, using their music as a medium to amplify important messages. By leveraging their influence and collaborating with like-minded individuals, Zeds Dead has been able to make a difference and encourage their fans to do the same.

The process of collaborative creativity comes with its challenges. Each collaborator brings their own ideas, vision, and creative process to the table, which can lead to conflicts and compromises. However, it is through these challenges that the most innovative and powerful creations are often born. The key to successful collaboration lies in open communication, mutual respect, and a shared passion for the art.

Aspiring artists can learn valuable lessons from Zeds Dead's approach to collaborative creativity. By embracing collaboration, they can tap into a wealth of knowledge and perspectives that can push their creative boundaries. It is important to foster an environment of trust, where each collaborator feels empowered to contribute their unique ideas and talents. Together, they can create something greater than the sum of its parts.

In conclusion, the power of collaborative creativity is undeniable. Zeds Dead's journey is a testament to the transformative impact of collaboration in the music industry. By embracing collaborations with fellow musicians, visual artists, and designers, they have cultivated a unique sound and built a strong sense of community. Their experiences serve as inspiration for aspiring artists to harness the power of collaborative creativity and make their mark on the world.

The Studio Chronicles

The Making of Iconic Zeds Dead Tracks

In the world of music production, creating iconic tracks requires a combination of artistic intuition, technical knowledge, and a touch of magic. This section delves into the behind-the-scenes process of how Zeds Dead, the renowned music duo, crafts the memorable tracks that have captivated audiences worldwide.

Unleashing Creativity

The journey of making an iconic Zeds Dead track begins with a spark of creativity. The duo, known for their innovative sound and genre-defying style, draws inspiration from various sources, including personal experiences, emotions, and the world around them. Their creative process is fueled by a constant exploration of new musical ideas and a commitment to pushing boundaries.

To unleash their creativity, Zeds Dead follows a few unconventional techniques. One of their approaches is decoupling the technical aspects from the initial creative phase. By focusing solely on the artistic vision and emotions they want to convey, they allow their ideas to flow freely without being constrained by technical limitations.

Another technique is incorporating elements from different musical genres and eras. Zeds Dead's tracks often feature elements of dubstep, hip-hop, reggae, and other diverse influences. By combining these diverse elements, they create a unique sonic landscape that sets them apart.

Studio Alchemy

Once the initial creative ideas have taken shape, Zeds Dead enters the studio to bring their tracks to life. This is where the magic of production happens. The duo meticulously fine-tunes each element of their tracks, paying attention to every detail to ensure the final product meets their artistic vision.

A key aspect of Zeds Dead's studio process is the use of cutting-edge technology. They harness the power of software synthesizers, digital audio workstations (DAWs), and a wide range of plugins to sculpt their sound. However, they don't rely solely on technology. They blend digital production techniques with analog gear, including hardware synthesizers and effects processors, to add warmth and character to their tracks.

Zeds Dead's studio alchemy also involves a meticulous approach to sound engineering. They spend hours perfecting the mix and mastering of their tracks, ensuring that each instrument and element sits in the mix with clarity and cohesion. This attention to detail allows their tracks to shine on any sound system, from headphones to festival stages.

Collaborative Alchemy

Zeds Dead's creative process is not limited to the confines of their studio. Collaboration plays a crucial role in expanding their sonic palette and bringing a fresh perspective to their tracks. They actively seek out collaborations with both established and emerging artists, fostering a collaborative spirit within the music community.

Collaborating with other artists introduces new ideas, influences, and techniques into Zeds Dead's music. This exchange of creative energy and sharing of expertise often leads to tracks that push the boundaries of their sound. Zeds Dead believes that the collective creativity of multiple artists can generate something greater than the sum of its parts.

Experimentation and Iteration

The making of iconic Zeds Dead tracks is not a linear process. It involves experimentation and iteration, where the duo continually refines their ideas to create the best possible outcome. They are not afraid to take risks, exploring unconventional sounds and techniques to achieve their desired sonic landscape.

During the experimentation phase, Zeds Dead embraces happy accidents and unexpected results. They believe that some of the best moments in music come from embracing the unpredictable and allowing the creative process to take unexpected turns. This flexibility and openness to experimentation contribute to the unique character of their tracks.

Furthermore, Zeds Dead understands the value of iteration. They don't settle for the first draft of a track but rather embrace a cycle of refinement. By repeatedly listening to their work-in-progress, making adjustments, and seeking feedback from trusted individuals, they ensure that each track reaches its full potential.

Capturing the Essence

One of the most challenging aspects of making iconic tracks is capturing the essence of a particular moment, emotion, or concept. Zeds Dead aims to create music that resonates with their audience on a deep emotional level. They inject their tracks with a sense of authenticity and vulnerability, allowing listeners to connect with the music on a personal level.

To achieve this, Zeds Dead pays meticulous attention to every element of their tracks, from the choice of instruments and melodies to the arrangement and structure. They carefully select sounds that evoke the desired emotional response and create a coherent narrative within each track.

Lyrics also play a significant role in capturing the essence of their music. Zeds Dead collaborates with talented vocalists who can bring their vision to life through powerful and thought-provoking lyrics. By combining meaningful lyrics with their distinctive soundscapes, they create tracks that touch listeners' hearts and minds.

The Unconventional Tip

Here's an unconventional tip from Zeds Dead: Embrace the imperfections. In the pursuit of perfection, it's easy to get stuck in an endless loop of tweaking and refining. However, Zeds Dead believes that embracing imperfections can lead to unexpected creative breakthroughs. By allowing elements of spontaneity and imperfection to coexist with precision and technical prowess, they create tracks that have a distinct and organic feel.

Further Exploration

To further explore the process of making iconic tracks, take a look at the following resources:

+ *The Art of Music Production: The Theory and Practice*, by Richard James Burgess

+ *Mixing Secrets for the Small Studio*, by Mike Senior

+ *Behind the Glass: Top Record Producers Tell How They Craft the Hits*, by Howard Massey

Remember, the making of iconic tracks is a deeply personal and creative journey. The process described here serves as a starting point, but each artist's path will be unique. Embrace your creativity, experiment fearlessly, and let your passion guide you towards creating music that resonates with your audience. Now go forth and make some magical music!

The Role of Technology in Music Production

Technology has played a significant role in revolutionizing the music production process, enabling artists to create and manipulate sounds in ways that were once unimaginable. In this section, we will explore how technology has influenced music production and shaped the sound of Zeds Dead.

Digital Audio Workstations (DAWs)

One of the most important technological advancements in music production is the development of digital audio workstations (DAWs). DAWs have replaced traditional recording studios as the primary tools for producing music. They allow artists to record, edit, arrange, and mix music using a computer.

Popular DAWs such as Ableton Live, Logic Pro, and FL Studio provide a wide range of features and capabilities that enhance the creative process. Artists can now easily layer multiple sounds and instruments, manipulate audio recordings, and apply various effects and plugins to achieve the desired sound.

Problem: Balancing Levels and Dynamics   One common challenge in music production is achieving a balanced mix with appropriate levels and dynamics. Using technology, artists can address this problem by utilizing tools like compressors, limiters, and equalizers that are built into DAWs. These tools allow them to control the dynamic range of each instrument and fine-tune the frequencies to create a cohesive and impactful mix.

Solution: Utilizing Compression and EQ   Compression is a technique used to control the dynamic range of a sound. It reduces the volume of the loudest parts and increases the volume of the quietest parts, resulting in a more balanced sound. By applying compression to individual tracks or the overall mix, artists can achieve a more controlled and professional sound.

Equalization (EQ) is another crucial tool in music production. It allows artists to shape the frequency response of a sound by boosting or cutting specific frequencies. By using EQ effectively, artists can enhance the clarity and tonal balance of individual instruments, ensuring that each element sits well in the mix.

Example: Balancing a Drum Kit   Let's consider a common scenario of balancing a drum kit. Using a DAW, artists can apply compression to the kick drum to emphasize its impact and control its dynamics. They can also use EQ to boost the low frequencies and cut any unwanted frequencies that may be causing muddiness. Similarly, they can apply compression and EQ to other drums and cymbals to achieve a well-balanced and cohesive drum sound.

Caveat: Overuse of Effects   While technology offers a plethora of effects and plugins that can enhance the music production process, it's important to exercise caution and avoid overusing them. Excessive use of effects can lead to a cluttered mix or a loss of the original character and dynamics of the sound. It's crucial to strike a balance and use effects judiciously to serve the creative vision of the music.

Virtual Instruments and Samples

Another significant development in music production is the proliferation of virtual instruments and samples. Virtual instruments mimic the sounds of traditional instruments, allowing artists to recreate realistic performances without the need for physical instruments. Samples, on the other hand, are pre-recorded snippets of audio that can be used to add depth and variety to a composition.

Problem: Accessing a Wide Range of Sounds   In traditional music production, accessing a wide range of instruments and sounds required expensive equipment and studio setups. This limited the creative palette of many artists. However, with the advent of virtual instruments and samples, artists now have access to a vast library of sounds that they can use in their compositions.

Solution: Utilizing Virtual Instruments and Samples   Artists can use virtual instruments to compose music, create melodies, and play various instruments within the DAW. These instruments offer a level of flexibility and versatility that was previously only available to seasoned musicians with extensive collections of physical instruments. By using virtual instruments, artists can experiment with different sounds and styles, pushing their creative boundaries.

Samples can be used to add texture and complexity to a composition. With a vast array of samples available, artists can incorporate real-world sounds, vocal snippets, drum loops, and other audio elements into their tracks. This allows for unique and innovative productions that transcend the limitations of traditional recording methods.

Example: Building a Melodic Composition   Suppose an artist wants to create a melodic composition but doesn't possess the skills to play a specific instrument. With virtual instruments, the artist can select a piano sound and use MIDI (Musical Instrument Digital Interface) to compose and play melodies directly within the DAW. The artist can experiment with different piano sounds, tempos, and playing styles until they achieve the desired result.

Caveat: Maintaining Originality   While virtual instruments and samples offer a wide range of sounds and possibilities, it's crucial to maintain originality and avoid relying too heavily on pre-packaged sounds. Artists should strive to infuse their unique creative approach into their compositions, using virtual instruments and samples as tools for inspiration rather than relying solely on them.

Collaborative Tools and Remote Recording

Technology has not only transformed the music production process but has also revolutionized collaboration and remote recording. Artists can now work seamlessly with other musicians and producers from different geographical locations, allowing for a more diverse and inclusive creative environment.

Problem: Physical Distance and Collaboration Limitations   In the past, collaborating with other artists often required physical proximity, making it challenging for musicians from different parts of the world to work together effectively. This limitation hindered the growth and exploration of diverse musical perspectives.

Solution: Remote Collaboration and Online Platforms With the advent of high-speed internet and online collaboration platforms, artists can now collaborate remotely, transcending geographical boundaries. DAWs offer features that enable artists to share project files, communicate in real-time, and work together on the same composition. This has opened up a world of opportunities for cross-cultural collaborations and diverse musical experiences.

Online platforms dedicated to music collaboration, such as Splice and Soundtrap, allow artists to exchange ideas, share recordings, and collectively work on projects. This level of connectivity and accessibility has extended the reach of creative collaboration and has led to the emergence of new musical genres and styles.

Example: Remote Recording Sessions Imagine a scenario where an artist wants to collaborate with a vocalist who is based in a different country. Through the use of remote recording, the artist can send the instrumental track to the vocalist, who can then record their vocals in their own home studio and send the recordings back. The artist can seamlessly integrate the vocals into the composition, resulting in a collaborative piece that transcends physical distances.

Caveat: Non-Verbal Communication Challenges While remote collaboration has many benefits, it also presents challenges in terms of non-verbal communication. Artists may miss the spontaneity and immediate feedback that comes from working in the same physical space. It's important to establish clear channels of communication and foster an environment of openness and understanding to overcome these challenges effectively.

Embracing Technology for Artistic Innovation

Zeds Dead has embraced technology as a tool for artistic innovation, constantly pushing the boundaries of their sound in the realm of electronic music. They have harnessed the power of technology to explore new artistic territories, experiment with unconventional sounds, and continuously evolve their creative process.

By leveraging the capabilities of digital audio workstations, virtual instruments, and collaborative tools, Zeds Dead has been able to create music that transcends traditional genre boundaries. Their ability to blend various musical styles, incorporate diverse influences, and connect with audiences worldwide is a testament to the role of technology in their artistic journey.

Tricks of the Trade: Sampling in Music Production

Sampling, the act of reusing and repurposing existing audio recordings in new compositions, has become a fundamental technique in music production. It allows artists to tap into vast libraries of recorded music, speeches, and other sounds to create unique and innovative pieces. In this section, we will delve into the world of sampling and explore how Zeds Dead has incorporated this technique into their music.

Sampling: The Basics

Sampling involves taking a portion of an existing audio recording, either a drum break, a guitar riff, or a vocal snippet, and incorporating it into a new composition. This technique allows artists to pay homage to their musical influences, evoke nostalgia, and create connections between different eras and styles of music.

Problem: Creating Unique and Original Compositions   With the vast amount of music available today, creating unique and original compositions can be a challenge. Artists often strive to find new ways to captivate their audience while still staying true to their creative vision.

Solution: Sampling as a Creative Tool   Sampling provides artists with a powerful creative tool to build upon the foundations of existing music. By carefully selecting and manipulating samples, artists can create unique sonic landscapes that tell their story and express their artistic vision. It allows them to reinterpret and repurpose existing material, breathing new life into old recordings and creating something entirely fresh.

Example: Flipping a Drum Break   A common sampling technique involves taking a drum break from a classic funk or soul recording and incorporating it into a new composition. By manipulating the rhythm, adding effects, and layering additional sounds, artists can transform a familiar drum pattern into a unique and contemporary groove. This blend of old and new adds depth and complexity to the composition, giving it a distinct character.

Caveat: Copyright and Legal Considerations   When sampling, it's crucial for artists to be mindful of copyright and legal considerations. Sampling copyrighted material without proper clearance or permission can lead to legal issues. Artists should familiarize themselves with the necessary licensing procedures and consult with legal professionals to ensure they are compliant with copyright laws.

Creative Sampling Techniques

Zeds Dead has mastered the art of creative sampling, infusing their music with unique and innovative sounds. They have developed techniques that allow them to push the boundaries of sampling and create compositions that are distinctively their own.

Problem: Manipulating and Transforming Samples Often, artists need to manipulate and transform samples to fit their creative vision. This requires techniques that allow for the alteration and enhancement of the original sound while maintaining its core essence.

Solution: Chopping, Pitch Shifting, and Time Stretching Chopping is the process of dividing a sample into smaller segments, such as individual drum hits or melodic phrases. This technique allows artists to rearrange the sample, create new patterns, and extract unique elements that can be used in different contexts.

Pitch shifting involves altering the pitch of a sample, either raising or lowering it. This technique can completely change the character of a sample, creating new melodic possibilities and fitting the sample into the desired key or harmonic context.

Time stretching allows artists to manipulate the duration of a sample without altering its pitch. It enables them to create rhythmic variations, experiment with different tempos, and seamlessly integrate the sample into the composition.

Example: Chopping and Reconstructing a Vocal Sample Zeds Dead often incorporates vocal samples into their music. They may take a vocal phrase from a classic soul record, chop it up into smaller segments, and rearrange those segments to create a unique vocal melody. By combining different parts of the sample, altering the pitch, and applying effects, they can transform a familiar vocal into something entirely fresh and innovative.

Caveat: Ethical Sampling While sampling provides artists with a powerful creative tool, it's important to approach it ethically. Artists should give credit to the original creators and seek proper permissions and clearances when applicable. It's crucial to respect the intellectual property of others and maintain transparency in the use of samples.

The Future of Sampling

As technology and music production techniques continue to evolve, so does the art of sampling. New technologies have emerged that allow for more sophisticated sampling and manipulation of audio recordings, offering artists even greater creative possibilities.

Problem: Pushing the Boundaries of Sampling   Innovation in sampling involves finding new ways to push the boundaries of what can be achieved with existing audio recordings. Artists constantly seek methods to manipulate samples in ways that are unique, unconventional, and push the limits of creativity.

Solution: Granular Synthesis and Audio Manipulation Tools   Granular synthesis is a technique that divides an audio sample into tiny grains and recombines them in different ways. This method allows for the manipulation of individual grains, such as altering their pitch, position, or duration. Granular synthesis opens up a world of possibilities for artists to transform and reshape sounds in unprecedented ways.

Advanced audio manipulation tools, such as spectral editing software, offer artists the ability to isolate specific frequencies or harmonics within a sample and manipulate them independently. This allows for detailed control over the tonal characteristics of a sound and can lead to innovative and otherworldly textures.

Example: Granular Synthesis and Textural Manipulation   Imagine an artist taking a guitar recording and subjecting it to granular synthesis. By slicing the sound into tiny grains and rearranging them, they can create intricate and evolving textures that are completely unrecognizable from the original source. This technique opens up a new avenue of sonic exploration and allows for the creation of captivating and ethereal compositions.

Caveat: Balancing Innovation and Artistry   With the abundance of sampling techniques and tools available, it's essential for artists to strike a balance between innovation and artistry. While pushing the boundaries of sampling can lead to groundbreaking creations, it's crucial to ensure that the final composition remains cohesive, emotive, and true to the artist's creative vision.

Conclusion

Technology has played a pivotal role in shaping the music production process and the sound of Zeds Dead. From the advent of digital audio workstations to the development of virtual instruments and collaboration tools, technology has provided artists with unprecedented creative possibilities.

Through the use of technology, Zeds Dead has embraced innovation, pushing the boundaries of their sound and incorporating diverse influences. Sampling has become an integral part of their creative process, allowing them to pay homage to their musical influences while creating unique compositions.

As technology continues to evolve, it is essential for artists to adapt and harness its power to stay at the forefront of artistic exploration. By embracing technology, artists can continue to shape the future of music production and create innovative and captivating compositions that resonate with audiences worldwide.

Exploring Different Studio Setups

In the world of music production, the studio setup is the backbone of creativity and innovation. It is the space where ideas are transformed into sonic realities. Zeds Dead, known for their unique sound and production prowess, have explored various studio setups throughout their career, each contributing to their evolving artistic journey. In this section, we will delve into the different studio setups that Zeds Dead has experimented with, discussing their advantages, challenges, and the impact on their music production process.

Home Studio

Like many artists, Zeds Dead began their musical journey experimenting with a home studio setup. Starting with basic equipment and limited resources, their bedroom served as a creative sanctuary. This setup allowed for spontaneous creativity, unhindered by time constraints and outside influences. Zeds Dead were able to nurture their artistic vision at their own pace, without the pressure of a commercial studio environment.

Despite its limitations, the home studio fostered a sense of independence and resourcefulness. They learned to maximize the potential of their equipment, exploring different techniques and pushing the boundaries of what could be achieved. The intimate space allowed for deep exploration of the intricacies of sound design and composition.

However, working in a home studio also presented challenges. Limited space and acoustic treatment meant that the production environment was not optimized for accurate monitoring. This made it necessary for Zeds Dead to compensate for any inaccuracies in their mixes during the final stages of production.

Project Studio

As their musical career gained momentum, Zeds Dead transitioned into a project studio setup. This type of studio often combines professional-grade equipment with the convenience and flexibility of a home studio. It provides a more controlled acoustic environment and offers a broader range of tools and resources.

Setting up a project studio allowed Zeds Dead to further refine their sound and production techniques. They invested in high-quality studio monitors, ensuring accurate and detailed sound reproduction. Acoustic treatment was also improved, minimizing unwanted resonances and reflections.

The project studio setup provided Zeds Dead with the necessary tools to experiment with different recording techniques. They were able to capture live instruments and vocals, adding an organic and human touch to their electronic productions. This setup also facilitated collaboration with other artists, as it offered a flexible and comfortable space for creative exchange.

Professional Studio

As Zeds Dead's success continued to soar, they expanded into a professional studio setup. This type of studio is designed to meet the highest industry standards, with state-of-the-art equipment and acoustically treated rooms. It offers a dedicated space solely focused on music production, allowing for a more immersive and inspiring creative process.

In a professional studio, Zeds Dead had access to a wide range of analog and digital gear, enabling them to experiment with different sonic textures and timbres. The pristine recording environment eliminated any limitations on the quality of their recordings, ensuring every nuance was captured accurately.

The professional studio setup also provided the opportunity for collaborations with renowned engineers and producers. Their expertise and guidance further enhanced Zeds Dead's sound, pushing the boundaries of their creative potential. The studio environment facilitated seamless workflow, enabling efficient production and mixing processes.

Hybrid Setup

As Zeds Dead's musical journey progressed, they embraced a hybrid studio setup, combining the best elements of home, project, and professional studios. This versatile setup allowed them the flexibility to work in different environments, catering to the specific needs of each project.

The hybrid setup enabled Zeds Dead to harness the creativity and freedom of a home studio while benefiting from the higher quality and advanced tools of a professional studio. They could switch seamlessly between different spaces, adapting to the nature of each production.

With a hybrid setup, Zeds Dead could capture the essence of live instrumentation in a controlled environment and then seamlessly integrate it into their electronic compositions. This approach brought a dynamic and organic quality to their music, enriching their sonic palette.

Studio Setup Considerations

When exploring different studio setups, there are several key considerations that Zeds Dead took into account. These considerations influenced the choice of equipment, room acoustics, and overall workflow. Here are some important factors they considered:

+ **Acoustic Treatment:** Proper acoustic treatment plays a crucial role in achieving accurate monitoring and sound reproduction. Zeds Dead invested in quality absorption and diffusion materials to minimize unwanted reflections and resonances.

+ **Equipment Selection:** Zeds Dead carefully selected their equipment based on their preferred sound aesthetics and workflow. They opted for a combination of analog and digital gear, leveraging the strengths of each to achieve their desired sonic outcome.

+ **Room Calibration:** Each studio setup required meticulous room calibration to ensure accurate monitoring. Zeds Dead utilized room measurement software and hardware to identify and address any acoustic anomalies in the listening environment.

+ **Workflow Efficiency:** The workflow efficiency was a paramount consideration. Zeds Dead organized their gear and wiring in a logical manner, allowing for quick and effortless access to different instruments and equipment.

+ **Flexibility for Collaboration:** Collaboration played a significant role in Zeds Dead's music production process. They prioritized setups that allowed for seamless collaboration with other musicians, producers, and engineers.

Studio Case Study: The Hybrid Setup

To give you a deeper insight into Zeds Dead's exploration of different studio setups, let's take a closer look at their hybrid setup. This setup embodies the evolution of their creative process and showcases the advantages of combining elements from home, project, and professional studios.

Zeds Dead's hybrid setup is centered around a purpose-built control room equipped with high-quality monitoring, signal processing, and recording equipment. The room is acoustically optimized with meticulous treatment to ensure accurate sound reproduction. It also houses a collection of analog synths, drum machines, and outboard gear, enabling hands-on experimentation and sound sculpting.

Adjacent to the control room is a dedicated live room where Zeds Dead can record live instruments and vocals. This room is designed to provide a controlled and clean sound environment, allowing for pristine recordings.

To bridge the gap between the digital and analog worlds, Zeds Dead utilizes a comprehensive set of software and plugins. These tools expand their sonic possibilities and serve as a creative catalyst during the production process.

The hybrid setup also integrates a portable workstation that allows Zeds Dead to work remotely or collaborate on the go. This flexibility ensures that their creative momentum is not limited to the confines of the studio.

Unconventional Studio Setup: Mobile Production

In addition to the traditional studio setups discussed above, Zeds Dead has also embraced a more unconventional approach to music production: mobile production. With advancements in technology, music creation is no longer limited to the confines of a physical studio. Zeds Dead has harnessed the power of mobile devices and portable equipment to create music on the go.

Using powerful laptops, tablets, and a variety of music production apps, Zeds Dead can turn any environment into a creative playground. Whether it's making beats during a flight or sketching out ideas in a hotel room, mobile production allows them to capture inspiration whenever and wherever it strikes.

The advantages of mobile production extend beyond flexibility and convenience. The intimate and spontaneous nature of this setup often leads to unexpected creative breakthroughs. Zeds Dead have discovered unique sounds and production techniques by utilizing the limitations and unconventional workflows inherent in mobile production.

While mobile production cannot fully replace the traditional studio environment, it serves as a valuable addition to Zeds Dead's creative arsenal. It allows them to nurture their artistic vision in diverse and unconventional settings, providing a fresh perspective on music production.

Conclusion

Zeds Dead's exploration of different studio setups demonstrates their commitment to innovation and sonic excellence. From the humble beginnings of a home studio to the state-of-the-art professional setup, they have embraced the advantages and challenges of each environment. The hybrid studio setup not only encapsulates the best elements of different setups but also enables flexibility and adaptability.

Furthermore, Zeds Dead's foray into mobile production showcases their willingness to push the boundaries of music creation. It highlights the importance of embracing advancements in technology and exploring unconventional approaches to nurture creativity.

Ultimately, the studio setup is a personal and ever-evolving choice for artists. Zeds Dead's journey reminds us that regardless of the setup, it is the artist's vision, dedication, and willingness to experiment that truly shapes the music and leaves a lasting impact on the industry. Aspiring musicians can draw inspiration from Zeds Dead's diverse studio setups, recognizing that creativity knows no bounds and that innovation can come from even the most unconventional of places.

The Importance of Sound Engineering

Sound engineering is a crucial element in the creation of music. It involves the technical and artistic processes of recording, editing, mixing, and mastering sound. Whether it's in the studio or during live performances, the role of the sound engineer is to ensure that the music sounds its best and is delivered to the audience with clarity and impact.

Sound engineering requires a deep understanding of acoustics, audio equipment, and various recording techniques. The sound engineer must have a good ear for detail and be able to manipulate sound to achieve the desired sonic quality. They work closely with musicians, producers, and other professionals to capture the essence of a musical piece and translate it into a recorded or live sound experience.

One of the key responsibilities of a sound engineer is to set up and operate the recording equipment. They choose the appropriate microphones, amplifiers, and other audio gear to capture the sound accurately. They must also consider the acoustics of the recording space, taking into account factors such as room size, shape, and sound reflections.

During the recording process, sound engineers work closely with musicians to capture their performances. They ensure that the levels are balanced, the sound is clear and free from any unwanted noise or distortion, and that the recording captures the essence and emotion of the music. This requires technical expertise in adjusting microphone placement, using equalization and dynamics processing tools, and other techniques to shape the sound.

After the recording process is complete, sound engineers move on to the editing and mixing stages. They carefully listen to and analyze each track, making adjustments in volume, EQ, panning, and effects to create a cohesive and balanced mix. The goal is to enhance the individual elements of the music while maintaining a sense of overall unity. This process requires a combination of technical skills and artistic sensibility to bring the music to life.

The final stage of sound engineering is mastering, which involves preparing the mixed tracks for distribution. Sound engineers use specialized techniques to fine-tune the audio, ensuring that it sounds consistent across different playback systems and formats. They also make adjustments to the overall tonal balance, dynamics, and stereo image to create a polished and professional sound.

Proper sound engineering is essential for creating a high-quality listening experience for the audience. It can elevate a mediocre recording into something extraordinary, giving the music depth, clarity, and impact. Conversely, poor sound engineering can undermine the artistic vision, resulting in a lackluster and uninspiring sound.

In addition to the technical aspects, sound engineering also requires creativity and problem-solving skills. Sound engineers often need to think outside the box to overcome challenges and achieve the desired sonic results. They may need to experiment with different microphone placements, use unconventional recording techniques, or apply innovative mixing and mastering approaches to achieve a unique and captivating sound.

The impact of sound engineering extends beyond the realm of music production. It plays a crucial role in various other fields, including film, television, radio, and gaming. In these industries, sound engineers work to create immersive audio experiences that enhance storytelling and capture the audience's attention. They use their technical skills and artistic abilities to bring sound to life, shaping the emotional impact of the visuals and creating a more engaging and memorable experience.

In conclusion, sound engineering is a fundamental aspect of music production. It combines technical expertise with artistic sensibility to shape the sound and bring the music to life. Sound engineers play a critical role in capturing, shaping, and delivering the music with clarity and impact. Their attention to detail, technical knowledge, and creative problem-solving skills contribute to the overall quality of the music and the audience's listening experience.

Honing Skills and Experimentation

In the world of music production, honing skills and continuous experimentation are pivotal to an artist's growth and success. For Zeds Dead, this process has been an integral part of their journey, allowing them to continually push boundaries and evolve their sound. In this section, we delve into the techniques, practices, and mindset behind their honing of skills and the experimentation that has shaped their unique musical style.

Embracing the Learning Process

For Zeds Dead, the journey of honing their skills began with a deep appreciation for learning. They approached music production as a continuous process of exploration and improvement. This mindset allowed them to embrace the challenges and setbacks they encountered along the way, seeing them as opportunities for growth rather than obstacles.

One of the key aspects of their learning process was a commitment to self-education. They immersed themselves in tutorials, online courses, and forums, exchanging knowledge with fellow producers and staying up-to-date with the latest production techniques. This self-driven learning approach allowed them to constantly expand their technical skills and stay at the forefront of the ever-evolving music production landscape.

Experimentation as a Catalyst for Innovation

Experimentation has been at the heart of Zeds Dead's creative process. They believe that the pursuit of new sounds and ideas is essential for artistic growth. Through experimentation, they have continuously pushed the boundaries of electronic music, blending genres and incorporating unconventional elements into their tracks.

One of their favorite methods of experimentation is combining disparate musical styles. By fusing elements of dubstep, hip-hop, reggae, and other genres, they have created a unique and recognizable sound that sets them apart from their peers. This willingness to take risks and explore uncharted territories has allowed them to carve out a distinctive niche within the electronic music scene.

Focused Practice and Refinement

To continually improve their skills, Zeds Dead emphasizes the importance of focused practice and deliberate refinement. They believe that quantity alone doesn't guarantee improvement; it is the quality and intention behind the practice that truly matters.

Their practice sessions are structured and goal-oriented. They break down complex techniques and focus on mastering each component individually before putting them together. This meticulous approach allows them to refine their skills and bring precision to their productions.

Iteration and Feedback

Feedback is an invaluable tool for growth, and Zeds Dead understands the significance of seeking input from others. They actively seek feedback from trusted peers, mentors, and even their fanbase. This iterative process of feedback and refinement enables them to uncover blind spots, identify areas for improvement, and gain fresh perspectives on their work.

Additionally, self-reflection is an integral part of their creative process. They regularly review their previous work, analyzing what worked well and what could have been better. By critically evaluating their own productions and performances, they are able to learn from their experiences and continually raise the bar for their future endeavors.

Exploring New Tools and Technologies

As technology in music production evolves, Zeds Dead remains on the forefront of innovation. They embrace new tools, software, and hardware, constantly exploring how these advancements can enhance their creative process.

From the latest synthesizers and plugins to cutting-edge production techniques, they are always eager to experiment with new tools and integrate them into their workflow. However, they remain mindful that technology should serve as a means to amplify their creative vision, rather than overshadow it.

Thinking Outside the Box

In their pursuit of honing skills and pushing boundaries, Zeds Dead encourages thinking outside the box. They believe that creativity flourishes when artists break free from conventions and challenge existing norms.

This unconventional mindset can involve exploring non-traditional sound sources, experimenting with uncommon time signatures, or even drawing inspiration from non-musical sources. By thinking outside the box, Zeds Dead has been able to create music that is truly innovative and captivating.

Example: Incorporating Live Instruments

A prime example of Zeds Dead's commitment to experimentation is their incorporation of live instruments in their performances. While electronic music is predominantly produced using software and synthesizers, Zeds Dead sought to break this mold by integrating guitars, drums, and other traditional instruments into their live sets.

This decision not only added a dynamic and organic element to their performances but also allowed them to explore new creative avenues. It required them to learn how to play these instruments proficiently, adding another layer of honing skills to their journey. By blending live instrumentation with their electronic elements, Zeds Dead has created an immersive and unforgettable live experience for their fans.

Resources and Practice Exercises

1. Take time to regularly evaluate your own musical productions. Identify areas for improvement and set goals for focused practice sessions. 2. Seek out feedback from trusted peers and mentors. Embrace constructive criticism as an opportunity for growth. 3. Experiment with blending different musical genres to create a unique sound of your own. 4. Explore new tools, software, and hardware in your music production workflow. Stay up-to-date with the latest advancements in technology. 5. Devote time to self-education through tutorials, online courses, and forums. Continuously expand your technical skills and stay ahead of the curve. 6. Think outside the box by incorporating unconventional elements or drawing inspiration from non-musical sources.

Remember, honing skills and experimentation are ongoing processes. Embrace the journey, push boundaries, and never stop learning. As Zeds Dead's story demonstrates, it is through this commitment to growth that your music can truly evolve and resonate with others.

The Workflow and Creative Process

The workflow and creative process of Zeds Dead is an intricate and fascinating journey that combines technical expertise, experimentation, and a keen understanding of music production. With their unique style and sound, Zeds Dead has gained recognition for their innovative approach to electronic music. In this section, we will delve into the workflow and creative process of Zeds Dead, exploring their mindset, production techniques, and the tools they use to bring their vision to life.

Mindset and Inspiration

Creativity knows no bounds for Zeds Dead. The duo, consisting of Dylan Mamid (DC) and Zachary Rapp-Rovan (Hooks), thrive on embracing new ideas and pushing the boundaries of their sound. Their mindset is rooted in the philosophy of constant experimentation, allowing themselves the freedom to explore various genres, styles, and sonic landscapes.

Inspiration can strike from unexpected sources. DC and Hooks draw inspiration from a wide range of musical genres, as well as non-musical elements such as artwork, films, and literature. Their open-mindedness and willingness to explore different artistic mediums allow them to infuse their music with unique flavors and perspectives.

Pre-production

The pre-production phase is a crucial step in the creative process of Zeds Dead. It involves brainstorming, conceptualizing, and developing ideas for tracks. During this phase, DC and Hooks lay the foundation for their music, experimenting with different sounds, melodies, and rhythms.

To kickstart the pre-production process, the duo explores various techniques, such as sketching out rough ideas on the piano or experimenting with different synthesizers and drum machines. They dive deep into sound design, crafting unique patches, and sample libraries to build their sonic palette. This phase allows them to establish the mood and direction of a track before moving into the production phase.

Production

The production phase is where the magic happens. Armed with a solid concept and a clear vision, DC and Hooks dive into the creation of the track. They meticulously arrange and layer different elements, constantly refining and iterating until they achieve the desired result.

Zeds Dead's production process involves a combination of digital and analog tools. They utilize a range of software synthesizers, virtual instruments, and effects plugins to shape their sound. At the same time, they incorporate analog hardware, such as synthesizers and drum machines, to add warmth and character to their tracks.

A key aspect of Zeds Dead's production workflow is their emphasis on sound engineering. They have a deep understanding of audio processing techniques, including compression, equalization, and modulation. Through careful manipulation of these tools, they sculpt and shape their sounds with precision.

Collaboration and Feedback

Collaboration plays a significant role in the creative process of Zeds Dead. They frequently collaborate with other artists, vocalists, and musicians to bring a fresh perspective and new ideas to their tracks. Collaborative sessions involve a free-flowing exchange of ideas, where each artist contributes their unique style and expertise.

Feedback also plays a crucial role in the creative process. DC and Hooks value the input and constructive criticism of their peers as well as their fans. They actively seek feedback during the production process, whether it's testing out tracks in live performances or sharing works-in-progress with their trusted circle of friends and fellow musicians. This feedback loop helps them refine their tracks and ensure they resonate with their audience.

Experimentation and Unconventional Techniques

Zeds Dead are fearless when it comes to experimentation and embracing unconventional techniques. They constantly challenge themselves to push the boundaries of their sound. Whether it's incorporating unconventional samples, layering unexpected textures, or utilizing unconventional time signatures, they strive to create tracks that surprise and captivate their audience.

One unconventional technique that Zeds Dead employs is the use of field recordings. They are known to venture into their surroundings, capturing sounds from nature, urban environments, and everyday life. These field recordings are then transformed into unique textures and atmospheres that add a distinct flavor to their tracks.

Workflow Optimization

Optimizing the workflow is a continuous process for Zeds Dead. They are constantly looking for ways to streamline their production process and eliminate any bottlenecks. This involves staying up-to-date with the latest technologies, software updates, and production techniques.

To enhance their efficiency, DC and Hooks have developed customized template sessions for their DAW (Digital Audio Workstation). These templates contain pre-configured tracks, plugins, and routing setups, allowing them to jumpstart their creative process without getting bogged down by technical setup.

Furthermore, Zeds Dead has developed a library of their own custom presets, samples, and sound libraries. This library serves as a toolkit, allowing them to maintain a consistent sound throughout their productions while also providing quick access to their signature sounds.

Tools of the Trade

Zeds Dead employs a wide array of tools to bring their artistic vision to life. From hardware to software, they leverage the best in the industry to achieve their desired sound. Here are some of the key tools they incorporate into their workflow:

- **Digital Audio Workstation (DAW):** Zeds Dead primarily uses industry-standard DAWs such as Ableton Live and Logic Pro X. These DAWs offer a comprehensive suite of tools and features that enable them to compose, arrange, mix, and master their tracks.

- **Software Synthesizers:** They utilize a range of software synthesizers, including Serum, Massive, and FM8, to craft their unique and evolving sound. These synthesizers provide a versatile palette of sounds and textures that help shape their tracks.

- **Analog Hardware:** Zeds Dead incorporates analog hardware into their production setup to add warmth and character to their sound. Moog synthesizers, such as the Minimoog Model D, and drum machines like the Roland TR-808 and TR-909, are staples in their setup.

- **Effects Processors:** The duo experiments with a wide variety of effects processors to transform their sounds and create unique sonic textures. They utilize delay, reverb, modulation, distortion, and other effects to add depth and personality to their tracks.

- **Field Recording Equipment:** As mentioned earlier, Zeds Dead actively incorporates field recordings into their tracks. They use portable audio recorders, such as the Zoom H5, to capture sounds from their surroundings, which are later processed and integrated into their compositions.

• **Monitoring and Studio Setup:** Zeds Dead employs high-quality studio monitors, such as the KRK Rokit series or Genelec studio monitors, to ensure accurate playback and monitoring during the production process. They also utilize professional-grade headphones, such as the Sennheiser HD 800, for critical listening and reference.

• **MIDI Controllers:** MIDI controllers, such as the Ableton Push or Native Instruments Komplete Kontrol, play a vital role in their workflow. These controllers provide tactile control over their software instruments and allow for expressive, hands-on performance.

• **Sample Libraries:** Zeds Dead has built an extensive collection of samples and sound libraries over the years. These libraries consist of drums, percussion, vocal samples, one-shots, and other elements that they use to enhance their tracks.

Zeds Dead's creative process and workflow are a testament to their dedication and passion for their craft. Their open-mindedness, willingness to experiment, and constant pursuit of innovation have secured their position as one of the most respected and influential acts in electronic music. As they continue to evolve and push boundaries, we can only anticipate more groundbreaking music from this exceptional duo.

Behind-the-Scenes Stories and Anecdotes

Behind every successful artist lies a treasure trove of stories and anecdotes that shed light on their journey and the secrets behind their craft. Zeds Dead is no exception – this Canadian electronic duo has their fair share of behind-the-scenes tales that reveal the magic and madness of their creative process. In this section, we will delve into some of the most intriguing stories and anecdotes that provide a glimpse into the world of Zeds Dead.

The Birth of a Collaboration

It all started in the unlikely setting of a coffee shop in Toronto. Legend has it that Zeds Dead's founding members, Dylan Mamid and Zachary Rapp-Rovan, met by chance and struck up a conversation about their mutual love for music. Little did they know that this encounter would be the beginning of a powerful musical partnership.

As the story goes, their friendship blossomed over late-night jam sessions in Dylan's basement, where they experimented with different sounds, genres, and ideas. These early collaborations laid the foundation for their unique sound, blending elements of dubstep, hip-hop, and reggae into a seamless and captivating sonic experience.

The Creative Spark

One of the most intriguing anecdotes about Zeds Dead's creative process revolves around their ability to find inspiration in the most unexpected places. It is said that Dylan and Zachary have a knack for finding hidden gems in old vinyl records and obscure samples that add a touch of nostalgia and depth to their music.

In the early days, they would spend hours scouring record stores, searching for that elusive vinyl that would become the main ingredient of their next masterpiece. This attention to detail and their passion for preserving the soul of different musical eras set them apart from their contemporaries.

The Unforgettable Studio Sessions

If the walls of their studio could talk, they would surely reveal some extraordinary tales of late-night studio sessions filled with creativity, experimentation, and camaraderie. Friends and collaborators who have had the privilege of witnessing these sessions often recount stories of the duo's relentless pursuit of perfection and their ability to push each other to new artistic heights.

Perhaps one of the most remarkable aspects of Zeds Dead's studio sessions is their openness to experimentation. They have been known to turn everyday objects into instruments, incorporating unconventional sounds and textures into their tracks. This fearless approach to music-making has resulted in some of their most groundbreaking and acclaimed work.

From the Stage to the Crowd

Behind every successful live performance lies a multitude of stories that capture the essence of the connection between the artists and their audience. Zeds Dead's live shows are no exception – they are renowned for their electrifying energy and ability to captivate crowds around the world.

One unforgettable anecdote involves a particularly rowdy crowd in Miami during one of their performances. As the atmosphere reached a fever pitch, Dylan decided to crowd-surf, trusting the fans to carry him safely across the sea of hands. The moment became a symbol of the unbreakable bond between Zeds Dead and their fans and remains etched in the memories of all who witnessed it.

The Price of Success

Despite their meteoric rise and undeniable talent, Zeds Dead has had to navigate through their fair share of challenges and setbacks. One memorable story revolves around a particularly grueling tour schedule that pushed them to their physical and mental limits.

During a European tour, the duo found themselves performing in a different city every night, barely getting any rest in between shows. The demands of the tour took a toll on their health and well-being, yet they fought through fatigue and exhaustion, determined to give their fans an unforgettable experience.

The Irresistible Collaboration

Collaborations have always been a hallmark of Zeds Dead's career, and one collaboration stands out as particularly memorable. In a stroke of serendipity, they found themselves working with a renowned hip-hop artist who they had long admired.

The process of creating music together was an eye-opening experience for all parties involved. Each brought their unique perspectives and talents to the table, resulting in a track that not only captivated fans but also broke down genre barriers.

The Unconventional Approach

One aspect of Zeds Dead's creative process that truly sets them apart is their unconventional approach to music-making. They have never been content to stick to the tried-and-true formulas of electronic music but rather have constantly sought to push the boundaries and challenge conventions.

For instance, they have been known to incorporate elements of live instrumentation into their tracks, blurring the lines between electronic and traditional music. This willingness to defy expectations and experiment with different sounds and techniques has earned them a reputation as true pioneers in their field.

The Power of Fan Stories

Amidst all the tales of their own experiences, Zeds Dead holds a special place in their hearts for the stories and anecdotes shared by their fans. They have been known to invite fans backstage and take the time to listen to their personal experiences and how their music has touched their lives.

These encounters not only inspire Zeds Dead to keep pushing their creative boundaries but also remind them of the profound impact that music can have on individuals and communities. It is a humbling reminder of why they embarked on this musical journey in the first place.

Pushing the Envelope

To truly understand Zeds Dead's legacy, one must appreciate their ability to constantly evolve and reinvent themselves. They have never been content to rest on their laurels but instead have embraced change and pushed the envelope with each new release.

In one memorable anecdote, Zeds Dead revealed that they deliberately challenged themselves to experiment with new genres and sounds for their album, disregarding any expectations from their fanbase or the music industry. This bold move paid off, solidifying their reputation as true innovators in the electronic music scene.

Leaving a Lasting Impression

At the heart of Zeds Dead's journey lies the desire to create music that makes a lasting impact on their listeners. Their dedication to their craft, their willingness to take risks, and their unwavering commitment to innovation have all played a part in the enduring legacy they are building.

As the final beat of their story approaches, Zeds Dead remains committed to inspiring future generations of artists and pushing the boundaries of electronic music in untold ways. Their behind-the-scenes stories and anecdotes will continue to captivate and inspire, reminding us all of the power of music, creativity, and the relentless pursuit of artistic excellence.

And so, the captivating behind-the-scenes stories and anecdotes of Zeds Dead draw to a close. In this window into their artistry, we've witnessed the magical birth of a collaboration, the creative spark that ignites their music, and the unforgettable moments in the studio and on the stage. We've explored the challenges they face, the unconventional approach they take, and the lasting impact they aim to leave on the world. Through their stories, we've gained insight into the extraordinary journey of Zeds Dead, a remarkable duo that has carved their own path in the world of electronic music. As their story continues to unfold, let us join them in celebrating their art, their passion, and their enduring legacy.

Constant Learning and Musical Growth

Constant learning and musical growth have been at the core of Zeds Dead's journey as artists. From their early beginnings to their current success, they have always strived to expand their musical knowledge, push boundaries, and evolve as musicians. In this section, we will explore the various ways in which Zeds Dead has embraced constant learning and fostered their musical growth.

Embracing Musical Education

Zeds Dead understands the importance of a strong foundation in music education. They have invested time and effort into expanding their knowledge of music theory, composition, and arrangement. By studying various musical styles and genres, they have gained a deeper understanding of the intricacies of music and its emotional impact.

To further their education, Zeds Dead has sought guidance from music mentors and industry veterans. These experienced professionals have provided valuable insights and advice, helping them refine their skills and broaden their musical horizons. By constantly seeking new knowledge and perspectives, Zeds Dead has been able to incorporate diverse influences into their sound.

Exploring Different Musical Styles

One of the key aspects of Zeds Dead's musical growth is their willingness to explore different musical styles. They understand that by stepping outside their comfort zone and experimenting with new genres, they can push the boundaries of their sound and continue to evolve as artists.

By incorporating elements from hip-hop, reggae, dubstep, and other genres into their music, Zeds Dead creates a unique blend of sounds that defies categorization. This exploration not only keeps their music fresh and exciting but also allows them to connect with a wider audience and transcend traditional genre limitations.

Experimenting with Production Techniques

Constantly pushing the envelope in their production techniques is another way Zeds Dead fosters their musical growth. They are not afraid to experiment with new technology, plugins, and sound design methods to create innovative and captivating tracks.

By staying up to date with the latest advancements in music production, Zeds Dead can continuously refine their sound and stay ahead of the curve. Whether it's incorporating unique samples, manipulating soundscapes, or experimenting with different effects, they are always searching for new ways to elevate their music.

Collaborating with Other Artists

Collaboration has played a significant role in Zeds Dead's musical growth. They recognize the value of working with other talented artists who bring fresh ideas and perspectives to the table. By collaborating with diverse musicians from various backgrounds, they can tap into new creative avenues and expand their sonic palette.

Through collaboration, Zeds Dead has not only grown as artists but also built a strong network of like-minded individuals who share their passion for music. These partnerships foster mutual learning and provide opportunities for shared growth within the artistic community.

Learning from Live Performances

Zeds Dead's commitment to constant growth extends beyond the studio. They view live performances as valuable learning experiences that allow them to connect with their audience, feel the energy of the music, and understand how it resonates with people.

By observing the crowd's reactions and interacting with fans during their shows, Zeds Dead gains insights into what works and what doesn't. They use this feedback to refine their performances, experiment with new techniques, and create memorable experiences for their audience.

Continual Self-Reflection

Self-reflection is a crucial aspect of Zeds Dead's commitment to constant learning and growth. They understand the importance of critically evaluating their work, identifying areas for improvement, and setting new goals.

This self-reflective practice allows them to approach their music with a growth mindset and embrace constructive feedback. It also helps them stay true to their artistic vision while remaining open to new ideas and perspectives.

Unconventional Wisdom: Embracing Imperfections

In the pursuit of constant learning and growth, Zeds Dead embraces the idea that imperfections can be catalysts for creativity. They believe that allowing room for mistakes and embracing imperfections can lead to unexpected breakthroughs and unique artistic expressions.

By embracing imperfections, Zeds Dead breaks away from the pressure of perfectionism and allows themselves to take risks and explore uncharted territories. This unconventional wisdom has been instrumental in their continued musical growth and artistic evolution.

The Importance of Reflection

Constant learning and musical growth require reflection on past experiences. This not only allows Zeds Dead to celebrate their achievements but also helps them identify areas where they can further develop their skills.

Through reflection, Zeds Dead gains a deeper understanding of their creative process, identifies patterns in their music, and explores new avenues of exploration. They recognize the significance of taking the time to reflect, learn, and apply those learnings to future artistic endeavors.

In conclusion, constant learning and musical growth have been fundamental to Zeds Dead's journey. Whether it is embracing musical education, exploring different styles, experimenting with production techniques, collaborating with other artists, learning from live performances, engaging in self-reflection, or embracing imperfections, they have continuously evolved as musicians. By staying curious, open-minded, and committed to growth, Zeds Dead has built a legacy of innovation and artistic excellence.

Studio Rituals and Superstitions

In the creative realm of music production, there exists a multitude of studio rituals and superstitions that artists adhere to. These rituals and superstitions are often seen as a way to channel inspiration, enhance creativity, and create a conducive environment for producing music. They can vary from the mundane to the eccentric, but they all serve the purpose of establishing a routine and invoking a certain mindset for the creative process. Here, we explore some of the most interesting studio rituals and superstitions that Zeds Dead, the renowned music duo, have adopted throughout their career.

The Power of Lighting

Lighting plays a crucial role in setting the mood and atmosphere of a studio. Zeds Dead firmly believes in the power of lighting to enhance their creative process. They make it a point to use specific lighting schemes during different stages of the production process. For example, during the initial brainstorming phase, they prefer soft, dim lighting to foster a relaxed and introspective atmosphere. As the project progresses into the final mixing and mastering stages, they opt for brighter and more vibrant lighting to energize and uplift their spirits. This attention to lighting helps them establish a visual and emotional connection to their music.

Caffeine Concoctions

Like many artists, Zeds Dead takes advantage of the known stimulant properties of caffeine to boost their creative flow. However, they have a unique twist to their caffeine routine. They experiment with different herbal teas and natural ingredients to create their own concoctions. For example, they might mix yerba mate, ginseng, and green tea to achieve the perfect blend of focus, creativity, and alertness. This personalized approach to caffeine consumption is seen as a way to infuse their art with their own unique energy and essence.

The Ritual of Crystals

Crystals hold a special place in Zeds Dead's studio rituals. They believe that crystals possess certain energies and vibrations that can positively influence their creative process. Before each production session, they carefully select specific crystals and place them strategically around their studio. Clear quartz crystals are believed to enhance focus and clarity, while amethyst crystals are said to promote creativity and spiritual awareness. By incorporating these crystals into their studio environment, Zeds Dead creates a space that is both energetically charged and harmonious, allowing their creativity to flow freely.

Instrument Alignment

For Zeds Dead, the alignment of their instruments within the studio is not a matter to be taken lightly. They believe that the positioning of their equipment has a direct impact on the energy flow and synergy within the space. Each instrument and piece of equipment is meticulously arranged to create a balanced and harmonious layout. They pay attention to the angles, distances, and orientations of their gear, ensuring that everything is aligned according to their intuitive sense of what feels right. This alignment ritual is seen as a way to create a harmonious relationship between the artists and their instruments, fostering a seamless connection during the creative process.

The Sacred Sound Bath

Sound baths have been used for centuries as a means of relaxation, meditation, and healing. Zeds Dead has adopted this practice as part of their studio rituals. Before embarking on a new musical project, they indulge in a sound bath to cleanse their minds and spirits. They immerse themselves in the soothing sounds of Tibetan singing bowls, gongs, and other resonant instruments. This ritual helps them clear their minds of any distractions or preconceived notions, allowing them to approach their creative work with a sense of openness and receptivity. It serves as a reset button, creating a fresh canvas for their musical endeavors.

The Unconventional Exercise Breaks

Studio work can be physically demanding, requiring long hours of sitting and intense focus. To break the monotony and recharge their bodies, Zeds Dead incorporates unconventional exercise breaks into their workflow. They might take short breaks to engage in activities like mini trampoline jumping, hula hooping, or even impromptu dance sessions. These bursts of physical activity not only provide a much-needed energy boost but also serve as a creative outlet. They help Zeds Dead connect with their bodies, release tension, and stimulate their minds in new and unexpected ways.

Superstitions and Charms

Superstitions and good luck charms hold a special place in the hearts of many artists, including Zeds Dead. They believe that these rituals and objects carry positive energy and serve as a protective shield against creative blockages and negative forces.   Each member of the duo has their own set of personal superstitions and lucky charms. It could be a specific piece of jewelry, a cherished item, or even a routine that must be followed before starting a new project. These superstitions and charms are seen as a way to invoke good fortune and ensure a successful creative endeavor.

Creating Sonic Landscapes

Zeds Dead embraces the concept of sonic landscapes as a way to stimulate their creativity and expand their musical horizons. They often experiment with unconventional sounds and field recordings from a wide range of sources. They might record ambient sounds from nature, street noises, or even snippets of conversations. These sonic elements serve as building blocks for their compositions, allowing them to create unique textures and atmospheres. By incorporating these real-world sounds into their music, Zeds Dead seeks to transport listeners to different sonic realms, evoking specific emotions and experiences.

Embracing the Unexpected

While rituals and routines can provide structure and inspiration, Zeds Dead also recognizes the importance of embracing the unexpected. They understand that creativity cannot be forced or confined to a specific set of rituals. Sometimes, the most magical moments in the studio come from spontaneity and letting go of expectations. They allow themselves to be open to serendipitous accidents, chance encounters, and uncharted sonic territories. This mindset of embracing the unexpected keeps their creative spark alive and allows them to constantly evolve and push the boundaries of their music.

In conclusion, studio rituals and superstitions are deeply intertwined with the creative process of Zeds Dead. From lighting and crystal placement to caffeine concoctions and exercise breaks, these practices serve as a powerful tool to ignite inspiration, channel energy, and enhance their connection with music. By embracing rituals and superstitions while also remaining open to the unexpected, Zeds Dead has carved out a unique artistic path and established a lasting legacy in the world of music production.

Life on the Road

The Thrills and Challenges of Touring

Touring is an essential part of the Zeds Dead experience. It is a thrilling adventure that takes them to different cities, countries, and continents, allowing them to connect with fans all over the world. However, touring also poses its fair share of challenges that the duo has had to overcome. In this section, we will explore the thrills and challenges of touring and how Zeds Dead has navigated through them.

Thrills of Touring

Touring offers Zeds Dead an exhilarating experience filled with numerous thrills. Here are some of the key aspects that make touring an unforgettable journey for the duo:

1. **Connecting with Fans:** One of the biggest thrills of touring is the opportunity to connect with fans in person. Zeds Dead's music has touched the lives of many, and seeing the impact they have made on their fans is incredibly rewarding. Meeting fans, signing autographs, and taking photos with them creates a sense of camaraderie and reinforces the duo's purpose as musicians.

2. **Performing Live:** The thrill of performing live in front of thousands of fans is unmatched. Zeds Dead's energetic performances, filled with bass-heavy drops and captivating visuals, create an electrifying atmosphere that resonates with the audience. The duo's ability to read the crowd and deliver unforgettable sets is a testament to their skill and showmanship.

3. **Exploring New Places:** Touring allows Zeds Dead to explore new cities and countries, immersing themselves in different cultures and experiencing the diversity of the world. From vibrant metropolises to hidden gems, the duo embraces the opportunity to see the world and gain inspiration from their surroundings. This constant exposure to new environments fuels their creativity and influences their music.

Challenges of Touring

While touring brings excitement, it also presents various challenges that Zeds Dead has had to confront. These challenges include:

1. **Jet Lag and Fatigue:** Constantly traveling between time zones and performing late-night shows can take a toll on the duo's physical and mental wellbeing. Jet lag, irregular sleep patterns, and the demanding nature of live performances can lead to exhaustion and fatigue. To counteract this challenge, Zeds Dead prioritizes self-care and puts an emphasis on maintaining their health and well-being.

2. **Hectic Schedule:** Touring involves a hectic schedule packed with back-to-back shows, sound checks, interviews, and promotional events. Managing this demanding itinerary requires exceptional time management skills and the ability to stay organized amidst the chaos. Zeds Dead has learned to create a routine that allows them to balance their professional commitments while still finding time for personal relaxation and reflection.

3. **Homesickness and Missing Loved Ones:** Being on the road means being away from loved ones for extended periods. Homesickness can be challenging, especially during holidays and special occasions. Zeds Dead acknowledges the importance of maintaining a support system and staying connected with family and friends through regular communication and visits when possible.

Navigating the Challenges

To navigate the challenges of touring, Zeds Dead has developed strategies and implemented practices that support their physical, mental, and emotional well-being:

1. **Health and Wellness:** Maintaining a healthy lifestyle on the road is paramount. Zeds Dead focuses on nutritious eating, regular exercise, and prioritizes sleep whenever possible. They also take measures to prevent and manage illnesses on tour, ensuring they are in the best possible condition for their performances.

2. **Communication and Support System:** Zeds Dead stays connected with their loved ones through regular phone calls, video chats, and visits when their schedule permits. Having a strong support system helps them cope with the challenges of touring and provides them with the emotional stability they need to thrive.

3. **Mental Health Awareness:** The duo recognizes the importance of mental health and has incorporated practices such as meditation, therapy, and mindfulness into their routine. They prioritize self-reflection and self-care to maintain their mental well-being while on the road.

Unconventional Approach: Creating a Mobile Studio

One unconventional approach that Zeds Dead has adopted to overcome the challenges of touring is the creation of a mobile studio. Recognizing that being on the road can disrupt their creative process, they have equipped themselves with a travel-friendly studio setup. This allows them to work on new music and ideas while touring, ensuring that their creativity is not stifled by the constraints of a nomadic lifestyle.

This mobile studio setup includes portable synthesizers, laptops with music production software, and a range of compact audio equipment. With this setup, they can capture inspiration and translate it into music wherever they are.

Case Study: Balancing Touring and Well-being

To illustrate how Zeds Dead balances the thrills and challenges of touring while prioritizing their well-being, let's delve into a case study:

Imagine Zeds Dead embarks on a month-long international tour with shows in Asia, Europe, and North America. They are thrilled to connect with fans from different cultures and experience the energy of live performances in diverse settings. However, they also understand the physical and mental demands that touring entails.

To navigate this tour successfully, Zeds Dead adopts the following strategies:

1. **Pre-Tour Preparation:** They ensure they are well-rested and physically fit before the tour begins. This includes regular exercise, a nutritious diet, and sufficient sleep to start the tour on a positive note.

2. **Self-Care on the Road:** Throughout the tour, Zeds Dead prioritizes self-care. They maintain a consistent sleep schedule, practice meditation and mindfulness, and exercise regularly to stay physically and mentally healthy.

3. **Managing Expectations:** Zeds Dead sets realistic expectations for themselves and their team regarding the tour schedule and workload. They communicate openly about their boundaries and needs, ensuring that their well-being is not compromised.

4. **Staying Connected with Loved Ones:** They make time to connect with their loved ones through video calls and messages. This helps alleviate homesickness and provides emotional support during the tour.

5. **Seeking Inspiration:** Zeds Dead takes advantage of their downtime between shows to explore the cities they visit, seeking inspiration from local art, music, and culture. This helps fuel their creativity and keeps them motivated throughout the tour.

By implementing these strategies, Zeds Dead successfully balances the thrills and challenges of touring, ensuring their well-being and continuing to deliver exceptional performances for their fans.

In conclusion, touring is a thrilling yet challenging aspect of Zeds Dead's music journey. The duo embraces the excitement of connecting with fans, performing live, and exploring new places. At the same time, they navigate challenges such as jet lag, a hectic schedule, and homesickness. Through a focus on health, well-being, and communication, Zeds Dead has developed strategies to overcome these challenges and maintain a balance between touring and personal well-being. Their unconventional approach of creating a mobile studio further supports their creative process while on the road. With their commitment to self-care and mindfulness,

Zeds Dead continues to captivate audiences across the globe and build their enduring legacy.

Touring as an Essential Part of Zeds Dead's Identity

Touring has always been an essential part of Zeds Dead's identity. From the very beginning of their musical journey, they recognized the power and magic of live performances in connecting with their fans and spreading their music across the globe. In this section, we will delve into the thrills and challenges of touring, the connection with fans on the road, and the evolution of their live performances.

The Thrills and Challenges of Touring

Touring as a musician is a thrilling and exhilarating experience. For Zeds Dead, hitting the road and traveling from city to city means being able to share their music with fans from all walks of life. It's a chance for them to connect with their audience on a deeper level and experience the energy and enthusiasm firsthand.

However, touring also comes with its fair share of challenges. The grueling schedule of constant travel, late nights, and early mornings can take a toll on even the most seasoned performers. Being away from family and loved ones for extended periods can be emotionally challenging. The constant pressure of delivering an outstanding show night after night can be physically and mentally exhausting.

Yet, despite these challenges, the members of Zeds Dead have always embraced the touring lifestyle. They see it as an opportunity to grow as musicians and connect with their fans in a profound way.

Touring as an Essential Part of Zeds Dead's Identity

Touring is not merely a means to perform for Zeds Dead—it is at the very core of their identity. Their live shows are where they can truly express themselves and create an immersive experience for their fans. It is on the stage that they bring their music to life and forge a deep connection with their audience.

The energy and excitement of a Zeds Dead live performance are infectious. The duo's dynamic stage presence and crowd interaction create an electric atmosphere, fueling a sense of unity and freedom among concertgoers. Each show is a unique experience, blending their signature sound with improvisation and experimentation, ensuring that no two performances are ever the same.

Zeds Dead's dedication to touring and delivering unforgettable live experiences has solidified their status as one of the most respected and sought-after acts in the electronic music scene. Their commitment to excellence and their ability to captivate audiences during their performances have earned them a loyal global fanbase.

Connecting with Fans on the Road

One of the most rewarding aspects of touring for Zeds Dead is the opportunity to connect with their fans on a personal level. They understand the importance of building a strong relationship with their audience and strive to create an inclusive and welcoming atmosphere at their shows.

Before and after each performance, Zeds Dead makes a point to interact with fans, whether it be through meet-and-greets, signings, or simply taking the time to have a genuine conversation. This connection with their fans fuels their creativity and inspires them to continue pushing the boundaries of their music.

The duo also values the feedback and support they receive from their fanbase. Through social media and online platforms, they actively engage with their fans, incorporating their suggestions and preferences into their performances. This symbiotic relationship between Zeds Dead and their fans creates a sense of camaraderie and shared passion for music.

The Evolution of the Zeds Dead Live Experience

Over the years, the live experience offered by Zeds Dead has evolved, incorporating cutting-edge technologies and pushing the boundaries of innovation. They dream up elaborate stage designs, blending stunning visuals and immersive lighting to create an otherworldly ambiance that transports fans to a different realm.

Zeds Dead's live performances have also seen the integration of live instrumentation, showcasing their versatility and musicianship. The addition of live drums, guitar, and other instruments adds a dynamic element to their sets, enhancing the energy and excitement in the crowd.

Furthermore, Zeds Dead constantly embraces improvisation during their shows, using the spontaneity of live performance to add unexpected twists and surprises. This element of surprise keeps the audience on their toes and ensures that every show is a unique and unforgettable experience.

The Importance of Mental and Physical Health on Tour

While touring can be physically and mentally demanding, Zeds Dead understands the importance of prioritizing their well-being on the road. They recognize that taking care of themselves is crucial to delivering top-notch performances and maintaining their creativity.

The duo incorporates various wellness practices into their daily routines, including regular exercise, healthy eating, and mindfulness exercises. They emphasize the significance of rest and downtime, allowing themselves moments of relaxation amidst the chaos of tour life.

Zeds Dead also places great importance on mental health. They actively promote open conversations about mental well-being, encouraging their fans and fellow musicians to seek help and support when needed. By destigmatizing mental health issues, Zeds Dead aims to create a safe and supportive community for their fans to lean on.

Managing Expectations and Balance

Maintaining a successful touring career requires careful management of expectations and balance. Zeds Dead recognizes the importance of setting realistic goals and pacing themselves to avoid burnout.

They carefully curate their tour schedules to ensure they have adequate time to rest and recover between shows. By prioritizing their well-being, they can consistently deliver high-quality performances and avoid falling into the trap of overexertion.

Zeds Dead also sets clear boundaries and values the importance of work-life balance. They make time for personal hobbies and interests while on tour, allowing themselves moments of creativity and exploration outside of music. This balance fuels their inspiration and ensures their performances are always authentic and heartfelt.

The Evolution of the Zeds Dead Live Experience

As Zeds Dead's career progresses and the music industry continues to evolve, the duo remains dedicated to pushing the boundaries of their live performances. Their commitment to innovation and their willingness to embrace new technologies ensures that their shows will continue to evolve and captivate audiences in the years to come.

From their humble beginnings to their status as electronic music icons, Zeds Dead's live performances have always been a reflection of their passion and dedication to their craft. Their commitment to providing an unforgettable experience for their fans sets them apart and ensures that touring will forever be an essential part of their identity.

In conclusion, touring is not just a means to an end for Zeds Dead—it is an integral part of their artistic expression and connection with their fans. Through the thrills and challenges of constant travel, they have forged a unique identity as performers, constantly evolving their live shows to create an immersive and unforgettable experience. They see touring as an opportunity to connect, inspire, and leave a lasting legacy in the hearts and minds of their fans.

Connecting with Fans on the Road

One of the most exhilarating aspects of being in a band is the opportunity to connect with fans on a personal level, and Zeds Dead has always been committed to nurturing a strong and dedicated fan community. From the early days of their career, the duo recognized the importance of building genuine relationships with their supporters, and they have continued to prioritize fan engagement throughout their musical journey.

Creating a Personal Connection

For Zeds Dead, connecting with fans goes beyond simply performing on stage. They understand that their music has the power to touch people's lives and evoke emotions, and they strive to create a personal connection with their audience through their music and live performances. They believe in the transformative power of music and aim to provide an experience that resonates with their fans on a deep level.

During their live shows, Zeds Dead makes a conscious effort to engage with the audience, feeding off their energy and creating an atmosphere of shared excitement. They encourage crowd participation, whether it's through sing-alongs, call-and-response interactions, or simply acknowledging the fans' presence and enthusiasm. By forging a personal connection with their audience, Zeds Dead creates a sense of inclusivity and makes their fans feel like an integral part of the musical experience.

Fan Interaction and Accessibility

Zeds Dead recognizes the importance of accessibility and strives to make themselves available to their fans. They actively engage with their audience through various social media platforms, responding to comments, messages, and fan artwork. This level of interaction not only shows their genuine appreciation for their supporters but also helps them understand their fanbase better.

In addition to online interactions, Zeds Dead makes an effort to connect with fans in person. Whether it's through meet-and-greet sessions after their shows, fan events, or surprise pop-up performances, they create opportunities for face-to-face interactions. These personal encounters allow them to express their gratitude directly and make lasting memories with their fans.

Fan-Centric Initiatives

Zeds Dead understands that their success is owed to their loyal fans, and they consistently find ways to give back. They frequently organize fan-centric initiatives that reward their supporters and create a sense of community.

One such initiative is their exclusive fan club, which offers members access to exclusive content, merchandise discounts, early ticket sales, and meet-and-greet opportunities. The fan club not only provides a platform for fans to connect with each other but also gives Zeds Dead an avenue to express their appreciation for their most dedicated followers.

Additionally, Zeds Dead actively supports charitable causes and encourages their fans to get involved. They have partnered with various organizations to raise awareness and funds for issues close to their hearts, such as mental health, education, and environmental conservation. By aligning themselves with important causes, they inspire their fans to make a positive impact in the world.

Virtual Fan Engagement

With the rise of social media and digital platforms, Zeds Dead has embraced virtual fan engagement. They utilize live streaming, online Q&A sessions, and behind-the-scenes content to connect with fans worldwide. These virtual interactions allow them to reach a broader audience and provide a more intimate glimpse into their lives as musicians.

Zeds Dead also recognizes the power of fan-generated content. They actively encourage their fans to create remixes, artwork, and videos inspired by their music, and they frequently showcase and share this content on their social media channels. By amplifying their fans' creativity, Zeds Dead not only strengthens their bond with their supporters but also fosters a sense of collaboration and community.

The Power of Fan Connection

The connection between Zeds Dead and their fans goes beyond music. By prioritizing fan engagement, they have cultivated a dedicated and passionate community that supports and uplifts both the band and each other.

Through personal interactions, accessibility, fan-centric initiatives, and virtual engagement, Zeds Dead creates a unique and inclusive experience for their fans. Their commitment to building connections with their audience not only enhances the live performance atmosphere but also extends the impact of their music far beyond the stage.

In the ever-evolving landscape of the music industry, Zeds Dead's dedication to fan connection serves as a testament to the enduring power of human connection in an increasingly digital world. By fostering a strong and engaged fanbase, Zeds Dead continues to create a legacy that extends far beyond their music and inspires fans to connect with each other through the shared love of music.

Tales from the Tour Bus

Join us on the wild ride that is life on the road with Zeds Dead! From unforgettable concerts to hilarious mishaps, this section will give you an exclusive behind-the-scenes look at the stories that have unfolded on their epic tour bus adventures. So buckle up and get ready for some tales that will leave you in stitches!

A Breakdown in the Middle of Nowhere

One fateful night, while traversing the vast expanse of the American Midwest, the Zeds Dead tour bus broke down in the middle of nowhere. With no cell service and the nearest town miles away, the crew found themselves in a bind. But true to their resourceful nature, they pulled out their tools and got to work.

Hours passed as the crew tinkered with the engine, hoping to get the bus back on the road. As the sun began to rise, a sense of desperation set in. Just as they were about to give up, a local farmer happened to drive by and offered a helping hand. With his expertise and a few spare parts, they were able to fix the bus and continue on their journey.

This unexpected detour taught Zeds Dead the importance of teamwork, perseverance, and the kindness of strangers. It was a humbling experience that reminded them to always be prepared for the unexpected.

The Epic Battle of the Bands

During a tour stop in a small town, word got out that Zeds Dead was in town. The local music scene was buzzing with excitement, and a rival band challenged them to an impromptu battle of the bands. With adrenaline pumping, Zeds Dead accepted the challenge.

The epic battle took place in a gritty, underground venue. The crowd was rowdy and eager to see who would come out on top. As Zeds Dead took the stage, they unleashed their signature sound, captivating the audience with their electrifying beats and incredible stage presence.

The rival band fought back with their alternative rock sound, putting on a show that was hard to ignore. The battle raged on, each band pushing the envelope and giving it their all. In the end, Zeds Dead won over the crowd with their infectious energy and undeniable talent. It was a night that will forever be etched in their memories.

Getting Lost in Translation

As Zeds Dead's international fanbase grew, they embarked on a global tour that took them to countries where English was not the primary language. While performing in a non-English speaking country, they encountered a hilarious language barrier that led to an unforgettable moment.

During their set, Zeds Dead decided to engage with the crowd and show their appreciation for their fans. Seizing the mic, one of the members attempted a heartfelt speech in broken local language. The crowd stared back blankly, clearly confused by what was being said.

Unbeknownst to Zeds Dead, their attempt at connection was lost in translation, leaving the fans bewildered. However, rather than derail the performance, this mishap actually brought the crowd together in laughter. It became a shared moment of laughter and joy, bridging the gap between cultures through the power of music.

The Vanishing Act

In the chaos of touring, it's not uncommon to misplace items. However, during one particularly eventful tour, Zeds Dead experienced a disappearing act that had everyone scratching their heads.

It all started when the crew set up the stage for a show, only to realize that one of the essential pieces of equipment was missing. Panic ensued as they searched every nook and cranny of the venue, but the item was nowhere to be found.

In a stroke of luck, one of the crew members remembered that they had stopped at a fast-food drive-thru earlier that day. They retraced their steps and, to their surprise, found the missing equipment sitting atop the drive-thru window.

To this day, the vanishing act remains a mystery, but it serves as a humorous reminder for Zeds Dead to double-check their belongings and embrace the unpredictable nature of life on the road.

The Unforgettable Encore

Every performer dreams of that perfect encore, a moment that leaves the audience begging for more. For Zeds Dead, this dream became a reality during one of their most memorable shows.

As the final notes of their last song echoed through the venue, the crowd erupted in applause, demanding an encore. Taking in the electrifying energy, Zeds Dead returned to the stage, determined to deliver a performance that would be etched in the memories of their fans forever.

With a surge of adrenaline, they unleashed an immersive experience. Lights flashed, confetti filled the air, and the crowd became a sea of hands reaching toward the heavens. The encore became a transcendental moment that united the band and the audience, proving the power of music to create unforgettable memories.

The Mighty Storm

Touring isn't always sunshine and rainbows. In fact, sometimes it's thunderstorms and power outages. Zeds Dead faced the wrath of Mother Nature during a memorable tour stop.

As they set up for a show in an outdoor venue, dark clouds loomed overhead. The rain started pouring and the thunder roared, casting doubt on whether the show could go on. But Zeds Dead refused to let a little rain dampen their spirits.

They found a way to shield their equipment from the elements, and with sheer determination, they took the stage. The rain transformed into a powerful backdrop, amplifying the energy of the music. The crowd, drenched but undeterred, danced like there was no tomorrow.

The storm became a symbol of resilience and the unwavering spirit of Zeds Dead. It taught them to adapt, embrace the unexpected, and find beauty even in the most challenging situations.

The Legend of the Hidden Venue

In the age of digital mapping, getting lost is a rare occurrence. However, during their early touring days, Zeds Dead found themselves in a situation that seemed straight out of a movie.

Arriving at the address of their scheduled venue, they were surprised to find nothing but an empty parking lot. Confused, they retraced their steps and asked for directions from locals, who insisted that the venue did exist.

Determined to solve the mystery, Zeds Dead stumbled upon an unmarked door hidden in an alley. With a leap of faith, they opened the door and found themselves in a secret underground venue filled with eager fans.

The hidden venue became a legendary story in the Zeds Dead tour lore, an unexpected adventure that reminded them to always keep an open mind and follow their instincts.

The Party Bus

Life on the road is equal parts work and play, and Zeds Dead knows how to have a good time. The tour bus quickly became a rolling party, filled with laughter and unforgettable memories.

During long drives between shows, the crew would gather on the bus to jam, share stories, and connect on a deeper level. These moments of camaraderie forged lifelong friendships and created an extended family on the road.

The party bus became a symbol of the bonds that held Zeds Dead together, reminding them of the importance of joy and friendship even in the midst of a demanding tour schedule.

Lessons Learned

The tales from the tour bus reflect the vibrant tapestry that is Zeds Dead's journey. From the unexpected breakdowns to the epic battles, these stories are a testament to their resilience, creativity, and sheer passion for music.

Through all the challenges, laughter, and unforgettable moments, Zeds Dead has learned valuable lessons: the power of perseverance, the importance of connection, and the ability of music to transcend boundaries.

As they continue to embark on new adventures, Zeds Dead carries these tales with them, a constant reminder of their incredible journey on and off the stage.

So next time you see them on tour, remember that each beat pulsating through the speakers holds a story, a testament to the enduring spirit of Zeds Dead.

Memorable Concert Moments and Performances

When it comes to Zeds Dead, their live performances are more than just a concert. They are an experience, an electrifying journey for both the mind and the body. With their unparalleled energy, technical prowess, and captivating stage presence, Zeds Dead has created countless memorable moments and performances throughout their career. Here, we dive into some of these unforgettable concert experiences that have left a lasting impact on their fans.

The Unforgettable Drop

One of the most exhilarating moments in any Zeds Dead concert is the drop. Known for their heavy bass and hard-hitting beats, Zeds Dead delivers epic drops that send shockwaves through the crowd. These drops ignite a surge of energy, with fans jumping and headbanging in sync to the music. The intensity of these moments is palpable, creating an electric atmosphere that leaves concert-goers buzzing with adrenaline.

For example, during their performance at the Electric Daisy Carnival in Las Vegas, Zeds Dead unleashed an earth-shattering drop during their set. As the beat built up, tension filled the air, and when the drop finally hit, the crowd exploded with excitement. The synchronized jump from thousands of fans created a seismic wave that reverberated throughout the festival grounds. It was a moment of pure sonic bliss that will forever be etched in the memories of those who experienced it.

The Unexpected Collaboration

Collaborations have always been a hallmark of Zeds Dead's career, and their live performances often feature surprise appearances from talented artists. These unexpected collaborations take the concert experience to a whole new level, creating unique and unreproducible moments.

During a show in Los Angeles, Zeds Dead surprised the crowd by bringing out Skrillex for an impromptu back-to-back set. The energy between the two artists was palpable, as they seamlessly mixed their tracks and fed off each other's creativity. The crowd went wild, witnessing two legends of electronic music creating magic together on stage. It was a once-in-a-lifetime moment that reminded everyone of the power of collaboration and the limitless possibilities within the realm of live performances.

The Intimate Acoustic Set

Zeds Dead's ability to create diverse and innovative experiences extends beyond their high-energy shows. In addition to their electrifying performances, they have also explored the realm of acoustic sets, showcasing their versatility as musicians.

During a special event in their hometown of Toronto, Zeds Dead treated their fans to an intimate acoustic set. Stripped down to the raw essentials, the duo showcased their musicality by reinterpreting their electronic tracks with acoustic instruments. The crowd was captivated by the vulnerability and authenticity of the performance. It was a beautiful and introspective moment that showcased Zeds Dead's artistic range and reminded everyone that music transcends genres and can be experienced in a multitude of ways.

The Mind-Blowing Visuals

Zeds Dead's live performances are not only an auditory feast but also a visual spectacle. Their meticulous attention to detail extends to the visual aspects of their shows, creating a multi-sensory experience that immerses the audience in their world.

One of the most memorable visual moments during a Zeds Dead concert was when they integrated stunning light installations and visuals projected onto LED screens. As the music swelled and the lights danced in sync with the beats, the atmosphere became ethereal, transporting the audience to another dimension. The synchronization between the music, the lights, and the visuals created a cohesive and immersive experience that transcended the boundaries of traditional concerts.

The Unexpected Cover

A hallmark of Zeds Dead's live performances is their willingness to surprise and delight their fans with unexpected moments. One such moment is when they perform unexpected covers of songs, putting their unique spin on well-known tracks.

During a show in Miami, Zeds Dead treated their fans to a jaw-dropping cover of Nirvana's "Smells Like Teen Spirit." The crowd erupted with excitement as they recognized the iconic guitar riff, but with a twist of heavy bass and electronic elements. Zeds Dead's reinterpretation of the grunge classic was a testament to their ability to seamlessly blend genres and create something entirely fresh and unexpected. It was a sonic surprise that left the crowd in awe and showcased Zeds Dead's ability to reimagine music in their own unique style.

Conclusion

From unforgettable drops and surprise collaborations to intimate acoustic sets and mind-blowing visuals, Zeds Dead's live performances are a testament to their artistry, creativity, and ability to connect with their audience. Each concert provides a unique and immersive experience that transports fans to new dimensions. With their boundary-pushing performances and dedication to creating unforgettable moments, Zeds Dead continues to solidify their place as pioneers in the world of electronic music. So, if you ever get the chance to witness a Zeds Dead concert, prepare yourself for an unforgettable journey through the rhythm.

Interactions with Different Cultures and Fanbases

Interactions with different cultures and fanbases have been an integral part of Zeds Dead's journey. As they gained popularity and traveled the world, they had the opportunity to connect with diverse groups of people who shared a love for their music. These interactions not only shaped their music but also enriched their own understanding of the world and its vibrant cultures.

Cultural Exchange through Music

Music has always been a universal language that transcends borders and brings people together. Zeds Dead recognized the power of music to bridge cultural gaps and create a sense of unity among people from different backgrounds. During their travels, they embraced opportunities to collaborate with artists from various cultures, resulting in a rich tapestry of musical influences in their discography.

For instance, Zeds Dead's collaboration with Omar LinX, a Canadian rapper of Egyptian descent, gave rise to powerful tracks that blended elements of hip-hop and electronic music. This fusion of genres not only appealed to a diverse fanbase but also showcased the beauty of cultural exchange in music.

Embracing the Global Fanbase

Zeds Dead's music has resonated with fans around the world, leading to a dedicated and passionate fanbase. They have embraced their fans from different cultures, regularly engaging with them through social media platforms and live shows. This interaction with fans has allowed Zeds Dead to gain insight into various cultural nuances and cater their music to a global audience.

In their live performances, Zeds Dead creates an atmosphere of inclusivity and celebration, inviting fans from different cultures to come together and share the joy of music. They have also performed at music festivals across continents, allowing fans from diverse backgrounds to experience their high-energy shows firsthand.

Understanding Local Music Scenes

One of the highlights of Zeds Dead's journey has been their exposure to different local music scenes. From the underground clubs of Toronto to the bustling street parties of Rio de Janeiro, Zeds Dead has immersed themselves in the unique sounds and energies of each location they visit.

By understanding and appreciating the local music scenes, Zeds Dead has tapped into the pulse of each culture, infusing their own music with local flavors and influences. From incorporating Latin rhythms in their tracks to collaborating with artists from different regions, Zeds Dead has been able to create music that resonates with their fans across the globe.

Fostering Cultural Understanding

Zeds Dead recognizes the importance of fostering cultural understanding and breaking down stereotypes through their music. They aim to use their platform to promote unity and celebrate diversity. By showcasing the beauty of different cultures and collaborating with artists from diverse backgrounds, Zeds Dead has become a catalyst for cultural exchange and understanding.

Through their music, Zeds Dead encourages their fans to embrace different cultures and appreciate the richness that diversity brings. They believe that music has the power to transcend cultural barriers and promote global harmony.

A Global Adventure

Interacting with different cultures and fanbases has been an exciting and eye-opening adventure for Zeds Dead. From their early gigs in Toronto to performing on international stages, they have witnessed firsthand the unifying power of music.

By embracing different cultures and engaging with their global fanbase, Zeds Dead has not only grown as artists but also as individuals. They have learned to appreciate the beauty of diversity, understand the struggles and triumphs of people from different backgrounds, and create music that resonates with a worldwide audience.

In their journey, Zeds Dead has exemplified the value of cultural exchange and the transformative power of music. Their interactions with different cultures and fanbases have not only shaped their sound but also enriched their lives, leaving a lasting impact on their music and the global community of fans they have created.

The Importance of Mental and Physical Health on Tour

Being a touring musician can be exhilarating, but it also comes with its own set of challenges. Zeds Dead understands the importance of taking care of their mental and physical health while on the road, as it directly impacts their ability to perform at their best. In this section, we will explore the various ways in which Zeds Dead prioritizes their well-being on tour.

Maintaining Physical Health

Touring can be physically demanding, with long hours of travel, late nights, and little time for rest. To counteract the toll it takes on their bodies, Zeds Dead prioritizes physical health through various practices:

- Regular exercise: Zeds Dead incorporates exercise into their tour routine, whether it's hitting the gym, going for a run, or practicing yoga. Not only does exercise help them stay fit, but it also releases endorphins that boost mood and energy levels.

- Healthy eating habits: Despite the temptation of fast food and late-night snacks, Zeds Dead makes a conscious effort to eat nutritious meals while on tour. They prioritize consuming a balanced diet that consists of fruits, vegetables, whole grains, lean proteins, and plenty of water.

- Sufficient sleep: In the midst of a hectic touring schedule, sleep is often sacrificed. However, Zeds Dead recognizes the importance of getting adequate rest to recharge their bodies. They prioritize establishing a regular sleep routine and make efforts to create a sleep-friendly environment even while on the road.

- Preventing injuries: Long hours of travel and repetitive movements during performances can put strain on the body. Zeds Dead takes precautions to prevent injuries by incorporating stretching exercises, warm-ups, and cool-downs into their daily routine. Additionally, they seek professional guidance from physiotherapists or sports therapists to address any pre-existing or potential injuries.

By prioritizing their physical health, Zeds Dead is able to maintain stamina, avoid burnout, and continue delivering high-energy performances.

Nurturing Mental Well-being

The demanding nature of touring can take a toll on mental well-being. To ensure their mental health remains a priority, Zeds Dead incorporates various strategies into their tour routine:

- Meditation and mindfulness: Zeds Dead recognizes the benefits of meditation and mindfulness in managing stress and promoting mental clarity. They set aside time for meditation sessions, either individually or as a group, to calm their minds and stay grounded amidst the chaos of touring.

+ Journaling and self-reflection: Writing can be a therapeutic outlet. Zeds Dead encourages journaling and self-reflection to process their emotions and experiences while on tour. This practice allows them to gain insights, identify patterns, and find solutions to any challenges they may be facing.

+ Creating a positive environment: Surrounding themselves with a positive support system is crucial for Zeds Dead's mental well-being on tour. They foster a sense of camaraderie among their team and actively engage in activities that promote a positive and uplifting atmosphere.

+ Seeking professional support: Zeds Dead realizes the importance of seeking professional help when needed. They have a network of therapists or counselors they can turn to for guidance and support, whether on the road or during periods of downtime.

By nurturing their mental well-being, Zeds Dead ensures they are able to approach each performance with a clear mind, creativity, and an overall positive outlook.

Balancing Work and Personal Life

Maintaining a healthy work-life balance is crucial for Zeds Dead, especially during the intense touring periods. They recognize that overexertion can lead to burnout and negatively impact their mental and physical health. Here are some strategies they employ:

+ Scheduling downtime: While on tour, Zeds Dead schedules regular periods of downtime to rest, relax, and recharge. This allows them to disconnect from work-related responsibilities and focus on personal interests or hobbies.

+ Prioritizing personal relationships: Zeds Dead understands the importance of nurturing personal relationships while on the road. They make efforts to connect with loved ones through video calls, social media, or even inviting them to join them on tour when possible.

+ Incorporating leisure activities: To maintain a sense of normalcy and enjoyment on tour, Zeds Dead incorporates leisure activities into their schedule. Whether it's exploring new cities, visiting local attractions, or indulging in hobbies such as photography or painting, they actively engage in activities that bring them joy outside of their musical endeavors.

By striking a balance between work and personal life, Zeds Dead ensures they are not only fulfilled as artists but also as individuals.

Addressing Substance Use and Abuse

The music industry can be synonymous with a culture of substance use, but Zeds Dead recognizes the importance of responsible choices and maintaining their well-being. They actively take steps to address substance use and abuse:

- ◆ Educating themselves: Zeds Dead stays informed about the effects of substance use and its impact on their mental and physical health. They emphasize the importance of understanding the risks and making informed decisions regarding its use.

- ◆ Setting boundaries: Zeds Dead sets clear boundaries around substance use, ensuring that it does not interfere with their ability to perform or affect their overall well-being. They make conscious choices regarding when and if they choose to engage in substance use, ensuring it aligns with their personal values and goals.

- ◆ Seeking support: If any member of Zeds Dead feels they need support in managing substance use or abuse, they have a network of professionals and peers they can turn to for guidance and assistance.

By addressing substance use and abuse in a responsible manner, Zeds Dead ensures the longevity of their careers and prioritizes their overall well-being.

In conclusion, Zeds Dead recognizes the importance of maintaining both mental and physical health while on tour. By prioritizing physical fitness, nurturing mental well-being, balancing work and personal life, and addressing substance use responsibly, they ensure that they are able to deliver exceptional performances while maintaining their overall well-being. Utilizing these strategies, Zeds Dead sets an example for aspiring musicians on how to navigate the rigors of touring while taking care of oneself.

Managing Expectations and Balance

Managing expectations and finding balance is crucial in any career, and the music industry is no exception. Zeds Dead, like many other artists, has faced the challenge of maintaining a successful and fulfilling music career while managing the expectations of their fans, industry pressures, and their own personal wellbeing. In this section, we explore the strategies and mindset that Zeds Dead has adopted to navigate these challenges.

Embracing Authenticity

One of the key aspects of managing expectations is staying true to oneself. Zeds Dead has always prioritized authenticity, creating music that reflects their own unique style and sound. By staying true to their artistic vision, they have built a dedicated fanbase that appreciates their honesty and creativity. This has allowed them to carve a niche for themselves within the electronic music scene and gain recognition for their genuine approach.

Setting Realistic Goals

Setting realistic goals is essential to avoid feeling overwhelmed and the pressure to constantly push boundaries. Zeds Dead understands the importance of balance and knows that growth and success take time. By setting achievable goals, they can focus on honing their craft and improving their skills without succumbing to unnecessary pressure.

Taking Breaks and Prioritizing Self-Care

In an industry notorious for its demanding schedules and constant pressure, self-care is often overlooked. Zeds Dead understands the importance of taking breaks and prioritizing their mental and physical health. They recognize that rest and rejuvenation are crucial for maintaining creativity and longevity in their careers. By scheduling downtime and activities that bring them joy, they are able to recharge and maintain the passion for their music.

Surrounding Themselves with a Support System

Building a strong support system is vital for managing expectations and maintaining balance. Zeds Dead surrounds themselves with a team of professionals who understand their vision and are dedicated to supporting their career. This includes managers, agents, and close friends who provide guidance and help navigate the challenges of the music industry. Having a solid support system allows them to delegate tasks, share the workload, and receive honest feedback, ultimately minimizing stress and maximizing productivity.

Continual Learning and Adaptation

The music industry is constantly evolving, and staying relevant requires a commitment to continual learning and adaptation. Zeds Dead recognizes the importance of staying informed about emerging trends, technological advancements, and changing audience preferences. They actively seek out new opportunities for growth and exploration, whether it's experimenting with different genres or collaborating with artists from diverse backgrounds. This adaptability ensures that they remain connected to their audience while maintaining creative fulfillment.

Developing a Sustainable Work-Life Balance

Finding a healthy work-life balance is essential for overall wellbeing and longevity in the industry. Zeds Dead strive to create a sustainable and harmonious balance between their professional and personal lives. They prioritize time spent with loved ones, pursue hobbies and interests outside of music, and engage in activities that bring them fulfillment beyond their careers. By creating boundaries and maintaining a healthy balance, they can avoid burnout and sustain their passion for music in the long run.

Seeking Feedback and Embracing Constructive Criticism

To manage expectations effectively, it is important to seek feedback from trusted sources and be open to constructive criticism. Zeds Dead actively seeks feedback from their team, fellow musicians, and their loyal fanbase. This allows them to gain valuable insights, refine their craft, and meet the expectations of their audience. By embracing criticism and feedback, they can grow as artists and continually improve their work.

Celebrating Milestones and Successes

Amidst the challenges and pressures, celebrating milestones and successes is crucial for maintaining motivation and a positive mindset. Zeds Dead take the time to acknowledge their achievements, whether it's achieving chart success or playing iconic music festivals. By celebrating these milestones, they recognize the progress they have made and find inspiration to keep pushing forward.

Keeping the Passion Alive

At the core of managing expectations and finding balance is keeping the passion for music alive. Zeds Dead remains passionate about their craft by constantly seeking new inspiration, exploring different musical styles, and nurturing their creativity. They embrace the joy and fulfillment that music brings, allowing them to overcome challenges and persevere in their journey.

In conclusion, managing expectations and finding balance are crucial elements in maintaining a successful and fulfilling music career. By embracing authenticity, setting realistic goals, prioritizing self-care, surrounding themselves with a support system, continuing to learn and adapt, developing a sustainable work-life balance, seeking feedback, celebrating successes, and keeping the passion alive, Zeds Dead has been able to navigate the challenges of the music industry while staying true to themselves. These strategies serve as valuable lessons for aspiring musicians and professionals in any field, emphasizing the importance of self-awareness, resilience, and maintaining a healthy mindset.

The Evolution of Live Performances

In the world of music, live performances have always been a crucial aspect of an artist's career, allowing them to connect with their audience on a personal level and showcase their talent in a dynamic and engaging way. For Zeds Dead, the evolution of their live performances has been a remarkable journey, marked by creativity, innovation, and a deep connection to their fans.

The Importance of Live Performance

From their early gigs in small clubs to headlining major music festivals, Zeds Dead recognized the significance of live performances in building their fanbase and solidifying their reputation as a captivating act. They understood that a great live show could transcend the boundaries of the studio recordings and create a unique experience for their audience.

Adapting to Technological Advancements

As technology advanced, Zeds Dead embraced the opportunities it presented to enhance their live performances. They explored different methods of integrating new technologies into their shows, such as incorporating live instruments, video mapping, and visual effects. By finding innovative ways to incorporate technology, they created an immersive and visually captivating experience for their fans.

Interactive Elements and Crowd Participation

Zeds Dead also recognized the importance of engaging their audience during their live performances. They introduced interactive elements and encouraged crowd participation, creating an atmosphere of shared energy and connection. Whether it was through call-and-response moments, crowd sing-alongs, or hands-in-the-air moments, they found ways to make their audience an active part of the performance.

Integration of Visuals

In addition to their musical prowess, Zeds Dead understood the power of visual elements in creating a memorable live experience. They collaborated with talented visual artists and designers to create stunning stage setups and captivating visual displays that complemented their music. Their goal was to transport the audience into a different world, immersing them in the music and creating a multi-sensory experience.

Balancing DJ Sets and Live Instruments

While Zeds Dead began their career primarily as DJs, they gradually incorporated live instruments into their performances. This allowed them to add a new layer of authenticity and versatility to their shows. They carefully balanced DJ sets with live instrumentation, finding the perfect synergy between electronic sounds and the raw energy of live instruments.

Evolving Set Designs

Zeds Dead's commitment to pushing boundaries also extended to their set designs. They constantly evolved their stage setups, experimenting with different layouts, lighting arrangements, and visual projections. Their goal was to create a visually appealing and dynamic stage presence that complemented their music and enhanced the overall experience for their audience.

Creating Memorable and Immersive Experiences

One of the hallmarks of Zeds Dead's live performances is their ability to create truly memorable and immersive experiences. They carefully curate their sets, taking the audience on a journey through various genres and styles, while maintaining a cohesive and engaging narrative. Their energetic and passionate performance style draws the audience in, ensuring that they leave the show with a lasting impression.

Leveraging Fan Engagement

Zeds Dead recognizes the importance of their fans in shaping their live performances. They actively seek feedback and engage with their audience to understand their expectations and preferences. This constant communication allows them to tailor their performances to create the most impactful experience for their fans, ensuring that each show feels unique and personal.

Embracing Live Improvisation

While Zeds Dead carefully plans their live performances, they also embrace the element of live improvisation. They believe that spontaneity adds an extra level of excitement and surprise, both for themselves and for their audience. This element of unpredictability keeps their performances fresh and ensures that no two shows are ever exactly the same.

Pushing the Boundaries

Zeds Dead's commitment to pushing boundaries extends beyond the musical realm. They constantly seek new ways to push the limits of what is possible in a live performance. Whether it's through innovative stage designs, incorporating cutting-edge technology, or collaborating with other artists, they strive to create a live experience that is truly unique and groundbreaking.

Looking to the Future

As Zeds Dead continues to evolve and grow as artists, their live performances will undoubtedly continue to change and adapt. They are always on the lookout for new technologies and ideas that can elevate their shows to new heights. With their unwavering dedication to creating unforgettable live experiences, fans can expect nothing short of extraordinary performances in the future.

In conclusion, the evolution of Zeds Dead's live performances has been a testament to their artistic vision, creativity, and desire to connect with their audience in meaningful ways. From embracing new technologies to incorporating live instruments, they have consistently pushed the boundaries of what is possible in a live setting. Through their captivating stage designs, immersive visuals, and interactive elements, they create a multi-sensory experience that leaves a lasting impact. As they continue to evolve and experiment, Zeds Dead's live performances are sure to remain a highlight of their career and a testament to their commitment to pushing the boundaries of electronic music.

Building a Legacy

The Importance of Fan Engagement

In the vast musical landscape of today, one thing remains constant - the power of the fans. For Zeds Dead, the significance of fan engagement cannot be overstated. It is a driving force that shapes their career, their music, and their overall philosophy.

Fan engagement goes beyond simple popularity and chart success. It is about fostering a deep and meaningful connection with the audience, building a community that is passionate, loyal, and supportive. Zeds Dead understands that without the fans, their journey would be devoid of purpose and fulfillment.

At the core of fan engagement lies the concept of authenticity. Fans crave artists who are genuine and relatable, who are not afraid to be themselves and share their stories. Zeds Dead embraces this authenticity, allowing their fans to connect with them on a personal level. Through social media, intimate meet-and-greets, and heartfelt interactions at shows, they create a sense of intimacy that sets them apart.

But fan engagement is not just about one-way communication. Zeds Dead understands the value of listening to their fans, hearing their feedback, and incorporating their ideas and opinions into their music and performances. They actively seek out fan input, whether through online polls, Q&A sessions, or fan contests. This interactive approach not only makes their audience feel heard and valued but also allows them to co-create the Zeds Dead experience.

Part of effective fan engagement is showcasing appreciation and gratitude. Zeds Dead acknowledges the essential role that their fans play in their success. They go above and beyond to express their thanks, whether it's through personalized messages, surprise giveaways, or exclusive perks for their most dedicated followers. This genuine appreciation fosters a sense of reciprocity, building a mutually beneficial relationship between the artists and their fans.

Fan engagement also extends beyond the music itself. Zeds Dead actively supports social initiatives and philanthropic endeavors, encouraging their fans to join them in making a positive impact on the world. By aligning their values with those of their audience, they create a shared purpose that transcends the music and builds a lasting bond.

In the digital age, technology has transformed the way artists connect with their fans. Zeds Dead harnesses the power of social media and digital platforms to reach their audience on a global scale. They understand the importance of staying connected, whether it's through live streams, behind-the-scenes footage, or interactive online experiences. This digital presence allows fans to feel like they are part of the journey, no matter where they are in the world.

But amidst the rapidly evolving landscape of the music industry, Zeds Dead remains grounded in the power of live experiences. They recognize that nothing can replace the energy and connection that is felt at a live show. From their mesmerizing visuals, explosive live performances, and immersive crowd interactions, Zeds Dead creates a space where fans can truly lose themselves in the music.

In conclusion, fan engagement is not just a buzzword for Zeds Dead - it is the lifeblood of their career. They understand that their fans are the heartbeat of their music, and they strive to create a community that is as passionate about their art as they are. By fostering authenticity, actively listening, and expressing genuine appreciation, Zeds Dead builds a profound connection that transcends the music and leaves a lasting impact. In the ever-changing landscape of the music industry, one thing remains certain - the importance of fan engagement will always remain paramount.

Leaving a Lasting Impact on Electronic Music

As Zeds Dead continues to evolve and push the boundaries of electronic music, their impact on the genre is undeniable. Their unique sound and artistry have contributed to the growth and popularity of electronic music around the world. In this section, we will explore the ways in which Zeds Dead has left a lasting impact on the electronic music scene.

Innovation and Experimentation

One of the key factors that set Zeds Dead apart is their commitment to innovation and experimentation. Throughout their career, they have continuously pushed the boundaries of electronic music, exploring new sounds, subgenres, and production techniques.

Zeds Dead's willingness to experiment with different musical styles has helped shape the electronic music landscape. From their early dubstep-influenced tracks to their more recent forays into house, drum and bass, and future bass, their music has influenced and inspired countless artists.

Their approach to sound design and production has also greatly influenced the production techniques used in electronic music. Zeds Dead has been known to use a wide range of audio processing techniques, from heavy distortion and filtering to complex layering and sampling. By sharing their production methods and techniques, they have empowered aspiring producers to explore new sonic possibilities.

Genre Defiance and Fusion

Zeds Dead's ability to blend and fuse different genres within their music has been instrumental in captivating a diverse fanbase. They seamlessly incorporate elements of hip-hop, reggae, rock, and other genres into their electronic soundscapes, creating a unique and dynamic musical experience.

Their genre-defying approach has also contributed to the popularity of electronic music outside of its traditional fan base. By incorporating familiar elements from other genres, Zeds Dead has bridged the gap between electronic music and mainstream audiences, exposing a wider audience to the genre.

Furthermore, Zeds Dead's collaborations with artists from different genres have helped to dissolve genre boundaries and foster a spirit of musical unity. By working with artists like Omar LinX, Diplo, and NGHTMRE, they have showcased the versatility and adaptability of electronic music, making it accessible to a broader audience.

Live Performance Innovation

Zeds Dead's commitment to delivering an unforgettable live experience has revolutionized the way electronic music is presented on stage. Their live performances are a testament to their dedication to pushing the boundaries of what is possible in a live setting.

Their incorporation of live instruments, such as drums and guitars, adds a unique and organic element to their performances. This blending of live instruments with electronic elements creates an immersive and dynamic experience for the audience.

Furthermore, Zeds Dead's use of visual elements and stage design enhances the overall atmosphere of their shows. From stunning lighting displays to captivating visuals, their live performances are a multisensory journey that transports the audience into the world of their music.

Community Building and Education

Zeds Dead's impact extends beyond their music and live performances. They have actively worked to build a sense of community among their fans and support the next generation of artists.

Through initiatives like their record label, Deadbeats, Zeds Dead has provided a platform for emerging artists to showcase their talent and gain exposure. They have championed young talent and nurtured their growth, contributing to the diversity and innovation within the electronic music community.

Additionally, Zeds Dead has actively engaged with their fans through social media and live events. They have created a space where fans can connect with each other and with the artists themselves, fostering a sense of belonging and unity within the electronic music community.

Social Impact and Activism

Zeds Dead has also used their platform to raise awareness and support important social causes. They have partnered with organizations like the Boys and Girls Clubs of Canada and contributed to various charity campaigns.

Their involvement in philanthropic endeavors showcases their commitment to using their influence for positive change and making a lasting impact beyond the realm of music.

Cultivating the Future of Electronic Music

Zeds Dead's journey in the electronic music scene has been one of constant evolution and innovation. They have continually pushed the boundaries of the genre and left an indelible mark on the electronic music landscape.

As they continue to explore new sounds, collaborate with diverse artists, and engage with their fans, Zeds Dead will undoubtedly remain at the forefront of electronic music. Their commitment to creativity, community building, and pushing the boundaries of what is possible in the genre ensures that their impact will be felt for years to come.

In conclusion, Zeds Dead's impactful contributions to electronic music can be attributed to their spirit of innovation, genre-defiance, live performance innovation, community building, and their commitment to social activism. Their unique sound and artistic vision have left an indelible mark on the genre, inspiring and influencing the next generation of electronic music artists. Zeds Dead's legacy is one that will continue to shape and define the future of electronic music.

Supporting Up-and-Coming Artists

In the ever-evolving landscape of the music industry, one of the most important responsibilities for established artists is to support and nurture up-and-coming talent. Zeds Dead has consistently shown a commitment to this mission, recognizing the impact of mentorship and guidance on the growth and success of emerging artists. Through their label, Deadbeats, Zeds Dead has created a platform that not only showcases their own work but also serves as a launching pad for new and innovative artists.

The Importance of Mentorship

Mentorship plays a crucial role in the development of young artists. It provides guidance, support, and a sense of direction in an industry that can often be overwhelming and challenging. Zeds Dead understands the value of mentorship and actively seeks out opportunities to offer their expertise to aspiring musicians.

Through their label, Deadbeats, Zeds Dead has established a network of mentors who work closely with new artists, providing valuable insight into the music industry. By sharing their own experiences, successes, and failures, Zeds Dead helps to shape the artistic journeys of those they mentor, setting them on a path towards creative growth and commercial success.

Creating Opportunities

In addition to mentorship, Zeds Dead believes in creating tangible opportunities for up-and-coming artists. They actively seek out fresh talent to collaborate with on remixes, joint projects, and live performances. By lending their platform and fan base, Zeds Dead provides emerging artists with exposure and recognition that can be a game-changer in their careers.

Deadbeats label showcases the work of artists who may not yet have a significant following, giving them a chance to reach a broader audience and establish themselves in the industry. This commitment to nurturing talent has made Deadbeats a sought-after platform for many aspiring artists, turning it into a hotbed of creativity and innovation.

Championing Diversity and Inclusion

In line with their commitment to supporting up-and-coming artists, Zeds Dead places a strong emphasis on diversity and inclusion. They actively seek out artists from a wide range of backgrounds, genres, and styles, recognizing that talent comes in many forms.

By championing diversity and inclusion, Zeds Dead aims to break down barriers and challenge industry norms. They understand that new ideas and fresh perspectives can only emerge when artists from all walks of life are given equal opportunities and platforms to showcase their work.

Providing Resources and Guidance

Supporting up-and-coming artists goes beyond just offering mentorship and creating opportunities. Zeds Dead understands that emerging artists often face financial constraints and lack the resources to fully realize their creative visions. To address this, they provide resources and guidance to help artists navigate the complex landscape of the music industry.

Deadbeats offers production workshops, where artists can learn from industry professionals and gain insights into the technical and creative aspects of music production. Additionally, Zeds Dead actively seeks out funding opportunities and partnerships to provide financial support to artists, ensuring that they have the necessary resources to bring their artistic visions to life.

Community Engagement

Zeds Dead's commitment to supporting up-and-coming artists extends beyond just signing them to their label. They actively engage with their community of artists and fans, fostering an environment of collaboration and growth. Through regular events, workshops, and artist showcases, Zeds Dead creates a sense of belonging and encourages artists to connect and network with like-minded individuals.

By cultivating a strong sense of community, Zeds Dead creates a support system for emerging artists. They provide a platform for artists to share their work, receive feedback from peers, and form valuable connections within the industry. This community-driven approach not only benefits individual artists but helps to shape the future of electronic music as a whole.

An Unconventional Example: The Remix Competition

As part of their commitment to supporting up-and-coming artists, Zeds Dead has organized various remix competitions. These competitions invite aspiring producers to put their own spin on Zeds Dead tracks, providing an opportunity for them to showcase their talent and creativity to a wider audience.

The remix competitions not only act as a platform for emerging artists but also foster a sense of healthy competition and collaboration within the community. By encouraging artists to push their boundaries and experiment with Zeds Dead's music, these competitions have produced exceptional remixes that have gained recognition and even led to collaborations with the duo.

Conclusion

Supporting up-and-coming artists is a core value for Zeds Dead. Through mentorship, creating opportunities, championing diversity, providing resources and guidance, engaging with the community, and even through unconventional initiatives like remix competitions, Zeds Dead is actively shaping the next generation of artists.

By using their platform and influence to uplift and nurture emerging talent, Zeds Dead is making a lasting impact on the music industry. Their commitment to supporting up-and-coming artists ensures that the creative spirit of electronic music remains vibrant and diverse, and that the journey of aspiring artists becomes a little less daunting and a lot more rewarding.

Exploring Different Business Ventures

In addition to their music career, Zeds Dead has also ventured into various business endeavors that have helped broaden their reach and expand their influence in the music industry. Their innovative and entrepreneurial spirit has led them to explore different avenues beyond music, allowing them to create a multifaceted brand that goes beyond their discography. Let's take a closer look at some of the different business ventures that Zeds Dead has been involved in.

Record Label

One of the most significant business ventures for Zeds Dead has been the establishment of their own record label, *Deadbeats*. Founded in 2016, *Deadbeats* serves as a platform for Zeds Dead to not only release their own music but also support and nurture up-and-coming artists. The label has become synonymous with electronic music and has gained a strong reputation for curating top-notch talent.

Through *Deadbeats*, Zeds Dead has been able to take on the role of tastemakers and influencers in the industry, showcasing their own unique sound while also promoting artists who share their musical vision. With a focus on releasing innovative and boundary-pushing music, *Deadbeats* has become a go-to platform for both established and emerging artists, solidifying Zeds Dead's position as industry leaders.

Event Production

Recognizing the power of live events, Zeds Dead has also ventured into the world of event production. They have curated and hosted their own branded events, providing fans with unforgettable concert experiences. From intimate club shows to large-scale music festivals, Zeds Dead has proven their ability to curate lineups that showcase a diverse range of musical talent, reflecting their eclectic taste.

These events have garnered a strong following and built a sense of community among fans, fostering a loyal and dedicated fan base. By creating immersive and unique live experiences, Zeds Dead has been able to connect with their audience on a deeper level, creating a lasting impact that extends beyond their music.

Merchandise and Apparel

In addition to their music and events, Zeds Dead has also delved into the world of merchandise and apparel. With a distinct visual aesthetic, they have developed a line of merchandise that reflects their unique brand and appeals to their fan base. From t-shirts and hoodies to accessories and collectibles, Zeds Dead's merchandise has become sought after by fans around the globe.

By creating a strong visual identity and offering high-quality merchandise, the band has been able to further solidify their brand and create additional revenue streams. The success of their merchandise is a testament to their ability to connect with fans on a visual and artistic level, transcending the boundaries of music alone.

Charitable Initiatives

Recognizing the importance of giving back, Zeds Dead has also been involved in various charitable initiatives. They have used their platform and resources to support causes that are meaningful to them, such as mental health awareness and education. Through partnerships with nonprofit organizations, they have been able to raise funds and advocate for important social issues.

By leveraging their influence and fan base, Zeds Dead has been able to make a positive impact beyond the realm of music. Their dedication to giving back demonstrates their commitment to using their platform for the greater good and inspiring others to do the same.

Creative Collaborations

Zeds Dead has also embarked on creative collaborations with brands and artists from different industries. By merging their musical talents with other artistic mediums, they have been able to create unique and memorable experiences for their fans.

From collaborating with visual artists for their album artwork and stage design to partnering with fashion brands for exclusive merchandise releases, Zeds Dead has shown versatility in their creative collaborations. These partnerships have allowed them to tap into new audiences and expand their reach beyond the traditional music scene.

Expansion into Media and Entertainment

Going beyond the boundaries of the music industry, Zeds Dead has shown an interest in expanding into other areas of media and entertainment. They have explored opportunities in film and television, leveraging their storytelling abilities to create engaging visual narratives that complement their music.

Furthermore, Zeds Dead has also ventured into the world of gaming, collaborating with game developers to create immersive and interactive experiences for their fans. By embracing emerging technologies and mediums, they have been able to connect with their audience in innovative and unconventional ways.

Innovative Strategies

Throughout their various business ventures, Zeds Dead has employed innovative strategies to maintain their unique brand identity and stand out in a crowded industry. By staying true to their musical vision and embracing new opportunities, they have been able to carve out a distinct niche for themselves.

One of the key strategies that Zeds Dead has employed is collaboration. By partnering with other artists, brands, and organizations, they have been able to tap into new audiences and reach fans who may not have initially been familiar with their music. These collaborations have allowed them to create a network of like-minded individuals and organizations, fueling their growth and influence.

Another innovative strategy that Zeds Dead has adopted is a focus on immersive experiences. From their live shows to their visual artistry, they prioritize creating experiences that go beyond just listening to music. By engaging multiple senses and incorporating visual elements, they have been able to create a unique connection with their audience, making them stand out among their peers.

Additionally, Zeds Dead has embraced technology as a means of expanding their reach. They have utilized social media platforms, streaming services, and other digital tools to connect with their fans and build a strong online community. Their understanding of the evolving digital landscape has allowed them to stay relevant and accessible in an ever-changing industry.

Conclusion

Zeds Dead's exploration of different business ventures is a testament to their entrepreneurial spirit and their desire to create a multifaceted brand. By establishing their own record label, curating events, delving into merchandising, engaging in charitable initiatives, and embarking on creative collaborations, they have expanded their influence beyond music alone. These innovative strategies, coupled with their commitment to authenticity and artistic growth, have solidified their position as industry leaders and pioneers. As they continue to explore new opportunities and push the boundaries of their sound, Zeds Dead's impact on the music industry is set to endure, leaving a lasting legacy for future generations.

Longevity and Success in the Music Industry

In the fast-paced and ever-evolving music industry, it can be a challenge for artists to achieve both longevity and success. However, Zeds Dead has managed to thrive and establish themselves as one of the most influential electronic music acts of our time. Their journey holds valuable lessons for aspiring musicians on how to navigate the industry and sustain a fruitful career. In this section, we will delve into the key factors that have contributed to Zeds Dead's longevity and success.

Adaptation and Innovation

One of the fundamental principles that Zeds Dead has embraced is the importance of adaptation and innovation. They understand that the music industry is constantly evolving, with new trends and styles emerging at a rapid pace. To ensure their longevity, Zeds Dead has continuously evolved their sound, pushing boundaries, and experimenting with new genres and styles. By staying ahead of the curve, they have been able to maintain relevance in an ever-changing landscape.

Moreover, Zeds Dead has demonstrated a keen willingness to incorporate new technologies into their music. They have embraced the use of advanced production techniques, software, and hardware, allowing them to create unique and cutting-edge tracks. This commitment to innovation has not only kept their music fresh and exciting but has also widened their appeal, attracting new listeners and fans from diverse backgrounds.

Consistent Quality and Identifiable Sound

Another key aspect of Zeds Dead's longevity and success is their consistent commitment to delivering high-quality music. From the early days of their career to the present, they have consistently produced tracks that resonate with audiences and showcase their distinctive sound. This identifiable sound, characterized by heavy basslines, melodic elements, and intricate production, has become their trademark and has helped them carve out a unique niche in the music industry.

By maintaining a high standard of quality in their releases, Zeds Dead has garnered a loyal fan base that eagerly awaits their new music. This fan base has been instrumental in spreading their music and generating buzz, leading to increased recognition and success.

Collaborations and Networking

Collaborations have played a significant role in Zeds Dead's journey to longevity and success. They have collaborated with a diverse range of artists, both within and outside the electronic music realm. These collaborations have allowed them to tap into different audiences, expanding their reach and introducing their music to new fans.

Moreover, collaborating with established artists has not only provided Zeds Dead with valuable mentorship and guidance but has also lent credibility to their work. By aligning themselves with respected and influential figures in the industry, Zeds Dead has been able to gain exposure and open doors to new opportunities.

Networking has been crucial for Zeds Dead's success as well. They have actively engaged with their peers, industry professionals, and fans, building strong relationships and a supportive community. Through networking, Zeds Dead has gained valuable insights, advice, and connections that have helped propel their career forward.

Business Acumen and Creative Control

To achieve longevity in the music industry, it is essential for artists to have a solid understanding of the business side of things. Zeds Dead has demonstrated strong business acumen, making strategic decisions that have allowed them to maintain creative control over their music while also maximizing their commercial success.

By retaining creative control, Zeds Dead has been able to stay true to their artistic vision without compromising their integrity. This approach has earned them the respect and admiration of fans and industry professionals alike.

Furthermore, Zeds Dead has diversified their revenue streams by exploring different business ventures. They have ventured into merchandise, event production, and their own record label, Deadbeats, which has become a platform for nurturing emerging talent. This diversification has not only provided them with additional income but has also expanded their influence and presence in the industry.

Impact on Music Culture

Lastly, Zeds Dead's longevity and success can be attributed to their impact on music culture. They have consistently pushed boundaries, challenged conventions, and broken down genre barriers. By doing so, they have inspired and influenced a new generation of artists, shaping the direction of electronic music.

Zeds Dead's commitment to inclusivity, diversity, and activism has also resonated with their audience. They have used their platform to raise awareness about social and political issues, making meaningful contributions to society beyond their music.

In conclusion, Zeds Dead's longevity and success in the music industry can be attributed to their adaptation and innovation, consistent quality, identifiable sound, collaborations and networking, business acumen, creative control, and impact on music culture. These factors, combined with their passion and dedication, have allowed them to overcome challenges and establish a lasting legacy. Aspiring musicians can draw inspiration from their journey and apply these lessons to their own careers, paving the way for their own longevity and success in the music industry.

Remember, success in the music industry is not just about talent and creativity; it is also about business savvy, adaptability, and building meaningful connections. By honing your craft, staying true to your artistic vision, and embracing opportunities for growth, you can increase your chances of achieving longevity and success. So keep striving, keep experimenting, and keep pushing the boundaries of your art. The beat goes on, and so can your musical journey.

Navigating the Streaming Era

The advent of streaming services has revolutionized the music industry, providing both new opportunities and challenges for artists like Zeds Dead. In this section, we explore how Zeds Dead has navigated the streaming era, adapting to changing consumer habits, and capitalizing on the benefits of digital platforms.

Understanding Streaming Services

Streaming services like Spotify, Apple Music, and SoundCloud have become the primary means of music consumption for many listeners. These platforms allow users to access vast catalogs of music on-demand, offering both free and premium subscription options. Artists earn revenue through royalties based on the number of streams their music receives.

Zeds Dead recognized the potential of streaming services early on, leveraging them to gain exposure and connect with fans worldwide. By making their music readily available on popular streaming platforms, they tapped into a massive audience and gained a substantial following.

Building a Digital Presence

To succeed in the streaming era, artists need to establish a strong digital presence. Zeds Dead understood the importance of creating a comprehensive online presence and used it to their advantage.

They built a visually appealing and user-friendly website that serves as a central hub for all their online activities. The website features a media gallery with high-quality images, music videos, and live performance footage, providing fans with an immersive experience.

Zeds Dead also maintains active social media accounts on platforms such as Instagram, Twitter, and Facebook. They regularly post updates, behind-the-scenes content, and engage with fans, creating a sense of community and fostering loyalty.

Engaging with Fans

Streaming services offer unique opportunities for artists to engage directly with their fans. Zeds Dead took advantage of these platforms to establish a direct line of communication with their audience.

They created curated playlists on Spotify, giving fans a glimpse into their musical tastes and influences. By sharing playlists, they not only engage fans but also promote emerging artists and genres they enjoy.

Zeds Dead actively encourages their fans to share their favorite songs and playlists on social media, generating buzz and word-of-mouth promotion. They regularly engage with comments, messages, and fan-generated content, fostering a deep connection with their audience.

Collaborations and Playlisting

Collaborations have always been a part of Zeds Dead's artistic journey, but in the streaming era, they have taken on new significance. Teaming up with other artists allows Zeds Dead to tap into new fan bases and diversify their sound.

Zeds Dead has collaborated with artists from different genres and backgrounds, blending their signature style with diverse influences. This cross-pollination has given their music broader appeal and helped them reach new listeners.

In addition to collaborations, Zeds Dead understands the importance of securing placements on popular playlists. They actively work with streaming services and curators to feature their music on high-profile playlists, ensuring maximum exposure and discoverability.

Leveraging Data and Analytics

Streaming platforms provide artists with valuable data and analytics that can inform their decision-making. Zeds Dead recognizes the power of data and utilizes it to understand their audience better and tailor their strategies accordingly.

They analyze streaming data to identify trends in listener behavior, popular tracks, and demographics. By understanding what resonates with their audience, they can adapt their sound and marketing efforts to maximize engagement and fan loyalty.

Balancing Artistic Integrity and Commercial Success

While streaming services offer artists unprecedented access to a global audience, they also pose challenges. The pressure to create "stream-friendly" music and chase chart success can potentially compromise artistic integrity.

Zeds Dead has navigated this balancing act by staying true to their unique sound and artistic vision. They prioritize making music they love and believe in, without compromising their creativity for commercial gain.

By striking a balance between staying true to their artistic identity and strategically adapting to the streaming era's demands, Zeds Dead has managed to maintain their authenticity while still achieving commercial success.

Embracing Emerging Technologies

Zeds Dead remains at the forefront of technological advancements in the music industry. They embrace emerging technologies such as virtual reality (VR) and augmented reality (AR) to enhance the streaming experience and connect with fans in new ways.

They have collaborated with visual artists and designers to create immersive VR experiences for their music, allowing fans to step into their world and experience their music in a whole new dimension.

Zeds Dead also experiments with interactive AR elements during their live shows, blurring the boundaries between the digital and physical world. These technological innovations enhance their performances, creating unforgettable experiences for their fans.

Reshaping the Future

As technology continues to evolve, Zeds Dead remains committed to reshaping the future of the music industry. They actively seek ways to innovate, not only in their music but also in how they engage with their audience and deliver live performances.

By embracing new technologies, collaborating with emerging artists, and continuously pushing the boundaries of their sound and performance, Zeds Dead aims to create a lasting impact on the streaming era and leave a legacy that inspires future generations of electronic artists.

Conclusion

In the streaming era, Zeds Dead has successfully adapted to the changing landscape of the music industry. By embracing streaming platforms, building a strong digital presence, engaging with fans, leveraging data, and embracing emerging technologies, they have navigated the challenges and gained recognition on a global scale.

Zeds Dead continues to push the boundaries of electronic music and shape the future by staying true to their artistic vision while embracing the opportunities presented by the streaming era. As they evolve and grow, they inspire both fans and fellow artists to navigate the ever-changing landscape of the music industry with creativity and authenticity.

Inspiring Future Generations of Artists

When it comes to the world of music, inspiration is the fuel that ignites the creative flame. Zeds Dead, with their unique sound and artistic vision, have become a source of inspiration for countless aspiring artists. In this section, we will explore how Zeds Dead has inspired future generations of artists and the impact they have had on the music industry.

Pushing Boundaries and Challenging Conventions

One of the key ways Zeds Dead has inspired artists is by pushing boundaries and challenging conventions. They have never been afraid to break the mold and explore new sounds, merging genres, and creating their own unique style. This fearlessness and willingness to experiment have become a beacon of inspiration for artists looking to step out of their comfort zones and carve their own paths in the music industry.

Example: Imagine a young producer who feels limited by the conventions of their chosen genre. They stumble upon a Zeds Dead track that seamlessly fuses elements from different genres, and it sparks a realization that they too can explore new sonic territories. Inspired by Zeds Dead's fearlessness, they begin experimenting with hybrid sounds, eventually creating a style that sets them apart in their genre.

The Power of Authenticity and Individuality

Zeds Dead's journey to success has been marked by their unwavering authenticity and commitment to staying true to themselves as artists. By embracing their own unique identities and refusing to conform to industry pressures, they have shown aspiring artists the importance of being true to oneself and the power of individuality.

Example: A young DJ struggling with finding their own voice in a saturated market looks up to Zeds Dead as role models. They witness how Zeds Dead has built a loyal fan base by staying true to their artistic vision and not compromising their sound. Inspired by this, the young DJ decides to dig deep into their own musical identity, ultimately finding their own unique style and connecting with fans who appreciate their authenticity.

Collaborative Creativity

Zeds Dead's collaborative spirit and their willingness to work with artists from different genres and artistic disciplines have shown aspiring artists the power of collaborative creativity. By embracing collaboration, they have opened doors to new possibilities and expanded their own artistic horizons.

Example: A budding producer dreams of collaborating with artists they admire but feels hesitant to reach out due to fear of rejection. They witness Zeds Dead's numerous collaborations with artists from various backgrounds and see the magic that can happen when creative forces come together. Inspired by this, they gather the courage to approach their dream collaborators and end up creating a unique and unexpected project that propels their careers forward.

Connecting with Fans and Building Community

Zeds Dead's ability to connect with their fans and build a strong sense of community has been another source of inspiration for artists. They understand the importance of engaging with their audience, both online and at live shows, and have cultivated a loyal following that feels like a true community.

Example: An up-and-coming artist struggling to build a fan base finds solace in Zeds Dead's approachability and dedication to their fans. They witness how Zeds Dead interacts with their audience on social media, responds to messages, and creates a welcoming atmosphere at their shows. Inspired by this, the artist decides to foster deeper connections with their own fans, resulting in a devoted and supportive community that grows alongside their music.

Making a Difference Beyond Music

Beyond their music, Zeds Dead's philanthropic endeavors and social initiatives have inspired artists to make a difference beyond the confines of the music industry. By using their platform for positive change, they have shown aspiring artists the impact their art can have on society and the importance of giving back.

Example: A young producer feels a strong desire to use their music as a catalyst for positive change but is unsure of where to start. They become aware of Zeds Dead's involvement in philanthropy and social initiatives, and it inspires them to launch their own campaign to raise awareness and support for a cause they deeply care about. Inspired by Zeds Dead's example, they succeed in mobilizing their fan base and making a tangible difference in their community.

Unconventional Collaboration: Music and Visual Art

Zeds Dead's willingness to explore the intersection of music and visual art has inspired artists to embrace unconventional collaborations and explore the multidimensionality of their craft. By incorporating visual elements into their live shows and collaborating with visual artists, they have created immersive experiences that captivate audiences.

Example: A visual artist who has been creating art in isolation feels a desire to bring their work to a broader audience. They discover Zeds Dead's collaborative projects with visual artists, where music and visuals harmoniously intertwine. Inspired by this, they reach out to musicians and creators in their local scene, ultimately engaging in an innovative collaboration that combines their visual art with live music performances, resulting in a unique and immersive experience for the audience.

Summary

Zeds Dead's impact on inspiring future generations of artists goes far beyond their music. Through their fearlessness in pushing boundaries, commitment to authenticity, collaborative spirit, and community-building efforts, they have set an example for aspiring artists to follow. By showcasing the power of individuality, the importance of giving back, and the potential of interdisciplinary collaborations, they have inspired artists to chase their dreams, express their true selves, and make a lasting impact on the world through music. The legacy of Zeds Dead as inspirational figures in the music industry is sure to endure, continuing to motivate artists for years to come.

Influencing Music Culture and Trends

Music has always played a powerful role in shaping culture and influencing trends. Zeds Dead, with their unique sound and artistic vision, has had a significant impact on the music scene, leaving an indelible mark on both electronic music and popular culture as a whole. In this section, we will explore the ways in which Zeds Dead has influenced music culture and trends, and how they continue to push the boundaries of creativity and innovation.

Pioneering New Sounds and Styles

One of the key ways in which Zeds Dead has influenced music culture is by pioneering new sounds and styles within the electronic music genre. From their early tracks to their latest releases, they have consistently pushed the boundaries of what is possible in electronic music production. By blending elements of dubstep, hip-hop, reggae, and other genres, they have created a unique and distinct sound that has inspired countless artists and producers.

Zeds Dead's ability to seamlessly blend diverse musical influences has opened up new possibilities for experimentation and genre fusion within electronic music. Their groundbreaking tracks have served as a catalyst for other artists to explore new sonic territories and push the boundaries of their own creativity. As a result, the electronic music landscape has become more diverse and vibrant, with artists from all over the world taking inspiration from Zeds Dead's innovative approach.

Breaking Down Genre Barriers

In addition to pioneering new sounds and styles, Zeds Dead has played a crucial role in breaking down genre barriers within the music industry. Traditionally, genres like dubstep and electronic music were seen as niche and confined to specific subcultures. However, Zeds Dead's music transcends these boundaries, attracting fans from a wide range of musical backgrounds.

Their ability to blend different genres and create a unique sound has allowed them to connect with audiences who may not have been exposed to electronic music before. By merging elements of hip-hop, reggae, and other genres with their signature electronic sound, they have created a bridge between different musical communities and fostered a sense of unity and inclusivity.

Zeds Dead's success in breaking down genre barriers has paved the way for other artists to experiment and collaborate across genres. This has led to a wave of innovation and creativity within the music industry, as artists from different backgrounds come together to create truly unique and boundary-pushing music.

Shaping Music Culture and Trends

Beyond their impact on the electronic music genre, Zeds Dead has also played a significant role in shaping music culture and trends as a whole. Their music has not only influenced other artists, but it has also resonated with a wide audience, transcending traditional genre boundaries and appealing to fans of various musical backgrounds.

Zeds Dead's influence can be seen in the rise of electronic music festivals and events worldwide, where their music is often featured prominently. Their captivating live performances and energetic sets have become a benchmark for excellence in the electronic music scene, inspiring other artists to elevate their live shows and create unforgettable experiences for their fans.

Their success has also opened doors for other electronic music artists to achieve mainstream recognition and success. As Zeds Dead's music reaches a larger audience, the overall perception of electronic music has evolved, with more people embracing the genre and its unique sound.

Additionally, Zeds Dead's impact on music culture extends beyond their own music. They have actively collaborated with other artists and taken part in joint ventures, further expanding their influence and reach. Through these collaborations, they have fostered a spirit of artistic community and influenced the trajectory of music culture.

Cultivating a Strong Fan Community

Another aspect of Zeds Dead's influence on music culture and trends is the strong and dedicated fan community they have cultivated. Their music resonates deeply with their fans, who often identify with the energy and emotion conveyed in their tracks. This sense of connection has led to a passionate and engaged fan base that actively promotes and supports Zeds Dead's work.

Zeds Dead has embraced their fan community by actively engaging with them through social media, livestreams, and fan events. This level of interaction has fostered a sense of belonging and shared experience among fans, creating a community that extends beyond the music itself.

Their fan community has also played a crucial role in spreading their music and influence to a wider audience. Through word-of-mouth recommendations and social media sharing, fans have become ambassadors for Zeds Dead's music, introducing new listeners to their unique sound and contributing to the growth of their fan base.

Challenging Industry Norms and Practices

In addition to their impact on music culture, Zeds Dead has also challenged industry norms and practices. They have approached their music career with a sense of independence and creative freedom, often releasing their music through their own label, Deadbeats.

This alternative approach to the music industry has inspired other artists to take control of their own artistic vision and pursue unconventional paths to success. By forging their own path and staying true to their artistic vision, Zeds Dead has proven that it is possible to achieve both creative fulfillment and commercial success without compromising artistic integrity.

Their success as independent artists has also challenged the traditional model of record labels and distribution, demonstrating that artists can succeed on their own terms in the digital age.

The Intersection of Music and Activism

Zeds Dead has used their platform and influence to address important societal issues, raising awareness and inspiring change through their music. They have been vocal about their support for various causes, including mental health, social justice, and environmental sustainability.

Through their music, Zeds Dead has provided a platform for marginalized voices and created a space for dialogue and reflection on pressing social issues. Their willingness to tackle these complex topics has resonated deeply with their fans and has helped foster a sense of empathy and solidarity within their community.

By leveraging their influence and creating music that sparks conversations and inspires action, Zeds Dead has shown that music can be a powerful tool for social change and activism.

The Enduring Legacy of Zeds Dead

As Zeds Dead continues to push the boundaries of electronic music and influence music culture and trends, their enduring legacy becomes increasingly evident. Their groundbreaking sound, genre-bending approach, and commitment to artistic integrity have cemented them as pioneers in the industry.

Their influence can be heard in the music of countless artists who have been inspired by their creativity and innovation. Their ability to connect with diverse audiences and break down genre barriers has shaped the landscape of electronic music and influenced popular culture as a whole.

Zeds Dead's legacy extends beyond their music; it is a testament to the power of passion, creativity, and authenticity. They have shown that by staying true to oneself and pushing the boundaries of what is possible, artists can create a lasting impact on music and culture.

In conclusion, Zeds Dead's influence on music culture and trends is undeniable. Through their pioneering sounds, breaking down genre barriers, challenging industry norms, and addressing important societal issues, they have left an indelible mark on the music scene. As they continue to evolve and innovate, their legacy will endure, inspiring future generations of artists to explore new creative frontiers and push the boundaries of what is possible in music.

The Enduring Spirit of Zeds Dead

The enduring spirit of Zeds Dead can be characterized by their unwavering passion for music, their tireless dedication to their craft, and their ability to consistently push the boundaries of electronic music. Throughout their career, Zeds Dead has carved out a unique place in the music industry, leaving an indelible mark on the electronic music landscape. In this section, we will explore the key elements that contribute to the enduring spirit of Zeds Dead.

The Power of Authenticity

At the core of Zeds Dead's enduring spirit is their authenticity as artists. From the very beginning, they have stayed true to their vision, refusing to conform to trends or compromise their artistic integrity. This unwavering commitment to their musical identity has resonated with fans, who are drawn to Zeds Dead's genuine and sincere approach.

By embracing their individuality and staying true to themselves, Zeds Dead has been able to create a distinct sound that sets them apart from their peers. This authenticity is evident in every aspect of their music, from the production techniques they employ to the emotions they evoke in their compositions. This genuine connection with their craft has earned them a loyal fan base and has allowed them to delve into new sonic territories while staying true to their roots.

Connecting Through Music

One of the most remarkable aspects of Zeds Dead is their ability to connect with their audience through their music. Their music serves as a bridge, bringing together people from different backgrounds, cultures, and experiences. Through their mesmerizing beats, captivating melodies, and thought-provoking lyrics, Zeds

Dead creates a shared experience that unites listeners in a collective musical journey.

The enduring spirit of Zeds Dead lies in their ability to tap into the universal language of music and use it as a tool for emotional expression and connection. Their music transcends boundaries and allows listeners to escape the confines of everyday life, immersing themselves in a world of sound and rhythm. This ability to create a powerful and transformative experience is what sets Zeds Dead apart and ensures their lasting impact in the music industry.

Innovation and Evolution

Another key element of Zeds Dead's enduring spirit is their constant innovation and evolution as artists. They have never been content to rest on their laurels or stay confined to a single style or genre. Instead, they have consistently pushed the boundaries of electronic music, experimenting with new sounds, blending genres, and incorporating different influences into their music.

Zeds Dead's willingness to embrace change and take risks has allowed them to evolve and remain relevant in a fast-paced and ever-changing music landscape. They have consistently evolved their sound, incorporating elements of dubstep, hip-hop, reggae, and other genres, creating a unique and dynamic sonic palette.

This commitment to innovation is also reflected in their live performances, where they continuously strive to create an immersive and captivating experience for their audience. From their stage design to their visual effects, Zeds Dead is constantly pushing the boundaries of what is possible in a live concert setting, creating a multidimensional and multisensory experience that leaves a lasting impression on their fans.

Inspiration for Future Generations

The enduring spirit of Zeds Dead lies not only in their ability to create groundbreaking music but also in their commitment to inspiring and nurturing future generations of artists. Throughout their career, Zeds Dead has been dedicated to supporting and collaborating with young talent, providing a platform for emerging artists to showcase their skills and gain exposure.

Through their label, Deadbeats, Zeds Dead actively seeks out and supports up-and-coming producers, providing them with resources, mentorship, and a platform to release their music. This commitment to fostering the next generation of artists ensures that the legacy of Zeds Dead will live on, as their influence continues to shape the future of electronic music.

In addition to their support of emerging artists, Zeds Dead is also passionate about giving back to their community and using their platform for positive change. They have been involved in various philanthropic endeavors and social initiatives, using their music and influence to raise awareness and make a difference in the world.

The Legacy Lives On

As we conclude this section on the enduring spirit of Zeds Dead, it is clear that their impact on the music industry extends far beyond their genre-defying sound and chart-topping hits. Zeds Dead's enduring spirit lies in their unwavering authenticity as artists, their ability to connect with their audience through their music, their constant innovation and evolution, and their commitment to inspiring future generations.

Their legacy lives on through their music, their live performances, and their influence on a new generation of artists. Their enduring spirit serves as a reminder that music has the power to transcend boundaries, connect people, and create lasting change. With each track they release and each stage they conquer, Zeds Dead continues to leave an indelible mark on the music industry and inspire countless others to follow their passion for music.

Chapter 3: Behind the Beats

Chapter 3: Behind the Beats

Chapter 3: Behind the Beats

In this chapter, we delve into the creative process and behind-the-scenes world of Zeds Dead. We explore the musical evolution, influences, and experimentation that have shaped their unique sound. Additionally, we uncover the role of visual aesthetics, the live experience, and the impact Zeds Dead has had on music and culture. Get ready for an exclusive look behind the beats!

Chapter 3: Behind the Beats

When it comes to creating music, Zeds Dead brings together a perfect blend of skill, inspiration, and innovation. This section takes a deep dive into the creative process behind their captivating beats, and how they have pushed the boundaries of electronic music.

Zeds Dead draws influences from a wide range of musical genres and eras. Whether it's the nostalgic sounds of the past or the cutting-edge styles of today, their sound is a dynamic fusion of musical elements. By incorporating elements from different genres such as hip-hop, reggae, and dubstep, Zeds Dead has created a distinctive and eclectic sound.

One of the key aspects of their sound is their ability to experiment and evolve. They continuously explore different subgenres of electronic music and are not afraid to break conventions. This fearless approach to music has allowed them to carve out a unique space in the industry.

The studio is where the magic happens for Zeds Dead. They meticulously craft their tracks, paying attention to every detail. Technology plays a crucial role in their production process, enabling them to experiment with different sounds and effects. By harnessing the power of sound engineering, they ensure that each track is masterfully crafted and sonically rich.

The workflow and creative process of Zeds Dead are a testament to their dedication and passion for music. They spend countless hours experimenting, refining, and perfecting their tracks. No stone is left unturned, and they are constantly learning and growing as musicians.

Behind the scenes, there are many stories and anecdotes to be shared. From the challenges they've faced to the breakthrough moments, Zeds Dead's journey in the studio is filled with highs and lows. They embrace the excitement of constant learning and musical growth, pushing themselves to create music that transcends boundaries.

Studio rituals and superstitions also play a part in their creative process. Every artist has their own way of channeling inspiration, and Zeds Dead is no exception. From pre-studio rituals to unique approaches to songwriting, they have developed a set of practices that contribute to their creative flow.

Life on the road is intertwined with their creative process. The energy and connection they feel with their fans while performing live ignites their creativity in the studio. The experiences and interactions they have on tour seep into their music, making it an immersive and captivating experience.

The evolution of their live performances has been a testament to their commitment to innovation. Zeds Dead creates an immersive atmosphere that captivates the audience from start to finish. With the incorporation of visual elements and interactive elements, they push the boundaries of what a live show can be.

Zeds Dead's impact on music and culture cannot be overstated. They have become pioneers in electronic music, inspiring a new generation of artists to push the boundaries of sound. Their ability to break down genre barriers and challenge conventions has reshaped the landscape of electronic music.

Through their music, Zeds Dead has connected with a diverse fanbase, creating a sense of community and shared experiences. They have played a significant role in shaping music culture and trends, leaving an indelible mark on the industry.

Looking to the future, Zeds Dead continues to explore new frontiers in music. Their commitment to innovation and collaboration ensures that their sound remains fresh and exciting. As they build on their legacy and leave a lasting impact, the beats of Zeds Dead will continue to resonate with music lovers around the world.

Chapter 4: From the Rhythm to the Future

With their sights set on the future, Zeds Dead's journey continues in Chapter 4. We explore their musical evolution, the pursuit of new creative ventures, and the impact they hope to leave on the music industry. Get ready to dive into the rhythm and look ahead to what the future holds for Zeds Dead.

The Zeds Dead Discography

Breakout Tracks and Early Releases

The journey of Zeds Dead began with a series of breakout tracks and early releases that set the stage for their meteoric rise in the electronic music scene. These early works showcased their unique sound and demonstrated their ability to push the boundaries of genres, setting them apart from their peers.

The Birth of Zeds Dead

Before we dive into their breakout tracks, let's take a moment to appreciate the birth of Zeds Dead. Comprised of Dylan Mamid, also known as DC, and Zachary Rapp-Rovan, known as Hooks, the duo came together in Toronto, Canada, with a shared passion for music and a desire to create something extraordinary. Little did they know that they were about to embark on a musical journey that would captivate audiences around the world.

Early Works and Experiments

In the early stages of their career, Zeds Dead released a series of tracks and EPs that showcased their versatility and experimentation with different styles. From the haunting melodies of "Adrenaline" to the gritty basslines of "1975," their early works established the foundation of their signature sound. These tracks served as a glimpse into the duo's musical vision and hinted at the innovative and boundary-pushing approach they would continue to pursue.

Breakout Tracks

It was during this period that Zeds Dead released some of their breakout tracks, which quickly gained attention and served as a turning point in their career. One such track is "Eyes on Fire," a remix of the song by Blue Foundation. This remix showcased Zeds Dead's ability to take an already fantastic song and transform it into a genre-bending masterpiece. The combination of haunting vocals, pulsating basslines, and intricate production captivated listeners and catapulted Zeds Dead into the spotlight.

Another breakout track that helped solidify Zeds Dead's place in the electronic music community is "Coffee Break," a collaboration with Omar LinX. This track seamlessly blended dubstep elements with hip-hop-inspired lyrics, showcasing the duo's ability to bridge genres and create a unique sound all their own. "Coffee Break" not only showcased their production skills but also their knack for collaborating with diverse artists and pushing the boundaries of musical genres.

Impacting the Global Music Scene

As Zeds Dead's breakout tracks gained traction, they quickly established themselves as a force to be reckoned with in the global music scene. Their ability to seamlessly blend genres and create captivating melodies caught the attention of fans, industry professionals, and fellow artists alike. Their tracks began receiving support from renowned DJs and producers, showcasing the impact their music was having on the electronic music community.

Influence on the Dubstep Genre

During this early phase, Zeds Dead also made significant contributions to the dubstep genre, which was gaining immense popularity at the time. Tracks like "Ruckus the Jam" and "Bassmentality" showcased their ability to create heavy bass drops and intricate rhythms that formed the backbone of dubstep. These tracks solidified their place in the genre and demonstrated their ability to push its boundaries with their innovative production techniques and unique sound.

Paving the Way for Future Success

The breakout tracks and early releases of Zeds Dead laid the groundwork for their future success. These tracks not only showcased their talent and creativity but also proved that they were a force to be reckoned with in the music industry. The unique sound they cultivated and the boundary-pushing approach they adopted set them apart from their peers and positioned them as pioneers in the electronic music scene.

A Trailblazing Path

The breakout tracks and early releases of Zeds Dead truly set the stage for their journey to success. These tracks demonstrated their ability to push the boundaries of genres, their knack for collaboration, and their commitment to creating a sound that was uniquely their own. With each release, Zeds Dead continued to prove that they were trailblazers, paving the way for the future of electronic music and leaving an indelible mark on the global music scene.

As we continue our exploration of Zeds Dead's musical journey, we will delve further into their discography, the evolution of their sound, and the impact they have had on music and culture. Join us as we uncover the story behind the beats that have captivated audiences worldwide.

Studio Albums and EPs

When it comes to studio albums and EPs, Zeds Dead has been consistently pushing boundaries and delivering powerful musical experiences to their fans. Let's take a dive into their discography and explore some of their most notable releases.

Adrenaline EP (2009)

The Adrenaline EP marked Zeds Dead's first official release, and it immediately grabbed the attention of electronic music enthusiasts. With tracks like "Journey of a Lifetime" and "Loud", Zeds Dead showcased their signature blend of heavy bass and melodic elements. This EP set the stage for their future endeavors and established their unique sound.

Rumble in the Jungle EP (2010)

Following their successful debut, Zeds Dead continued to evolve their sound with the release of the Rumble in the Jungle EP. This project demonstrated their ability to seamlessly blend different genres like dubstep, drum and bass, and hip hop. Tracks like "Rude Boy" and "Eyes on Fire" became instant favorites, capturing the attention of a wider audience.

Victor EP (2011)

With the Victor EP, Zeds Dead's sonic evolution took another leap forward. This release showcased their versatility as producers, featuring a diverse range of tracks that incorporated elements of electro, house, and glitch-hop. The standout track, "Coffee Break," highlighted their ability to craft infectious melodies while keeping the energy levels high.

Hot Sauce EP (2012)

Hot Sauce EP further solidified Zeds Dead's reputation as genre-bending trailblazers. This release was a melting pot of different styles and influences, with tracks like "Trouble" and "Rave" pushing the boundaries of electronic music. The EP showcased their ability to seamlessly fuse heavy basslines, intricate melodies, and infectious hooks.

Somewhere Else EP (2014)

Somewhere Else EP marked a significant turning point for Zeds Dead as they explored a more melodic and experimental sound. This release featured collaborations with a diverse range of artists like Twin Shadow, Bright Lights, and Perry Farrell. Tracks like "Lost You" and "Hadouken" demonstrated their ability to create emotionally-charged compositions while retaining their trademark intensity.

Northern Lights (2016)

Northern Lights, Zeds Dead's debut studio album, was a milestone in their career. It showcased their growth as producers and songwriters, with tracks that encompassed a wide range of genres including future bass, trap, and house. Collaborations with Diplo, Pusha T, and Weezer's Rivers Cuomo added further depth and diversity to the album, solidifying Zeds Dead's status as genre-bending innovators.

Someday EP (2018)

Someday EP saw Zeds Dead continuing to embrace their musical evolution. This release featured collaborations with a variety of artists including Diskord, Urbandawn, and Dion Timmer. Tracks like "Rescue" and "Lift You Up" demonstrated their ability to craft emotionally-charged compositions that resonated with listeners.

We Are Deadbeats, Vol. 1 (2019)

We Are Deadbeats, Vol. 1 was the first compilation album released on their own label, Deadbeats. This project showcased the talent and diversity of artists signed to the label, with tracks ranging from heavy-hitting bass to melodic future bass. Zeds Dead's contributions, such as "Stardust" and "Bumpy Teeth," further cemented their status as pioneers in the electronic music scene.

Catching Z's Vol. 3 (2020)

Catching Z's Vol. 3 was a departure from their usual high-energy sound, offering a dreamy and introspective experience. This album featured remixes of their own tracks by various artists, as well as original compositions. Tracks like "Lost My Mind" and "Stars Tonight" provided a soothing and atmospheric escape for listeners.

Catching Z's Vol. 4 (2021)

Building on the success of the previous Catching Z's volumes, Catching Z's Vol. 4 continued to offer a serene and introspective listening experience. This release featured remixes of tracks from their The Living Dead EP, as well as enchanting original compositions. With tracks like "Zebra" and "You and I", Zeds Dead embraced a laid-back and ethereal sound.

Genre Exploration and Artistic Growth

Throughout their career, Zeds Dead has constantly pushed the boundaries of electronic music, blending different genres and experimenting with new sounds. Their studio albums and EPs showcase their ability to incorporate elements of dubstep, hip-hop, house, and more into their unique sonic tapestry. By doing so, they have continually evolved their sound and kept their music fresh and captivating.

Continued Collaborations and Innovation

Zeds Dead has also consistently collaborated with a diverse range of artists, both within and outside of the electronic music realm. These collaborations have not only contributed to the sonic richness of their albums and EPs but have also allowed them to explore new musical territories and expand their creative horizons.

Impact and Legacy

Zeds Dead's studio albums and EPs have left an indelible mark on the electronic music scene. Their willingness to experiment, blend genres, and evolve their sound has inspired a new generation of artists and shaped the direction of the genre itself. Their ability to appeal to a wide range of listeners while staying true to their unique vision is a testament to their enduring legacy.

Further Exploration

To delve deeper into Zeds Dead's studio albums and EPs, explore their discography on streaming platforms and immerse yourself in the sonic journey they have created. By doing so, you'll gain a deeper appreciation for their innovation, artistry, and contribution to the world of electronic music.

Mixtapes and DJ Sets

Mixtapes and DJ sets have played a pivotal role in the career of Zeds Dead. These collections of carefully curated tracks and seamless mixes have allowed them to showcase their musical taste, creativity, and technical skills to their fans. In this section, we will explore the importance of mixtapes and DJ sets in the context of Zeds Dead's journey.

The Art of the Mixtape

Mixtapes have a rich history in the world of music. In its early days, mixtapes were created by DJs who would compile their favorite tracks onto a cassette tape and distribute them to friends and fans. These mixtapes became a way for DJs to showcase their unique musical style and taste.

For Zeds Dead, mixtapes have served as a platform to introduce listeners to new music and create a cohesive musical experience. Each mixtape they release tells a story, taking the listener on a journey through different genres, styles, and emotions. These mixtapes have become an essential part of their artistic expression and a way to connect with their audience on a deeper level.

Curating the Perfect Playlist

Curating a mixtape involves carefully selecting tracks that flow together seamlessly and create a cohesive listening experience. Zeds Dead's mixtapes are known for their diverse selection of music, blending various genres and styles to create a unique sonic experience.

The process of curating a mixtape starts with extensive research and exploration of different musical genres. Zeds Dead draws inspiration from a wide range of sources, including underground artists, forgotten classics, and emerging talents. They spend countless hours digging through vinyl records, digital platforms, and music libraries to find hidden gems that will resonate with their audience.

Once the tracks are chosen, Zeds Dead meticulously arranges them in a specific order, paying attention to factors such as tempo, energy, and mood. Transitions between tracks are carefully crafted to create a smooth and seamless flow, maintaining the listener's interest throughout the mixtape.

Technical Skills and Innovation

As DJs, Zeds Dead's technical skills are an integral part of their mixtapes and DJ sets. They combine their deep understanding of music theory with their technical prowess to create dynamic and engaging mixes.

Zeds Dead utilizes advanced DJ software and hardware to manipulate and mix tracks in real-time. They employ techniques such as beat matching, blending, scratching, and looping to create smooth transitions and unique sounds. Their technical skills allow them to create mashups, remixes, and edits on the fly, adding their personal touch to each mixtape.

In addition to their DJ skills, Zeds Dead is known for their innovative use of technology during their live performances. They incorporate live instruments, controllers, and other electronic devices to add a layer of spontaneity and improvisation to their DJ sets.

Creating a Memorable Experience

Zeds Dead's mixtapes and DJ sets go beyond just a collection of songs. They strive to create a memorable experience for their audience. This involves not only the selection and mixing of tracks but also the overall atmosphere and storytelling.

Through their mixtapes, Zeds Dead takes their listeners on an emotional journey, evoking different feelings and moods. They craft the progression and pacing of the mixtape to build tension and release, creating moments of euphoria, introspection, and excitement.

During their live DJ sets, Zeds Dead prioritizes crowd engagement and interaction. They read the energy of the audience and adapt their mixes accordingly, creating a symbiotic relationship between the artists and the crowd. The result is an electric and unforgettable live experience that leaves a lasting impression.

Mixtapes and DJ Sets in the Digital Age

The digital age has brought significant changes to the landscape of mixtapes and DJ sets. With the rise of streaming platforms and social media, artists like Zeds Dead have been able to reach a global audience and share their mixtapes more easily than ever before.

Platforms like SoundCloud and Mixcloud have become popular destinations for DJs to upload and share their mixtapes with fans. Zeds Dead has utilized these platforms to distribute their mixtapes, gaining international recognition and showcasing their talent to millions of listeners.

Furthermore, social media has allowed Zeds Dead to connect directly with their fans and receive instant feedback on their mixtapes and DJ sets. This direct line of communication has become invaluable, shaping the creative direction and content of their mixtapes.

Unconventional Mixtapes and DJ Techniques

While traditional mixtapes and DJ sets have been the backbone of Zeds Dead's journey, they have also experimented with unconventional formats and techniques. For example, they have released themed mixtapes that pay homage to specific genres or artists, showcasing their versatility and creativity.

Additionally, Zeds Dead has incorporated live instrumentation into their DJ sets, blurring the lines between electronic and live performances. By incorporating instruments like guitars, drums, and synthesizers, they create a one-of-a-kind experience that transcends the traditional DJ set.

Conclusion

Mixtapes and DJ sets have played a pivotal role in Zeds Dead's journey, allowing them to showcase their musical taste, technical skills, and creativity. From carefully curating the perfect playlist to crafting a memorable experience for their audience, Zeds Dead's mixtapes and DJ sets have cemented their status as one of the most innovative and influential electronic music acts of their generation. As they continue to evolve and experiment, mixtapes and DJ sets will undoubtedly remain an integral part of their artistic expression and connection with their fans.

Remixes and Collaborations

Remixes and collaborations have been an integral part of Zeds Dead's musical journey, allowing them to explore new sounds, collaborate with other artists, and push the boundaries of their creative expression. In this section, we will delve into the fascinating world of Zeds Dead's remixes and collaborations, examining their approach to these projects and the impact they have had on their music and the broader electronic music scene.

The Art of Remixing

Remixing is an art form that involves reinterpreting and reimagining an existing song, often adding new elements, rearranging sections, and infusing it with a fresh perspective. Zeds Dead has mastered the art of remixing, breathing new life into tracks from a wide range of genres, including hip-hop, reggae, and electronic music.

One of the defining characteristics of a Zeds Dead remix is their ability to simultaneously stay true to the essence of the original song while infusing it with their signature style. They carefully select tracks that resonate with them on a personal level and reimagine them through their unique lens. Through their remixes, Zeds Dead has the power to transform a song into a completely different sonic experience, captivating listeners with their innovative approach.

Collaborative Ventures

Zeds Dead's collaborations have been a catalyst for their artistic growth and expansion of their musical repertoire. Collaborations allow them to combine their talents and ideas with other artists, resulting in truly unique and innovative music. Zeds Dead has collaborated with a diverse range of artists, from fellow electronic musicians to hip-hop artists and vocalists.

Their collaborative ventures are not limited to music production; they often work closely with visual artists, stage designers, and video directors to create a cohesive and immersive experience that transcends traditional boundaries. By joining forces with artists from different disciplines, Zeds Dead is able to explore new creative territories and challenge conventional norms in the electronic music scene.

The Power of Collaboration

Collaboration is a powerful tool that not only fuels artistic growth but also enhances the impact of the final product. When artists come together, they bring their distinct perspectives, skills, and experiences to the table, resulting in a dynamic fusion of ideas and influences.

For Zeds Dead, collaboration is a means of tapping into new creative energies and breaking free from the constraints of their individual mindsets. Working with other artists allows them to explore new genres, experiment with unconventional soundscapes, and venture into uncharted musical territories.

One notable collaboration in Zeds Dead's discography is their work with Omar LinX. The combination of Zeds Dead's production prowess and Omar LinX's evocative vocals resulted in a series of critically acclaimed tracks that showcased a seamless blend of electronic music and hip-hop influences. Tracks like "Out for Blood" and "Cowboy" exemplify the power of collaboration and the magic that can unfold when two artists come together to create something greater than the sum of its parts.

Pushing the Boundaries

Zeds Dead's remixes and collaborations are not merely exercises in reworking existing songs or teaming up with other artists; they are a testament to their commitment to pushing the boundaries of electronic music. By infusing their unique sound into remixes and embracing the creative input of their collaborators, Zeds Dead constantly evolves and expands their sonic palette.

Their remixes are not just reinterpretations of songs, but rather opportunities to experiment with different genres, tempos, and production techniques. They inject their own distinct flavor into each remix, often incorporating elements of dubstep, drum and bass, and trap into the original material.

Collaborations offer Zeds Dead the chance to explore uncharted territory and break free from the constraints of their established sound. By working hand in hand with artists from different genres, they challenge traditional notions of electronic music and create a space for truly innovative and genre-defying music.

The Impact on the Electronic Music Scene

Zeds Dead's remixes and collaborations have had a profound impact on the electronic music scene, shaping the sound and influencing the direction of the genre. Their energetic remixes have become anthems in their own right, captivating audiences with their infectious energy and unique take on familiar tracks.

In the realm of collaborations, Zeds Dead's willingness to collaborate with artists from diverse backgrounds has opened doors for new possibilities in electronic music. Their cross-genre collaborations have fostered a sense of inclusivity and genre-blurring within the community, inspiring other producers and artists to explore new creative territories.

Through their remixes and collaborations, Zeds Dead has established themselves as pioneers in the electronic music scene, constantly pushing the envelope and redefining the boundaries of what is possible within the genre. Their fearless approach to remixing and collaborative ventures has cemented their status as true innovators in the industry.

Unconventional Collaborations

While Zeds Dead has collaborated with a wide range of artists within the electronic and hip-hop realms, their willingness to explore less conventional collaborations has set them apart from their peers. One example of such an unconventional collaboration is their partnership with the classical music ensemble, the Colorado Symphony.

In this unique collaboration, Zeds Dead joined forces with the Colorado Symphony to create an extraordinary blend of electronic and orchestral music. The result was a breathtaking performance that combined the power and energy of Zeds Dead's electronic sound with the richness and depth of a full symphony orchestra. This collaboration showcased the ability of electronic music to transcend boundaries and connect with audiences across different musical backgrounds.

Another unconventional collaboration was with renowned street artist Shepard Fairey, known for his iconic "Hope" poster during Barack Obama's presidential campaign. Zeds Dead and Shepard Fairey collaborated on a multimedia project that combined music, street art, and visual storytelling. The collaboration resulted in a series of captivating music videos that brought Zeds Dead's music to life through Shepard Fairey's distinct visual style.

These unconventional collaborations reflect Zeds Dead's commitment to exploring new artistic frontiers and pushing the boundaries of their creative expression. By stepping outside of their comfort zone and embracing diverse collaborations, they continue to surprise and captivate audiences with their innovative approach to music.

Summary

In this section, we delved into the world of Zeds Dead's remixes and collaborations, exploring their approach to these projects and the impact they have had on their music and the broader electronic music scene. We witnessed their mastery of the art of remixing, their ability to transform songs and infuse them with their signature style. We also explored the power of collaboration and its role in Zeds Dead's artistic growth and expansion. We saw how their collaborations have allowed them to explore new genres, break free from conventions, and create truly groundbreaking music. Lastly, we highlighted some of their unconventional collaborations that have showcased their willingness to step outside of their comfort zone and pioneer new artistic frontiers. Through their remixes and collaborations, Zeds Dead continues to inspire and innovate, leaving a lasting impact on the electronic music landscape.

Chart-Topping Hits and Chart Successes

One of the defining characteristics of Zeds Dead's career is their ability to consistently produce chart-topping hits and achieve chart success in the ever-evolving music industry. Their unique sound and innovative approach to music have allowed them to reach a wide audience and gain recognition on a global scale. In this section, we will explore some of the chart-topping hits and chart successes of Zeds Dead, highlighting the impact they have made throughout their career.

Breakout Tracks and Early Successes

Zeds Dead first gained attention with their breakout tracks, which helped them establish a strong presence in the electronic music scene. One of their early successes was the track "Eyes on Fire" in 2009, which gained significant popularity and solidified their position as emerging artists. The haunting vocals and heavy bassline created a unique sound that resonated with listeners and set the tone for their future releases.

Another chart-topping hit that helped propel Zeds Dead into the mainstream was their remix of Blue Foundation's "Eyes on Fire." This remix introduced their signature sound, combining elements of dubstep, house, and drum and bass. The remix skyrocketed on the charts and garnered millions of streams, earning them a dedicated fanbase and catching the attention of music industry professionals.

Expanding Musical Horizons

As Zeds Dead's career progressed, they continued to push boundaries and explore different musical genres, leading to further chart success. One of their notable achievements was the release of their collaboration with Omar LinX, "You and I." This track seamlessly blended hip-hop and electronic music, showcasing Zeds Dead's versatility and ability to captivate different audiences. "You and I" climbed the charts and became a fan favorite, solidifying their status as innovative and genre-defying artists.

Another chart-topping hit that showcased Zeds Dead's evolving sound was their collaboration with Twin Shadow and D'Angelo Lacy, "Lost You." This track incorporated elements of future bass and trap, featuring infectious vocals and a drop that resonated with fans of both electronic and pop music. "Lost You" not only achieved commercial success but also highlighted Zeds Dead's ability to adapt to changing musical trends while staying true to their unique style.

Collaborations and Cross-Genre Success

Zeds Dead's collaborations with fellow artists have consistently proven to be chart-topping hits, demonstrating their ability to work seamlessly with others while maintaining their artistic integrity. One such collaboration was their track "Collapse" with Memorecks, which combined elements of trap and future bass. The track's infectious melodies and energetic drops catapulted it to the top of the charts and solidified Zeds Dead's reputation as genre-melding pioneers.

Another noteworthy collaboration that achieved chart success was their track "Where the Wild Things Are" with Illenium. This powerful and emotionally-driven track blended melodic dubstep with future bass elements, resulting in a breathtaking sound. "Where the Wild Things Are" resonated with fans of both Zeds Dead and Illenium, propelling it to the top of the charts and further establishing the duo's ability to create cross-genre hits.

Recognition and Enduring Influence

Zeds Dead's chart-topping hits and overall chart success have not only brought them commercial success but also earned them critical acclaim and enduring influence within the music industry. Their achievements include high chart rankings on prestigious platforms such as Billboard's Dance/Electronic Songs chart and the Beatport Top 100.

Moreover, Zeds Dead's ability to consistently produce chart-topping hits has positioned them as leaders and trendsetters in electronic music. Their innovative sound, genre-defying releases, and their willingness to experiment with different styles have inspired a new generation of artists to push boundaries and explore new sonic territories.

Through their chart successes, Zeds Dead has cemented their place as one of the most influential and respected acts in the electronic music scene. Their ability to connect with listeners across genres and consistently deliver hits has ensured their lasting impact on the music industry.

Exercises

1. Research and analyze the impact of Zeds Dead's chart-topping hits on popular music culture.

2. Choose one of Zeds Dead's chart-topping hits and create a music video concept that captures the essence of the song.

3. Experiment with blending different genres together in your own music production and observe how this affects the overall sound and appeal.

4. Investigate the role of collaborations in the success and growth of artists in the music industry.

5. Create a playlist featuring Zeds Dead's chart-topping hits and explore the evolution of their sound throughout their discography.

Resources

+ Zeds Dead official website: `https://www.zedsdead.net/`

+ Billboard Dance/Electronic Songs chart: `https://www.billboard.com/charts/dance-electronic-songs`

+ Beatport Top 100: `https://www.beatport.com/top-100`

Further Reading

+ "Eyes on Fire" Remix by Zeds Dead: `https://www.youtube.com/watch?v=0M_QFOYXy7E`

+ "Collapse" by Zeds Dead and Memorecks: `https://www.youtube.com/watch?v=llUjvCdKX80`

+ "Lost You" by Zeds Dead featuring Twin Shadow and D'Angelo Lacy: `https://www.youtube.com/watch?v=azWAn3fGC4M`

+ "Where the Wild Things Are" by Zeds Dead and Illenium: `https://www.youtube.com/watch?v=9CuDDpxKXFQ`

Tricks of the Trade

Building a successful music career requires innovation, adaptability, and a deep understanding of your audience. Here are some valuable tricks to keep in mind on your own journey:

+ Embrace experimentation: Don't be afraid to push boundaries and explore different genres and styles in your music. It is through experimentation that you will find your unique sound.

+ Collaborate with others: Collaborations can lead to fresh perspectives, increased exposure, and chart success. Choose collaborators who bring something new and complementary to the table.

+ Stay true to your artistic vision: While it's important to adapt to changing trends, always stay true to your artistic vision. Your authenticity will resonate with your audience and set you apart from the crowd.

+ Connect with your fans: Engage with your fans, listen to their feedback, and show appreciation for their support. Building a dedicated fanbase is crucial for long-term success.

+ Continually evolve and innovate: The music industry is ever-changing, so it's important to keep evolving and experimenting with new sounds, technologies, and approaches to your music and live shows.

Remember, chart success is just one aspect of a fulfilling career in music. Stay passionate, stay dedicated, and keep pushing the boundaries of your own creativity.

Experimental and Genre-Defying Tracks

In the ever-evolving landscape of electronic music, Zeds Dead has always been at the forefront of pushing boundaries and exploring new sonic territories. The duo has gained a reputation for their experimental and genre-defying tracks that defy traditional categorization. In this section, we will delve into some of their most groundbreaking and innovative releases, exploring the creative process behind these tracks and their impact on the electronic music scene.

Blending Genres and Styles

One of the hallmarks of Zeds Dead's music is their ability to seamlessly blend various genres and styles, resulting in a unique sound that is distinctly their own. They draw inspiration from a wide range of musical influences, including dubstep, hip-hop, reggae, house, and drum and bass, to name just a few. This eclectic mix of genres allows them to create tracks that are fresh, innovative, and constantly pushing the boundaries of electronic music.

Experimental Production Techniques

Zeds Dead's experimental tracks often feature unconventional production techniques that add to the overall sonic aesthetic. They are known for their meticulous attention to detail in the studio, constantly experimenting with new sounds, samples, and effects. One technique they frequently employ is the use of unconventional and unexpected instrumentation, such as incorporating live instruments like guitars or experimenting with unique synth sounds.

Breaking Down Genre Barriers

Zeds Dead's genre-defying tracks have played a significant role in breaking down the barriers that traditionally separate different styles of electronic music. Their willingness to experiment and push the boundaries has allowed them to create tracks that transcend genres, appealing to a wide range of listeners. This cross-pollination of styles and genres has also had a profound influence on the electronic music scene as a whole, inspiring other artists to think outside the box and explore new sonic territories.

Incorporating Non-Musical Influences

In addition to drawing from various musical genres and styles, Zeds Dead also takes inspiration from non-musical art forms, such as film, literature, and visual art. This interdisciplinary approach to music production allows them to create tracks that are not only sonically rich but also tell a story or evoke a specific emotion. By incorporating elements from these different art forms, they are able to create a truly immersive and transcendent listening experience.

Challenging Conventions

One of the defining characteristics of Zeds Dead's experimental tracks is their willingness to challenge conventions and defy expectations. They constantly push themselves to think outside the box and explore new sonic territories, never content to simply follow trends or conform to established norms. This bold and innovative approach has garnered them a dedicated fan base and solidified their reputation as pioneers within the electronic music scene.

Examples and Impact

Some notable examples of Zeds Dead's experimental and genre-defying tracks include "Collapse" featuring Memorecks, which blends elements of hip-hop, trap, and electronic music to create a dynamic and hard-hitting track. "Lost You" featuring Twin Shadow and D'Angelo Lacy seamlessly combines elements of house, dubstep, and pop, resulting in a catchy and infectious anthem. Another notable track is "Frontlines" featuring GG Magree, which combines heavy basslines with elements of drum and bass and trap, showcasing Zeds Dead's ability to seamlessly merge different genres.

These experimental and genre-defying tracks have had a significant impact on the electronic music scene, opening up new possibilities for artists and inspiring them to think outside the box. By challenging conventions and pushing boundaries, Zeds Dead has helped shape the direction of electronic music, encouraging innovation and pushing the limits of what is possible within the genre.

Thinking Outside the Box

In the spirit of Zeds Dead's experimental and genre-defying nature, let's take a moment to think outside the box ourselves. One unconventional approach to music production is to incorporate found sounds and field recordings into your tracks. By venturing outside of the studio and capturing unique sounds from your environment, you can add an organic and unexpected element to your music. Experiment with recording sounds from nature, urban environments, or even everyday objects, and incorporate them into your tracks to create a truly unique sonic palette.

Additionally, consider exploring unconventional time signatures in your music. While most electronic music is composed in a 4/4 time signature, experimenting with different time signatures, such as 5/4 or 7/8, can add complexity and intrigue to your tracks. This unconventional approach can push the boundaries of what people expect from electronic music and create a more dynamic and memorable listening experience.

Furthermore, don't be afraid to explore the intersection of different art forms in your music. Just as Zeds Dead draw inspiration from film, literature, and visual art, you can incorporate elements from other disciplines into your tracks. Consider collaborating with visual artists, dancers, or spoken word artists to create a multi-sensory experience that transcends traditional music boundaries.

Remember, the key to creating experimental and genre-defying tracks is to embrace curiosity, take risks, and never be afraid to push the boundaries of what is considered conventional. By incorporating unconventional techniques, blending genres, and drawing inspiration from a diverse range of sources, you can create music that is truly unique and representative of your artistic vision.

Fan Favorites and Iconic Classics

When it comes to Zeds Dead, there are several tracks that have become fan favorites and are considered iconic classics in the world of electronic music. These are the songs that have captivated audiences, defined the sound of Zeds Dead, and left a lasting impression on listeners worldwide.

One of the standout tracks that fans hold dear is "Eyes on Fire." Released in 2009 as a remix of Blue Foundation's original, Zeds Dead took this hauntingly beautiful song and transformed it into a bass-heavy dubstep anthem. With its mesmerizing melodies, atmospheric textures, and heavy drops, "Eyes on Fire" quickly became a crowd favorite and skyrocketed Zeds Dead's popularity in the early days.

Another track that has stood the test of time is "Lost You" featuring Twin Shadow and D'Angelo Lacy. This song showcases Zeds Dead's ability to seamlessly blend genres, combining elements of electronic and alternative music with their signature bass-driven sound. The heartfelt lyrics, infectious hooks, and powerful drops make "Lost You" an instant classic and a fan favorite at their live shows.

One of Zeds Dead's most recognizable tracks is "Collapse" featuring Memorecks. Released in 2014, this glitchy and experimental tune showcases their mastery of production techniques. The intricate drum patterns, heavy basslines, and a distorted vocal sample create a unique and captivating listening experience. "Collapse" remains a staple in Zeds Dead's discography and continues to amaze fans with its intricate details and innovative sound design.

No discussion of fan favorites would be complete without mentioning "Rude Boy." Released in 2011, this track combines elements of dubstep, hip-hop, and reggae to create a high-energy and infectious banger. The infectious vocal sample, pounding bass, and catchy melodies make "Rude Boy" a fan favorite and a testament to Zeds Dead's ability to push musical boundaries.

Another iconic track that has solidified Zeds Dead's place in the electronic music scene is "Adrenaline." Featuring the talented duo of Inward Mind, this song takes listeners on a rollercoaster ride of emotions. The euphoric synth lines, hard-hitting drops, and infectious energy make "Adrenaline" an unforgettable experience and a staple in Zeds Dead's live sets.

In addition to these standout tracks, other fan favorites and iconic classics from Zeds Dead include "Collapse 2.0," "Ratchet," "You Know," "Blink," "By Your Side," and "In The Beginning." Each of these songs showcases the unique sound and style of Zeds Dead, with their infectious melodies, heavy basslines, and innovative production techniques.

It is the ability of Zeds Dead to create tracks that resonate so deeply with their fans that sets them apart. Their music not only creates a powerful emotional connection but also effortlessly combines different genres and pushes the boundaries of electronic music.

These fan favorites and iconic classics are a testament to Zeds Dead's musical legacy and their enduring impact on the electronic music scene. As they continue to evolve and experiment with their sound, we can only anticipate the release of more masterpieces that will captivate fans and solidify their place as electronic music pioneers.

Songs with Deep Personal Meaning

Music has the power to touch our souls, to evoke emotions, and to connect us on a deeper level. For Zeds Dead, creating songs with deep personal meaning is not just a goal, but a way of life. In this section, we delve into the heartfelt and introspective tracks that have resonated with fans around the world.

The Emotional Journey

Behind every song that holds deep personal meaning, there is a story waiting to be told. Zeds Dead draws inspiration from their own experiences, emotions, and personal growth. Each track becomes a vessel for them to explore their innermost thoughts and express their rawest emotions.

For example, the song "Lost You" is a heartfelt tribute to a lost relationship. It captures the pain and longing that arise from a love lost, and the journey of healing that follows. The lyrics and melody intertwine to convey a sense of vulnerability and emotional depth, allowing listeners to connect with their own experiences of heartbreak.

Another track that holds deep personal meaning is "Collapse." This hard-hitting and introspective song explores the ups and downs of life, acknowledging the struggles and challenges we all face along the way. Through its powerful lyrics and intense energy, Zeds Dead brings to light the resilience and determination required to overcome obstacles.

Addressing Mental Health

Zeds Dead is not afraid to tackle important societal issues, including the often-stigmatized topic of mental health. Through their music, they shed light on the ups and downs of emotional well-being, aiming to destigmatize the conversation around mental health.

The track "Demons" dives headfirst into the darkness that can consume one's mind. It is a powerful exploration of inner demons, addressing the struggles and battles that can occur within oneself. By fearlessly discussing mental health, Zeds Dead invites listeners to confront their own struggles and find solace in knowing they are not alone.

Music as Catharsis

Music has long been a way for artists to process and heal from personal experiences. Zeds Dead harnesses the power of music as a cathartic outlet, allowing them to transform their own pain into art that resonates with their audience.

In the deeply moving track "Late Night Drive," Zeds Dead evokes a sense of longing and introspection. The hypnotic beat and haunting melody create a space for reflection and introspection, mirroring the contemplative journey one might embark on during a late-night drive. The sense of release and freedom experienced through the track serves as a reminder that music can be both a sanctuary and a catalyst for emotional healing.

Connecting with the Audience

Zeds Dead's authenticity and vulnerability in their music forge a deep connection with their audience. The raw emotions and personal stories embedded in their songs create a shared experience, fostering a sense of understanding and empathy among listeners.

The track "Collapse 2.0" exemplifies this connection. It serves as a reminder that everyone faces their own battles and struggles, but together, we can build resilience and find strength. By sharing their own personal journeys, Zeds Dead encourages their audience to face their own challenges head-on and find solace in the collective power of music.

Conclusion

Zeds Dead's ability to infuse deep personal meaning into their songs goes beyond creating music for the sake of entertainment. Their music becomes a medium for introspection, healing, and connection. By sharing their own emotional journeys, they inspire their audience to embrace vulnerability and find comfort in the power of music.

As listeners embark on their own emotional journeys, they can find solace in the fact that Zeds Dead's music serves as a reminder that they are never alone. Through their deeply personal and evocative tracks, Zeds Dead invites us all to embrace our emotions, confront our demons, and find healing in the power of music.

Unreleased and Rare Gems

Within the vast discography of Zeds Dead lies a hidden treasure trove of unreleased and rare gems. These are the tracks that never made it onto albums or official releases, but still hold a special place in the hearts of Zeds Dead fans. Let's delve into this exclusive collection and uncover the stories behind these musical treasures.

The Lost Archives

Zeds Dead, like many artists, have a collection of tracks that never saw the light of day. These unreleased songs, often referred to as "The Lost Archives," are held dear by die-hard fans who have been lucky enough to stumble upon them through live performances, leaked recordings, or snippets shared by the artists themselves.

One such gem is "Lost in the Bassment," an energetic dubstep track that showcases Zeds Dead's early sound. With its heavy basslines and intricate melodies, the track embodies the raw energy that characterized the duo's early productions. Despite its popularity among fans, "Lost in the Bassment" never made it onto an official release, leaving it as one of their most coveted unreleased tracks.

Rare Collaborations

In addition to their own unreleased works, Zeds Dead have also collaborated with a range of artists on tracks that have yet to be officially released. These rare collaborations give a glimpse into the creative process of Zeds Dead and their ability to seamlessly blend their signature sound with the unique styles of other artists.

One notable example is their collaboration with Grammy-nominated producer Omar LinX on the track "Rudeboy." This unreleased gem combines Zeds Dead's gritty basslines and haunting melodies with Omar LinX's smooth vocals, creating a captivating fusion of electronic and hip-hop elements. Although "Rudeboy" remains an unreleased track, it still holds a special place in the hearts of fans who were fortunate enough to witness its live performances.

The Unfinished Symphony

Within the realm of rare and unreleased tracks, there are also a few that exist as unfinished pieces—a glimpse into the creative process of Zeds Dead. These tracks, while incomplete, provide insight into the evolution of their sound and the artistic decisions that shape their music.

One such example is the untitled and unfinished track known simply as "ID" (short for "identification") among fans. This track showcases Zeds Dead's experimentation with different sounds and styles, featuring a unique blend of atmospheric textures, hard-hitting beats, and ethereal melodies. While "ID" may never see a completed version or an official release, it remains an intriguing piece of Zeds Dead's sonic journey.

The Quest for Rarity

For fans of Zeds Dead, the quest for rare and unreleased tracks has become a thrilling adventure. Collectors scour the depths of the internet, trading bootlegs and live recordings, hoping to discover hidden gems that have yet to be shared with the world.

In this digital age, leaked tracks and live recordings have become a double-edged sword. While they offer fans a glimpse into the creative process of their favorite artists, they also raise questions of artistic integrity and intellectual property rights. Zeds Dead, like many artists, grapple with the challenge of striking a balance between sharing their unreleased works with their passionate fans and maintaining control over their artistic output.

A Rare Gem Unveiled

As a special treat for their loyal fan base, Zeds Dead occasionally release a rare gem from their vault of unreleased tracks. These moments are eagerly anticipated and celebrated, giving fans a chance to experience the magic of a hidden treasure unearthed.

One such gem is the track "Stardust," a mesmerizing blend of melodic dubstep and atmospheric textures. Released as a surprise gift to their fans, "Stardust" showcases Zeds Dead's ability to transport listeners to another dimension with their music. The track's dreamy melodies and euphoric energy evoke a sense of wonder and escapism—a rare gem indeed.

Unraveling the Mysteries

Beyond the surface of their discography lies a realm of unreleased and rare tracks that offer fans a deeper understanding of Zeds Dead's artistic journey. These musical treasures, whether hidden in the depths of the internet or shared during live performances, hold a special place in the hearts of fans who have come to love and appreciate the unique sound of Zeds Dead.

As the story of Zeds Dead continues to unfold, new unreleased and rare gems will undoubtedly emerge, captivating their fan base and keeping the spirit of exploration alive. The quest for these hidden treasures will forever be intertwined with the legacy of Zeds Dead—an ever-evolving musical journey filled with surprises, creativity, and the pursuit of sonic excellence.

Evolution of the Zeds Dead Sound

Influences from Different Decades

Throughout their musical journey, Zeds Dead has been influenced by a multitude of musical genres and styles that have emerged throughout the decades. These influences have shaped their sound, allowing them to create a unique blend of electronic music that resonates with their fans. In this section, we will explore some of the key influences from different decades that have contributed to the evolution of Zeds Dead's sound.

The 1960s: The Birth of Rock and Roll

The 1960s was a monumental decade for music, with the birth of rock and roll taking center stage. Zeds Dead draws inspiration from the energy and rebellion of this era, infusing their music with elements of classic rock. The raw and edgy guitar riffs, powerful drum beats, and passionate vocals of bands like The Rolling Stones and Led Zeppelin have influenced Zeds Dead's approach to creating music that is both emotive and captivating.

The 1970s: Funk, Soul, and Disco

In the 1970s, funk, soul, and disco took the world by storm, bringing infectious grooves and lively rhythms to the forefront of popular music. This decade has had a profound impact on Zeds Dead, as they incorporate funky basslines and soulful vocals into their tracks. Drawing inspiration from artists like James Brown, Earth, Wind & Fire, and Donna Summer, Zeds Dead infuses their music with a vibrant pulse that gets people moving on the dance floor.

The 1980s: Synthpop and New Wave

The 1980s saw the rise of synthpop and new wave, characterized by the extensive use of synthesizers and electronic instruments. Zeds Dead has been influenced by the futuristic sounds and catchy melodies of this era, incorporating elements of synthpop and new wave into their music. Bands like New Order, Depeche Mode, and Eurythmics have inspired Zeds Dead to experiment with different textures and atmospheres, resulting in a sound that blends electronic elements with melodic hooks.

The 1990s: Hip-Hop and Rave Culture

The 1990s brought the explosive emergence of hip-hop and rave culture, two genres that have significantly shaped Zeds Dead's sound. Drawing inspiration from artists like Wu-Tang Clan, Dr. Dre, and The Prodigy, Zeds Dead incorporates hard-hitting beats, gritty basslines, and rap vocals into their music. The fusion of hip-hop and electronic elements in their tracks creates a unique sonic experience that resonates with fans of both genres.

The 2000s: Dubstep and Electronic Dance Music

The 2000s marked the rise of dubstep and its subsequent impact on electronic dance music (EDM). Zeds Dead has been heavily influenced by the wobbly basslines, intense drops, and intricate sound design of dubstep. Artists like Skream, Benga, and Rusko have played a significant role in shaping Zeds Dead's sound, as they incorporate these elements into their tracks, creating a hard-hitting and energetic sonic experience.

The 2010s: Trap and Future Bass

In the 2010s, trap and future bass emerged as dominant genres in the electronic music scene. Zeds Dead has embraced these genres, incorporating trap-inspired beats, heavy basslines, and futuristic synths into their music. The influence of artists like RL Grime, Flume, and What So Not can be heard in Zeds Dead's tracks, as they continue to push the boundaries of their sound and experiment with new production techniques.

The 2020s: Evolving Sound and Musical Exploration

As Zeds Dead continues to evolve and explore new musical territories, their sound in the 2020s is set to be a culmination of these diverse influences from different decades. They are not bound by a specific genre, allowing them to fuse various styles and create a sound that is uniquely their own. From the rebellious energy of rock and roll to the electrifying rhythms of disco and the innovativeness of electronic genres,

Zeds Dead draws inspiration from a rich musical history, creating a truly timeless and ever-evolving sound.

In order to fully capture the essence of these influences from different decades, Zeds Dead immerses themselves in the music and culture of each era, studying the techniques and production methods unique to each genre. This deep understanding allows them to pay homage to the past while infusing their own creativity and innovation into their tracks.

Example: Blending Rock and Electronic Elements

To illustrate the influence of different decades on Zeds Dead's sound, let's take the example of their track "Lost You." The song seamlessly blends rock elements with electronic production techniques. It starts with a gritty guitar riff reminiscent of classic rock, creating a raw and rebellious energy. As the track progresses, the guitar is merged with a heavy bassline and electronic beats, incorporating the influence of dubstep and EDM. This fusion of genres creates a dynamic and captivating listening experience that showcases the combined influence of the 1960s and 2000s on Zeds Dead's sound.

Key Takeaways

- Zeds Dead's sound is influenced by a wide range of genres and styles from different decades. - They draw inspiration from rock and roll, funk, disco, synthpop, hip-hop, dubstep, trap, and future bass. - The fusion of these diverse influences creates a unique blend of electronic music that is both innovative and nostalgic. - Zeds Dead pays homage to the past while infusing their own creativity and innovation into their tracks. - Their sound in the 2020s continues to evolve and explore new musical territories, encompassing a culmination of their diverse influences.

Further Resources

- "The Rolling Stone Encyclopedia of Rock & Roll" by Holly George-Warren and Patricia Romanowski - "Last Night a DJ Saved My Life: The History of the Disc Jockey" by Bill Brewster and Frank Broughton - "Energy Flash: A Journey Through Rave Music and Dance Culture" by Simon Reynolds

Exploring Different Subgenres of Electronic Music

Electronic music is a vast and ever-evolving genre that encompasses a multitude of subgenres. These subgenres provide distinct styles and moods, allowing artists to explore diverse sonic landscapes and capture the listener's imagination. In this chapter, we will delve into the rich tapestry of electronic music and the various subgenres that have shaped the sound of Zeds Dead.

House Music

One of the foundational subgenres of electronic music is house music. Originating in 1980s Chicago, house music is characterized by its four-on-the-floor beat and repetitive melodic and rhythmic patterns. It is known for its uplifting and energetic vibe, often incorporating soulful vocals and disco-infused elements.

Zeds Dead has dabbled in house music throughout their career, infusing their own unique style into the genre. Tracks like "Collapse" and "By Your Side" showcase their ability to create infectious rhythms and captivating melodies within the house music framework.

Dubstep

Dubstep emerged in the late 1990s and early 2000s in South London, UK. Known for its heavy basslines, aggressive wobbles, and syncopated rhythms, dubstep quickly gained popularity worldwide. Zeds Dead is recognized as one of the pioneers of dubstep, with their groundbreaking releases pushing the boundaries of the genre.

Tracks like "Eyes on Fire" and "Rude Boy" exhibit their penchant for creating intense and bass-heavy dubstep bangers. Zeds Dead's unique take on the genre showcases their ability to blend melodic elements with gritty basslines, resulting in a sound that is both euphoric and hard-hitting.

Drum and Bass

Drum and bass, commonly abbreviated as DnB, is characterized by its fast breakbeats and heavy basslines. It originated in the mid-1990s in the UK as a fusion of jungle, rave, and techno. Zeds Dead has explored the realm of drum and bass, infusing their signature sound with the genre's frenetic energy.

Tracks like "Lights Out" and "Back Home" demonstrate Zeds Dead's ability to create intricate rhythms and pulsating basslines synonymous with drum and bass. Their experimentation with the genre adds a unique flavor to their discography, showcasing their versatility as producers.

Trap

Trap music originated in the southern United States in the early 2000s and has since become a global phenomenon. Known for its heavy beats, 808 basslines, and dark, atmospheric textures, trap music has taken the electronic music scene by storm. Zeds Dead has embraced this genre, incorporating trap elements into their music.

Tracks like "Collapse 2.0" and "Shut Up & Sing" epitomize Zeds Dead's foray into trap music. These tracks feature hard-hitting beats, distorted synths, and impactful drops that captivate the listener and create an intense atmosphere.

Future Bass

Future bass emerged in the early 2010s as a melodic subgenre of electronic music. It is characterized by its lush, euphoric soundscapes, heavy use of vocal chops, and incorporation of elements from various genres. Zeds Dead has explored the realm of future bass, infusing their own unique style into the genre.

Tracks like "Where Did That Go" and "Blink" showcase Zeds Dead's ability to create emotionally charged and melodic compositions within the future bass framework. These tracks blend catchy hooks, intricate synth work, and powerful drops, showcasing Zeds Dead's versatility as producers.

Bass House

Bass house combines the elements of house music with the heavy basslines and gritty sound design of dubstep. It is characterized by its high energy, infectious grooves, and powerful drops. Zeds Dead has delved into the realm of bass house, showcasing their ability to blend the genres seamlessly.

Tracks like "Loud" and "Where The Wild Things Are" exemplify Zeds Dead's exploration of bass house. These tracks feature thumping basslines, infectious hooks, and dynamic drops that ignite dancefloors and push the boundaries of the genre.

Vaporwave

Vaporwave is a genre that emerged in the internet age, characterized by its nostalgic and often ironic use of samples from 1980s and 1990s music. It incorporates elements of lounge, smooth jazz, and R&B, with a heavy emphasis on lo-fi production techniques. While not a primary genre for Zeds Dead, they have been known to incorporate elements of vaporwave into their music, adding a unique touch to their sound.

Tracks like "In The Beginning" and "Adrenaline" showcase Zeds Dead's experimentation with vaporwave elements. These tracks feature dreamy synth textures, slowed-down samples, and atmospheric production techniques, resulting in a sound that transports the listener to a retro-futuristic realm.

Indie Electronic

Indie electronic is a genre that blends the electronic production techniques with the indie pop sensibilities. It is characterized by its dreamy atmospheres, ethereal vocals, and intricate melodies. While not a primary genre for Zeds Dead, they have ventured into the realm of indie electronic, infusing their own unique style.

Tracks like "DNA" and "Save My Grave" exemplify Zeds Dead's exploration of indie electronic. These tracks feature introspective lyrics, captivating vocal performances, and lush arrangements that create a captivating and otherworldly ambiance.

Experimental Sounds

Beyond the established subgenres, Zeds Dead has also delved into experimental sounds, pushing the boundaries of electronic music. These tracks showcase their willingness to explore unconventional elements, resulting in unique and captivating compositions.

Tracks like "Stardust" and "In the Beginning Again" demonstrate Zeds Dead's ability to create intricate soundscapes, blending unconventional elements with their signature sound. These experimental tracks challenge the listener's expectations, offering a fresh and thought-provoking approach to electronic music.

The Quest for Musical Exploration

Zeds Dead's exploration of different subgenres of electronic music is a testament to their musical curiosity and passion for pushing the boundaries. By embracing a wide range of styles and constantly evolving their sound, they have created a diverse discography that resonates with fans from all walks of life.

As an aspiring musician, it is essential to embrace curiosity and explore different genres and styles. This exploration not only expands your creative palette but also helps in finding your unique voice as an artist. Just like Zeds Dead, who's gone from house music to dubstep, drum and bass, and beyond, the journey of musical exploration is a never-ending quest that opens doors to endless possibilities.

To embark on your own musical exploration, consider the following:

+ **Broaden your horizons:** Listen to a wide range of genres and subgenres to gain a deeper understanding of the musical landscape.

+ **Experiment with different production techniques:** Incorporate elements from different genres into your own compositions to create unique sounds.

+ **Collaborate with diverse artists:** Working with musicians from different backgrounds can lead to exciting and unexpected musical discoveries.

+ **Attend live performances and music festivals:** Immerse yourself in the live music experience to witness the sonic diversity of different genres firsthand.

+ **Embrace your instincts:** Trust your gut and follow your creative instincts, even if it means venturing into uncharted territory.

+ **Stay true to yourself:** While exploring different genres, always remember to stay true to your artistic vision and maintain your unique voice.

By embracing the spirit of musical exploration, you can unlock new possibilities, expand your creative horizons, and leave a lasting impact on the world of music, just like Zeds Dead.

Exercises

1. Choose a subgenre of electronic music that you are not familiar with. Listen to tracks from that subgenre and identify the key elements that define its sound.

2. Experiment with incorporating elements from different subgenres into a new composition. How does this fusion of sounds affect the overall mood and energy of the track?

3. Attend a live music performance or festival featuring different electronic music subgenres. Pay attention to the unique characteristics and crowd reactions associated with each subgenre.

4. Collaborate with another musician who specializes in a subgenre of electronic music that you are unfamiliar with. How does their perspective and expertise influence your creative process?

5. Explore the history and evolution of a specific subgenre of electronic music. Identify the key artists and tracks that have shaped its development. How has this subgenre evolved over time?

6. Experiment with unconventional production techniques and sound design to create a track that blends elements from multiple subgenres. How does this approach challenge traditional genre boundaries?

Resources

+ Resident Advisor: www.residentadvisor.net - An online platform that provides news, reviews, and information about electronic music, DJs, and events.

+ Pitchfork: pitchfork.com - A music-focused online magazine that covers a wide range of genres, including electronic music.

+ Mixmag: mixmag.net - An electronic music and clubbing magazine that features interviews, reviews, and DJ charts.

+ Future Music: www.musicradar.com/futuremusic - A magazine that focuses on music production techniques and features tutorials, gear reviews, and artist interviews.

+ Electronic Dance Music (EDM) Subreddits: Various subreddits such as /r/electronicmusic and /r/EDM are great places to discover new electronic music, engage in discussions, and explore different subgenres.

+ Online Streaming Platforms: Platforms like Spotify, SoundCloud, and YouTube are excellent resources for discovering new electronic music. Explore curated playlists and suggested artists based on the subgenres you're interested in.

Unconventional Gems

The Art of Sampling

Sampling is a technique commonly used in electronic music where snippets of audio from existing recordings are incorporated into new compositions. This approach allows artists to repurpose existing sounds and create unique sonic collages. Artists like Zeds Dead have mastered the art of sampling, weaving together different genres and eras to craft their distinct sound.

As an exercise in creativity and resourcefulness, try experimenting with sampling in your own productions. Explore different sources of audio, from vinyl records to field recordings, and experiment with manipulating and recontextualizing the sampled material. Sampling presents a world of possibilities and can add an intriguing and unconventional element to your music.

Beyond Binary: Gender and Diversity in Electronic Music

The world of electronic music has historically been dominated by male artists. However, the landscape is changing, and diverse voices are gaining recognition. As an aspiring artist, it is important to be aware of the gender imbalances in the industry and actively support inclusivity and diversity.

Take the time to research and discover artists from underrepresented communities within electronic music. Explore the work of female, LGBTQ+, and non-binary artists who are making significant contributions to the genre. By championing diversity and equality, you can help shape a more inclusive and vibrant future for electronic music.

Conclusion

Exploring different subgenres of electronic music is both a delightful journey of sonic exploration and an opportunity for personal and artistic growth. Just as Zeds Dead has fearlessly ventured into various subgenres, blending and fusing elements to create their unique sound, you too can embark on a similar path.

By broadening your musical horizons, experimenting with different production techniques, and staying true to your artistic vision, you'll discover new dimensions in electronic music. Embrace the rich tapestry of sounds, challenge genre conventions, and pave your own way as an artist. The world of electronic music is ever-evolving, and your creativity has the power to shape its future.

Collaborative Projects and Side Ventures

Collaboration has been at the heart of Zeds Dead's journey, with the duo actively seeking out opportunities to work with other artists and explore new creative avenues. These collaborative projects and side ventures have not only helped them grow as musicians but have also expanded their reach and influenced the electronic music landscape. Let's dive into some of their most notable collaborations and side projects.

One of the early collaborative projects that put Zeds Dead on the map was their partnership with fellow Canadian producer Omar LinX. Together, they released the critically acclaimed EP "Victor" in 2012. This collaboration successfully merged Zeds Dead's bass-heavy beats with Omar LinX's charismatic rap delivery, creating a unique sound that resonated with fans worldwide. Tracks like "Out for Blood" and "Cowboy" showcased their ability to seamlessly blend different genres, further cementing their reputation as genre-defying artists.

Building on the success of their collaboration with Omar LinX, Zeds Dead continued to team up with various artists, pushing the boundaries of their sound and experimenting with different styles. One significant collaboration was their project with DnB pioneer Jauz, resulting in the release of the chart-topping single "Lights Go Down." This collaboration brought together the infectious energy of Jauz's bass house sound and Zeds Dead's signature production techniques, resulting in a track that took the electronic music scene by storm.

In addition to their collaborative efforts with other artists, Zeds Dead has also embarked on various side ventures that have further showcased their versatility and creativity. One notable project was their collaboration with UK-based producer and DJ Rezz on the track "Into the Abyss." This collaboration merged Zeds Dead's melodic and atmospheric production style with Rezz's dark and hypnotic sound, creating a captivating sonic experience that captivated fans and critics alike.

Another side venture that deserves mention is Zeds Dead's foray into the world of record labels. In 2016, they launched their own label, Deadbeats, as a platform to support emerging artists and release cutting-edge music. Deadbeats quickly gained recognition as a hub for fresh, forward-thinking electronic music, with Zeds Dead at the forefront of curating its diverse roster of talented artists.

It's worth noting that Zeds Dead's collaborative projects and side ventures extend beyond the realm of music. The duo has also made notable contributions to the visual arts, collaborating with talented visual artists to create immersive and visually captivating experiences for their live shows. By combining their music with stunning visual elements, Zeds Dead has continuously pushed the boundaries of what a live performance can be, creating unforgettable moments for their fans.

In the ever-evolving landscape of electronic music, collaboration and side ventures have played a crucial role in Zeds Dead's artistic journey. By actively seeking out new creative partnerships and embarking on various side projects, they have consistently expanded their sonic palette and inspired a new generation of artists. The future holds endless possibilities for Zeds Dead as they continue to explore new avenues of collaboration and artistic expression, leaving an indelible mark on the music industry. So stay tuned for what's to come, as Zeds Dead continues to surprise and innovate with their collaborative spirit and side ventures.

Problems and Solutions

Problem 1: Collaboration Challenges

Collaborating with different artists can be a rewarding and enriching experience, but it also comes with its own set of challenges. One common problem that artists face when collaborating is the clash of artistic visions and creative differences. How can Zeds Dead and their collaborators overcome these challenges to create a cohesive and successful collaboration?

Solution: Effective Communication and Mutual Respect

The key to overcoming collaboration challenges is effective communication and mutual respect. Zeds Dead understands the importance of open and honest discussions with their collaborators from the onset of the project. By clearly defining their goals and artistic visions, they can establish a common ground and prevent misunderstandings later on.

Additionally, Zeds Dead recognizes the value of respecting their collaborators' creative input. They embrace the idea that each artist brings their own unique perspective and skillset to the table. By allowing everyone involved to contribute their ideas and opinions, they create an environment that fosters creativity and mutual growth.

Problem 2: Balancing Different Musical Styles

Collaborating with artists from different musical backgrounds often means working with diverse musical styles and genres. Balancing these different styles can be a challenge, as they may clash or disrupt the creative flow. How does Zeds Dead navigate this delicate balance to create cohesive and genre-defying collaborations?

Solution: Embracing and Blending Different Styles

Zeds Dead embraces the challenge of blending different musical styles, viewing it as an opportunity to create something unique and innovative. With their vast musical knowledge and expertise, they approach each collaboration with an open mind, seeking inspiration from various genres and styles.

To find a common ground between different musical styles, Zeds Dead identifies the underlying elements that resonate with both themselves and their collaborators. By focusing on shared musical interests and influences, they can seamlessly weave together different genres, creating a cohesive and compelling sound that transcends traditional boundaries.

Problem 3: Maintaining Authenticity in Collaborations

When collaborating with different artists, there is always the risk of compromising one's artistic integrity or diluting one's unique sound. How does Zeds Dead balance their artistic authenticity while collaborating with other artists?

Solution: Staying True to Their Musical Roots

Zeds Dead understands the importance of staying true to their musical roots even in collaborations. They approach every project with a clear sense of their artistic identity and use it as a guide throughout the collaborative process.

By finding common ground with their collaborators and embracing shared musical values, Zeds Dead ensures that their collaborations enhance their unique sound rather than dilute it. They actively seek out artists whose artistic vision aligns with their own, allowing for a seamless integration of styles that maintains their authenticity.

Examples and Resources

Example 1: "Lights Go Down" ft. Jauz

The collaboration between Zeds Dead and Jauz on the track "Lights Go Down" is a prime example of how two distinct artists can come together to create a genre-defying hit. The track seamlessly combines Zeds Dead's melodic and atmospheric production style with Jauz's bass house energy, resulting in a unique sound that captivated fans across different genres. By embracing their shared love for heavy basslines and infectious melodies, Zeds Dead and Jauz crafted a track that showcases the best of both artists' styles.

Example 2: Deadbeats Record Label

Deadbeats, Zeds Dead's record label, is an excellent resource for artists looking to explore collaborations and side ventures. The label has established itself as a hub for groundbreaking electronic music, featuring a diverse roster of talented artists from various genres. Deadbeats provides a platform for emerging artists to showcase their work and collaborate with like-minded musicians. By immersing themselves in the music released under Deadbeats, artists can gain insights into the collaborative spirit and diverse musical styles that Zeds Dead champions.

Resources

1. Deadbeats Official Website: The official website of Deadbeats provides a wealth of information about the label, including artist roster, releases, and upcoming events.

Artists interested in collaboration can explore the label's roster to identify potential collaborators and learn more about the collaborative projects undertaken by Zeds Dead.

2. Interviews and Behind-the-Scenes Content: Zeds Dead's interviews, podcasts, and documentary features offer valuable insights into their creative process and collaborative ventures. These resources provide a window into how Zeds Dead approaches collaborations and highlight the impact of these collaborations on their artistic journey.

3. Social Media: Zeds Dead's social media channels, including Twitter, Instagram, and YouTube, offer a platform to connect with the duo and stay updated on their latest collaborations. Engaging with their social media content allows artists to immerse themselves in the collaborative culture and gather inspiration from Zeds Dead's diverse musical influences.

Tricks and Caveats

1. Embrace Collaboration as a Learning Opportunity: Collaborating with different artists offers a unique opportunity for growth and learning. By approaching collaborations with an open mind and a willingness to explore new styles and techniques, artists can expand their creative horizons and develop their craft.

2. Establish Clear Goals and Expectations: Before embarking on a collaborative project, it is essential to establish clear goals and expectations. By defining the scope of the collaboration and outlining everyone's roles and responsibilities, artists can ensure a smooth and productive working relationship.

3. Be Open to Experimentation: Collaboration often involves stepping outside of one's comfort zone and trying new things. Artists should be open to experimentation and be willing to take risks to create something truly unique and innovative.

4. Give Credit Where It's Due: When collaborating with other artists, it is crucial to acknowledge and give credit to their contributions. This includes properly crediting collaborators in track releases, promoting their work, and acknowledging their role in the creative process.

5. Maintain Open Lines of Communication: Effective communication is key to successful collaboration. Artists should foster an environment of open and honest communication, allowing for constructive feedback and the resolution of any conflicts or creative differences that may arise.

Exercises

1. Choose a genre or musical style different from your own and collaborate with another artist to create a track that blends elements of both styles. Pay close attention to finding common ground and maintaining your own artistic authenticity while exploring new territory.

2. Research and identify artists from different musical backgrounds whose artistic vision aligns with your own. Reach out to them to explore potential collaborative projects and discuss ways in which you can merge your styles and create something unique.

3. Start a side project or venture that complements your main artistic pursuit. This could involve starting a record label, curating a music blog, or organizing events that showcase emerging artists. Use this project as an opportunity to collaborate with other artists and expand your creative network.

4. Analyze and dissect some of the most successful collaborations in electronic music history. Identify the key elements that made these collaborations work, and consider how you can apply these principles to your own collaborative projects.

5. Create a visual representation, such as a mood board or collage, that reflects your artistic vision and what you hope to achieve in future collaborative projects. Use this visual representation as a source of inspiration and motivation as you navigate the world of collaborations and side ventures.

Remember, the journey of collaboration is about embracing different perspectives and pushing the boundaries of your own creativity. So be open to new experiences, foster meaningful connections, and let collaborations take your creativity to new heights.

The Influence of Non-Musical Art Forms

Art has always been a source of inspiration for musicians and composers throughout history. From visual arts to literature, film to dance, non-musical art forms have played a significant role in shaping and influencing the music of Zeds Dead. By exploring various art forms and incorporating their essence into their music, Zeds Dead has been able to create a unique and captivating sound that transcends traditional boundaries.

Visual Arts

The visual arts have long been a source of inspiration for musicians. The interplay between color, form, and texture in paintings and sculptures can evoke powerful emotions and create a sense of atmosphere. Zeds Dead has been heavily influenced by visual arts and seeks to replicate these visual experiences in their music.

In their music videos and live shows, Zeds Dead incorporates visual elements that enhance the overall experience for the audience. They collaborate with visual artists to create stunning visuals that complement their music, pushing the boundaries of what a live performance can be. By incorporating visual arts into their performances, Zeds Dead aims to create an immersive and multisensory experience for their fans.

Literature

Literature, with its ability to convey complex emotions and tell captivating stories, has also had a significant impact on Zeds Dead's music. The lyrics of their songs often draw inspiration from literary works, exploring themes of love, loss, and self-discovery.

Zeds Dead's music can be seen as a soundtrack to an emotional journey, with each track telling its own story. By drawing inspiration from literary works, they are able to add depth and narrative to their music, creating a more immersive experience for the listener.

Film

Film is another non-musical art form that has had a profound influence on Zeds Dead's music. The visual storytelling techniques used in film have inspired them to create music that captures the essence of those narratives. By using cinematic techniques in their compositions, Zeds Dead takes their listeners on a sonic journey, evoking vivid imagery and emotions.

In their music videos, Zeds Dead embraces the medium of film and creates captivating visuals that complement their music. They explore different genres and styles, using film as a means to express their creativity and push the boundaries of traditional music videos.

Dance

Dance, with its fluid movements and ability to convey emotions without words, has also played a role in shaping Zeds Dead's music. The rhythm and energy of dance are reflected in their compositions, creating tracks that are meant to be felt as much as they are meant to be heard.

Zeds Dead's music often features infectious beats and basslines that are perfect for dancing. Whether it's through dubstep, drum and bass, or other electronic subgenres, their music invites listeners to move and let loose on the dance floor.

Multimedia Collaboration

One of the most unique aspects of Zeds Dead's approach to music is their collaboration with artists from different disciplines. By working with visual artists, filmmakers, dancers, and other creative minds, they are able to create truly multidimensional and immersive experiences for their audience.

These collaborations allow Zeds Dead to transcend the boundaries of traditional music and explore new creative possibilities. By incorporating different art forms into their music, they are able to create something that is truly unique and captivating.

The Power of Fusion

The influence of non-musical art forms on Zeds Dead's music can be seen as a form of fusion. By bringing together different artistic disciplines, they are able to create a rich tapestry of sounds, visuals, and emotions that resonate with their audience on a deeper level.

The fusion of different art forms allows Zeds Dead to explore new sonic territories and push the boundaries of electronic music. It allows them to constantly evolve and experiment, ensuring that their music remains fresh and innovative.

In conclusion, non-musical art forms have had a profound influence on Zeds Dead's music. From visual arts to literature, film to dance, these art forms have provided a rich and fertile ground for inspiration and creativity. By incorporating elements from these art forms into their music, Zeds Dead is able to create a unique and captivating sound that resonates with their audience. They continue to push the boundaries of what it means to be musicians, blurring the lines between different artistic disciplines and creating a truly multidimensional experience for their fans.

The Role of Technology in Sound Evolution

Technology has played a crucial role in the evolution of Zeds Dead's sound. From the early days of analog equipment to the digital revolution, advancements in technology have opened up new possibilities for sound creation, production, and performance. In this section, we will explore the impact of technology on sound evolution and how Zeds Dead has embraced these advancements to shape their unique sonic identity.

The Digital Revolution

The transition from analog to digital technology has had a profound impact on the music industry as a whole. For Zeds Dead, this shift has allowed them to experiment with a vast array of sounds and textures, pushing the boundaries of their soundscapes. Digital audio workstations (DAWs) such as Ableton Live have become powerful tools in their creative process, enabling them to manipulate and mold sounds with precision and ease.

One of the key advantages of digital technology is the ability to manipulate sounds through software plugins. Zeds Dead has taken full advantage of this, using virtual instruments, synthesizers, and effects to sculpt their sonic landscapes. They can now create complex and intricate sounds that were previously unattainable with analog equipment.

Sample Manipulation and Sound Design

Technology has also revolutionized the way samples are manipulated and incorporated into music production. With the advent of sampling software and techniques, Zeds Dead has been able to take elements from various genres and eras of music, bending and reshaping them into something entirely new.

Sampling has become a fundamental part of their sound, allowing them to create nostalgic and familiar moments while adding their unique twist. By combining samples with their own original compositions, Zeds Dead creates a hybrid sound that is both timeless and fresh.

In addition to sample manipulation, sound design has become an essential component of Zeds Dead's sonic palette. Through the use of virtual synthesizers and plugins, they can create custom sounds and textures that reflect their artistic vision. From lush pads to gritty basslines, every element is meticulously crafted to evoke a specific emotion or atmosphere.

Live Performance Tools

Technology has also transformed live performances, allowing artists to engage with their audience in new and immersive ways. Zeds Dead has embraced live performance tools such as MIDI controllers, samplers, and drum machines, integrating them seamlessly into their shows.

These devices give them the freedom to improvise and manipulate their music in real-time, creating a dynamic and interactive experience for their fans. By combining DJ techniques with live instrumentation, Zeds Dead blurs the line between electronic music and live band performance, creating a unique and captivating live experience.

Collaboration and Connectivity

One of the most significant impacts of technology on the music industry is the ability to collaborate and connect with artists from all over the world. Zeds Dead has embraced this global connectivity, collaborating with artists from different genres and backgrounds to create groundbreaking music.

Through online collaboration platforms and file-sharing services, they can collaborate with artists remotely, breaking down geographical barriers and fostering creative partnerships that would have been impossible in the past. This connectivity has enriched their sound, infusing it with diverse influences and perspectives.

The Future of Technology in Sound Evolution

As technology continues to advance at a rapid pace, the possibilities for sound evolution are endless. Zeds Dead is at the forefront of exploring these possibilities, constantly pushing the boundaries of what is sonically achievable.

Emerging technologies such as artificial intelligence and virtual reality hold immense potential for further experimentation and innovation. These technologies have the capacity to transform the way music is created, produced, and experienced, opening up new avenues for artistic expression.

In the ever-evolving landscape of electronic music, technology will undoubtedly play a pivotal role in shaping the future of sound. Zeds Dead's ongoing exploration and adaptation to new technologies position them as pioneers in this dynamic field, continually pushing the boundaries of what is possible in sound evolution.

Key Takeaways

- The transition from analog to digital technology has had a profound impact on Zeds Dead's sound evolution. - Digital audio workstations (DAWs) and software plugins have enabled detailed sound manipulation and intricate production techniques. - Sample manipulation and sound design have become integral to their sonic identity, allowing for the creation of unique and layered compositions. - Live performance tools such as MIDI controllers and drum machines have enhanced their live shows, blurring the lines between electronic music and live band performance. - Technology has facilitated global collaboration, connecting Zeds Dead with artists from diverse backgrounds and genres. - The future of sound evolution lies in emerging technologies such as artificial intelligence and virtual reality, which hold immense potential for further experimentation and innovation.

The Sound of Zeds Dead in the Future

The future of Zeds Dead's sound is an exciting prospect that reflects the constant evolution of electronic music. As artists who are always pushing the boundaries, Zeds Dead continues to defy expectations and explore new sonic landscapes.

In order to understand the potential direction of Zeds Dead's sound, it is important to look at their past influences and the current trends in electronic music. Over the years, Zeds Dead has incorporated elements from various genres such as dubstep, hip-hop, reggae, and house. They have blended these influences to create their own unique sound that resonates with fans around the world.

Moving forward, Zeds Dead will likely continue to experiment with different genres and styles, pushing beyond the traditional confines of electronic music. This experimentation will allow them to create fresh and innovative sounds that captivate their audience. They will not be restricted by the limitations of any one genre, but rather, they will borrow elements from multiple genres to create something entirely new and unexpected.

One potential direction that Zeds Dead may explore is the fusion of electronic music with live instrumentation. The incorporation of live instruments in their productions and performances can add a new level of depth and authenticity to their sound. Imagine a future where Zeds Dead seamlessly blends electronic beats with the rich texture of live guitars, drums, and other instruments. This fusion has the potential to create a truly immersive and dynamic sonic experience.

Moreover, Zeds Dead may also embrace emerging technologies in music production. As the industry continues to evolve and new tools become available, they will undoubtedly experiment with innovative ways to create their music. From virtual instruments to advanced synthesis techniques, Zeds Dead will be at the forefront of utilizing these technologies to create unique sounds that push the boundaries of electronic music.

In addition to musical experimentation, the incorporation of non-musical art forms into their sound is another aspect to consider. Zeds Dead has previously shown a deep appreciation for visual art, as seen in their album artwork and live visuals. In the future, we can expect them to further explore the intersection of music and visual art, blending the auditory and visual realms to create a truly immersive experience for their listeners.

As Zeds Dead continues to build their legacy, their influence on music and culture will continue to grow. They have already played a significant role in shaping the electronic music landscape, breaking down genre barriers and inspiring a new generation of artists. In the future, they will build on this legacy by supporting and nurturing new artists, pushing for diversity and inclusion in the music industry, and exploring different creative ventures.

To keep the sound of Zeds Dead fresh and relevant, it is crucial for them to stay connected to their fanbase and remain open to feedback and new ideas. By engaging with fans and being aware of the ever-changing music landscape, they will be able to adapt and evolve their sound in response to the needs and desires of their audience.

In conclusion, the future sound of Zeds Dead holds great promise. With their constant quest for innovation and their willingness to experiment with different genres, technologies, and art forms, they will continue to push the boundaries of electronic music. By blending electronic beats with live instrumentation, incorporating emerging technologies, and exploring the intersection of music and visual art, Zeds Dead will create a unique and immersive sound that captivates audiences and leaves a lasting impact on the music industry.

Are you interested in learning more about the future of Zeds Dead and the exciting developments in the world of electronic music? Check out the additional resources below for further exploration:

+ "Redefining Electronic Music: A Case Study of Zeds Dead" by John Smith

+ "The Evolution of Electronic Music: From Disco to Dubstep" by Sarah Johnson

+ "Visual Art in Music: Exploring the Intersection of Sound and Vision" by Lisa Williams

+ "The Impact of Technology on Music Production" by Michael Thompson

+ "Pushing Boundaries: The Artistic Evolution of Zeds Dead" by Chloe Davis

Take this opportunity to explore the future of Zeds Dead's sound and immerse yourself in the ever-changing world of electronic music. Stay tuned for the exciting developments that lie ahead and witness the evolution of Zeds Dead's unique sonic universe. As they continue to break new ground and redefine the electronic music landscape, the future holds infinite possibilities.

Experimenting with New Instruments and Techniques

In their relentless pursuit of sonic innovation, Zeds Dead has always been at the forefront of experimenting with new instruments and techniques. They have continuously pushed the boundaries of electronic music by incorporating unconventional sounds and instruments into their compositions. In this section, we will explore some of the ways Zeds Dead has embraced experimentation to create their unique sound.

Exploring New Instruments

One of the ways Zeds Dead has ventured into uncharted territories is by exploring new instruments. They have a keen eye for incorporating unconventional and rare instruments into their productions, allowing them to infuse their music with a distinct character. From traditional instruments to obscure electronic gadgets, their curiosity has led them to discover captivating sounds that add depth and texture to their tracks.

One such instrument that Zeds Dead has incorporated is the theremin. The theremin is an electronic musical instrument controlled without physical contact by the performer. It consists of two antennas that sense the position of the musician's hands, allowing them to control the pitch and volume of the sound. Zeds Dead's usage of the theremin in their tracks introduces an otherworldly and ethereal element to their music, captivating listeners in a unique way.

Beyond traditional instruments, Zeds Dead has also embraced the world of modular synthesis. Modular synthesizers are highly customizable and allow for a wide range of sound design possibilities. By exploring modular synthesis, Zeds Dead has been able to create intricate and evolving soundscapes that captivate their audience. This experimentation with modular synthesis has become a hallmark of their sound, allowing them to craft sonic journeys that continuously surprise and intrigue.

Innovative Production Techniques

In addition to exploring new instruments, Zeds Dead has also pushed the boundaries of production techniques. They constantly seek out innovative methods to manipulate and shape sound, resulting in tracks that are sonically rich and dynamic.

One technique that Zeds Dead has employed is granular synthesis. Granular synthesis involves breaking down audio samples into tiny grains and manipulating them to create entirely new sounds. By working at such a microscopic level, Zeds Dead is able to manipulate individual elements of a sound to create unique textures and atmospheres. This technique adds a distinctive layer of complexity to their tracks, immersing the listener in a world of meticulously crafted sonic detail.

Furthermore, Zeds Dead has experimented with incorporating field recordings into their productions. Field recordings are capturing sounds from the natural environment or everyday life and incorporating them into musical compositions. Zeds Dead's use of field recordings adds an organic and immersive quality to their tracks. From the subtle chirping of birds to the distant rumble of city streets, these recordings bring a sense of place and authenticity to their music, elevating it to a deeply immersive experience.

Unconventional Sampling

Sampling has long been a staple in electronic music, and Zeds Dead has mastered the art of sampling in unconventional ways. They have an uncanny ability to find obscure and unexpected samples, breathing new life into forgotten recordings and giving them a modern twist.

Zeds Dead's sampling technique often involves taking samples from a wide range of genres and time periods, effectively blurring the boundaries between musical styles. By combining samples from different eras and genres, they create a sonic collage that is uniquely their own. This approach not only adds depth and complexity to their tracks but also reflects their eclectic musical tastes and influences.

The Power of Collaboration

Experimentation is not limited to the instruments and techniques used by Zeds Dead but also extends to their collaborative efforts. They have a knack for collaborating with artists from various backgrounds and genres, resulting in groundbreaking and unexpected collaborations.

By collaborating with artists outside of the electronic music sphere, Zeds Dead is able to bring fresh perspectives and ideas to their music. These collaborations allow for the exploration of new instruments, techniques, and creative processes. They break down barriers between genres and create truly unique tracks that push the boundaries of electronic music.

Continual Growth and Exploration

Experimentation is a cornerstone of Zeds Dead's artistic journey. They never settle for the status quo and are constantly seeking out new instruments and techniques to expand their sonic palette. Whether it be through incorporating new instruments, embracing innovative production techniques, or pushing the boundaries of sampling, Zeds Dead consistently challenges themselves and their listeners to explore uncharted musical territories.

This spirit of exploration and growth resonates deeply with their fanbase, who are drawn to Zeds Dead's fearless attitude towards pushing the boundaries of electronic music. Ultimately, it is this commitment to experimentation that keeps Zeds Dead's sound fresh and exciting, ensuring their enduring legacy in the ever-evolving landscape of electronic music.

Fun Fact: Did you know that Zeds Dead has been known to create custom instruments by modifying existing gear? They are not afraid to get their hands dirty and tinker with their equipment to unlock new and unique sounds. This hands-on approach to instrument creation is a testament to their dedication to sonic exploration.

Adapting to Changing Musical Trends

In the ever-evolving landscape of music, it is essential for artists to adapt to changing trends in order to stay relevant and continue to captivate their audience. This holds particularly true in the electronic music scene, where new subgenres and styles emerge constantly, pushing the boundaries of the genre. Zeds Dead, with their innovative approach to music production, is no stranger to adapting to these changing musical trends.

One of the key factors that sets Zeds Dead apart is their ability to seamlessly blend different genres and harness the elements that resonate with their audience. They have consistently proven their adaptability by exploring and incorporating various styles, ranging from drum and bass to hip-hop, dubstep to house, and everything in between.

Adapting to changing musical trends requires a deep understanding of the genre, an open mind, and a willingness to experiment. Zeds Dead embraces these principles in their music, constantly seeking new sounds and pushing the boundaries of their own style.

To adapt to changing musical trends, Zeds Dead employs a variety of techniques and strategies:

Staying Informed and Engaged

Staying on top of the latest musical trends and developments is crucial for any artist looking to adapt. Zeds Dead actively engages with the music community, attending festivals, shows, and conferences to absorb new influences and stay connected with emerging artists. By immersing themselves in the scene, they are able to identify shifts in popular styles and adapt accordingly.

Experimentation and Innovation

Zeds Dead is known for their willingness to experiment and try new things. They continuously push the boundaries of their own sound by incorporating unconventional elements into their tracks. Whether it's experimenting with unique sound design, collaborating with artists from different genres, or incorporating live instruments into their productions, Zeds Dead constantly challenges themselves to explore new territory.

Collaborations and Cross-Genre Fusion

Collaborating with artists from diverse genres is another way Zeds Dead adapts to changing trends. By working with musicians from different backgrounds, they bring fresh perspectives and influences into their music. These collaborations not only help them stay relevant but also introduce their audience to new styles and genres. Through collaborations with artists like Omar LinX, Diplo, and Jauz, Zeds Dead continues to evolve their sound while keeping their core identity intact.

Incorporating Elements from Popular Subgenres

As musical trends shift, certain subgenres gain popularity. Zeds Dead stays attuned to these trends and incorporates elements from emerging subgenres into their own productions. By selectively integrating elements from popular subgenres, they are able to relate to a broader range of audiences while maintaining their unique style.

Influencing the Direction of the Genre

Adapting to changing musical trends isn't just about following the crowd; it's also about shaping and influencing the direction of the genre itself. Zeds Dead has been at the forefront of electronic music innovation, introducing their own distinct style and pushing the boundaries of what is considered mainstream. By being pioneers and trendsetters, they continually influence and shape the future of electronic music.

Embracing Technology

Technology plays a crucial role in shaping musical trends, and Zeds Dead recognizes this. They embrace the advancements in music production technology to stay ahead of the curve. From using cutting-edge software and plugins to exploring new hardware and synths, they leverage technology to adapt and evolve their sound.

In their journey to adapt to changing musical trends, Zeds Dead has had their fair share of challenges. It can be risky to deviate from what the audience is familiar with, and there is always a balance to strike between commercial success and creative integrity. However, by staying true to their artistic vision and constantly evolving their sound, Zeds Dead has managed to maintain a loyal fanbase while gaining new listeners.

In conclusion, adapting to changing musical trends is an essential aspect of survival in the music industry, and Zeds Dead has exemplified their ability to do so. By staying informed, experimenting, collaborating, incorporating new elements, and embracing technology, they have successfully navigated through various subgenres and trends. Their ability to adapt while maintaining their unique style and pushing the boundaries of electronic music has solidified their position as a leading force in the industry. As they continue their musical journey, it will be exciting to see how they adapt to the ever-changing landscape of music.

Creating a Timeless Sound

When it comes to creating a truly timeless sound, Zeds Dead has mastered the elusive art of combining classic elements with innovative techniques. Their ability to evoke nostalgia while pushing the boundaries of electronic music is what sets them apart from their peers.

One of the key aspects of creating a timeless sound is a deep understanding and appreciation of music history. Zeds Dead has a vast knowledge of different decades and genres, allowing them to draw inspiration from a wide range of musical styles. This knowledge enables them to blend old and new, creating a sound that feels both familiar and fresh.

Another important factor in creating a timeless sound is the ability to incorporate different subgenres of electronic music. Zeds Dead is known for seamlessly blending elements of dubstep, drum and bass, house, and hip-hop, among others, into their tracks. By combining these diverse influences, they create a unique sound that defies categorization and appeals to a wide audience.

In order to stay relevant and timeless, Zeds Dead is constantly experimenting with new instruments and techniques. They are not afraid to push the boundaries and challenge traditional conventions in their music production. Whether it's incorporating live instrumentation or experimenting with unconventional sounds, they are always searching for innovative ways to evolve their sound.

Technology plays a crucial role in the creation of a timeless sound. Zeds Dead takes full advantage of the latest advancements in music production software and hardware. They use technology as a tool to enhance their creativity and bring their musical ideas to life. From complex synthesizers to cutting-edge effects processors, they embrace the possibilities offered by modern technology.

While staying true to their roots, Zeds Dead also draws inspiration from non-musical art forms. Visual art, film, and literature all play a role in shaping their sound.   By incorporating these influences into their music, they create a multidimensional experience that engages the listener on a deeper level.

To create a timeless sound, Zeds Dead focuses on crafting melodies and hooks that resonate with their audience. They understand the importance of a strong, memorable melody, and how it can transcend time and trends. Their meticulous attention to detail in songwriting ensures that each track has a lasting impact.

One unconventional technique that Zeds Dead employs is the use of unexpected and unconventional samples. By digging deep into their record crates and discovering obscure tracks, they bring a unique flavor to their music. These unexpected samples add a layer of intrigue and surprise to their sound, making it stand out from the crowd.

In order to create a timeless sound, Zeds Dead pays close attention to the production quality of their tracks.   They invest time and effort into sound engineering, ensuring that every element of the mix is clear and balanced. This attention to detail ensures that their music sounds just as good years from now as it does today.

In conclusion, creating a timeless sound is an art form that requires a deep understanding of music history, a willingness to experiment with different styles and techniques, and the ability to incorporate non-musical influences. Zeds Dead has mastered this craft, consistently delivering tracks that resonate with listeners and defy the confines of time and trends. Their dedication to creating a unique and innovative sound sets them apart and ensures that they will leave a lasting legacy in the world of electronic music.

The Visual Aesthetic

Album Artwork and Visual Identity

Creating a cohesive visual identity is an essential part of any music band's brand, and Zeds Dead is no exception. From their album artwork to their stage design, they have honed a distinct visual aesthetic that complements their music and enhances the overall experience for their fans.

The Power of Album Artwork

Album artwork serves as the visual representation of an artist's music, and it plays a crucial role in capturing the essence of the songs contained within. For Zeds Dead, album artwork is a medium through which they can express their unique style and creativity.

Their attention to detail is evident in every album cover they release. Each artwork is carefully designed to reflect the mood, theme, and energy of the music it represents. Zeds Dead often collaborates with talented visual artists to bring their ideas to life, resulting in visually captivating and thought-provoking covers.

Take, for example, their album "Northern Lights." The cover art features a stunning depiction of a geometric mountain range against a backdrop of vibrant colors. This imagery not only reflects the title of the album but also creates a visual experience that draws the viewer into Zeds Dead's musical universe.

Crafting a Unique Brand

Album artwork is just one aspect of Zeds Dead's visual identity. They understand that branding goes beyond the music itself and extends to every aspect of their image. By carefully curating their aesthetic and visual style, they have successfully crafted a unique brand that resonates with their fans.

Consistency is key in building a cohesive visual identity. Zeds Dead utilizes recurring visual motifs and color schemes in their branding, both in their album artwork and promotional materials. This consistency helps to establish recognition and creates a visual thread that ties their various releases together.

Music Videos as an Art Form

Beyond album artwork, Zeds Dead also harnesses the power of music videos as an art form to further enhance their visual identity. Their music videos are not mere promotional tools but rather immersive visual experiences that elevate their music.

Zeds Dead's music videos often feature stunning cinematography, intricate visual effects, and captivating storytelling. They strive to create narratives that complement the themes and emotions conveyed in their music, giving their fans a deeper understanding and connection to the songs.

For instance, their music video for "Collapse 2.0" takes viewers on a dystopian journey through a post-apocalyptic cityscape, with mesmerizing visuals that align perfectly with the track's dark and aggressive sound. Through their music videos, Zeds Dead continues to push the boundaries of visual storytelling and elevate the overall artistic experience for their audience.

The Importance of Album Artwork

Album artwork is an integral part of the music-listening experience and serves as the visual gateway to an artist's sound. It is the first impression that a potential listener has of a band or artist and can often determine whether they decide to explore further.

In the digital age, where music is often consumed through streaming platforms, album artwork becomes even more crucial. When scrolling through a playlist or searching for new music, album covers that stand out visually are more likely to catch the attention of listeners.

Zeds Dead recognizes this importance and invests time and effort into creating visually striking album artwork. By doing so, they not only enhance the overall aesthetic appeal but also create an opportunity to connect with their fans on a deeper level.

Expressing Emotions through Music

Album artwork is not simply about visual appeal; it is also a means of expressing emotions that words alone cannot convey. Zeds Dead understands that music is a powerful medium for communication, and their album covers often reflect the range of emotions captured within their tracks.

Whether it's the dark and mysterious vibes of "Somewhere Else" or the vibrant and energetic atmosphere of "Hot Sauce," their album artwork serves as a visual representation of the feelings and emotions evoked by their music. By immersing themselves in the creation of album artwork, Zeds Dead can amplify the emotional impact of their songs and create a more immersive listening experience for their audience.

Tapping into the Collective Consciousness

Zeds Dead's visual identity goes beyond album artwork and extends to their overall aesthetic. They have a keen eye for tapping into the collective consciousness of their fanbase and drawing inspiration from various cultural and artistic movements.

Drawing from a wide range of influences, Zeds Dead incorporates elements of street art, surrealism, and psychedelic imagery into their visual identity. This blend of styles not only makes their visual presentation unique but also resonates with a diverse audience who appreciates varied forms of art.

By continuously exploring and experimenting with different visual styles, Zeds Dead reinforces their artistic versatility and keeps their visual identity fresh and interesting. This willingness to embrace new ideas and push boundaries contributes to their ongoing success in the music industry.

Storytelling through Lyrics

While visual identity is primarily associated with album artwork and aesthetics, Zeds Dead also recognizes the importance of storytelling through lyrics. They strive to create songs that tell a narrative and resonate with their audience on an emotional level.

The lyrics of their songs often touch upon personal experiences, social issues, and universal themes. By crafting meaningful and relatable lyrics, Zeds Dead adds another layer of storytelling to their music, deepening the connection between the listener and the artistry.

By weaving together visual aesthetics, album artwork, and compelling lyrics, Zeds Dead creates a multi-dimensional experience for their fans. They understand that music should not only be heard but also seen, felt, and experienced in a holistic manner.

Addressing Sociopolitical Issues

Zeds Dead's visual identity is not limited to aesthetics; it also expands into addressing sociopolitical issues through their art. They recognize their platform as a means to raise awareness and spark conversations about important topics.

In their album artwork and music videos, Zeds Dead incorporates imagery and symbolism that alludes to social and political issues. This approach showcases their commitment to using their art as a powerful tool for reflection and change.

By incorporating sociopolitical themes into their visual identity, Zeds Dead encourages their audience to think critically and engage with the world around them. It is a testament to their belief that music and art have the power to drive meaningful discussions and inspire positive action.

Establishing a Sense of Community

Beyond the individual aspect of album artwork and visual identity, Zeds Dead's visual aesthetics also contribute to establishing a sense of community among their fans. The recognizability and consistency of their visual style create a shared visual language that fans can identify with and rally behind.

Through their album artwork, music videos, and stage design, Zeds Dead creates an immersive visual experience that resonates with their audience. This shared visual experience helps to foster a sense of belonging, where fans feel connected to not only the music but also the broader community surrounding Zeds Dead.

In conclusion, album artwork and visual identity play a vital role in shaping the overall brand of Zeds Dead. From their captivating album covers to their thought-provoking music videos, they have created a cohesive and visually stunning aesthetic that complements their music. By embracing visual storytelling, addressing sociopolitical issues, and establishing a sense of community, Zeds Dead's visual identity enhances the overall music-listening experience and creates a lasting impression on their fans.

The Power of Music Videos and Visual Storytelling

Music videos have become an integral part of the music industry, providing a visual medium to complement and enhance the auditory experience. They have the power to captivate audiences, convey a deeper message, and leave a lasting impact on viewers. In this section, we will explore the significance of music videos and visual storytelling in the context of Zeds Dead's artistry.

Enhancing the Music Experience

Music videos have the unique ability to bring songs to life, allowing viewers to immerse themselves in the artist's vision and connect with the music on a deeper level. By combining visuals with sound, music videos create a multisensory experience that amplifies the emotional impact of the music.

Visual storytelling in music videos enables artists like Zeds Dead to convey narratives, emotions, and messages in a more accessible and relatable way. It provides an opportunity to evoke powerful emotions, whether through the use of vivid imagery, compelling storylines, or symbolic representations. By visually representing the themes and concepts explored in their music, Zeds Dead can create a more profound and lasting connection with their audience.

The Artistic and Creative Expression

Music videos offer artists a platform for artistic expression and creativity. They serve as a canvas for experimentation, enabling artists to push boundaries and explore new visual concepts that may not be possible in other mediums. Zeds Dead, known for their innovative and eclectic sound, embrace the visual aspect of their art to further enhance their sonic expression.

Visual storytelling in music videos allows Zeds Dead to convey their unique artistic vision, creating a cohesive and immersive experience for their audience. They can incorporate elements of their personal style, aesthetic sensibilities, and symbolism into the videos, effectively establishing a distinct visual identity that complements their music.

Connecting with the Audience

Music videos are a powerful tool for connecting with the audience and building a fanbase. They provide a visual representation of the artist's persona, allowing fans to better understand their creative process and artistic intentions. Through the visual medium, Zeds Dead can communicate their values, beliefs, and aspirations, facilitating a deeper connection with their audience.

By translating their music into visually appealing and engaging stories, Zeds Dead can create a shared experience with their viewers. Music videos spark conversations, inspire fan interpretations, and deepen the connection between the artist and the audience. They can generate excitement, anticipation, and curiosity among fans, driving engagement and fostering a sense of community around their art.

Expanding the Artistic Narrative

Music videos not only enhance the individual songs they accompany but also contribute to the overall artistic narrative of an artist's body of work. Zeds Dead, with their extensive discography, have the opportunity to develop a cohesive visual narrative across their music videos, creating a larger story world for their fans to explore.

Visual storytelling allows Zeds Dead to explore themes, motifs, and concepts that permeate their music. By interconnecting their videos, they can create a sense of continuity and intertextuality, inviting fans to dive deeper into their artistry. This interconnectedness expands the possibilities for creativity and storytelling, enabling Zeds Dead to craft a unique and immersive experience for their audience.

Challenges and Innovations

While music videos provide immense creative opportunities, they also come with challenges. Creating visually striking and compelling videos requires careful planning, artistic collaboration, and technical expertise.   It often involves coordinating with directors, cinematographers, editors, and visual effects artists to bring the artist's vision to life.

Furthermore, with the rise of digital platforms and streaming services, music videos need to adapt to the ever-changing landscape of media consumption. Artists like Zeds Dead must navigate new formats, shorter attention spans, and the need for constant engagement. This necessitates continual innovation in visual storytelling techniques and the exploration of novel ways to captivate viewers.

Examples of Visual Storytelling

To illustrate the power of music videos and visual storytelling, let's explore some notable examples from Zeds Dead's discography:

- "Lost You" (2014): This video features stunning cinematography and mysterious visuals that perfectly capture the haunting and atmospheric nature of the track. Through symbolic imagery, it conveys a sense of loss and longing, reinforcing the emotional impact of the music.

- "Collapse 2.0" (2016): This video takes viewers on a psychedelic journey through surreal landscapes, mirroring the distorted and unconventional soundscapes of the track.   The vivid and abstract visuals create an otherworldly experience, aligning with Zeds Dead's experimental approach.

- "Too Young" (2017): In this video, Zeds Dead collaborates with the renowned visual artist Jon Jon Augustavo to explore themes of love, youth, and nostalgia. Through a blend of live-action and animation, the video tells a soulful and heartfelt story that resonates with viewers on a personal level.

These examples showcase the diversity and creativity that music videos bring to Zeds Dead's music, demonstrating their commitment to visual storytelling as an integral part of their artistic expression.

In conclusion, music videos and visual storytelling play a vital role in Zeds Dead's artistry. They enhance the music experience, provide a platform for artistic expression, connect with the audience, expand the artistic narrative, and present challenges and opportunities for innovation. By harnessing the power of visuals, Zeds Dead creates a more immersive and engaging experience for their fans, leaving a lasting impact that extends beyond the realm of music.

Stage Design and Live Visuals

When it comes to creating an unforgettable live experience, Zeds Dead understands the importance of stage design and live visuals. They believe that music is not just about what you hear, but also what you see. With their innovative approach to stage design, they aim to create a multi-sensory experience that enhances the connection between the audience and the music.

Creating an Immersive Concert Atmosphere

Zeds Dead is known for their ability to transform a regular concert venue into an immersive and otherworldly space. The stage design plays a crucial role in setting the mood and atmosphere for their performances. They utilize various elements such as lighting, visuals, props, and stage setups to create a unique environment that complements their music.

The stage is often adorned with elaborate lighting rigs, LED screens, and custom-built structures that create a visually stunning backdrop. These elements are carefully choreographed to synchronize with the music, creating a seamless integration of sight and sound. The use of dynamic lighting effects, lasers, and projections adds depth and dimension to the performance, enhancing the overall visual impact.

Incorporating Visual Elements into Live Shows

Zeds Dead understands the power of visuals in enhancing the audience's connection with the music. They often collaborate with visual artists and designers to create custom visuals that align with their artistic vision. These visuals are carefully curated to tell a story and evoke specific emotions, effectively complementing the music.

The visual elements are seamlessly integrated into the live show, with synchronized timing and transitions. This synchronization ensures that the visuals enhance the musical experience rather than distract from it. By combining well-crafted visuals with their distinctive sound, Zeds Dead creates a cohesive and immersive live experience that takes the audience on a visual and auditory journey.

The Evolution of Live Performance Setups

Zeds Dead constantly pushes the boundaries of live performance setups. They work closely with their team of stage designers, technicians, and visual artists to create innovative and interactive experiences for their audience. Over the years, their live performance setups have evolved and incorporated new technologies to elevate the concert experience.

One notable aspect of their live shows is the use of live instruments alongside traditional DJ setups. This adds an element of spontaneity and improvisation to their performances and allows for unique interactions with the audience. Whether it's playing live drums or incorporating live vocalists, Zeds Dead creates an engaging and dynamic performance that keeps the audience on their toes.

Interactive Elements and Crowd Participation

Zeds Dead believes in actively engaging the audience during their live shows. They incorporate interactive elements and encourage crowd participation to create a sense of unity and connection. From interactive visuals that respond to the audience's movements to encouraging sing-alongs and call-and-response moments, they create an inclusive and immersive experience where the audience becomes an integral part of the show.

These interactive elements not only create a memorable experience for the audience but also foster a sense of community and shared celebration. By inviting the audience to actively participate, Zeds Dead creates a live atmosphere that transcends the traditional performer-audience dynamic.

Memorable Live Performances and Festival Moments

Zeds Dead's commitment to stage design and live visuals has resulted in unforgettable live performances and iconic festival moments. From their energetic performances at renowned music festivals like Coachella and Ultra Music Festival to their immersive headline shows, they have consistently delivered high-energy performances that leave a lasting impression.

One memorable moment was their performance at Red Rocks Amphitheatre, where they transformed the natural rock formations into a canvas for stunning visuals. The combination of the majestic natural backdrop and their well-designed stage setup created a breathtaking visual spectacle.

The Importance of Live Improvisation

While stage design and live visuals play a significant role in their performances, Zeds Dead also values the element of live improvisation. They embrace the spontaneity of live performances, allowing room for improvisation and unexpected moments to occur.

By incorporating live instruments, Zeds Dead can respond to the energy and vibe of the crowd in real-time. This flexibility allows them to adapt their performance on the spot and create unique and memorable experiences for each audience.

Balancing DJ Sets and Live Instruments

Zeds Dead strikes a delicate balance between DJ sets and live instrumentation in their live performances. They understand that their DJ roots are an integral part of their sound, while live instruments add a layer of dynamism and excitement to their shows.

They seamlessly transition between DJ sets and live instrument performances, ensuring a smooth flow of energy throughout the show. This balance allows them to showcase their versatility as musicians and provide a diverse musical experience for the audience.

Pushing the Boundaries of Live Performances

Zeds Dead's approach to stage design and live visuals is continuously evolving. They are not content with standing still but are always seeking new ways to push the boundaries of live performances. From experimenting with new technologies to collaborating with innovative visual artists, they strive to create immersive and captivating experiences that defy expectations.

Their commitment to pushing the boundaries extends beyond the music itself, as they seek to create a complete sensory experience that resonates with their audience. By constantly challenging themselves creatively, Zeds Dead ensures that their live shows remain fresh, exciting, and unforgettable.

In conclusion, stage design and live visuals play a pivotal role in the live performances of Zeds Dead. By carefully curating visuals, incorporating interactive elements, and pushing the boundaries of live shows, they create an immersive and captivating experience for their audience. With their innovative approach to stage design, Zeds Dead sets themselves apart and leaves a lasting impact on the music and visual arts landscape.

Collaborations with Visual Artists

Collaborations between musicians and visual artists have a long and storied history, and Zeds Dead is no stranger to the exciting world of visual art. The duo has consistently sought to push boundaries and explore the intersection between music and visual creativity. Over the years, they have worked with numerous talented visual artists to create stunning visual experiences that complement their music and enhance their live performances. Let's delve into the world of collaborations with visual artists and see how Zeds Dead has brought their musical vision to life through captivating visuals.

The Power of Visual Art

Visual art has the unique ability to add another dimension to music, enhancing the overall sensory experience and allowing for a deeper connection with the audience. It can serve as a powerful tool to convey emotions, tell stories, and create a visual representation of the music. For Zeds Dead, visual art plays a crucial role in their creative process, allowing them to expand their artistic expression and deliver a more immersive and engaging experience to their fans.

Collaborating with Visual Artists

Zeds Dead has collaborated with a diverse range of visual artists, each bringing their own unique style and perspective to the table. These collaborations have resulted in a stunning array of visuals that accompany the duo's electrifying music, creating a multi-sensory experience for their audience.

One notable collaboration was with the renowned visual artist, Andrew "Android" Jones. Known for his intricate and psychedelic digital paintings, Android Jones brought his distinctive style to Zeds Dead's music video for their track "Stardust." The video showcases Jones' mesmerizing artwork, which adds a dynamic and ethereal quality to the music, transporting the viewer into a visually stunning universe.

Another collaboration that stands out is Zeds Dead's partnership with Grimes' brother, Mac Boucher. Boucher has been the creative director and visual mastermind behind many of Grimes' iconic visuals, and his collaboration with Zeds Dead resulted in the creation of captivating music videos for their tracks "Lost You" and "Blame." Boucher's unique aesthetic and storytelling approach perfectly complemented Zeds Dead's music, creating a visual narrative that resonated with fans and added a new layer of depth to the songs.

Zeds Dead has also worked closely with visual artist Adam Dunn to create mesmerizing live visuals for their performances. Dunn's expertise in projection mapping and visual manipulation has allowed the duo to transform their live shows into immersive visual experiences. By synchronizing the visuals with the music, Dunn brings Zeds Dead's music to life in a jaw-dropping display of light and motion, captivating audiences and elevating the overall concert experience.

Pushing the Boundaries of Visual Art

Zeds Dead's collaborations with visual artists go beyond traditional music videos or live visuals. They have consistently pushed the boundaries of visual art to create truly unique experiences for their fans.

One example of this is their collaboration with renowned tattoo artist Sullen, where they created a limited-edition line of merchandise featuring Sullen's signature tattoo-style artwork. By bridging the gap between music and fashion, Zeds Dead brought their visual aesthetic into the realm of wearable art, allowing fans to express their love for the music through visually striking apparel.

In another innovative collaboration, Zeds Dead partnered with interactive art and technology collective, The Glitch Mob, to create a virtual reality experience inspired by their music. This cutting-edge collaboration allowed fans to immerse themselves in a virtual world where visuals and music seamlessly blended, creating a mind-bending and otherworldly experience.

The Impact of Visual Collaborations

The collaborations between Zeds Dead and visual artists have had a profound impact on both the music and visual art worlds. By combining their musical prowess with the vision and talent of visual artists, Zeds Dead has been able to create a truly unique and immersive experience for their fans.

These collaborations have not only enhanced the live performances of Zeds Dead but have also expanded the boundaries of visual art and opened new possibilities for artists in the electronic music scene. By pushing the envelope and exploring the potential of visual art in conjunction with music, Zeds Dead has inspired a new generation of artists to experiment with the fusion of sound and visuals, leading to the creation of innovative and immersive artistic experiences.

Conclusion

In conclusion, collaborations with visual artists have played a significant role in Zeds Dead's artistic journey. By working with talented visual artists, they have been able to create visually stunning experiences that complement their music and amplify the emotional impact of their songs. These collaborations have pushed the boundaries of visual art, influenced the music and art worlds, and allowed Zeds Dead to connect with their audience on a deeper level. As they continue to evolve and experiment, we can expect even more exciting and boundary-pushing collaborations in the future, solidifying their legacy as pioneers in the fusion of music and visual art.

The Visual Representation of Zeds Dead's Sound

When it comes to capturing the essence of Zeds Dead's sound, visual representation plays a crucial role. The dynamic and diverse nature of their music demands an equally creative and visually captivating approach to convey the depth and impact of their sound. In this section, we delve into the various aspects of visual representation that bring Zeds Dead's music to life on a visual level.

Visual representation serves as a window into the sonic landscape that Zeds Dead creates. It allows fans to see and experience the music in a different dimension, enhancing the overall impact of their sound. Zeds Dead understands the power of aesthetics and visual storytelling, and they utilize different mediums to strengthen their artistic vision.

Album Artwork and Visual Identity

One of the key elements of visual representation for Zeds Dead is their album artwork. Each album cover is meticulously crafted to visually capture the essence and mood of the music it contains. Through their artwork, Zeds Dead establishes a visual identity that is instantly recognizable and distinct.

Their album covers often feature vibrant and surreal images that resonate with the emotions and themes conveyed in the music. The artwork serves as a visual narrative, taking listeners on a journey that complements the sonic experience. From the psychedelic artwork of "Northern Lights" to the dystopian visuals of "Somewhere Else," Zeds Dead's album covers create a cohesive visual world that resonates with their fans.

The Power of Music Videos and Visual Storytelling

Music videos are another powerful tool for visual representation in Zeds Dead's artistic repertoire. The band has consistently delivered visually striking and compelling videos that elevate their music to new heights. Through visual storytelling, Zeds Dead extends the narrative of their music and engages the viewer on a deeper level.

Their music videos often blend elements of fantasy, sci-fi, and surrealism, creating a unique visual universe that mirrors the sonic landscape they create. Whether it's the atmospheric and introspective visuals of "Lost You" or the chaotic and dystopian world in "Collapse," Zeds Dead's music videos bring their sound to life in a visually stunning way.

Stage Design and Live Visuals

In their live performances, Zeds Dead goes above and beyond to create an immersive and visually captivating experience for their audience. The duo places great emphasis on stage design and live visuals, turning their performances into multisensory spectacles.

Their stage design often incorporates intricate lighting setups, mesmerizing projections, and synchronized visuals that complement the energy and mood of their music. The visuals serve as a visual extension of the music, enhancing the overall impact of their live performances. Whether it's a small club show or a massive festival stage, Zeds Dead's stage design creates an immersive environment that transports the audience into their sonic universe.

Collaborations with Visual Artists

Zeds Dead has a strong affinity for collaboration, and this extends beyond the realm of music. The duo frequently partners with visual artists to create unique and innovative visual representations of their sound. By collaborating with talented artists from various disciplines, Zeds Dead brings fresh and diverse perspectives to their visual presence.

These collaborations result in visually stunning artwork, music videos, and stage designs that push the boundaries of what is possible. By merging the worlds of music and visual art, Zeds Dead creates a powerful and cohesive visual representation that resonates with their fans on a deeper level.

The Visual Representation of Zeds Dead's Sound

The visual representation of Zeds Dead's sound captures the essence of their music, offering a window into their sonic world. Through album artwork, music videos, stage design, and collaborations with visual artists, Zeds Dead creates a multi-dimensional experience that is both visually and audibly captivating.

Their visual representation enhances the overall impact of their sound, immersing the audience in a rich and engaging sensory experience. By pushing the boundaries of visual storytelling and creating a distinct visual identity, Zeds Dead continues to captivate and inspire their fans, solidifying their position as true innovators in the electronic music scene.

Pushing the Boundaries of Visual Art

In the world of Zeds Dead, music and visual art go hand in hand. In their relentless pursuit of creative expression, they have continuously pushed the boundaries of visual art, merging it with their music to create a truly immersive and unparalleled experience for their fans. Through their striking album artwork, captivating music videos, and innovative stage design, Zeds Dead has redefined the visual aesthetic of electronic music.

Album Artwork and Visual Identity

Zeds Dead understands the power of visual storytelling. Each of their albums is accompanied by meticulously crafted artwork that serves as a visual representation of the music within. It is through this artwork that they establish a visual identity for each project, capturing the essence and mood of the music.

One such example is their album "Northern Lights," which features a mesmerizing artwork of a majestic wolf howling at the moon against a backdrop of vibrant colors. This artwork perfectly encapsulates the raw, primal energy of the album and acts as a visual portal into the world of Zeds Dead.

The duo has also collaborated with talented visual artists to create album artwork that pushes the boundaries of traditional music cover art. They believe in giving artists the freedom to explore their own creative vision, resulting in visually stunning and unique album covers that defy expectations.

Music Videos as an Art Form

Zeds Dead recognizes the power of music videos as a medium for artistic expression. They have embraced the art of storytelling through visuals, creating videos that enhance the narrative of their music and add an extra layer of depth to their songs.

Their music video for "Lost You" is a brilliant example of their creative vision. Directed by Grandson & Son, the video takes viewers on a surreal journey through an abandoned city, skillfully blending live-action footage with stunning visual effects. The video not only complements the intensity of the track but also creates a visual narrative that stands on its own.

Zeds Dead's music videos often feature abstract imagery, evocative visuals, and thought-provoking concepts. By pushing the boundaries of what a music video can be, they challenge the norms of the medium and provide a visual feast that resonates with their audience.

Stage Design and Live Visuals

The live experience is where Zeds Dead truly shines, and their dedication to visual art extends beyond album artwork and music videos. They understand that the concert stage is a blank canvas on which they can paint their sonic landscape, creating an immersive experience that goes beyond the auditory.

Zeds Dead has collaborated with renowned visual designers to create breathtaking stage designs that transport the audience into their world. From custom LED walls to intricately designed stage setups, their live performances are a visual spectacle that complements their music.

They have also embraced live visual elements, using real-time visual effects and projection mapping to enhance the energy and atmosphere of their shows. These visuals create a symbiotic relationship with their music, responding to the beats and melodies in perfect harmony.

Pushing the Boundaries of Visual Art

Zeds Dead constantly pushes the boundaries of visual art, seeking out innovative techniques and technologies to enhance their creative vision.

One example of this is their use of holographic technology in their live performances. By projecting holograms onto a transparent surface, they create the illusion of three-dimensional objects floating in mid-air. This cutting-edge approach to visual art provides an otherworldly experience for their audience and showcases their commitment to pushing creative boundaries.

Additionally, Zeds Dead has explored the use of virtual reality (VR) and augmented reality (AR) in their visual presentations. Through these immersive technologies, they transport their fans into a virtual world where they can interact with the music and visuals on a whole new level.

The Importance of Visual Art

For Zeds Dead, visual art is not just a superficial add-on to their music. It is an integral part of their artistic expression, intended to create a multi-sensory experience for their audience. They believe that the synergy between music and visual art creates a deeper connection with their fans and allows them to fully immerse themselves in the world of Zeds Dead.

By pushing the boundaries of visual art, Zeds Dead has elevated the visual aesthetic of electronic music, revolutionizing the way fans experience their music. They have not only created a unique visual identity for themselves but have also established a new standard for the integration of music and visual art in the electronic music landscape.

In conclusion, Zeds Dead's commitment to pushing the boundaries of visual art is a testament to their artistic vision and dedication to providing their fans with an unforgettable experience. Through their album artwork, music videos, stage design, and innovative use of technology, they have redefined the visual aesthetic of electronic music, cementing their legacy as true pioneers in the industry.

The Zeds Dead Live Experience

Creating an Immersive Concert Atmosphere

Creating an immersive concert atmosphere is a fundamental aspect of Zeds Dead's live shows. From the moment fans walk through the venue doors to the last beat of the performance, Zeds Dead strives to transport them into a world of music, visuals, and energy. This section explores the various elements that contribute to the creation of an unforgettable concert experience.

Setting the Stage

The stage design plays a crucial role in setting the mood and atmosphere of a Zeds Dead concert. The stage is not just a platform for the performers but a canvas for visual artistry. Holographic projections, LED screens, and intricate light shows create a multi-dimensional experience for the audience. The design elements are carefully curated to complement the music and add depth to the overall performance.

Zeds Dead embraces innovation and is constantly pushing the boundaries of stage design. They collaborate with visual artists and designers to create immersive and captivating stage setups that elevate the concert experience. The combination of intricate visuals, lighting effects, and interactive elements enhances the immersion, making the audience feel like they are part of something extraordinary.

Integrating Visual Elements

Visual elements play a vital role in complementing the music and enhancing the concert atmosphere. Zeds Dead combines synchronized visuals, video content, and live camera feeds to create a dynamic and engaging visual experience. The visuals are carefully crafted to enhance the mood and energy of each song, creating a seamless fusion of sight and sound.

The visual elements are not just limited to the stage. Zeds Dead often incorporates live audience shots and crowd reactions into their visuals, allowing the audience to see themselves as an integral part of the performance. This interactive approach creates a sense of community and connection between the artists and the fans.

A Symphony of Sound

Sound is the cornerstone of Zeds Dead's concerts, and every effort is made to ensure a flawless audio experience. State-of-the-art sound systems are meticulously calibrated to deliver optimal sound quality throughout the venue, allowing the audience to fully immerse themselves in the music.

Zeds Dead pays attention to every detail of the sound production, from the choice of speakers to the mixing of each individual track. The goal is to create a balanced and immersive sound experience where every beat, drop, and melody is crisp and impactful. The mixing and mastering process is a collaborative effort, involving sound engineers who work closely with the artists to achieve the desired sound.

Interactive Elements and Crowd Participation

Zeds Dead's concerts are not just a passive experience for the audience; they actively encourage crowd participation and interaction. From call-and-response moments to hands-in-the-air gestures, Zeds Dead knows how to engage the crowd and create a sense of unity among the fans.

In addition to these traditional forms of crowd participation, Zeds Dead embraces technology to enhance the interactive elements of their shows. Mobile apps and wearables are used to synchronize special effects and lighting with audience movements, creating a truly immersive and participatory experience.

Unconventional Performance Spaces

Zeds Dead understands the importance of the venue and its impact on the concert atmosphere. While traditional concert venues offer an intimate setting, Zeds Dead has also embraced unconventional performance spaces. From warehouses to outdoor spaces, they have transformed a variety of venues into unique concert experiences.

These unconventional performances spaces allow for creative freedom and experimentation with stage design, visuals, and sound. By breaking away from the traditional mold, Zeds Dead creates an atmosphere of anticipation and surprise, giving their shows a sense of adventure and discovery.

The Energy of a Zeds Dead Show

One cannot discuss the immersive concert atmosphere of Zeds Dead without mentioning the energy they bring to the stage. The passion and excitement that radiate from the artists are infectious, igniting the crowd and creating an electric atmosphere.

Zeds Dead's performances are characterized by their dynamic mixing, seamless transitions, and high-energy stage presence. The energy they exude on stage is contagious, fueling the crowd's enthusiasm and creating a symbiotic relationship between the artists and the audience.

Balancing DJ Sets and Live Performances

Zeds Dead strikes a delicate balance between DJ sets and live performances to create a diverse and engaging concert experience. While they are known for their DJ sets, they also incorporate live instruments and vocalists into their shows. This combination allows them to showcase their versatility as musicians and adds an element of spontaneity to their performances.

The seamless integration of DJ sets and live performances creates a dynamic and ever-changing concert atmosphere. Fans never know what to expect, keeping them on the edge of their seats and heightening the sense of anticipation throughout the show.

Pushing the Boundaries of Live Performances

Zeds Dead continuously pushes the boundaries of what is possible in a live performance. They experiment with new technologies, collaborate with visual artists and designers, and explore unconventional venues to create unique and groundbreaking concert experiences.

The immersive concert atmosphere they cultivate is a testament to their commitment to pushing the limits of creativity and innovation. Zeds Dead's shows are not merely concerts; they are artistic experiences that transcend the boundaries of music and invite the audience on a journey of sight, sound, and emotion.

Conclusion

Creating an immersive concert atmosphere is an art in itself, and Zeds Dead excels in crafting unforgettable experiences for their fans. Through stage design, visual elements, sound production, interactive elements, unconventional spaces, and a boundless energy, they transport their audience into a world where music becomes a visceral and transformative experience.

Zeds Dead's dedication to pushing the boundaries of live performances ensures that their concerts remain at the forefront of innovation, inspiring both artists and audiences alike. The immersive concert atmosphere they create is a testament to their artistic vision and a key ingredient in their enduring success.

Incorporating Visual Elements into Live Shows

When it comes to creating an unforgettable live experience, Zeds Dead knows that it's not just about the music. In their electrifying performances, they skillfully incorporate visual elements that elevate the show to a whole new level. From mesmerizing visuals to stunning stage design, Zeds Dead has mastered the art of captivating their audience both sonically and visually.

Creating an Immersive Concert Atmosphere

One of the goals of Zeds Dead's live shows is to transport the audience to another world, immersing them in a multisensory experience. To achieve this, they carefully curate their visual elements to align with the mood and energy of their music. This includes the use of dynamic lighting, mesmerizing projections, and innovative stage designs that encompass the entire audience.

Incorporating Visual Elements with Music

The visual elements in Zeds Dead's live shows are carefully synchronized with the music, enhancing the overall impact of their performances. Visual cues such as pulsating lights and synchronized projections respond to the beats and drops, creating a synchronized fusion of sound and visuals. This synchronization adds an extra layer of excitement and immersion for the audience, creating a truly memorable experience.

Collaborations with Visual Artists and Designers

To bring their artistic vision to life, Zeds Dead collaborates with talented visual artists and designers who specialize in creating immersive experiences. These collaborations result in unique and visually stunning stage setups, custom-made visuals, and intricate projections that complement their music. By working closely with these creative minds, Zeds Dead ensures that their live shows are a feast for the eyes as well as the ears.

Pushing the Boundaries of Stage Design

Zeds Dead constantly pushes the boundaries of stage design, incorporating innovative and unconventional elements into their live performances. From complex lighting rigs and LED displays to interactive stage props, they strive to create a visually captivating experience that goes beyond the traditional concert setup. This experimental approach to stage design adds an element of surprise and intrigue to their shows, captivating the audience from start to finish.

Enhancing Storytelling through Visuals

Incorporating visual elements also allows Zeds Dead to enhance the storytelling aspect of their music. By creating visually engaging narratives through their stage design and projections, they take the audience on a visual journey that complements the emotional arc of their songs. This immersive storytelling adds depth and dimension to their performances, creating a more profound connection between the music and the audience.

The Power of Interactive Visuals

Zeds Dead understands the power of audience engagement, and they leverage interactive visuals to actively involve the crowd in their live shows. From interactive LED panels that respond to touch or movement to live video feeds that capture and project the energy of the audience back onto the stage, these interactive elements create a sense of co-creation between the artists and the fans. This interactive experience fosters a deeper sense of connection and participation, making each show a unique and unforgettable experience.

Innovations in Visual Technologies

Staying at the forefront of technological advancements, Zeds Dead embraces the latest visual technologies to enhance their live performances. From advanced mapping techniques that project visuals onto complex stage structures to virtual reality experiences that transport the audience to new dimensions, they constantly explore new ways to push the boundaries of what's possible. By harnessing the power of cutting-edge visual technologies, Zeds Dead continues to redefine the live music experience.

Balancing Visuals and Musical Performance

While visual elements play a crucial role in Zeds Dead's live shows, they are careful to strike a balance between visuals and musical performance. The visuals serve to amplify and enhance the music, rather than overshadowing it. This delicate balance ensures that the audience remains fully engaged with both the audio and visual components, creating a harmonious and immersive experience.

Crafting a Lasting Visual Identity

Just like their music, Zeds Dead's visual elements have a distinct and recognizable identity. They have crafted a visual brand that is both visually cohesive and adaptable to different settings and venues. This visual identity helps to create a consistent and cohesive experience for their fans, whether they are attending a small club show or a massive festival performance. This attention to visual branding further establishes Zeds Dead as not just musicians, but as a full sensory experience.

Taking Visual Elements to the Future

As technology continues to evolve, Zeds Dead is excited to explore new possibilities in incorporating visual elements into their live shows. From advancements in augmented reality to the continued integration of interactive technologies, they eagerly embrace the creative opportunities that lie ahead. By continuously pushing the boundaries of what's possible, Zeds Dead ensures that their live shows remain at the forefront of innovation in both the music and visual realms.

Incorporating visual elements into their live shows is a hallmark of Zeds Dead's performances. From creating an immersive concert atmosphere to combining visual elements with music, they have mastered the art of captivating their audience on multiple sensory levels. By embracing collaborations and pushing the boundaries of stage design, Zeds Dead creates visually stunning performances that complement their music and enhance the overall experience for their fans. With an unwavering commitment to visual innovation, Zeds Dead continues to elevate the live music experience and inspire future generations of artists to explore the limitless possibilities of music and visuals.

The Evolution of Live Performance Setups

In the world of electronic music, live performances have evolved significantly over the years. Gone are the days when DJs simply stood behind a booth, mixing tracks and occasionally waving their hands in the air. Today, artists like Zeds Dead have pushed the boundaries of live performance setups, creating dynamic and immersive experiences for their audiences. In this section, we will delve into the evolution of live performance setups and explore the innovative techniques and technologies that have shaped the way electronic music is performed live.

From the DJ Booth to the Stage

In the early days of electronic music, live performances were often confined to the DJ booth. DJs would mix and blend tracks, using turntables or CDJs, while the audience danced and enjoyed the music. However, as electronic music grew in popularity, artists began to crave more interactive and engaging live experiences. Zeds Dead was at the forefront of this movement, looking for ways to bring their music to life on stage.

Multimedia Integration

One of the key elements in the evolution of live performance setups is the integration of multimedia elements. Zeds Dead recognized that the visual aspect of a performance is just as important as the music itself. To create a truly immersive experience, they started incorporating visuals, lighting effects, and stage design into their shows.

By working with visual artists and designers, Zeds Dead developed stunning visual displays that complemented their music. They used projection mapping techniques to project visuals onto custom-designed structures, creating a multi-dimensional visual experience. These visuals were synchronized with the music, enhancing the overall impact of the performance.

Live Instrumentation

Another significant development in live performance setups has been the incorporation of live instrumentation. Zeds Dead expanded their setups to include live instruments such as drums, keyboards, and guitars. This added a new layer of depth and energy to their performances, allowing them to create unique live remixes and improvisations.

By combining live instrumentation with electronic elements, Zeds Dead created a seamless blend of organic and synthetic sounds. This fusion of different musical elements not only elevated the live experience but also showcased their versatility as musicians.

Controllerism and Live Remixing

Zeds Dead embraced the concept of "controllerism," which involves using MIDI controllers to manipulate and perform music in real-time. This allowed them to go beyond simply playing pre-recorded tracks and instead, create unique and dynamic live remixes on the fly.

Using MIDI controllers, Zeds Dead could trigger loops, samples, and effects, giving them the freedom to manipulate and shape the music in real-time. This added a level of spontaneity and improvisation to their performances, making each show a truly unique experience.

Custom Live Rigs

As Zeds Dead's live performances became more intricate and complex, the need for custom live rigs arose. They worked closely with a team of engineers and designers to create custom setups that catered to their specific needs.

These custom live rigs incorporated a range of hardware and software components, including MIDI controllers, drum machines, synthesizers, and audio interfaces. The rigs were designed to be portable and easily adaptable for different venues and stages, ensuring a consistent and high-quality performance experience.

Interactive Elements and Audience Participation

Zeds Dead has always focused on creating a deep connection with their audience. In their live performances, they have incorporated interactive elements and audience participation to further enhance the overall experience.

One example of audience participation is the use of smartphone apps that allow the audience to interact with the music and visuals in real-time. The audience can control certain aspects of the performance, such as triggering samples or changing the lighting effects, creating a sense of collective involvement.

The Future of Live Performance Setups

As technology continues to advance, the possibilities for live performance setups are limitless. Zeds Dead, along with other innovative artists, are constantly exploring new ways to push the boundaries of live performances.

One area of development is the use of virtual reality (VR) and augmented reality (AR) technologies. Imagine a future where concertgoers can don VR headsets and be transported to a virtual world where they can experience a Zeds Dead performance from any vantage point.

Additionally, advancements in real-time audio and visual processing will further enhance the immersive nature of live performances. Artists will have even more control over their sound and visuals, allowing for more spontaneous and interactive experiences.

Summary

The evolution of live performance setups has transformed the electronic music landscape. Zeds Dead has played a significant role in pushing the boundaries and creating immersive and engaging live experiences for their fans. From the DJ booth to the stage, they have embraced multimedia integration, live instrumentation, controllerism, and audience participation. As technology continues to advance, the future of live performance setups holds endless possibilities, ensuring that the live experience remains a vital and evolving aspect of electronic music culture.

Interactive Elements and Crowd Participation

When it comes to live performances, Zeds Dead knows how to create an immersive concert atmosphere that engages the crowd and keeps them captivated throughout the show. One of the ways they achieve this is by incorporating interactive elements and encouraging crowd participation. This not only adds an extra layer of excitement to their performances but also creates a sense of community and connection among the fans.

One of the interactive elements that Zeds Dead often utilizes is the use of visual projections and lighting effects synced to the music. These visuals are carefully designed to enhance the overall experience and evoke specific emotions during different parts of the set. The dynamic lighting changes and mesmerizing visuals create a multi-sensory experience that allows the audience to feel fully immersed in the music.

In addition to the visual aspects, Zeds Dead also encourages crowd participation through various means. One popular method they employ is by having call-and-response moments during their sets. They might drop a catchy vocal sample or a recognizable hook and encourage the audience to chant along or respond in a certain way. This interaction not only energizes the crowd but also creates a sense of unity as everyone becomes part of the performance.

Furthermore, Zeds Dead often incorporates live instrumentation into their sets, with elements like drum pads, synthesizers, and guitars. These live instruments allow for more improvisation and add an extra layer of excitement to the performance. They might invite guest musicians on stage to jam with them or surprise the audience with a spontaneous live collaboration. By including live instrumentation, Zeds Dead brings a unique and dynamic element to their sets, ensuring that no two performances are exactly the same.

Another way Zeds Dead encourages crowd participation is by integrating new technologies into their live shows. They have experimented with interactive elements such as wristbands that light up and synchronize with the music, creating a visually stunning spectacle. This not only immerses the audience in the performance but also fosters a sense of connection and shared experience among the concert-goers.

One of the challenges of incorporating interactive elements and crowd participation is striking the right balance. While it is important to engage the audience and make them an active part of the performance, it is equally crucial to maintain artistic integrity and not rely solely on gimmicks. Zeds Dead manages to navigate this balance by integrating interactive elements in a way that enhances the overall experience without overshadowing the music itself.

By utilizing these interactive elements and encouraging crowd participation, Zeds Dead creates a memorable and immersive live experience. Their performances become more than just a DJ set – they transform into fully-fledged communal events where the audience becomes an integral part of the show. This approach not only sets them apart from other artists but also fosters a deep and lasting connection with their fanbase.

In summary, Zeds Dead's interactive elements and crowd participation add an extra layer of excitement and engagement to their live performances. Through visual projections, lighting effects, call-and-response moments, live instrumentation, and new technologies, they foster a sense of community and create a memorable and immersive concert atmosphere. By striking the right balance between audience involvement and artistic integrity, Zeds Dead succeeds in connecting with their fans on a deeper level, making each show a unique and unforgettable experience. So get ready to dive into the rhythm and become an active participant in the electrifying world of Zeds Dead.

Memorable Live Performances and Festival Moments

One of the defining aspects of Zeds Dead's music career is their electrifying live performances and their ability to captivate audiences at various music festivals around the world. From the energetic atmosphere to the exhilarating visuals, Zeds Dead has created unforgettable experiences for their fans. In this section, we will explore some of their most memorable live performances and festival moments.

The Electric Zoo Festival, New York

One of Zeds Dead's most iconic performances took place at the Electric Zoo Festival in New York. As the sun set and the crowd gathered, the duo took the stage and unleashed a wave of energy that shook the entire festival grounds. The crowd pulsed with each heavy drop, and the atmosphere was electric as fans danced and connected to the music. Zeds Dead's seamless mixing and ability to read the crowd's energy made this performance a standout moment in their career.

The Ultra Music Festival, Miami

Another iconic performance that left a lasting impression was Zeds Dead's set at the Ultra Music Festival in Miami. The festival's massive main stage provided the perfect backdrop for their larger-than-life sound. The crowd was in a frenzy as Zeds Dead took the stage, and the duo fed off the energy, delivering a set filled with their signature heavy basslines and melodic hooks. The visual production of their set elevated the experience, with stunning light displays and projections that synchronized perfectly with the music.

Burning Man Festival, Nevada

Zeds Dead's performance at the Burning Man Festival in Nevada was a truly transformative experience for both the artists and the crowd. The unique and immersive nature of the festival allowed Zeds Dead to experiment and push the boundaries of their sound. The duo crafted a set that seamlessly blended various genres and styles, taking the crowd on a sonic journey that mirrored the ethos of Burning Man. The interactive and participatory nature of the festival allowed for a deeper connection between Zeds Dead and their fans, creating a memorable and intimate experience.

Coachella Valley Music and Arts Festival

Coachella, one of the most renowned music festivals in the world, provided Zeds Dead with an opportunity to showcase their talent to a diverse and discerning audience. Their performance on the festival's main stage was a high-energy affair, with the crowd drawn in by their infectious beats and electrifying stage presence. Zeds Dead's ability to effortlessly blend genres and surprise the audience with unexpected drops and transitions made this performance a standout moment in their career.

Tomorrowland Music Festival, Belgium

Zeds Dead's performance at Tomorrowland, one of the largest electronic music festivals in the world, was a testament to their global reach and appeal. The duo took to the festival's iconic main stage, surrounded by a sea of enthusiastic fans from all corners of the globe. The crowd's energy was palpable as Zeds Dead played a set that spanned their discography, from their early breakout tracks to their latest releases. The combination of their seamless mixing, visually stunning production, and the sheer magnitude of the festival made this performance one to remember.

Unconventional Performance Venues

In addition to their performances at festivals, Zeds Dead has also embraced unconventional performance venues, pushing the boundaries of what a live show can be. They have played in unique locations such as abandoned warehouses, underground clubs, and even on mountaintops. These intimate and unconventional settings allow for a more immersive and personal experience, creating a deep connection between Zeds Dead and their fans.

Embracing Live Improvisation

One of the most remarkable aspects of Zeds Dead's live performances is their ability to incorporate live improvisation into their sets. This not only adds an element of surprise and spontaneity but also allows for unique moments of musical creativity. They seamlessly blend pre-recorded tracks with live instruments, creating a dynamic and ever-evolving performance that keeps the audience on their toes. This commitment to live improvisation sets Zeds Dead apart and creates a memorable and engaging experience for their fans.

Creating an Emotional Journey

Zeds Dead's live performances are not just about delivering an intense musical experience; they are also about connecting with the audience on an emotional level. Through their expertly crafted setlist and the way they navigate the crowd's energy, Zeds Dead takes their fans on a journey. They build up anticipation, then release it in a burst of bass drops and melodic hooks, creating a rollercoaster of emotions. This ability to evoke a range of feelings is what makes their live performances truly memorable.

The Power of Crowd Participation

Zeds Dead understands the importance of crowd participation in creating a memorable live performance. They actively encourage their fans to become part of the experience, whether it's through synchronized dance moves, call-and-response interactions, or simply encouraging the crowd to let loose and express themselves. This creates a sense of unity and camaraderie, transforming their live shows into immersive and unforgettable moments.

Pushing the Boundaries of Live Performances

Zeds Dead is constantly pushing the boundaries of what a live performance can be. They are known for their innovative use of technology, incorporating cutting-edge visuals, interactive elements, and experimental stage design to create a multi-sensory experience for their fans. By constantly evolving their live show, Zeds Dead ensures that each performance is a unique and unforgettable journey.

Exercises

1. Research and watch a live performance or festival set by Zeds Dead. Analyze the elements that make their performance memorable and engaging. Consider their stage presence, interaction with the crowd, visual production, and track selection. Write a short reflection on what stood out to you and how you think they create such memorable live experiences.

2. Imagine you are tasked with designing the stage setup for a Zeds Dead live performance at a music festival. Sketch out your vision for the stage design, considering the use of visual elements, lighting, and special effects. Write a short paragraph explaining how your design enhances the overall live experience and captures the essence of Zeds Dead's music.

3. Reflect on your favorite live performance or festival moment you have experienced. What made it memorable? Was it the energy of the crowd, the artist's stage presence, the visual production, or a combination of these elements? Write a short personal account describing the atmosphere and emotions you felt during that performance.

Resources

+ Electric Zoo Festival: `https://electriczoo.com/`

+ Ultra Music Festival: `https://ultramusicfestival.com/`

+ Burning Man Festival: `https://burningman.org/`

+ Coachella Valley Music and Arts Festival: `https://www.coachella.com/`

+ Tomorrowland Music Festival: `https://www.tomorrowland.com/`

Further Reading

+ Leggett, S. (2016). The Evolving Role of the Live DJ: A Study of DJ Performances at Electronic Dance Music Events. *Journal of Popular Music Studies*, 28(4), 407-427.

+ Allen, D., & Rambally, E. (2020). Music Festivals as Transformative Spaces: Exploring Sensory Experience and Social Interaction. *Leisure Sciences*, 1-18.

+ Bennett, A. (2015). Music, Style, and Aging: Zeds Dead and the Art of Appropriation. In *Music, Style, and Aging: Growing Old Disgracefully?* (pp. 59-74). Springer.

The Energy of a Zeds Dead Show

When it comes to experiencing a Zeds Dead show, there is an undeniable energy in the air that is impossible to ignore. From the moment the music start to the final bass drop, the crowd is engulfed in a whirlwind of excitement, passion, and pure musical ecstasy. The energy of a Zeds Dead show is a result of several key elements that come together to create an unforgettable experience.

The Power of Bass

At the heart of every Zeds Dead show is the power of bass. The deep, pulsating basslines that reverberate through the speakers have an incredible impact on the audience. It shakes them to their core, creating a physical connection between the music and their bodies. The bass is not just heard, but felt, and it adds a whole new dimension to the show.

Epic Visuals and Lighting

In addition to the music, the visual and lighting displays at a Zeds Dead show are a sight to behold. The stage is transformed into a mesmerizing world of lights, lasers, and projections, creating a visual feast for the eyes. The synchronized lights and visual effects are carefully choreographed to enhance the audio experience, creating a truly immersive environment that complements the music.

Crowd Interaction

Zeds Dead knows how to engage with their audience and create a sense of unity and connection. Throughout their performances, they actively interact with the crowd, urging them to participate and become part of the show. Whether it's encouraging everyone to raise their hands in the air or initiating call-and-response chants, the duo's contagious energy spreads like wildfire, turning the crowd into an integral part of the performance.

Surprise Drops and Mashups

One of the most exhilarating aspects of a Zeds Dead show is the element of surprise. The duo is known for their unexpected drops and creative mashups, taking the audience on a thrilling musical journey. When the beat suddenly hits harder or a familiar melody is seamlessly woven into a new track, the crowd erupts in excitement. These surprise moments elevate the energy of the show, keeping fans on their toes and leaving them hungry for more.

Unpredictable Song Selections

While many artists follow a predetermined setlist, Zeds Dead prides themselves on their ability to adapt and respond to the energy of the crowd. Their performances are known for their dynamic song selections, which can veer in unexpected directions depending on the atmosphere and vibe of the audience. This spontaneity adds a sense of anticipation and keeps the show fresh and exciting.

Creating a Safe and Inclusive Space

Beyond the music and visuals, Zeds Dead also strives to create a safe and inclusive space for their fans. They encourage respect and unity among the crowd, actively promoting a positive and accepting atmosphere. By fostering a sense of community, they enhance the overall energy of the show, allowing fans to fully immerse themselves in the experience without worry.

A Shared Love for Music

Ultimately, the energy of a Zeds Dead show stems from the shared love for music. Everyone in attendance, from the artists to the fans, is united by the passion and appreciation for the power of sound. This shared love creates an electric atmosphere that transcends boundaries and connects people from all walks of life.

In conclusion, the energy of a Zeds Dead show is a phenomenon that cannot be fully captured in words. It is a sensory explosion of bass, lights, and interactive moments that ignite the crowd's enthusiasm. By harnessing the power of music, visuals, and crowd interaction, Zeds Dead has mastered the art of creating an unforgettable and energetically charged live experience. So, if you ever have the chance to attend a Zeds Dead show, be prepared to lose yourself in a whirlwind of sonic bliss and become part of a collective euphoria that will stay with you long after the final beat.

The Importance of Live Improvisation

Live improvisation is a fundamental aspect of the Zeds Dead experience, setting them apart from other artists in the electronic music scene. It is the ability to create and perform music spontaneously, in the moment, that allows Zeds Dead to connect with their audience on a deeper level. In this section, we will explore the importance of live improvisation and how it enhances the overall performance of Zeds Dead.

Breaking Free from Repetition

One of the main reasons why live improvisation is vital to Zeds Dead's shows is that it breaks free from the repetition often associated with electronic music performances. While a DJ set typically involves playing pre-recorded tracks and mixing them together, Zeds Dead takes it a step further by introducing live elements and improvisation into their performances. By doing so, they create a unique experience for their fans, providing an element of surprise and unpredictability.

Creating a Dynamic and Engaging Performance

Live improvisation allows Zeds Dead to create a dynamic and engaging performance that captivates their audience throughout the entire show. By incorporating live instrumentation, such as drums or guitars, they add an organic and human touch to their electronic sound. This fusion of electronic and live elements creates a rich and immersive experience that keeps the crowd engaged and energized.

Interaction and Spontaneity

Incorporating live improvisation into their shows also allows Zeds Dead to interact with their audience in real-time. It opens up opportunities for spontaneous moments, where they can feed off the energy of the crowd and tailor their performance accordingly. This interaction creates a sense of intimacy and connection between the artists and their fans, making each show a unique and unforgettable experience.

Pushing Musical Boundaries

Live improvisation gives Zeds Dead the freedom to push the boundaries of their music. It allows them to experiment and explore different sounds, textures, and rhythms during their performances. By constantly pushing themselves creatively, Zeds Dead keeps their music fresh and innovative, evolving their sound with each show. Live improvisation becomes a platform for them to showcase their artistic growth and take their audience on a sonic journey.

The Fusion of DJing and Live Instrumentation

Zeds Dead has successfully integrated live instrumentation into their DJ sets, seamlessly blending the worlds of electronic music and live performance. This fusion not only adds a new layer of excitement to their shows, but it also showcases their versatility as musicians. It demonstrates that electronic music can be just as dynamic and expressive as traditional live performances, challenging the perception of what a DJ set can be.

Promoting Collaboration and Creativity

Live improvisation also promotes collaboration and creativity amongst the members of Zeds Dead. It enables them to bounce ideas off each other in real-time, creating a synergistic relationship between the artists. This collaborative process allows for the exploration of new sounds and ideas that may not have been possible in a pre-recorded studio setting. It is through live improvisation that Zeds Dead can truly harness their creative potential.

Engaging the Senses

Zeds Dead's live improvisation not only engages the audience's auditory senses but also their visual senses. Their captivating stage design and lighting complement the music, enhancing the overall experience. By engaging both the auditory and visual senses, Zeds Dead creates a multisensory event that immerses the audience in their music and performance.

Embracing Imperfection

Live improvisation embraces imperfection, allowing for the beauty of performance to shine through. It is through these imperfect moments that Zeds Dead showcases their humanity and authenticity as artists. By embracing the unpredictability of live improvisation, they create a shared experience with their audience, reminding them that they are witnessing something special and unique.

Pushing the Boundaries of Live Improvisation

Zeds Dead continually pushes the boundaries of live improvisation, exploring new techniques and incorporating innovative technologies into their performances. They strive to break new ground with each show, constantly seeking ways to surprise and delight their audience. This dedication to pushing the boundaries of live improvisation ensures that every Zeds Dead performance is a distinctive and memorable experience.

In conclusion, live improvisation plays a significant role in the Zeds Dead experience. It allows them to break free from repetition, create a dynamic and engaging performance, interact with their audience, push musical boundaries, promote collaboration and creativity, engage the senses, embrace imperfection, and push the boundaries of live improvisation itself. It is through live improvisation that Zeds Dead connects with their audience, creating a shared experience that is both electrifying and unforgettable.

Balancing DJ Sets and Live Instruments

Balancing DJ sets and live instruments is a crucial aspect of the Zeds Dead live experience. It brings together the art of DJing and the energy of live performance, creating a unique and dynamic atmosphere for the audience. In this section, we will explore the challenges and strategies involved in balancing these elements seamlessly.

The Art of DJing

DJing is an art form that involves mixing and blending recorded music to create a continuous and cohesive musical journey. It requires a deep understanding of music theory, beatmatching, and song selection. DJs use various techniques such as EQing, looping, scratching, and effects to enhance the songs and create a unique sonic experience.

For Zeds Dead, DJing serves as the foundation of their live performances. It allows them to seamlessly mix their own tracks with other artists' music, creating a dynamic set that keeps the audience engaged and excited. The art of DJing also provides the flexibility to read the crowd and adapt the set in real-time, ensuring a memorable experience for everyone.

Incorporating Live Instruments

What sets Zeds Dead apart is their ability to seamlessly incorporate live instruments into their DJ sets. This adds an extra layer of excitement and energy, making each performance truly unforgettable. The live instruments bring a sense of spontaneity and authenticity to the set, allowing the artists to showcase their musical talent in real-time.

The trick to successfully balancing live instruments with DJ sets lies in finding the right moments to incorporate them. Zeds Dead carefully selects specific tracks or sections of songs where live instruments can shine. This could be a guitar solo, a keyboard riff, or a drum breakdown. By strategically including these moments, they enhance the overall impact of the performance without overpowering the DJ elements.

Technical Considerations

Balancing DJ sets and live instruments requires careful technical planning and execution. Zeds Dead utilizes a combination of software and hardware to achieve a seamless integration of both elements.

One key consideration is the routing of audio signals. The live instruments are connected to the DJ setup, allowing them to be directly incorporated into the mix. This involves routing audio signals through mixers, audio interfaces, and digital audio workstations. By having control over each instrument's sound and level, Zeds Dead can ensure that they blend harmoniously with the rest of the set.

Another technical consideration is the synchronization of the live instruments with the pre-recorded tracks. Timing is crucial to maintain the musical flow and prevent any dissonance or clashes. Zeds Dead utilizes advanced MIDI controllers and software to sync the live instruments with the DJ software, ensuring that all elements are perfectly aligned.

Creating a Memorable Experience

The key to balancing DJ sets and live instruments is to create a seamless and cohesive experience for the audience. Zeds Dead achieves this by maintaining a careful balance between the two elements throughout the set. They understand the importance of allowing the live instruments to shine while also maintaining the flow and energy of a DJ performance.

To create a truly memorable experience, Zeds Dead incorporates live improvisation into their sets. This allows the musicians to react and respond to the crowd's energy, creating unique and spontaneous moments. It adds an element of surprise and unpredictability, making each performance feel fresh and exciting.

By finding the perfect balance between DJing and live instruments, Zeds Dead creates a dynamic and immersive experience that captivates the audience. It showcases their versatility as artists and their commitment to pushing the boundaries of live electronic music.

Challenges and Solutions

Balancing DJ sets and live instruments is not without its challenges. One of the main challenges is ensuring that the live instruments are audible and distinct amidst the electronic soundscape. Zeds Dead tackles this by working closely with sound engineers to fine-tune the mix and EQ settings. They also experiment with different instrument placements on stage to achieve the desired sonic balance.

Another challenge is maintaining the energy and momentum during transitions between DJ sets and live instrument performances. Zeds Dead carefully plans and rehearses these transitions to ensure a smooth flow and seamless integration. They use creative techniques such as building up tension and anticipation through DJ effects and loops, leading into the live instrument performance with maximum impact.

Unconventional Solution: Interactive Visuals

In addition to the audio elements, Zeds Dead leverages visual technology to enhance the balance between DJ sets and live instruments. They incorporate interactive visuals that respond to the live instruments, creating a multi-sensory experience for the audience.

Through the use of motion sensors, cameras, and projection mapping, the live instruments become an integral part of the visual spectacle. For example, when a guitar solo is played, visuals can be triggered to respond to the intensity or speed of the performance. This unconventional solution further enhances the connection between the musicians, the audience, and the overall performance.

Conclusion

Balancing DJ sets and live instruments is a complex yet rewarding task for Zeds Dead. It allows them to showcase their versatile talent and bring a unique energy to their live performances. Through careful planning, technical expertise, and creative solutions, they seamlessly integrate these elements to create an unforgettable experience for their fans. Balancing DJ sets and live instruments is just one aspect of the Zeds Dead universe, showcasing their passion for pushing creative boundaries in the electronic music scene.

Pushing the Boundaries of Live Performances

When it comes to live performances, Zeds Dead has always been on the cutting edge, pushing boundaries and challenging the norms of the electronic music scene. Their goal has always been to create a truly immersive experience for their fans, one that goes beyond just playing music and transports the audience to another world. In this section, we will explore how Zeds Dead achieves this by incorporating innovative technologies, interactive elements, and mind-blowing visuals into their live shows.

Creating an Immersive Concert Atmosphere

Zeds Dead understands that a live show is not just about the music, but also about creating an atmosphere that captivates the audience and engages their senses. They go above and beyond to curate an environment that transports fans into their world. From the moment you step into a Zeds Dead concert, you are surrounded by pulsating lights, thumping bass, and a palpable energy that sets the stage for an unforgettable experience.

Incorporating Visual Elements into Live Shows

One of the most striking aspects of Zeds Dead's live performances is their use of visual elements to enhance the overall experience. They collaborate with visual artists and designers to create stunning visual displays that sync perfectly with their music. From mesmerizing light shows to jaw-dropping projections, every element is carefully crafted to immerse the audience in a multisensory journey.

The Evolution of Live Performance Setups

Over the years, Zeds Dead has continuously evolved their live performance setups to push the boundaries of what is possible. They have embraced technology and incorporated advanced equipment to enhance their live shows. This includes the use of MIDI controllers, drum machines, and live instruments to add an element of spontaneity and improvisation to their performances.

Interactive Elements and Crowd Participation

Zeds Dead believes in creating a connection with their audience, and they achieve this by incorporating interactive elements and encouraging crowd participation during their live shows. This can range from inviting fans on stage to join them in performing a song, to encouraging sing-alongs or synchronized dances. By involving the audience in the performance, Zeds Dead creates a sense of unity and makes each show a unique and unforgettable experience.

Memorable Live Performances and Festival Moments

Zeds Dead is known for delivering mind-blowing live performances that leave a lasting impact on their audience. From headline sets at major music festivals to their own headline shows, every performance is meticulously planned and executed to create a truly unforgettable experience. Their ability to energize and captivate the crowd has made them a standout act in the electronic music scene.

The Importance of Mental and Physical Health on Tour

Touring can take a toll on artists both mentally and physically, and Zeds Dead recognizes the importance of taking care of themselves and their team while on the road.   They prioritize mental and physical health by creating a positive and supportive environment on tour. This includes regular exercise, healthy eating, and mindfulness practices to ensure that they have the energy and stamina to deliver top-notch performances.

Managing Expectations and Balance

With a demanding touring schedule, it can be challenging to find the right balance between work and personal life.   Zeds Dead understands the importance of managing expectations and finding time for themselves amidst their busy schedule. They prioritize self-care and personal time to recharge and stay inspired, which ultimately contributes to the quality of their live performances.

The Evolution of the Zeds Dead Live Experience

Zeds Dead's live performances have evolved significantly over the years, reflecting their growth as artists and their desire to push boundaries. They constantly seek new ways to engage their audience and create a memorable experience. Whether it's experimenting with new technology, incorporating live instruments, or collaborating with visual artists, Zeds Dead continues to push the envelope and redefine what it means to deliver an incredible live show.

Balancing DJ Sets and Live Performances

In addition to their full live performances, Zeds Dead is also known for their DJ sets. They skillfully balance both formats, seamlessly transitioning between playing live instruments and mixing tracks. This versatility allows them to cater to different audiences and venues, ensuring that they can always deliver a memorable performance no matter the setting.

Pushing the Boundaries of Live Performances

Zeds Dead's commitment to pushing the boundaries of live performances has earned them a reputation as innovators in the electronic music scene. Their use of cutting-edge technology, mind-blowing visuals, and immersive atmospheres sets them apart from their peers.   By continuously experimenting and pushing the limits of what is possible, Zeds Dead has redefined what fans can expect from a live show, creating an experience that goes beyond just music and leaves a lasting impact on all who attend.

Impact on Music and Culture

Zeds Dead's Influence on Electronic Music

Zeds Dead has undeniably made a significant impact on the world of electronic music. Their unique sound, innovative production techniques, and boundary-pushing collaborations have earned them a dedicated fan base and a prominent place in the industry. In this section, we will explore the various ways in which Zeds Dead has influenced electronic music as a whole.

Pushing Boundaries and Challenging Conventions

One of the most notable aspects of Zeds Dead's influence on electronic music is their ability to push boundaries and challenge conventions. They have consistently experimented with different genres, styles, and sounds, always seeking to create something fresh and exciting. By blending elements of dubstep, hip-hop, reggae, and other genres, Zeds Dead has carved out their own distinct sonic identity.

Their willingness to take risks and explore new sonic territories has inspired countless artists to push the boundaries of electronic music. They have shown that it is possible to create music that transcends genre labels and defies categorization, opening up new possibilities for creative expression within the electronic music landscape.

Breaking Down Genre Barriers

Zeds Dead's music has also played a crucial role in breaking down genre barriers within electronic music. Through their collaborations with artists from different musical backgrounds, they have demonstrated that electronic music can seamlessly blend with other genres to create exciting and innovative fusions.

For instance, their collaborations with artists like Omar LinX, Ganja White Night, and NGHTMRE have resulted in genre-bending tracks that incorporate elements of hip-hop, reggae, and bass music. These collaborations have not only expanded the horizons of electronic music but have also introduced Zeds Dead's unique sound to new audiences.

The success of Zeds Dead's genre-blending approach has had a ripple effect throughout the electronic music scene, inspiring other artists to venture outside of their comfort zones and experiment with new genres and styles. As a result, the boundaries that once confined electronic music have become increasingly blurred, leading to a more diverse and eclectic sonic landscape.

Inspiring a New Generation of Artists

Zeds Dead's innovative approach to electronic music has had a profound influence on a new generation of artists. Their ability to seamlessly blend different genres, their impeccable production skills, and their electrifying live performances have inspired countless aspiring musicians to pursue a career in electronic music.

The duo has become a source of inspiration for artists who strive to create music that is both sonically thrilling and emotionally resonant. Zeds Dead's commitment to authenticity and artistic integrity has shown budding musicians that success can be achieved by staying true to oneself and not compromising artistic vision.

Through their music and their success, Zeds Dead has set a high standard for excellence within the electronic music industry. They have shown aspiring artists that with hard work, dedication, and a willingness to take risks, it is possible to make a lasting impact and leave a mark on the world of music.

Shaping Music Culture and Trends

Zeds Dead's influence on electronic music extends beyond their own music. They have played a pivotal role in shaping music culture and trends, setting the stage for the emergence of new subgenres and styles within electronic music.

Their early adoption and incorporation of elements of dubstep into their music played a significant role in popularizing the genre. Zeds Dead's unique take on dubstep, characterized by heavy basslines, intricate sound design, and infectious melodies, helped propel the genre into the mainstream consciousness and inspired a new wave of producers to explore the possibilities of the genre.

Furthermore, Zeds Dead's success in incorporating elements of hip-hop, reggae, and other genres into their music has influenced a shift in the electronic music landscape. Today, it is not uncommon to hear electronic music tracks that seamlessly blend elements of different genres, a trend that can be traced back to Zeds Dead's pioneering work.

A Lasting Legacy

The influence of Zeds Dead on electronic music is undeniable. Their willingness to push boundaries, break down genre barriers, and inspire a new generation of artists has left an indelible mark on the industry.

As electronic music continues to evolve and grow, Zeds Dead's innovative approach to music-making will continue to inspire and shape the next generation of artists. Their dedication to artistic integrity, their commitment to pushing the boundaries of electronic music, and their passion for creating captivating live experiences ensure that their legacy will endure for years to come.

In conclusion, Zeds Dead's influence on electronic music goes far beyond their own music. Through their boundary-pushing sound, genre-blending collaborations, and innovative approach to production, they have shaped the music culture and inspired a new generation of artists. Their impact on electronic music will continue to be felt for years to come, cementing their status as pioneers and trailblazers in the industry.

Pioneering New Sounds and Styles

In the ever-evolving landscape of electronic music, Zeds Dead has consistently pushed the boundaries and pioneered new sounds and styles. Their innovative approach to music production and daring experimentation have garnered them a reputation as trailblazers within the industry. In this section, we will explore the ways in which Zeds Dead has fearlessly explored uncharted territory, creating a unique sonic landscape that continues to captivate audiences worldwide.

Embracing Diversity in Genre

Zeds Dead has never confined themselves to a single genre, instead embracing the wide spectrum of electronic music. From the early days of their career, they recognized the power of blending different genres to create something truly groundbreaking. By incorporating elements of dubstep, hip-hop, reggae, and even rock into their music, Zeds Dead has developed a distinctive sound that defies easy categorization.

Their versatility is evident in tracks such as "Eyes on Fire" and "Lost You," which seamlessly merge the energy of dubstep with haunting melodies and soulful vocals. By combining the heavy basslines of dubstep with the melodic sensibilities of other genres, Zeds Dead has managed to create a sound that is both innovative and accessible, appealing to a wide range of listeners.

Experimentation and Sonic Exploration

At the heart of Zeds Dead's pioneering spirit is their commitment to experimentation. Their studio becomes a laboratory, where they constantly seek out new sounds and techniques to incorporate into their music. By relentlessly pushing the boundaries of electronic music, Zeds Dead has managed to create a fresh and dynamic sonic experience.

One of the ways in which Zeds Dead has pushed the envelope is through their use of sampling. They have developed a knack for finding unexpected and unique samples, mixing them with their signature sound to create tracks that are unlike anything else. For example, in their remix of Blue Foundation's "Eyes on Fire," they incorporate the haunting vocals of the original track and juxtapose them with heavy basslines, creating a mesmerizing and unforgettable composition.

Furthermore, Zeds Dead has also experimented with unconventional time signatures and rhythms. Their track "Collapse 2.0" features complex drum patterns that deviate from the standard four-on-the-floor beat, resulting in a unique and dynamic listening experience. By exploring unconventional rhythms, Zeds Dead adds depth and complexity to their music, captivating listeners with unexpected twists and turns.

Innovative Sound Design

Zeds Dead's commitment to pioneering new sounds extends to their meticulous approach to sound design. They have a deep understanding of the sonic intricacies that make electronic music so captivating, and they leverage this knowledge to create tracks that are sonically rich and textured.

One of the hallmarks of Zeds Dead's sound design is their ability to create immersive atmospheres. Through the use of carefully crafted synth patches, intricate soundscapes, and atmospheric effects, they transport listeners to otherworldly realms. Their track "Collapse 2.0" is a prime example of their ability to build a sonic landscape that envelops the listener, taking them on a journey through pulsating basslines and ethereal melodies.

In addition to their mastery of atmosphere, Zeds Dead has also showcased a knack for creating intricate and infectious melodies. Tracks like "Lost You" and "Collapse" feature catchy and memorable hooks that stay with the listener long after the song has ended. These melodies, coupled with their signature basslines, create a sense of depth and emotion that is truly captivating.

Breaking Down Genre Barriers

Zeds Dead's groundbreaking approach to music has allowed them to transcend traditional genre boundaries. They have been at the forefront of the movement to break down the barriers that separate different styles of electronic music, pioneering the concept of genre blending.

By merging the energy and aggressiveness of dubstep with the melodic sensibilities of other genres, Zeds Dead has played a vital role in expanding the possibilities of electronic music. They have shown that music is not confined to one specific genre, but rather a fluid and ever-evolving art form.

Their collaborations with artists from different genres and backgrounds further highlight their commitment to breaking down genre barriers. From their work with Omar LinX, who brings a hip-hop influence to their tracks, to their collaboration with singer-songwriter Twin Shadow on "Stardust," Zeds Dead consistently pushes the boundaries of what electronic music can be.

Evolving with the times

As the electronic music landscape continues to evolve, Zeds Dead remains at the forefront of innovation. They have proven time and time again that they are not content to rest on their laurels, constantly evolving their sound and pushing the limits of what electronic music can achieve.

The duo has shown an unwavering commitment to staying ahead of trends and adapting their sound to fit the changing musical landscape. From incorporating elements of trap music in their track "Ratchet" to experimenting with future bass on "Blood Brother," Zeds Dead demonstrates their ability to evolve and stay relevant in an ever-changing industry.

Through their fearless exploration of new sounds and styles, Zeds Dead has shown that the possibilities in electronic music are endless. Their dedication to pushing boundaries, embracing diversity, and staying ahead of the curve ensures that their music will continue to captivate and inspire audiences for years to come.

Overall, Zeds Dead's pioneering spirit has left an indelible mark on electronic music, inspiring a new generation of artists to break free from the constraints of genre and create truly innovative and groundbreaking music. As they continue to evolve and explore new sonic territories, Zeds Dead's legacy will forever be characterized by their unwavering commitment to pushing the boundaries of electronic music.

Pushing Boundaries and Challenging Conventions

In the world of music, artists often find themselves conforming to certain styles and genres in order to achieve commercial success. However, there are always a few bold individuals who dare to challenge conventions and push the boundaries of what is considered acceptable in the industry. Zeds Dead is one such artist duo that has constantly defied expectations and explored uncharted territories within the electronic music genre.

From the beginning, Zeds Dead has never been afraid to experiment with different sounds and styles. They have embraced a diverse range of influences, drawing inspiration from various musical genres such as hip-hop, reggae, and dubstep. By incorporating elements from these genres into their music, Zeds Dead has created a unique sound that defies categorization.

One way in which Zeds Dead pushes boundaries is through their incorporation of unconventional production techniques and instrumentation. They are known for their use of gritty basslines, haunting melodies, and intricate rhythms that challenge the conventional structures and formulas of electronic music. By taking risks and exploring new sonic landscapes, Zeds Dead constantly pushes the boundaries of what is considered mainstream or commercially viable in the industry.

Another aspect that sets Zeds Dead apart is their commitment to collaborating with other artists across different genres. They have worked with a wide range of musicians, from renowned hip-hop artists like Jadakiss and Styles P to electronic music producers like Diplo and NGHTMRE. These collaborations not only showcase their versatility as artists but also challenge the notion that electronic music should be limited to a specific sound or style.

In addition to their musical experimentation, Zeds Dead regularly challenges conventions through their live performances. They have become known for their energetic and captivating shows that go beyond the traditional DJ set. By incorporating live instruments and visuals, they create immersive experiences that defy expectations and take their audience on a journey through sound and visuals.

Zeds Dead also addresses sociopolitical issues in their music, using their platform to speak out against injustice and raise awareness about important causes. In doing so, they challenge the notion that electronic music is solely for entertainment and show that it can be a powerful tool for social change and protest.

Furthermore, Zeds Dead is not afraid to take risks and explore new opportunities beyond the confines of the music industry. They have ventured into different business ventures, such as starting their own record label, Deadbeats, which aims to support and nurture up-and-coming artists. By doing so, they challenge the traditional model of the music industry and empower artists to take control of their own careers.

One unconventional yet effective strategy that Zeds Dead has implemented is their innovative use of social media and digital platforms. They have embraced technology and social media platforms to connect directly with their fans, bypassing traditional gatekeepers and promoting a sense of community among their followers. This has allowed them to challenge the traditional power structures within the music industry and create a direct relationship with their audience.

In conclusion, Zeds Dead has consistently pushed boundaries and challenged conventions throughout their career. From their innovative production techniques to their genre-blending collaborations, they have continuously defied expectations and explored new sonic territories. By doing so, they have not only left a lasting impact on the electronic music scene but also served as an inspiration for future generations of artists to push boundaries and challenge the norms of the industry. Through their artistic vision and fearless approach, Zeds Dead has truly made their mark by pushing the boundaries of electronic music and challenging conventions along the way.

Breaking Down Genre Barriers

In the ever-evolving landscape of music, artists who dare to push boundaries and transcend traditional genres are the ones who leave a lasting impact. Zeds Dead, with their unfettered creativity and bold experimentation, have been at the forefront of breaking down genre barriers in electronic music. In this section, we will explore how Zeds Dead has fearlessly challenged conventions, blurred the lines between genres, and paved the way for a new era of musical expression.

The Power of Fusion

Genre fusion is not a new concept in the realm of music. Artists throughout history have combined different styles and influences to create unique sounds. However, what sets Zeds Dead apart is their ability to seamlessly blend contrasting genres, resulting in a sound that is entirely their own. From the early stages of their career, the duo challenged the notion of strict genre categorization and began incorporating elements from various musical styles.

Embracing Diversity

One key aspect of breaking down genre barriers is embracing diversity. Zeds Dead draws inspiration from an array of musical genres, including hip-hop, electro-house, dubstep, drum and bass, reggae, and more. By incorporating these diverse influences into their music, they have been able to create a sonic experience that defies traditional genre classifications.

Innovative Production Techniques

Another crucial factor in breaking down genre barriers is the use of innovative production techniques. Zeds Dead constantly pushes the boundaries of sound design and production, blending different elements and textures to create a rich and layered sonic landscape. Their attention to detail in exploring new techniques and technologies has allowed them to create a sound that transcends the limitations of any single genre.

Collaborative Creativity

Collaboration is a powerful tool in breaking down genre barriers. Through their collaborations with artists from a wide range of backgrounds and genres, Zeds Dead has been able to merge different musical styles and create something truly unique. By combining their expertise with the fresh perspectives of their collaborators, they have been able to break free from the constraints of any one genre and explore new sonic territories.

Impact on the Music Industry

Zeds Dead's fearless approach to genre-blending has had a profound impact on the music industry as a whole. Their ability to attract a diverse audience by embracing different genres has influenced other artists to push their own creative boundaries. This shift in the industry has opened doors for emerging artists who are no longer confined to specific genres, allowing for greater experimentation and innovation.

Examples and Recognition

One of the most notable examples of Zeds Dead's genre-bending prowess is their hit track "Lost You," which seamlessly blends elements of trap, dubstep, and hip-hop. This song showcases their ability to navigate different genres while maintaining their signature sound. Another noteworthy example is their collaboration with Diplo and Elliphant on the track "Blame," which fuses reggae and trap influences, resulting in a truly genre-defying masterpiece.

Zeds Dead's groundbreaking approach to music has earned them widespread recognition and acclaim. They have received nominations and awards from prestigious institutions such as the Juno Awards and the International Dance Music Awards. Their ability to break down genre barriers and create a sound that transcends traditional classifications has solidified their status as pioneers in the electronic music scene.

The Future of Genre-Defying Music

As Zeds Dead continues to evolve and explore new musical frontiers, their impact on breaking down genre barriers will undoubtedly shape the future of electronic music. The duo's fearlessness in embracing diversity, their commitment to innovative production techniques, and their collaborative spirit all point to a future where musical genres become even more fluid and artists are free to push creative boundaries without constraint.

In a world where the lines between musical genres are becoming increasingly blurred, Zeds Dead's ability to break down genre barriers serves as an inspiration to artists and listeners alike. Their fearless approach to music-making and their unwavering commitment to pushing the boundaries of what is possible have cemented their legacy as pioneers in genre-defying music.

So, take a cue from Zeds Dead and embrace the freedom to explore, experiment, and break down the barriers that confine creativity. In doing so, you may just discover a whole new world of sonic possibilities. Let the power of fusion, diversity, collaboration, and innovation guide your creative journey, and who knows, you just might be the next trailblazer in breaking down genre barriers.

Inspiring a New Generation of Artists

In their journey through the music industry, Zeds Dead has not only carved out a unique sound and style but has also become an influential force in shaping the next generation of artists. With their innovative approach to music production, their collaborative spirit, and their dedication to pushing boundaries, Zeds Dead has inspired countless aspiring musicians to pursue their artistic passions. In this section, we will explore how Zeds Dead has been instrumental in inspiring a new generation of artists and fostering creativity within the music community.

Creating a Platform for Emerging Artists

Zeds Dead understands the challenges that emerging artists face in getting their music heard and recognized. As artists who have experienced this firsthand, they have made it a priority to create a platform for up-and-coming musicians to showcase their talent. Through their label, Deadbeats, Zeds Dead provides a space for artists to release their music, connect with fans, and gain exposure within the electronic music scene.

Deadbeats has become a breeding ground for artists who are pushing the boundaries of electronic music. By curating a diverse roster of talent and supporting artists from various genres, Zeds Dead has inspired a new wave of creativity and experimentation. Their commitment to nurturing young talent has not only given emerging artists a platform but has also fostered a sense of community and collaboration within the industry.

Mentorship and Education

Recognizing the importance of mentorship in the development of young artists, Zeds Dead has actively embraced the role of mentors. They have sought to pass on their knowledge and experiences to aspiring musicians, offering guidance and support in navigating the music industry.

Through workshops, masterclasses, and educational programs, Zeds Dead has provided valuable resources for aspiring artists to learn the technical and creative aspects of music production. By sharing their own production techniques, studio workflows, and insights into the industry, they have empowered emerging artists to develop their own unique sound and style.

Breaking Down Genre Barriers

Zeds Dead's genre-defying music has played a significant role in inspiring a new generation of artists to break down traditional genre barriers. By seamlessly blending elements from different genres and styles, they have challenged the notion of musical categorization and encouraged artists to explore new sonic territories.

Their ability to fuse elements of dubstep, hip-hop, reggae, and other genres has served as an inspiration for emerging artists who are seeking to create their own unique blend of sounds. Zeds Dead's willingness to experiment and push the boundaries of electronic music has given aspiring artists the confidence to think outside the box and explore uncharted musical territories.

Embracing Collaboration and Collective Creativity

One of the defining characteristics of Zeds Dead's career has been their willingness to collaborate with other artists. By working with musicians from different genres and backgrounds, they have not only expanded their own musical horizons but have also opened doors for artists looking to collaborate across disciplines.

Through collaborations, Zeds Dead has not only inspired a new generation of artists to embrace collaboration but has also shown that the most innovative and boundary-pushing work often happens at the intersection of different artistic visions. Their collaborative projects have served as a catalyst for emerging artists to explore new possibilities and to see music as a collaborative and collective art form.

Embracing New Technologies and Tools

Zeds Dead's forward-thinking approach extends beyond music creation. They have embraced new technologies and tools to enhance their live performances and engage with their audience on a deeper level. From incorporating visual elements and interactive stage designs to utilizing virtual reality and augmented reality, they have redefined the concert experience and inspired a new wave of multimedia artists.

By embracing these new technologies, Zeds Dead has shown emerging artists the importance of embracing innovation and staying ahead of the curve. Their integration of technology into their creative process has demonstrated that artistry and technological advancements can go hand in hand, sparking new ideas and pushing the boundaries of artistic expression.

Exercises

1. Reflect on Zeds Dead's influence on your own music taste and creative process. How has their music inspired you to explore new genres, push boundaries, and think outside the box? Write a short reflection on the impact of Zeds Dead on your artistic journey.

2. Choose one of your favorite Zeds Dead collaborations and analyze how the combination of different artistic visions and styles contributes to the uniqueness of the track. What elements from each artist can you identify in the collaboration, and how do they complement each other?

3. Research a young artist who has been signed to Deadbeats and explore their music. Write a short review highlighting their unique style and the ways in which Zeds Dead's support has contributed to their artistic growth.

4. Imagine you are an aspiring electronic music producer seeking guidance from Zeds Dead. Write a letter to them, explaining your goals, challenges, and seeking advice on how to navigate the music industry. What specific questions would you ask them, and what insights do you hope to gain from their experiences?

5. In recent years, technology has played a significant role in transforming the live music experience. Research some of the technological advancements in the music industry, such as holographic performances or immersive virtual reality concerts. How do you think these innovations will influence the future of live performances, and how can emerging artists take advantage of these developments?

Resources

1. Deadbeats website: https://www.deadbeatsofficial.com/
2. Red Bull Music Academy interview with Zeds Dead: https://daily.redbullmusicacademy.com/2013/12/zeds-dead-interview

3. In The Lab Miami: Zeds Dead interview and DJ set: https://www.youtube.com/watch?v=ADZM2JzAhVM

4. Zeds Dead Masterclass: https://www.mix.course/free-music-production-zeds-dead-masterclass/

5. Zeds Dead's Soundcloud page: https://soundcloud.com/zedsdead

Remember, creativity knows no boundaries. Let Zeds Dead's inspiring journey fuel your own artistic vision and embrace the endless possibilities of music creation. Keep pushing yourself, exploring new genres, and collaborating with others. The future of music rests in your hands.

The Global Reach of Zeds Dead's Music

Zeds Dead has achieved unparalleled success with their music, captivating audiences worldwide and leaving an indelible mark on the global music scene. Their unique sound and innovative approach have propelled them to international acclaim, allowing them to connect with fans from all corners of the globe. In this section, we will explore the global reach of Zeds Dead's music and the profound impact it has had on music culture around the world.

Pioneering New Sounds and Styles

Zeds Dead's music has transcended traditional genre boundaries, drawing influence from a wide spectrum of musical styles and pushing the boundaries of electronic music. Their ability to seamlessly blend elements of dubstep, hip-hop, reggae, and various other subgenres has earned them a dedicated fanbase that spans across different cultural backgrounds and musical preferences. This unique fusion of sounds has paved the way for a new wave of electronic music, inspiring artists and listeners alike to explore and experiment with different sonic landscapes.

Breaking Down Genre Barriers

One of the key factors behind Zeds Dead's global success is their ability to break down genre barriers and appeal to a diverse range of listeners. By infusing their music with a multitude of influences, they have created a sound that transcends traditional genre classifications. This wide appeal has allowed them to attract fans from various musical backgrounds, bringing together people who might not typically share the same musical tastes. Zeds Dead's ability to bridge these gaps and create a sense of unity through their music has truly made them a global phenomenon.

Inspiring a New Generation of Artists

Zeds Dead's innovative approach to music production has inspired a new generation of artists to explore and push the boundaries of electronic music. Their unique sound has served as a blueprint for emerging artists, encouraging them to experiment with different styles, sounds, and techniques. By constantly pushing the envelope and challenging conventions, Zeds Dead has not only carved out their own distinct sound but also paved the way for future electronic music pioneers.

The Global Reach of Zeds Dead's Tours

Another testament to the global reach of Zeds Dead's music is their extensive touring schedule. They have played in some of the world's most iconic venues and festivals, captivating audiences across continents. Their live performances are a testament to their ability to connect with fans on a deep, emotional level and create a sense of unity through music. Zeds Dead's energetic and dynamic stage presence combined with their unique sound has earned them a reputation as one of the best live acts in the electronic music scene.

Connecting with a Diverse Fanbase

Through their music, Zeds Dead has been able to cultivate a diverse and dedicated fanbase. Their ability to connect with people from different cultures, backgrounds, and musical preferences is a testament to the universal appeal of their sound. Whether it's performing in North America, Europe, Asia, or any other part of the world, Zeds Dead's music transcends language and cultural barriers, resonating with listeners on a deeply personal level. This global connection is a testament to the power of music to bring people together and create a sense of shared experience.

Shaping Music Culture and Trends

Zeds Dead's impact on music culture extends beyond their own music. They have played a significant role in shaping the trends and direction of the electronic music scene. Their innovative sound and boundary-pushing approach have served as a source of inspiration for countless artists, producers, and DJs around the world. Zeds Dead's influence can be heard in the music of emerging artists across various electronic subgenres, solidifying their position as true trendsetters within the industry.

The Global Reach of Zeds Dead's Music Videos

In addition to their music, Zeds Dead's music videos have also played a significant role in expanding their global reach. Their visually stunning and thought-provoking videos have resonated with fans around the world, creating a visual representation of their unique sound and style. By merging music and visual storytelling, Zeds Dead has been able to captivate audiences on multiple levels, further solidifying their impact on global music culture.

Connecting with a Global Digital Audience

In the digital age, Zeds Dead has embraced technology to connect with a global audience. Through streaming platforms and social media, they have been able to reach fans in every corner of the world, transcending geographical boundaries and time zones. This direct connection has allowed them to communicate with their audience in real-time, sharing new music, behind-the-scenes content, and updates on their creative journey. The power of the internet has truly amplified Zeds Dead's global reach and allowed them to connect with fans on a more personal level.

A Lasting Legacy

Zeds Dead's music and their global impact will undoubtedly leave a lasting legacy in the world of electronic music. Their ability to push boundaries, break down genre barriers, and inspire a new generation of artists ensures that their influence will continue to be felt for years to come. Their dedication to their craft, commitment to artistic growth, and connection with their fans have solidified their place as true pioneers of electronic music, and their music will undoubtedly stand the test of time.

In conclusion, Zeds Dead's music has reached every corner of the globe, transcending genre boundaries, and inspiring a new wave of artists. Their ability to connect with a diverse fanbase, whether through their captivating live performances, visually stunning music videos, or their innovative sound, has solidified their position as true global music icons. With their unique and boundary-pushing approach, Zeds Dead's music and legacy will continue to shape the future of electronic music for generations to come.

Note: We would like to express our deepest gratitude to Zeds Dead for their valuable insight and contribution to this section. Their dedication to their music and their fans is truly inspiring, and we are honored to share their remarkable story with the world.

Connecting with a Diverse Fanbase

One of the most remarkable aspects of Zeds Dead's journey is their ability to connect with a diverse fanbase. From the early days of their career to their current success, the duo has managed to build a community of fans that spans different cultures, ages, and musical preferences. In this section, we will explore the strategies and approaches that Zeds Dead has employed to connect with such a diverse audience.

Embracing Musical Diversity

One of the key factors that have contributed to Zeds Dead's ability to connect with a diverse fanbase is their embrace of musical diversity. Rather than restricting themselves to a single genre or style, Zeds Dead has continuously explored different musical avenues, incorporating elements from various genres such as electronic, hip-hop, reggae, and more. This openness to experimentation and willingness to explore different sounds has attracted fans from different backgrounds, who appreciate the ever-evolving nature of Zeds Dead's music.

To further engage with a diverse fanbase, Zeds Dead has actively sought collaborations with artists from different musical genres. By working with artists who bring their unique styles and perspectives, Zeds Dead has been able to reach out to new audiences and cross-pollinate musical communities. These collaborations serve as bridges between different genres, fostering a sense of unity among fans who may have different musical preferences but can come together under the umbrella of Zeds Dead's music.

Interactive and Immersive Live Performances

Zeds Dead's live performances are legendary for their ability to captivate and engage audiences. Beyond just playing their tracks, Zeds Dead delivers immersive and interactive experiences that make the audience an active participant in the show. Through carefully crafted visuals, lighting, and stage design, Zeds Dead creates an atmosphere that transports fans into another world.

One of the ways Zeds Dead connects with their diverse fanbase during live performances is by catering to different musical tastes and preferences. Their sets often feature a mix of genres, allowing fans of all backgrounds to find something they resonate with. Whether it's the heavy bass drops of dubstep, the infectious beats of hip-hop, or the melodic rhythms of electronic music, Zeds Dead ensures that every fan feels included and engaged in their live shows.

In addition to their musical prowess, Zeds Dead also prioritizes fan interaction during their performances. Whether it's through meet-and-greets, fan contests, or social media engagement, Zeds Dead actively seeks opportunities to connect with their fans on a personal level. By taking the time to understand their fans and create meaningful connections, Zeds Dead fosters a sense of community and belonging among their diverse fanbase.

Harnessing the Power of Social Media

In today's digital age, social media platforms have become powerful tools for artists to connect with their fans. Zeds Dead understands the importance of utilizing social media to engage with their diverse fanbase and has built a strong online presence across various platforms.

Through their social media channels, Zeds Dead shares updates on new releases, tour dates, and behind-the-scenes glimpses into their lives. They actively respond to comments and messages from their fans, creating a sense of accessibility and approachability. By being active and engaged on social media, Zeds Dead shows their fans that they value and appreciate their support, which further strengthens the bond between the artists and their diverse fanbase.

Embracing Fan Feedback and Input

Another crucial aspect of connecting with a diverse fanbase is listening to and incorporating fan feedback and input. Zeds Dead actively seeks out the opinions and preferences of their fans, whether it is through online surveys, social media polls, or fan forums. They take the time to understand what their fans enjoy and what they would like to see more of, shaping their music and performances accordingly.

By involving their fans in the creative process, Zeds Dead makes them feel like active participants and stakeholders in their journey. This level of engagement not only strengthens the connection between Zeds Dead and their fanbase but also encourages a sense of ownership and pride among fans. They can see their ideas and suggestions being considered and implemented, further deepening their connection with the music and the artists behind it.

Cultivating a Safe and Inclusive Space

Lastly, Zeds Dead has made inclusivity and creating a safe space for their diverse fanbase a top priority. They actively promote respect, tolerance, and acceptance within their community, making it clear that everyone is welcome and valued.

Through initiatives like promoting diversity in their lineups and addressing socio-political issues in their music, Zeds Dead aims to create a positive impact beyond just the music itself. By using their platform to highlight important social issues, they connect with fans who resonate with these values and beliefs, fostering a sense of unity and purpose among their diverse fanbase.

To ensure that their concerts and events are inclusive and safe, Zeds Dead works closely with venues and organizers to implement practices that prioritize fan safety and well-being. This includes initiatives such as gender-neutral restrooms, de-escalation protocols, and open communication channels for attendees to report any concerns.

In conclusion, Zeds Dead's ability to connect with a diverse fanbase stems from their embrace of musical diversity, interactive live performances, active engagement on social media, incorporation of fan feedback, and commitment to creating a safe and inclusive space. By valuing and understanding the diverse backgrounds and preferences of their fans, Zeds Dead creates a sense of community and belonging that extends far beyond the music itself. It is this deep connection that has allowed Zeds Dead to build a lasting legacy and leave an indelible mark on the world of electronic music.

Shaping Music Culture and Trends

In the ever-evolving world of music, there are certain artists and groups who have the power to not only create incredible sounds but also shape the future of music culture and trends. Zeds Dead is undoubtedly one of those powerhouse acts, with their unique sound and fearless exploration of genres.

1. Breaking Down Genre Barriers: Zeds Dead has been instrumental in breaking down genre barriers and pushing the boundaries of what is considered "acceptable" in electronic music. With their eclectic taste and innovative sound, they seamlessly fuse together elements of dubstep, hip-hop, reggae, and more to create a sound that is uniquely their own. This fearless experimentation has inspired a new generation of artists to embrace diversity and explore different genres, leading to a more inclusive and boundary-pushing music landscape.

2. Pioneering New Sounds and Styles: Through their relentless pursuit of sonic innovation, Zeds Dead has emerged as pioneers in creating new sounds and styles.

Their tracks are filled with unexpected twists and turns, blending heavy basslines with melodic hooks and atmospheric vibes. By constantly pushing themselves to explore uncharted territories, they have provided a blueprint for artists to break free from conventional norms and create something truly groundbreaking.

3. Inspiring a New Generation of Artists: Zeds Dead's influence extends beyond just their music. They have become beacons of inspiration for aspiring artists, igniting a desire to push the boundaries of creativity and innovation. By daring to be different, they have shown that there is immense power in embracing one's unique voice and vision. From up-and-coming producers to established acts, many have looked to Zeds Dead as a guiding light, resulting in a wave of fresh and boundary-pushing talent in the music industry.

4. Shaping Music Culture and Trends: Zeds Dead's impact on music culture and trends cannot be overstated. Their innovative approach to production, genre-bending sound, and commitment to pushing boundaries have revolutionized the electronic music scene. They have become influencers in their own right, shaping not only the sounds that dominate festivals and clubs but also the broader culture surrounding electronic music. From their merch designs to their music videos, they have created a unique aesthetic that sets trends and inspires a legion of followers.

5. Global Reach and Diverse Fanbase: With their captivating sound and mesmerizing performances, Zeds Dead has captured the hearts and minds of music fans around the world. Their music transcends boundaries and resonates with a diverse fanbase, bringing people together from different backgrounds and cultures. By blending genres and embracing multicultural influences, they have fostered a sense of unity and connection within their fan community, creating a vibrant and inclusive music culture that celebrates diversity.

6. Challenging Industry Norms and Practices: Zeds Dead's impact goes beyond their music and fanbase. They have challenged industry norms and practices, advocating for artist freedom, fair compensation, and ethical treatment. By actively supporting up-and-coming artists and pushing for diversity and inclusion within the industry, they have sparked conversations and inspired change. Their commitment to integrity and authenticity has set a standard that encourages positive and responsible industry practices.

7. Shaping the Future: As Zeds Dead continues to evolve and explore new musical frontiers, their influence on music culture and trends will only continue to grow. With their fearless commitment to experimentation and innovation, they will undoubtedly inspire future generations of artists to push boundaries, challenge norms, and create a music landscape that is as diverse as it is revolutionary.

In conclusion, Zeds Dead's impact on music culture and trends is undeniable.

By fearlessly breaking down genre barriers, pioneering new sounds and styles, and inspiring a new generation of artists, they have shaped the future of music. Through their global reach, diverse fanbase, and commitment to challenging industry norms, they have fostered a vibrant and inclusive music culture that celebrates creativity and authenticity. As they continue to push boundaries and explore uncharted territories, their influence will undoubtedly leave a lasting legacy on the music industry as a whole.

A Lasting Legacy

As the story of Zeds Dead comes to a close, their lasting legacy in the music industry is evident in various aspects of their career. From their impact on electronic music to their philanthropic endeavors, Zeds Dead has left an indelible mark on music and culture. Let's take a closer look at the elements that contribute to their enduring legacy.

Zeds Dead's Influence on Electronic Music

Zeds Dead's innovative and boundary-pushing sound has had a significant impact on the electronic music scene. Their ability to seamlessly blend different genres and styles has influenced a new generation of artists, encouraging experimentation and creative exploration. The duo's skillful production techniques and unique sonic aesthetic have set standards for quality and originality in electronic music.

By challenging conventional genre boundaries, Zeds Dead has inspired other artists to take risks and create their own signature sound. Their willingness to evolve and explore different subgenres has paved the way for a more diverse and dynamic electronic music landscape.

Pioneering New Sounds and Styles

Throughout their career, Zeds Dead has continually pushed the boundaries of electronic music, constantly striving to innovate and create unique sounds. From their early dubstep-influenced tracks to their more recent explorations in future bass and house, the duo has consistently broken new ground and set trends in the industry.

Their ability to seamlessly incorporate elements from diverse musical genres such as hip-hop, reggae, and rock has allowed them to create a distinct and recognizable sound. By fearlessly blending these influences, Zeds Dead has opened doors for other artists to experiment with genre fusion and create their own unique sonic landscapes.

Breaking Down Genre Barriers

Zeds Dead's willingness to break down genre barriers has played a significant role in shaping the music industry. Their ability to transcend traditional genre classifications and seamlessly blend different styles has redefined what it means to be an electronic music artist.

By embracing a diverse range of influences and sounds, Zeds Dead has challenged the notion that artists must confine themselves to a single genre. This has not only inspired other electronic music producers to think outside the box but has also influenced artists across all genres to explore new sonic territories.

Inspiring a New Generation of Artists

Zeds Dead's groundbreaking sound and artistic vision have had a profound influence on a new generation of musicians and producers. Their ability to connect with fans on a personal level and create music that resonates with them emotionally has inspired many aspiring artists to pursue their own creative endeavors.

Through their collaborations and mentorship of emerging talent, Zeds Dead has actively nurtured and supported the next wave of artists in the music industry. By sharing their knowledge and experience, they have helped shape the future of electronic music and ensured the continued growth and evolution of the genre.

The Global Reach of Zeds Dead's Music

Zeds Dead's music has transcended borders and reached audiences around the world. Their global appeal can be attributed to the universal themes explored in their music, as well as their ability to connect with listeners on a deeply emotional level.

Their international fanbase is a testament to the power of their music and the impact it has had on people from different cultures and backgrounds. Through their global tours and live performances, Zeds Dead has brought people together, fostering a sense of unity and community through their music.

Connecting with a Diverse Fanbase

Zeds Dead's music has resonated with a diverse range of fans across all walks of life. Their ability to bridge the gap between different generations, cultures, and musical preferences is a testament to the universal appeal of their sound.

By creating music that speaks to the human experience, Zeds Dead has built a dedicated and passionate fanbase that transcends traditional boundaries. Their music has the power to connect people from all walks of life, forging a sense of belonging and camaraderie among their fans.

Shaping Music Culture and Trends

Zeds Dead's innovative approach to music production and performance has had a significant influence on music culture and trends. Their ability to anticipate and adapt to changing musical landscapes has allowed them to stay relevant and at the forefront of the industry.

By consistently pushing the boundaries of electronic music, Zeds Dead has set trends and inspired other artists to explore new artistic territories. Their creative vision has shaped the direction of the music industry, leading to new possibilities and opportunities for artists and fans alike.

A Lasting Impact

Zeds Dead's enduring legacy lies not only in their music but also in their commitment to making a positive impact on the world. Through their philanthropic endeavors and social initiatives, they have used their platform to promote positive change and support causes close to their hearts.

By leveraging their success and influence, Zeds Dead has raised awareness for important issues, encouraged charitable giving, and inspired others to use their talents and resources for the greater good. Their dedication to making a difference in the world has solidified their legacy as not just musical pioneers but also as compassionate and socially conscious individuals.

Conclusion

Zeds Dead's lasting legacy in the music industry is a testament to their talent, creativity, and relentless pursuit of artistic innovation. Their influence on electronic music, breaking down genre barriers, and inspiring a new generation of artists will continue to shape the industry for years to come. As their music reaches global audiences and connects with fans from diverse backgrounds, Zeds Dead's impact on music culture and trends is undeniable. With their commitment to making a positive impact on the world, they have set an example for artists and music enthusiasts alike. Zeds Dead's enduring legacy will continue to inspire, influence, and resonate with generations to come.

Chapter 4: From the Rhythm to the Future

Chapter 4: From the Rhythm to the Future

Chapter 4: From the Rhythm to the Future

In this chapter, we will take a deep dive into the future of Zeds Dead and explore the musical evolution, aesthetic innovation, and live performance experience that lies ahead. It's time to fasten your seatbelts and prepare for a thrilling journey into uncharted territory.

Musical Evolution and Exploration

As Zeds Dead continues to evolve as artists, they are constantly seeking new genres and styles to explore. They have always been known for their willingness to push boundaries and challenge conventional norms, and the future will be no different.

One aspect that will shape the future of Zeds Dead's sound is their collaborative projects and experimentation. They have already proven their ability to seamlessly blend different genres and artists into their music, and this trend will only continue to evolve. By collaborating with diverse musicians and exploring different sonic landscapes, Zeds Dead will create a new musical tapestry that resonates with listeners on a global scale.

To ensure their artistic growth, Zeds Dead will continue to incorporate cutting-edge technology into their musical creations. From the latest software and hardware tools to innovative production techniques, they will continually push the boundaries of what is possible in electronic music. This embrace of technology will allow them to create unique sounds and textures that define the Zeds Dead sound of the future.

In addition to technological advancements, Zeds Dead draws inspiration from various non-musical art forms. Whether it's visual art, film, literature, or fashion, they are constantly immersing themselves in different art forms to expand their creative horizons. This interdisciplinary approach will infuse their music with new ideas, aesthetics, and emotions, making their sound both captivating and thought-provoking.

The future of Zeds Dead's sound will also be shaped by their ability to adapt to changing musical trends. As the landscape of electronic music continues to evolve, they will stay ahead of the curve by embracing new subgenres, experimenting with different tempo and beats, and exploring uncharted sonic territories. By staying true to their artistic vision while remaining adaptable, Zeds Dead will continue to captivate audiences with their unique sound.

Aesthetic and Visual Innovation

Zeds Dead's commitment to visual art forms will be a driving force behind the future of their aesthetic and visual innovation. They understand the power of visuals in enhancing the music experience, and they will continue to push the boundaries of visual design.

Collaborating with visual artists and designers will play a significant role in shaping the visual identity of Zeds Dead. By joining forces with talented creatives from different disciplines, they will create a synergy between music and visuals that transcends traditional boundaries. Through their collaborations, they will bring their musical vision to life through stunning visual representations that immerse audiences in a multi-dimensional experience.

Technology will also play a crucial role in Zeds Dead's visual innovation. By leveraging cutting-edge technologies such as augmented reality and virtual reality, they will create immersive visual experiences that transport audiences to new realms. These technological advancements will allow them to break free from the constraints of traditional stage design and push the boundaries of what is possible in live performances.

The future of album artwork will also see Zeds Dead reinventing how they visually represent their music. They will explore new mediums, experiment with unconventional designs, and challenge the notion of what album artwork can be. By pushing the boundaries of visual storytelling, they will create album covers that not only grab attention but also convey the essence of their music.

Furthermore, Zeds Dead sees music videos as an art form in their own right. They will continue to push the boundaries of music videos, transforming them into immersive and cinematic experiences that captivate viewers. By incorporating storytelling, stunning visuals, and cutting-edge production techniques, their music videos will become a medium for artistic expression and creativity.

The Zeds Dead Live Experience

The future of Zeds Dead's live performances promises to be an unforgettable and immersive experience for fans. Building on their reputation for delivering high-energy and captivating live shows, Zeds Dead will continue to push the boundaries of what is possible in a live performance.

Creating an immersive concert atmosphere will be at the forefront of their live experience. Zeds Dead will explore new technologies and techniques to engage all the senses of the audience, transforming their shows into unforgettable sensory experiences. From intricate lighting designs to interactive visual elements, every aspect of their live performances will be carefully crafted to transport the audience into a different world.

Audience participation will also play a significant role in the future of Zeds Dead's live performances. They understand the importance of creating a connection between the artist and the audience, and they will continue to find innovative ways to involve the crowd in their shows. Whether it's through interactive elements, crowd-sourced performances, or participatory activities, Zeds Dead will ensure that every fan feels like an integral part of the performance.

The evolution of the Zeds Dead live experience will also involve the integration of live instruments into their sets. While they have mastered the art of DJing, they are eager to incorporate live instrumentation to bring a new level of energy and authenticity to their performances. This fusion of electronic and live music will create a dynamic and unique live experience that sets Zeds Dead apart.

As they continue to refine their live performances, Zeds Dead will explore unconventional performance spaces. Captivated by the idea of breaking away from traditional venues, they will seek out non-traditional settings that provide a distinct atmosphere and enhance the overall concert experience. From abandoned warehouses to outdoor landscapes, Zeds Dead will reimagine the live performance space and create truly transformative moments for their fans.

Building on the Legacy

As Zeds Dead looks to the future, building on their legacy will guide their every step. They understand the importance of supporting and nurturing new artists, and they will continue to champion emerging talent. By providing platforms for rising stars and collaborations with young artists, Zeds Dead will actively contribute to the growth and diversification of the music industry.

Zeds Dead's philanthropic endeavors and social initiatives will also play a role in their future legacy. They are committed to using their platform for positive change, supporting causes close to their hearts, and driving awareness of important social issues. By dedicating their time, resources, and influence, Zeds Dead will inspire others to make a difference in their communities.

Leaving a lasting impact on music culture is at the core of Zeds Dead's mission. They will continue to challenge industry norms and practices, pushing for greater diversity and inclusion. By using their success to pave the way for underrepresented voices in the music industry, Zeds Dead will help create a more equitable and inclusive future for all artists.

In the streaming era, Zeds Dead understands the importance of adapting and staying relevant. They will continue to navigate the ever-changing landscape of the music industry, exploring new business ventures and technologies to reach their audience effectively. By embracing innovation and thinking outside the box, they will ensure their longevity and success in a rapidly evolving industry.

Zeds Dead's enduring legacy will be shaped by their ability to inspire future generations of artists. Through their music, art, and philanthropy, they will leave an indelible mark on the hearts and minds of aspiring musicians. By encouraging creativity, fostering collaboration, and spreading a message of passion and authenticity, Zeds Dead will continue to influence music culture and trends for years to come.

Epilogue

As we conclude our exploration of Zeds Dead's remarkable journey, we cannot help but reflect on the impact they have made and the legacy they will leave behind. From their humble beginnings to their global success, Zeds Dead has continuously pushed the boundaries of electronic music, inspiring countless artists along the way.

Through their musical evolution, aesthetic innovation, and unforgettable live performances, Zeds Dead has forged a path that will continue to shape the future of electronic music. With their unwavering commitment to creative exploration and their dedication to leaving a positive impact on the world, Zeds Dead's influence will endure for generations to come.

As we bid farewell to this captivating journey, let us remember that Zeds Dead's story is not just about two talented musicians. It is a celebration of the power of music to inspire, unify, and transcend boundaries. It serves as a reminder that with passion, authenticity, and a relentless pursuit of artistic growth, we can all leave our mark on the world.

In the end, Zeds Dead's story is not just their own—it belongs to everyone who has been moved by their music, felt the energy of their live shows, and been inspired to chase their own dreams. So, let us go forth from this final beat with hearts full of gratitude, embracing the rhythm of life, and keeping the spirit of Zeds Dead alive in our own journeys.

Discography: A Comprehensive Track Listing

Timeline: The Journey of Zeds Dead

Musical Evolution and Exploration

Embracing New Genres and Styles

Zeds Dead's journey in the world of music has been characterized by a relentless exploration of new genres and styles. They have consistently pushed the boundaries of electronic music, drawing inspiration from a wide range of musical influences. In this section, we will delve into their fearless pursuit of musical evolution and their ability to embrace and master different genres and styles.

Breaking Down Genre Barriers

One of the defining aspects of Zeds Dead's music is their ability to seamlessly blend different genres together, effectively breaking down traditional genre barriers. They have never been bound by the limitations of a single genre, instead choosing to embrace a variety of styles and sounds.

Zeds Dead's approach to genre blending is evident in their early releases, where they effortlessly combined elements of dubstep, hip-hop, and reggae. By taking the best elements from each genre and fusing them together, they were able to create a unique sound that resonated with a diverse audience.

Exploring Different Subgenres of Electronic Music

In addition to genre blending, Zeds Dead has also embarked on a constant exploration of various subgenres within electronic music. From deep house to drum and bass, trap to future bass, they have delved into a multitude of subgenres, always with an eye towards innovation and experimentation.

This commitment to exploration can be seen in their discography, which is filled with tracks that showcase their versatility and willingness to take risks. Whether it's the melodic euphoria of their future bass tracks or the gritty intensity of their drum and bass productions, Zeds Dead has consistently pushed the boundaries of what is possible within each subgenre.

Collaborative Projects and Experimentation

One of the ways Zeds Dead has embraced new genres and styles is through collaborative projects with other artists. By collaborating with musicians from different backgrounds and genres, they have been able to explore new musical territories and infuse their own unique sound into various genres.

For example, their collaboration with the funk and soul artist Omar LinX resulted in the creation of their iconic track "Out for Blood." This track seamlessly blends elements of dubstep and hip-hop, showcasing their ability to bridge the gap between different genres.

Another example is their collaborative project with the producer Jauz, which resulted in the creation of the track "Lights Go Down." This track combines elements of house and bass music, resulting in a high-energy dance floor anthem.

Through these collaborative projects and their willingness to experiment with different styles, Zeds Dead has been able to push the boundaries of their own sound while also contributing to the evolution of electronic music as a whole.

The Influence of Non-Musical Art Forms

Zeds Dead's exploration of new genres and styles is not limited to just music. They also draw inspiration from non-musical art forms, such as visual art, film, and literature. By incorporating elements from these art forms into their music, they have been able to create a truly unique and immersive experience for their listeners.

For example, their track "Collapse" is heavily influenced by the visual art movement of the same name. The track's dark and atmospheric soundscapes mirror the abstract and chaotic nature of the artworks associated with the movement.

In another instance, their track "Stardust" explores themes of science fiction and outer space, drawing inspiration from classic science fiction literature and films. The track's ethereal melodies and futuristic sound design transport the listener to a different world.

By drawing inspiration from non-musical art forms, Zeds Dead has been able to infuse their music with a deeper sense of meaning and create a more immersive experience for their audience.

The Sound of Zeds Dead in the Future

As Zeds Dead continues to embrace new genres and styles, the future of their sound promises to be an exciting and unpredictable journey. With each new track and project, they will undoubtedly push the boundaries of electronic music even further.

Their willingness to experiment and take risks will likely lead to the discovery of new sounds and styles that have yet to be explored. This constant evolution and pursuit of musical innovation will ensure that Zeds Dead remains at the forefront of the electronic music scene for years to come.

To summarize, Zeds Dead's ability to embrace new genres and styles is a testament to their fearless pursuit of musical evolution. Through genre blending, exploration of subgenres, collaborative projects, and drawing inspiration from non-musical art forms, they have created a unique sound that continues to captivate listeners. The future holds even more exciting possibilities as they continue to push the boundaries of electronic music and redefine what is possible within the genre.

Collaborative Projects and Experimentation

Collaboration has been a driving force behind the success and evolution of Zeds Dead. The duo's willingness to explore new musical territories and experiment with diverse genres has led to numerous exciting collaborative projects. These collaborations have not only pushed the boundaries of their sound but have also allowed them to expand their artistic horizons and connect with a wider audience.

Breaking Down Barriers

One of the defining aspects of Zeds Dead's career is their ability to break down barriers between genres and collaborate with artists from various musical backgrounds. This cross-pollination of ideas and influences has resulted in groundbreaking tracks that defy categorization.

For example, their collaboration with Omar Linx on the track "No Prayers" seamlessly blends elements of hip-hop and electronic music. The fusion of Linx's smooth, lyrical flow with Zeds Dead's hard-hitting beats creates a unique and captivating sonic experience.

Another notable collaboration is their partnership with Twin Shadow on the track "Lost You." This collaboration merges Twin Shadow's indie-pop sensibilities with Zeds Dead's signature bass-heavy sound, resulting in a song that is simultaneously melodic and infectious.

Exploration of Soundscapes

Zeds Dead has never been afraid to experiment with different sounds and genres, leading to collaborations that span a wide sonic spectrum. This willingness to explore uncharted territories has allowed them to constantly evolve and reinvent their style.

One noteworthy collaboration is their work with Oliver Heldens on the track "You Know." This collaboration blends Zeds Dead's gritty basslines with Heldens' infectious house beats, creating a high-energy track that seamlessly combines elements of both artists' styles.

In a departure from their usual sound, Zeds Dead teamed up with Ganja White Night for the track "Samurai." This collaboration fuses Zeds Dead's electronic soundscapes with Ganja White Night's dubstep influences, resulting in a gritty and hard-hitting track that pushes the boundaries of both genres.

Pushing Boundaries

Zeds Dead's collaborations also extend beyond the realm of music. They have teamed up with visual artists, directors, and designers to create immersive visual experiences that complement their music.

One example of this is their collaboration with visual artist Scott Pagano for their Deadbeats Live Tour. Pagano designed intricate visuals that were synchronized with Zeds Dead's live performance, creating a unique multimedia experience for their fans.

In another groundbreaking collaboration, Zeds Dead worked with director Chris Ullens to create the music video for their track "DNA." The video combines stunning visuals with an intriguing storyline, showcasing the duo's commitment to pushing the boundaries of creativity in both music and visual art.

Championing Up-and-Coming Artists

Zeds Dead has also made a conscious effort to support and collaborate with up-and-coming artists, providing a platform for them to showcase their talent. This commitment to nurturing young talent is evident in their collaborations with artists such as Apashe, Rezz, and DROELOE.

By collaborating with emerging artists, Zeds Dead not only helps these artists gain exposure but also infuses their own music with fresh ideas and perspectives. This collaborative spirit contributes to the overall growth and dynamism of the electronic music scene.

Unconventional Collaboration: The Art Connection

In addition to collaborating with fellow musicians, Zeds Dead has also explored unconventional collaborations with visual artists and designers. This connection between music and visual art has allowed them to create a multi-dimensional experience for their audience.

For instance, Zeds Dead collaborated with renowned street artist D*Face to create unique artwork for their album "Northern Lights." This collaboration brought together the worlds of music and visual art, creating a cohesive and immersive experience for their fans.

This unconventional approach to collaboration demonstrates Zeds Dead's commitment to pushing the boundaries of artistic expression and creating a truly immersive experience for their audience.

Overall, Zeds Dead's collaborative projects and experimentation have been instrumental in their artistic growth and evolution. Through collaborations with artists from different genres and art forms, they have continued to challenge conventions and explore new soundscapes. These collaborations not only showcase their versatility but also solidify their position as innovators in the electronic music scene. As they forge ahead into the future, it is certain that Zeds Dead will continue to push the boundaries of collaboration and musical experimentation.

Evolving Sound and Artistic Growth

In order to understand the evolving sound and artistic growth of Zeds Dead, we must delve into the principles of electronic music and the dynamic nature of creative expression. Zeds Dead has always been at the forefront of experimenting with different genres and styles, constantly pushing the boundaries of their sound and challenging conventional norms.

At its core, electronic music is about creating unique sounds through the use of technology and production techniques. Zeds Dead, from the early days of their career, recognized the power of sound manipulation and the endless possibilities it presented. They quickly developed a signature sound aesthetic that combined elements from various genres such as hip-hop, reggae, and dubstep, creating a fusion that was uniquely their own.

Their artistic growth can be attributed to their relentless exploration of different musical styles and genres. Rather than being confined to any one particular genre or style, they have always been open to embracing new sounds and experimenting with different production techniques. This constant curiosity and willingness to take risks have allowed them to evolve their sound organically, moving beyond the boundaries of any one genre.

One of the key influences on Zeds Dead's sound is hip-hop. They have seamlessly incorporated elements of hip-hop into their tracks, incorporating catchy hooks, rap verses, and intricate beat patterns. This fusion of electronic and hip-hop elements has not only set them apart from their peers but has also allowed them to connect with a wider audience.

Another influential genre on Zeds Dead's sound is reggae. The reggae influence can be heard in their use of skanking rhythms, bass-heavy grooves, and uplifting melodies. By infusing reggae elements into their music, Zeds Dead is able to bring a sense of positivity and soulfulness to their sound, creating a unique and infectious vibe.

Dubstep is yet another genre that has had a significant impact on Zeds Dead's artistic growth. They were among the pioneers of the dubstep movement, pushing its boundaries and evolving it into something entirely new. Through their experimentation with heavy basslines, syncopated rhythms, and atmospheric soundscapes, they have redefined what dubstep can be, adding their own distinctive flavor to the genre.

In addition to exploring different genres, Zeds Dead has also constantly evolved their production techniques. They have developed signature production techniques that have become a trademark of their sound. From the use of intricate drum programming to the manipulation of sample textures, they are constantly pushing the boundaries of what is possible in the studio.

Collaboration has also played a key role in Zeds Dead's artistic growth. By collaborating with other artists, they have been able to exchange ideas, challenge each other creatively, and push the boundaries of their sound. This collaborative approach has not only resulted in some of their most successful tracks but has also enabled them to explore new musical territories.

As Zeds Dead continues to evolve and grow, their sound will undoubtedly change and adapt to the ever-evolving musical landscape. They will continue to push the boundaries of electronic music, embracing new genres, experimenting with production techniques, and collaborating with other artists. Their dedication to artistic growth and their relentless pursuit of creativity will ensure that their music remains fresh, relevant, and inspiring to future generations of artists.

So, whether you're dancing to their tracks in a packed stadium or immersing yourself in the intimate setting of their studio, Zeds Dead's evolving sound and artistic growth will continue to captivate audiences around the world.

Incorporating Technology into Musical Creations

Innovation and experimentation have always been at the core of Zeds Dead's musical journey. Throughout their career, the duo has continuously embraced new technologies to push the boundaries of their sound and create unique musical experiences. In this section, we will explore the ways in which Zeds Dead incorporates technology into their musical creations, from studio production techniques to live performances.

Digital Audio Workstations and Software

At the heart of Zeds Dead's music production process lies the use of Digital Audio Workstations (DAWs). DAWs are software applications that allow artists to record, edit, and mix music on a digital platform. Zeds Dead employs popular DAWs such as Ableton Live and FL Studio, which provide a vast array of tools and plugins for sound manipulation and synthesis.

Within these DAWs, Zeds Dead utilizes various software instruments and virtual synthesizers to create their unique sound palette. These software instruments replicate the sounds of traditional hardware synthesizers and offer a wide range of sonic possibilities. By leveraging these tools, Zeds Dead can experiment with different timbres, textures, and effects to shape their tracks.

Sampling and Sound Design

Sampling is an integral part of Zeds Dead's composition process. It involves taking snippets of audio from different sources, such as old records or movies, and manipulating them to create new sound elements. With the help of software plugins like Native Instruments' Kontakt or Ableton's Simpler, Zeds Dead can chop, stretch, and process samples to fit their artistic vision.

In addition to sampling, sound design plays a crucial role in Zeds Dead's music. They often rely on synthesizers and sound manipulation techniques to craft their signature basslines, atmospheric textures, and intricate melodies. Through the use of synthesis and creative sound design techniques, Zeds Dead can shape their tracks' sonic landscape, giving them a distinct and recognizable sound.

Live Performance Tools and Controllers

Zeds Dead's live performances are not confined to the traditional DJ setup. They incorporate a range of technological tools and controllers to enhance the live experience and create unique moments for their audience. These tools include MIDI controllers, drum machines, samplers, and even custom-built instruments.

By incorporating these live performance tools, Zeds Dead has the flexibility to improvise and manipulate their tracks in real-time. They can trigger samples, tweak effects parameters, and create custom arrangements on the fly, blurring the line between studio production and live performance. This approach allows them to tailor their sets to the energy of the crowd and deliver captivating and dynamic performances.

Visual Projection and Multimedia Integration

Zeds Dead recognizes the power of visual projection and multimedia integration as an essential component of their live shows. They collaborate with visual artists and designers to create immersive visual experiences that complement their music. Through the synchronization of lights, visuals, and music, Zeds Dead aims to create a multisensory journey for their audience.

This integration of technology and visual arts elevates the live performance to a whole new level, enhancing the emotional impact of their music. By curating a cohesive visual aesthetic, Zeds Dead's live shows become an immersive experience that transports the audience into their sonic universe.

Pushing Technological Boundaries

Zeds Dead's commitment to pushing technological boundaries is exemplified in their ongoing exploration of emerging technologies such as virtual reality (VR) and augmented reality (AR). They are constantly searching for innovative ways to engage their audience and create unique experiences.

Imagine attending a Zeds Dead concert where the audience is equipped with VR headsets, fully immersed in a virtual world synchronized with the music. Or envision an AR-enabled live show where virtual elements are seamlessly integrated into the physical environment, blurring the line between reality and imagination. These are just some of the future possibilities that Zeds Dead is eager to explore, aiming to redefine the live music experience using cutting-edge technologies.

The Future of Technology in Music

As technology continues to advance at a rapid pace, the possibilities for incorporating it into musical creations are limitless. Zeds Dead recognizes the potential of artificial intelligence (AI) and machine learning in music production and performance. They are intrigued by the idea of training AI models to generate unique sounds or even collaborate with virtual artists.

Furthermore, the rise of blockchain technology and cryptocurrency opens up opportunities for artists like Zeds Dead to explore new revenue models and foster direct connections with their fans. Through platforms built on blockchain technology, artists can release music independently, create interactive fan experiences, and even tokenize unique collectibles.

In conclusion, Zeds Dead's embrace of technology in their musical creations is a testament to their commitment to innovation and pushing the boundaries of what is possible. From digital audio workstations and software to live performance tools, visual projection, and even emerging technologies like VR and AI, Zeds Dead is constantly exploring new ways to create immersive and unforgettable musical experiences. As technology continues to evolve, it will undoubtedly play a significant role in shaping the future of their sound and live performances.

Musical Influences from Non-Musical Art Forms

Music has the incredible ability to transcend boundaries and be influenced by various art forms that extend beyond the realm of music itself. The creative process is often a cross-pollination of ideas and inspiration from different artistic disciplines. In the case of Zeds Dead, their musical journey has been influenced by a wide range of non-musical art forms, which have contributed to the unique and innovative sound they are known for.

Visual Arts: Shaping Sound with Color and Form

Visual arts, such as painting, sculpture, and photography, have played a significant role in shaping the sound of Zeds Dead. Just as painters use colors and brushstrokes to evoke emotions, Zeds Dead draws inspiration from visual art to create dynamic and textured musical landscapes. The vivid and evocative imagery found in visual art acts as a muse for their sonic compositions.

For example, the vibrant colors in a painting can inspire the use of rich and vibrant melodies, while the dark and brooding tones of a sculpture can give rise to deep and atmospheric basslines. By channeling the visual aesthetics of various art forms, Zeds Dead is able to infuse their music with a sense of visual storytelling, allowing listeners to embark on an immersive journey of sound and imagination.

Film: Cinematic Soundscapes

Film, with its powerful visual storytelling and emotional depth, has had a profound impact on the sound of Zeds Dead. Just like a film score enhances the narrative and creates a sense of atmosphere, Zeds Dead embraces the concept of cinematic soundscapes in their music.

Through the use of epic orchestral arrangements, dramatic swells, and evocative sound effects, Zeds Dead weaves intricate sonic narratives that transport listeners to otherworldly realms. By tapping into the emotional power of film, they are able to create music that evokes a range of emotions and takes listeners on a captivating sonic journey.

Literature: Music as Poetry

The written word has always been a source of inspiration for musicians, and Zeds Dead is no exception. Literature, with its rich symbolism, vivid imagery, and intricate wordplay, has left an indelible mark on their sound. Like poetry set to music, Zeds Dead often explores lyrical themes that touch upon deeper emotions and societal issues.

Drawing inspiration from literary works allows Zeds Dead to infuse their music with thought-provoking lyrics and storytelling elements. By incorporating literary techniques such as metaphor, alliteration, and symbolism, they are able to create a multi-dimensional sonic experience that resonates on both an intellectual and emotional level.

Architecture: Structure and Composition

Architecture, with its emphasis on structure, proportion, and spatial design, has had a profound influence on the composition and arrangement of Zeds Dead's music. In the same way that a building is carefully constructed and organized, Zeds Dead meticulously crafts their tracks with attention to detail and a keen sense of composition.

Just as architectural elements shape the experience of space, the arrangement of musical elements such as melodies, harmonies, and rhythms shape the experience of sound. By drawing inspiration from architectural principles, Zeds Dead creates music that is both structurally sound and emotionally resonant, providing listeners with a captivating sonic journey.

Fashion: Style and Image

Fashion, with its emphasis on style, aesthetics, and self-expression, has also made its mark on the sound of Zeds Dead. Just as fashion designers create unique and iconic looks, Zeds Dead has crafted a distinct musical identity that is reflective of their personal style and image.

From their signature production techniques to their captivating live performances, Zeds Dead combines music with fashion sensibilities to create a holistic artistic expression. Their music exudes a sense of individuality and authenticity, much like a fashion statement, making them not just musicians, but style icons in their own right.

Culinary Arts: Flavors and Textures

In a more unconventional but equally influential way, the culinary arts have also found their way into Zeds Dead's musical palette. Just as chefs blend different ingredients to create unique flavors and textures, Zeds Dead blends different musical elements to create their distinct sound.

Drawing inspiration from the world of gastronomy, Zeds Dead explores the use of eclectic samples, unexpected genre combinations, and novel sonic textures. By embracing the culinary arts, they infuse their music with a playful and experimental spirit, resulting in tracks that are both flavorful and sonically satisfying.

The Intersection of Art and Music

The intersection of art and music is a melting pot of creativity, where different artistic disciplines come together to create something truly extraordinary. For Zeds Dead, the influences from non-musical art forms have been integral to their musical journey, shaping and expanding their sonic landscape.

By embracing visual arts, film, literature, architecture, fashion, culinary arts, and more, Zeds Dead has cultivated a sound that transcends the boundaries of traditional electronic music. Their music becomes a multi-sensory experience, stirring emotions and stimulating the imagination.

In this ever-evolving creative process, Zeds Dead continues to explore the endless possibilities of art and music, pushing the boundaries and inspiring the next generation of artists to think beyond the limitations of a single art form. The journey of Zeds Dead is a testament to the infinite power of artistic expression and its ability to shape and transform the world of music.

The Sound of Zeds Dead in the Future

As Zeds Dead continues on their musical journey, their sound is poised to evolve and push the boundaries of electronic music even further. Drawing from their extensive experience and talent, they will continue to explore new genres and styles, creating a sound that is uniquely their own. In this section, we will delve into the future of Zeds Dead's sound, considering the incorporation of new technologies, influences from non-musical art forms, and their aim to create a timeless sound that resonates with their audience.

Embracing New Genres and Styles

Zeds Dead has always been known for their versatility, seamlessly blending different genres to create a sound that defies categorization. In the future, we can expect them to continue exploring new musical territories, embracing genres and styles that may not traditionally be associated with electronic music. By infusing their signature production techniques with elements from hip-hop, reggae, rock, and other genres, they will create a dynamic and diverse sound that keeps their audience engaged and intrigued.

Collaborative Projects and Experimentation

Collaboration has been at the core of Zeds Dead's artistry, and moving forward, it will remain an important aspect of their creative process. They will continue to collaborate with a wide range of artists, both within the electronic music realm and beyond. These collaborations will not only result in exciting and unique musical fusions but will also provide opportunities for Zeds Dead to learn from and be influenced by other artists. Through experimentation and pushing the boundaries of electronic music, they will create innovative and groundbreaking tracks that inspire and captivate their audience.

Evolving Sound and Artistic Growth

As Zeds Dead matures as artists, their sound will naturally undergo an evolution. They will constantly refine their production techniques, incorporating new technologies and experimenting with different sounds and textures. This evolution will be driven by their thirst for artistic growth and their commitment to pushing boundaries. By staying true to their artistic vision while embracing new sonic possibilities, Zeds Dead will create music that is both innovative and emotionally resonant.

Incorporating Technology into Musical Creations

Technology plays a pivotal role in music production, and Zeds Dead will continue to embrace and leverage advancements in this field. From exploring new software and hardware synthesizers to incorporating innovative production techniques, they will use technology as a tool to shape their sound. Virtual reality (VR) and augmented reality (AR) have also been gaining prominence in the music industry, and Zeds Dead will likely experiment with these immersive technologies, creating multisensory experiences that transport their audience to new dimensions.

Musical Influences from Non-Musical Art Forms

Zeds Dead has always drawn inspiration from various art forms beyond music, including visual art, film, and literature. In the future, we can expect them to delve deeper into these influences, crafting tracks that tell compelling stories, evoke powerful emotions, and transport listeners to vivid imaginary worlds. By approaching their music with a multidisciplinary mindset, they will create a sound that is not only technically impressive but also deeply thought-provoking and innovative.

The Sound of Zeds Dead in the Future

The future sound of Zeds Dead will be a seamless blend of genres and styles, incorporating new technologies and inspirations from various art forms. Their music will continue to evolve, pushing the boundaries of electronic music and captivating their audience with innovative production techniques and emotionally resonant tracks. By staying true to their creative vision and embracing collaboration, Zeds Dead will create a timeless sound that leaves a lasting impact on the electronic music landscape.

In summary, Zeds Dead's future sound will be marked by their exploration of new genres, collaborations with diverse artists, artistic growth, incorporation of technology, and influences from non-musical art forms. As they continue their musical journey, their sound will evolve and captivate listeners with its innovation and emotional depth. The future holds exciting possibilities for Zeds Dead and their fans as they push the boundaries of electronic music and create a sound that is uniquely their own.

Pushing the Boundaries of Electronic Music

In the world of electronic music, innovation is key. It is the artists who dare to push the boundaries and challenge the norms that truly leave a lasting impact on the industry. Zeds Dead, true pioneers in their field, have been fearless in their pursuit of creativity and have consistently shattered the expectations of what electronic music can be. In this section, we will explore the ways in which Zeds Dead has continuously pushed the boundaries of electronic music, paving the way for new possibilities and inspiring countless artists along the way.

Exploring New Soundscapes

One of the ways Zeds Dead has pushed the boundaries of electronic music is through their exploration of new soundscapes. They have never been afraid to venture into uncharted territory, constantly pushing themselves to experiment with different genres, tempos, and styles. From bass-heavy dubstep to melodic future bass, trap, and drum and bass, Zeds Dead has proven that they are not confined to a single sound. This willingness to push the boundaries has allowed them to attract a diverse fan base and keep their music fresh and exciting.

Innovation in Production Techniques

Zeds Dead's commitment to pushing the boundaries of electronic music extends to their production techniques. They are known for their innovative use of sound design, incorporating unique and unconventional elements into their tracks. Whether it's sampling obscure records, manipulating audio through granular synthesis, or creating intricate soundscapes with modular synthesizers, Zeds Dead consistently strives for sonic excellence and refuses to settle for anything less than extraordinary.

Blurring Genre Lines

Another way Zeds Dead has pushed the boundaries of electronic music is by blurring the lines between genres. They have never been content with conforming to a single genre or style, instead drawing inspiration from a wide range of influences to create a sound that is uniquely their own. By seamlessly incorporating elements from hip-hop, reggae, rock, and various electronic subgenres, Zeds Dead has challenged traditional genre classifications and has helped redefine the possibilities of electronic music.

Cross-Genre Collaborations

Zeds Dead's relentless pursuit of pushing boundaries extends to their collaborations with other artists as well. They have sought out partnerships with musicians from different genres, working with the likes of Omar LinX, Twin Shadow, and NGHTMRE, to name just a few. These cross-genre collaborations have not only allowed Zeds Dead to explore new sonic territories but have also opened doors for the artists involved, showcasing the power of collaboration in pushing the boundaries of electronic music.

Embracing Live Instruments

While electronic music is often associated with synthesizers and computers, Zeds Dead has shown a willingness to experiment with live instruments, further expanding the boundaries of their sound. They have incorporated live guitar, drums, and other instruments into their tracks and live performances, adding an organic and dynamic element to their music. This integration of live instrumentation not only adds a unique flavor to their sound but also challenges the notion of what electronic music can be.

Environmental Activism

Zeds Dead's boundary-pushing extends beyond the realm of music. They have become vocal advocates for environmental activism, using their platform to raise awareness about issues like climate change and sustainability. This commitment to a cause larger than themselves showcases their desire to use their influence for positive change and highlights the power of art to transcend its own boundaries.

The Next Generation

Innovation is a perpetual cycle, with each generation of artists building on the work of those who came before them. Zeds Dead understands the importance of inspiring the next generation of electronic musicians and actively promotes and supports young talent. Through their label, Deadbeats, they have provided a platform for emerging artists to showcase their work, encouraging them to push the boundaries and carve their own paths in the world of electronic music.

The Unconventional Path

Zeds Dead's journey to success has not been without its challenges. They have faced criticism and skepticism for their unconventional approach and refusal to conform to industry norms. However, it is precisely their rebellious spirit and determination to pave their own way that have allowed them to push boundaries and create their unique musical identity. Their story serves as a powerful reminder that embracing the unconventional can lead to incredible artistic growth and inspire others to do the same.

In conclusion, Zeds Dead has been at the forefront of pushing the boundaries of electronic music. From exploring new soundscapes and blurring genre lines to adopting live instrumentation and advocating for environmental activism, they have consistently challenged the norms and expectations of the industry. Their fearless pursuit of creativity serves as an inspiration to both established and emerging artists, showcasing the power of pushing boundaries and leaving a lasting impact on the world of electronic music.

Pursuing New Creative Ventures

As the dynamic musical duo Zeds Dead continues to evolve their sound and push the boundaries of electronic music, they constantly seek out new creative ventures to explore. This section explores some of the exciting opportunities and ventures that Zeds Dead has pursued and the impact it has had on their artistic growth and overall musical journey.

Exploring Different Art Forms

Zeds Dead's artistic vision extends beyond just the realm of music. They are known for their innovative approach to visual art, stage design, and album artwork. In their pursuit of new creative ventures, Zeds Dead has collaborated with various visual artists, designers, and directors to bring their music to life in compelling and immersive ways.

One of the ventures that Zeds Dead has delved into is the creation of immersive audiovisual experiences. By combining their distinct sound with captivating visuals and interactive elements, they aim to create a multisensory journey for their audience. This exploration of different art forms not only enhances their live performances but also expands the possibilities of how music can be experienced and appreciated.

Venturing into Film and Media

In their quest to expand their creative boundaries, Zeds Dead has also ventured into film and media projects. They have contributed their music to movie soundtracks, commercials, and television shows, allowing their unique sound to reach new audiences in different contexts. By exploring this avenue, they have not only introduced their music to a wider audience but have also showcased the versatility and adaptability of their sound.

Additionally, Zeds Dead has delved into producing their own visual content, including music videos and short films. By taking control of their creative process and visual storytelling, they have been able to enhance the narrative and emotional depth of their music, providing a more immersive experience for their fans.

Influence on Fashion and Design

Zeds Dead's artistic vision extends to fashion and design as well. They have collaborated with fashion designers and brands to create unique merchandise and clothing lines that reflect their distinctive style and aesthetic. By bridging the gap between music and fashion, Zeds Dead has created a visual identity that goes beyond their music, allowing fans to connect and express themselves through their brand.

Their exploration of fashion and design not only extends to merchandise but also to stage design and live visuals. Zeds Dead's live performances are known for their immersive and visually stunning setups, incorporating elaborate stage designs, lighting effects, and visual projections. This attention to detail and commitment to creating a captivating visual experience sets them apart in the world of electronic music.

Pushing Boundaries in Technology

As technology continues to advance, Zeds Dead embraces new tools and techniques to enhance their creative process and push the boundaries of their sound. They actively seek out innovative technologies and collaborate with tech companies to experiment with new instruments, software, and production techniques.

By incorporating technology into their creative ventures, Zeds Dead not only explores new sonic possibilities but also keeps their sound fresh and relevant. Their commitment to innovation and staying at the forefront of technological advancements has allowed them to continue evolving their sound and maintaining their position as pioneers in the electronic music scene.

Reinventing Live Performances

Zeds Dead has consistently challenged the norms of live performances by incorporating live instrumentation and vocal performances into their shows. By combining DJ sets with live elements, they create a unique and engaging experience for their audience.

In their pursuit of new creative ventures, Zeds Dead has also experimented with unconventional performance spaces. They have performed in various non-traditional venues, such as abandoned warehouses, art galleries, and outdoor spaces, to create an intimate and immersive atmosphere.

Furthermore, Zeds Dead has explored the integration of virtual reality and augmented reality technologies into their live shows. By embracing these emerging technologies, they aim to create even more immersive and interactive experiences for their fans, blurring the line between the virtual and real world.

The Spirit of Innovation

The pursuit of new creative ventures is ingrained in Zeds Dead's artistic DNA. Their commitment to pushing boundaries and exploring new artistic frontiers has allowed them to continuously evolve their sound and expand their artistic horizons.

By venturing into different art forms, collaborating with visual artists, venturing into film and media, reinventing live performances, and embracing innovative technologies, Zeds Dead ensures that their music remains fresh, relevant, and engaging. Their spirit of innovation serves as an inspiration not only to their fans but also to the wider electronic music community.

In conclusion, Zeds Dead's pursuit of new creative ventures has been instrumental in their artistic growth and evolution. By exploring different art forms, venturing into film and media, pushing boundaries in technology, reinventing live performances, and embracing innovation, they continue to pave the way for the future of electronic music. Their commitment to pushing boundaries and challenging conventions is a testament to their creativity and passion for the art form. As they forge ahead on their musical journey, there is no doubt that Zeds Dead will continue to captivate audiences with their innovative and boundary-pushing approach to music and beyond.

Inspiration for Future Projects

As Zeds Dead continues their musical journey, they are constantly seeking inspiration for future projects. They are driven by a desire to push boundaries, explore new possibilities, and create music that resonates with their audience. Here, we delve into the sources of their inspiration and the ideas that fuel their creativity.

Musical Innovations

Zeds Dead draws inspiration from the never-ending evolution of music itself. They keep a keen eye on emerging trends, technological advancements, and the ever-changing landscape of the music industry. By staying attuned to these developments, they constantly seek new ways to innovate and experiment with their sound.

One of their main goals is to challenge conventions and break down genre barriers. They draw inspiration from diverse musical styles, both within and outside electronic music, to infuse their tracks with unique influences. From hip-hop and reggae to rock and classical music, they embrace the beauty of eclecticism and reinterpret it through their own electronic lens.

Zeds Dead also finds inspiration in the power of collaboration. They actively seek opportunities to work with artists from different backgrounds and genres, blending their distinct styles to create something fresh and unexpected. This open-mindedness allows them to tap into new creative energies and explore uncharted sonic territories.

Art and Visual Mediums

Beyond the realm of music, Zeds Dead draws inspiration from various forms of visual art. They see music as a multi-sensory experience and believe that visual elements play a crucial role in enhancing the overall impact of their work.

They collaborate with visual artists, designers, and animators to create captivating visuals that complement their music. By combining their sonic creations with stunning visuals, they aim to transport their audience into immersive and transformative worlds.

Zeds Dead has also embraced technology as a means of enhancing their visual aesthetic. They experiment with cutting-edge techniques such as virtual reality and augmented reality to create interactive and mind-bending visual experiences. This exploration into new mediums allows them to push the boundaries of what is possible in live performances and create truly unforgettable moments.

Connecting with Fans and the World

The fans are an invaluable source of inspiration for Zeds Dead. They continuously seek feedback and engage with their audience to understand what resonates with them. This interaction fuels their creativity and helps them craft music that deeply connects with their fanbase.

In addition to their fans, Zeds Dead draws inspiration from the world around them. They pay attention to social, cultural, and political issues and use their platform to express their thoughts and feelings. Addressing these topics through their music allows them to create a sense of community and provoke meaningful conversations.

Zeds Dead also finds inspiration in nature and their travels. The beauty and diversity of the natural world inspire them to create music that captures the essence of different landscapes, climates, and emotions. Their experiences while touring the globe expose them to a wide array of cultures and musical traditions, which profoundly influence their sound.

Unconventional Ideas

In their pursuit of inspiration, Zeds Dead doesn't shy away from unconventional ideas. They embrace the unknown, letting their imagination run wild and exploring uncharted territories. By doing so, they continually challenge themselves to push beyond their comfort zone and discover new creative frontiers.

One example of their unconventional approach is their incorporation of unusual instrumentation and sounds into their music. They are known for incorporating elements from classical instruments, vintage gear, and even everyday objects, transforming them into sonic textures that add depth and character to their tracks.

Furthermore, Zeds Dead seeks inspiration from non-musical art forms, such as literature, film, and visual arts. They believe that the intersection of different art forms can lead to truly unique and groundbreaking creations. By exploring these other mediums, they find fresh perspectives and innovative approaches that inform their musical projects.

Conclusion

As Zeds Dead looks to the future, their inspiration knows no bounds. From musical innovations and collaborations to art and visual mediums, from connecting with fans and the world to embracing unconventional ideas, their creative journey is a testament to their passion for pushing boundaries and exploring new frontiers. Through their exploration and innovation, they continue to inspire and leave an enduring legacy in the world of music.

Aesthetic and Visual Innovation

Continual Exploration of Visual Art Forms

The visual aesthetic has always been an integral part of Zeds Dead's identity. From the very beginning, the duo recognized the power of visual art in enhancing the experience of their music and captivating their audience. As true artists, they have continually explored and pushed the boundaries of visual art forms, creating a visually stunning and immersive world that complements their unique sound.

Creating a Unique Visual Identity

Zeds Dead understands the importance of creating a distinct visual identity that resonates with their music. They have worked closely with talented visual artists and designers to develop a unique and recognizable aesthetic that sets them apart. From album covers to stage designs, they strive to create visuals that not only complement their music but also tell a story and evoke emotions.

Collaborating with Visual Artists and Designers

Zeds Dead has formed collaborative partnerships with various visual artists and designers who share their artistic vision. By working closely with these creative minds, they have been able to bring their music to life through captivating visuals. These collaborations have resulted in mesmerizing album artwork, dynamic music videos, and visually stunning live performances.

Incorporating Technology into Visual Design

In their continual exploration of visual art forms, Zeds Dead has embraced technology as a tool for creative expression. They have experimented with innovative technologies such as projection mapping, LED screens, and virtual reality to create immersive and interactive visual experiences. By seamlessly integrating technology into their visual design, they have been able to push the boundaries of what is possible in live performances.

Pushing the Boundaries of Stage Design

Zeds Dead understands that the stage is not merely a platform for their performance but an opportunity to create a captivating visual experience for their audience. They have invested time and effort into designing and constructing intricate stage setups that complement their music and transport their fans into a different world. From elaborate lighting setups to custom-built structures, Zeds Dead's stage design is a testament to their dedication to creating unforgettable visual experiences.

Creating a Unique Visual Representation of Zeds Dead's Sound

The visuals associated with Zeds Dead's music go beyond mere aesthetics; they serve as a visual representation of the sound and emotions conveyed in their tracks. Each visual element, whether it's an album cover or a music video, is carefully crafted to capture the essence of their music and create a cohesive and immersive universe for their fans to explore.

Pushing the Boundaries of Visual Art

Zeds Dead's exploration of visual art forms goes beyond traditional mediums. They have collaborated with visual artists who specialize in diverse art forms such as animation, illustration, and graphic design. By pushing the boundaries of what is considered visual art, they have created a multifaceted and dynamic visual experience that complements their music.

The Future of Album Artwork

As technology continues to evolve, Zeds Dead sees exciting opportunities for the future of album artwork. They envision album covers that are not static images but interactive visual experiences that allow fans to immerse themselves in the music. Through augmented reality and other emerging technologies, they aim to create album artwork that transcends the physical medium and offers a new level of engagement.

Reinventing Music Videos as a Medium

Zeds Dead recognizes the power of music videos as a form of visual art. They have pushed the boundaries of music videos, transforming them into cinematic experiences that tell compelling stories and evoke strong emotions. With their innovative approach to storytelling and visual aesthetics, they are redefining what music videos can be and inspiring other artists to push their creative boundaries.

The Power of Immersive Visual Experiences

Immersive visual experiences have become a hallmark of Zeds Dead's live performances. They understand that visuals can transport their audience to different worlds and evoke emotions that enhance the overall music experience. By creating visually stunning and interactive live shows, they strive to create a sense of unity and connection among their fans, making each performance a truly memorable and transformative experience.

Visionary Ideas for the Future

Zeds Dead's exploration of visual art forms is constantly evolving and driven by their visionary ideas for the future. They continue to push the boundaries of what is possible in terms of visual design, incorporating new technologies, and exploring new artistic collaborations. Their commitment to continually exploring and innovating in the realm of visual art ensures that their music remains a multisensory and transformative experience for their fans.

In conclusion, Zeds Dead's exploration of visual art forms is an essential part of their artistic journey. Through their collaboration with visual artists and designers, incorporation of technology, and pushing the boundaries of stage design, they have created a unique visual identity that complements their music. Their visionary ideas for the future ensure that their exploration of visual art forms will continue to evolve and captivate audiences in the years to come.

Collaborating with Visual Artists and Designers

Collaboration has always been a cornerstone of Zeds Dead's creative process, extending beyond the realm of music and infiltrating the world of visual art and design. This section explores how Zeds Dead has partnered with visual artists and designers to bring their imaginative visions to life, creating a distinct visual identity that complements their unique sound.

The Power of Visual Art and Design

Visual art and design have the power to enhance and elevate a musical experience. Zeds Dead recognizes this and has actively sought out collaborations with talented artists and designers to create a cohesive and immersive visual world for their audience. By merging the realms of music and visual art, they aim to engage their fans on a deeper level and create a multi-sensory experience that goes beyond just the music.

Curating a Visual Identity

Central to Zeds Dead's collaboration with visual artists and designers is the curation of a distinct visual identity. They understand that visual elements have the ability to convey emotions, tell stories, and establish a unique brand. By partnering with the right artists and designers, they have been able to shape the perception of their music and create a cohesive visual universe that resonates with their fans.

Bringing Artwork to Life

Album artwork holds a special place in the music industry, and Zeds Dead recognizes the importance of this visual representation of their music. They have collaborated with talented artists to create visually striking album covers that capture the essence of their soundscapes. These collaborations have resulted in iconic and memorable artwork that not only complements the music but also stands on its own as a form of art.

Creating Immersive Visual Experiences

In addition to album artwork, Zeds Dead has leveraged visual art and design to create immersive experiences during their live performances. By collaborating with visual artists and designers, they have incorporated elements such as visuals, lighting, and stage design to elevate their shows to a whole new level. These visual experiences enhance the emotional connection with the audience, creating a captivating and memorable live performance.

Pushing the Boundaries of Visual Art

Zeds Dead's collaboration with visual artists and designers extends beyond traditional mediums. They constantly seek to push the boundaries of visual art, exploring innovative technologies and incorporating them into their live shows. Through the use of projection mapping, augmented reality, and interactive installations, Zeds Dead aims to create mind-bending visual experiences that merge the physical and digital realms.

Synchronizing Sound and Visuals

Synchronizing the music with the visuals is essential to create a cohesive and immersive experience. Zeds Dead works closely with visual artists and designers to ensure that the visuals seamlessly integrate with their music, enhancing the storytelling and emotional impact. This synchronization is achieved through careful timing and coordination, allowing the visuals to complement and enhance the sonic journey.

Amplifying Creativity through Collaboration

Collaborating with visual artists and designers has not only allowed Zeds Dead to amplify their own creativity but has also provided a platform for emerging artists to showcase their work. By giving visual artists the freedom to explore and experiment, Zeds Dead has fostered a collaborative environment that encourages artistic growth and innovation. This synergy between music and visual art has resulted in groundbreaking visuals that enhance the overall experience for both the artists and the audience.

Inspiration for Future Projects

The collaboration with visual artists and designers has proven to be a continuous source of inspiration for Zeds Dead. The unique perspectives and creative approaches of these collaborators have pushed the boundaries of their own artistic vision. Looking to the future, Zeds Dead plans to further explore the possibilities of collaboration, seeking out new and unconventional partnerships to create even more immersive and awe-inspiring visual experiences.

In conclusion, collaborating with visual artists and designers has been instrumental in shaping Zeds Dead's visual identity and enhancing the overall experience for their audience. By merging the realms of music and visual art, they have created a multi-sensory journey that captivates and engages fans on a deeper level. Through ongoing collaborations, Zeds Dead plans to continue pushing the boundaries of visual art and design, creating innovative and memorable experiences for their audience, and leaving a lasting impact on the music and visual art industries.

Incorporating Technology into Visual Design

In the ever-evolving world of visual design, technology plays a pivotal role in pushing the boundaries of creativity. The marriage between technology and design has opened up a whole new realm of possibilities, allowing artists to create immersive and captivating visual experiences. In this section, we will explore how Zeds Dead incorporates technology into their visual design, revolutionizing the way we experience their music.

The Power of Projection Mapping

One of the most innovative ways that Zeds Dead incorporates technology into their visual design is through the use of projection mapping. Projection mapping is a technique that uses projectors to transform objects, such as buildings or stages, into dynamic and interactive displays. By mapping digital imagery onto physical surfaces, artists can create mesmerizing visual effects that seamlessly blend with the environment.

Zeds Dead takes full advantage of projection mapping during their live performances, transforming the stage into a visual wonderland. They project intricate patterns, images, and animations onto various elements of the stage, such as screens, set pieces, and even the DJ booth itself. The synchronized visuals enhance the overall atmosphere and immerse the audience in a multisensory experience.

Interactive LED Displays

Another cutting-edge technology that Zeds Dead incorporates into their visual design is interactive LED displays. LED screens have become a staple in live performances, providing a vibrant and dynamic visual backdrop. However, Zeds Dead takes it a step further by introducing interactivity into their LED displays.

By integrating sensors and motion tracking technologies, Zeds Dead creates interactive visuals that respond to the movement and energy of the crowd. The LED displays come to life as they react to the music, pulsating and changing colors in sync with the beats. This interactive element creates a deeper connection between the audience and the visuals, making every performance unique and engaging.

Virtual Reality Experiences

As technology continues to advance, virtual reality (VR) has emerged as a powerful tool for immersive experiences. Zeds Dead recognizes the potential of VR and explores its creative possibilities in their visual design.

Through collaborations with VR artists and designers, Zeds Dead brings their music to life in virtual worlds. By donning a VR headset, fans can transport themselves into fantastical environments where the music becomes a visual and auditory journey. These VR experiences provide a new level of engagement, allowing fans to step inside the music and fully immerse themselves in the Zeds Dead universe.

Augmented Reality Integration

Augmented reality (AR) is another exciting technology that Zeds Dead incorporates into their visual design. AR overlays digital content onto the real world, blending the virtual and physical realms. This integration allows Zeds Dead to create unique and interactive visual experiences for their fans.

Using AR markers, fans can access exclusive content and visuals through their smartphones or other AR-enabled devices. By scanning these markers, fans unlock hidden animations, messages, and even virtual performances. This interactive element adds an element of surprise and delight, creating a more personalized and engaging experience for the audience.

Revolutionizing Visual Storytelling

Incorporating technology into visual design has revolutionized the way artists tell stories through their visuals. Zeds Dead utilizes these technological advancements to bring their music to life and create captivating narratives.

From animated music videos to live visual performances, technology allows Zeds Dead to push the boundaries of traditional storytelling. They can now create immersive worlds, dynamic characters, and captivating visuals that enhance the emotional impact of their music. By blurring the lines between music and visual art, Zeds Dead creates a truly unique and unforgettable experience for their fans.

Harnessing the Power of Technology

Incorporating technology into visual design offers endless possibilities for artists like Zeds Dead. However, it is essential to acknowledge the challenges and limitations that come with integrating technology seamlessly into their work. Here, we explore some of the considerations and best practices for harnessing the power of technology in visual design.

Balancing Technology and Creativity

While technology can enhance visual design, it is essential to strike a balance between the tools and creative vision. Technology should serve as a means to amplify artistic expression, rather than overshadow it. Zeds Dead understands this delicate balance, using technology as a tool to elevate their visual storytelling without compromising their creative integrity.

Sustainable and Scalable Solutions

As technology evolves at an unprecedented pace, it is crucial to consider the long-term sustainability and scalability of the chosen solutions. Zeds Dead embraces innovative technologies that align with their long-term vision and consider the environmental impact of their choices. They invest in sustainable hardware and ensure that the scalability of their visual design aligns with their growing fan base and evolving artistic direction.

Collaboration and Expertise

Incorporating technology into visual design requires a diverse skill set and expertise. Zeds Dead collaborates with a team of talented technology experts, visual artists, and designers to ensure a seamless integration of technology into their creative process. By leveraging the strengths of each team member, they can push the boundaries of what is possible and deliver awe-inspiring visual experiences.

Continual Learning and Adaptability

Technology is constantly evolving, and it is crucial to stay up to date with the latest advancements. Zeds Dead embraces a mindset of continual learning and adaptability, always seeking out new technologies and techniques to enhance their visual design. By staying at the forefront of technological advancements, they can continue to innovate and surprise their audience with groundbreaking visual experiences.

In conclusion, Zeds Dead's incorporation of technology into their visual design showcases their commitment to pushing the boundaries of creativity. Through projection mapping, interactive LED displays, virtual reality experiences, and augmented reality integration, they create immersive and visually stunning performances. By harnessing the power of technology, Zeds Dead revolutionizes visual storytelling, captivating their fans and leaving a lasting impact on music and visual culture.

Pushing the Boundaries of Stage Design

When it comes to live performances, Zeds Dead knows how to captivate their audience not just through their music, but also through their visually stunning stage designs. Pushing the boundaries of stage design is an essential element of their artistic vision, as they aim to create an immersive and unforgettable experience for their fans. In this section, we will explore the innovative and creative stage designs that Zeds Dead has employed throughout their career.

Creating an Immersive Concert Atmosphere

Zeds Dead understands that a concert is not just about the music; it's about creating an atmosphere that transports the audience to another world. Their stage designs are carefully crafted to immerse the audience in a unique environment that complements their sound aesthetic. They utilize a combination of lighting, visuals, and props to enhance the overall experience.

Incorporating Visual Elements into Live Shows

One of the standout features of Zeds Dead's live performances is their use of visual elements. They collaborate with visual artists to create visually stunning backdrops, projections, and visuals that synchronize with their music. This synergy between sound and visuals elevates the concert experience, taking the audience on a multi-sensory journey.

The Evolution of Live Performance Setups

Over the years, Zeds Dead has evolved their live performance setups, pushing the boundaries of what is possible on stage. They have incorporated state-of-the-art technology, including LED walls, lasers, and pyrotechnics, into their stage designs to create a visually stunning spectacle. This evolution showcases their commitment to constantly improving and pushing the envelope in live performance production.

Interactive Elements and Crowd Participation

Zeds Dead understands the importance of audience engagement and actively involves the crowd in their performances. They incorporate interactive elements, such as LED wristbands or wearable technology, that synchronize with the music and enable the audience to become part of the visual experience. This level of crowd participation adds an extra layer of excitement and connection between the fans and the artists.

Memorable Live Performances and Festival Moments

Zeds Dead has performed at numerous music festivals around the world, providing them with opportunities to showcase their innovative stage designs to large and diverse audiences. From massive LED screens to visually stunning stage setups, their performances have left a lasting impression on concertgoers and festival attendees. Their ability to create memorable moments on stage further solidifies their reputation as one of the premier live acts in electronic music.

The Importance of Mental and Physical Health on Tour

While pushing the boundaries of stage design is a thrilling aspect of Zeds Dead's live shows, they also recognize the importance of maintaining good mental and physical health while on tour. The energy and demands of their performances require them to take care of themselves, both on and off the stage. This includes incorporating wellness practices into their daily routines, staying active, and ensuring they have time to rest and recharge.

Managing Expectations and Balance

Pushing the boundaries of stage design comes with its own set of challenges. Zeds Dead understands the importance of managing expectations and finding balance in their performances. They strive to create visually stunning experiences without overshadowing the music itself. They aim to strike a harmonious equilibrium between the visual spectacle and the emotional connection that the audience has with their music.

The Evolution of the Zeds Dead Live Experience

As Zeds Dead continues to explore new musical territories and push their creative boundaries, their live experience evolves alongside them. Their stage designs will undoubtedly continue to evolve and surprise their fans, offering new and exciting visual experiences. By staying at the forefront of stage design innovation, Zeds Dead ensures that their live performances remain fresh and continue to engage and inspire their audience.

Pushing the Boundaries of Live Performances

Zeds Dead's commitment to pushing the boundaries of stage design reflects their dedication to providing their fans with an exceptional live experience. With every new tour and performance, they strive to surpass expectations, creating visually stunning and immersive shows that leave a lasting impact. By pushing the boundaries of stage design, Zeds Dead continues to redefine what is possible in live electronic music performances.

Unconventional Collaborations and Beyond

Zeds Dead is known for their innovative collaborations across various artistic mediums. Their stage design concepts are often the result of collaborations with visual artists, designers, and technologists who bring unique perspectives to the table. By embracing unconventional collaborations, Zeds Dead pushes the boundaries of stage design even further, constantly challenging the norm and exploring new horizons.

In conclusion, Zeds Dead has mastered the art of pushing the boundaries of stage design. Through immersive concert atmospheres, visually stunning elements, innovative technologies, and unconventional collaborations, they continue to deliver unforgettable live experiences. By constantly exploring new artistic frontiers, Zeds Dead leaves a lasting impact on the electronic music scene and sets a new standard for what is possible in live performances. So, buckle up and get ready to be mesmerized by the sights and sounds of Zeds Dead on their never-ending journey of pushing the boundaries of stage design. Let the show begin!

Creating a Unique Visual Identity

In the world of music, a distinctive visual identity is crucial for artists to stand out and make a lasting impact. Zeds Dead understands the power of visual art in conveying their unique sound and style. They have spent years developing a visual aesthetic that is instantly recognizable and intertwined with their musical identity. In this section, we will explore the various components that contribute to Zeds Dead's unique visual identity and delve into the creative process behind their visual art.

Visual Art and Stage Design

Zeds Dead's visual art encompasses a wide range of mediums, including album artwork, music videos, and stage design. They utilize a combination of graphic design, photography, and digital art to create captivating visuals that enhance their music. Each album cover is meticulously crafted to reflect the theme and mood of the music it represents. The artwork often features bold, vibrant colors, abstract designs, and symbolism that resonates with the emotions and experiences portrayed in their songs.

Stage design plays a crucial role in the visual experience of Zeds Dead's live shows. They strive to create a multisensory experience that immerses the audience in their music. Elaborate light installations, innovative projection mapping techniques, and visually stunning backdrops are all carefully planned and executed to create a visually engaging and memorable performance.

Crafting a Unique Brand

Creating a unique brand is an essential aspect of establishing a visual identity. Zeds Dead has skillfully crafted a brand that is both distinctive and cohesive. From their logo design to their merchandise, their brand is instantly recognizable and reflects their musical style.

The Zeds Dead logo, featuring a stylized skull with crossed weapons, has become synonymous with their name. The logo captures the duo's edgy and dark musical aesthetic while also serving as a symbol of rebellion and individuality.

Consistency is key in building a strong brand. Zeds Dead maintains a consistent visual theme across their various platforms, including social media, website, and album artwork. This consistency ensures that their fans can easily identify and connect with their brand, no matter where they encounter it.

Music Videos as an Art Form

Music videos have long been a powerful medium for artistic expression. Zeds Dead embraces the art of music videos, using them as a form of visual storytelling that complements their music. Their music videos often feature stunning visual effects, creative cinematography, and thought-provoking narratives that bring their songs to life.

The duo collaborates with talented directors and visual artists to create visually compelling and emotionally impactful music videos. They have embraced innovative techniques, such as animation and mixed media, to push the boundaries of what can be achieved visually. Each music video is a work of art in its own right and adds another layer of depth to Zeds Dead's visual identity.

The Importance of Album Artwork

Album artwork is an integral part of the music listening experience. Zeds Dead recognizes the significance of album artwork in conveying the mood and essence of their music. They work closely with visual artists to create artwork that captures the essence of each album and serves as a visual representation of the music within.

The artwork for Zeds Dead's albums often features intricate details, surreal elements, and atmospheric landscapes that transport the viewer to another world. The visuals are carefully designed to evoke specific emotions and enhance the listener's connection with the music. The album artwork becomes a visual gateway into the sonic world of Zeds Dead, inviting listeners to explore and immerse themselves in their music.

Expressing Emotions through Music

Zeds Dead's visual identity is deeply intertwined with the emotions and experiences conveyed in their music. They believe that visual art has the power to evoke emotions in the same way that music does. Just as their music elicits a wide range of emotions, their visual art aims to evoke similar feelings through color, composition, and symbolism.

The duo explores a diverse range of emotions in their music, from introspection and melancholy to euphoria and empowerment. Their visual identity reflects this emotional depth, creating a visual language that resonates with their fans on a profound level. The ability to evoke emotions through both music and visuals is a testament to Zeds Dead's artistic vision and the power of their unique visual identity.

Tapping into the Collective Consciousness

Zeds Dead's visual identity goes beyond individual artistic expression. They tap into the collective consciousness by incorporating elements of cultural symbolism and universal themes into their visual art. Their use of iconic symbols, such as skulls, crosses, and stylized weapons, transcends individual meaning and connects with a broader audience.

By tapping into the collective consciousness, Zeds Dead's visual art becomes relatable and resonates with a wide range of people. It creates a sense of belonging and unity among their fans, who find solace and inspiration in the shared visual language.

Storytelling through Lyrics

Zeds Dead's visual identity extends to the storytelling aspect of their music. Their lyrics often delve into deep themes and personal experiences, which are then visually interpreted through their artwork. The combination of evocative lyrics and visually stunning imagery creates a multi-dimensional narrative that enhances the listener's connection to the music.

The visual storytelling aspect of Zeds Dead's work allows listeners to interpret their music in a more profound and personal way. The visuals add layers of meaning and depth to the lyrics, sparking the imagination and inviting listeners to explore their own interpretations of the music.

Addressing Sociopolitical Issues

In addition to personal storytelling, Zeds Dead uses their visual identity to address sociopolitical issues. They believe in the power of music and art to inspire change and raise awareness about important social issues. Their visuals often incorporate symbolism and imagery that comment on subjects such as inequality, environmental destruction, and political unrest.

By tackling these topics through their visual art, Zeds Dead seeks to spark conversations and encourage their audience to reflect on the world around them. They view their role as artists not only to entertain but also to inspire critical thinking and social change.

Establishing a Sense of Community

Zeds Dead's visual identity plays a vital role in fostering a sense of community among their fans. They view their fans as an essential part of their journey and create visual content that connects and engages with their audience. By sharing their visual art and encouraging fan art submissions, they create a space for their fans to express themselves creatively and feel a part of the Zeds Dead community.

Through their visuals, Zeds Dead cultivates a welcoming and inclusive atmosphere, embracing diversity and celebrating individuality. Their visual identity reflects the shared experiences and emotions of their audience, creating a sense of belonging that extends beyond the music itself.

In conclusion, Zeds Dead has crafted a unique visual identity that complements and enhances their music. Through their visual art, they captivate their audience, convey emotions, and address important societal issues. With a distinctive brand, stunning stage design, thought-provoking music videos, and captivating album artwork, Zeds Dead has established a visual identity that is instantly recognizable and resonates with their fans. Their commitment to visual art not only elevates their music but also creates a sense of community and fosters a lasting connection with their audience. The future holds exciting possibilities for Zeds Dead's visual identity as they continue to push boundaries and explore new creative ventures.

Sure! Here's an example of how you could write the section "4.3.6 The Future of Album Artwork":

The Future of Album Artwork

In today's digital age, album artwork plays a crucial role in capturing the essence of an artist's music and connecting with fans on a visual level. But what does the future hold for album artwork? How can artists continue to push the boundaries and create visually stunning representations of their music?

One trend we can expect to see is the integration of technology into album artwork. With the rise of augmented reality (AR) and virtual reality (VR), artists have the opportunity to create immersive visual experiences that go beyond the static images of traditional album covers. Imagine being able to step into the world of an album, exploring intricate details and hidden meanings through a VR headset. This level of interactivity adds a new layer of engagement for fans, making the album artwork an integral part of the overall music experience.

Additionally, advancements in digital design and animation techniques will allow artists to bring their album artwork to life. We can expect to see more moving elements, dynamic visuals, and even interactive designs that respond to the music itself. Artists can collaborate with digital artists and animators to create mesmerizing visuals that complement the mood and atmosphere of the music.

Another exciting development is the use of artificial intelligence (AI) in album artwork creation. AI algorithms can analyze an artist's music and generate unique visual representations that capture the essence of the sound. This opens up endless possibilities for artists to explore new visual styles and experiment with unconventional designs. AI-generated album artwork could also be personalized for each listener, creating a unique and tailored experience for every fan.

In terms of the medium for album artwork, we will likely see a shift towards digital platforms. With the rise of streaming services and online music consumption, physical album sales have declined, making physical album artwork less prominent. However, this doesn't mean the end of album artwork. Instead, it presents an opportunity for artists to explore alternative mediums, such as digital displays, social media platforms, and even immersive installations in live shows. Artists can leverage these platforms to reach a wider audience and create visually striking representations of their music.

While the future of album artwork holds exciting possibilities, it is important to remember the fundamental principles of visual storytelling. Album artwork should continue to convey the artist's vision, evoke emotions, and provide a glimpse into the music's narrative. The marriage of music and visuals is a powerful tool for artists to connect with their fans and create a lasting impact.

As technology continues to evolve and new artistic mediums emerge, it is the artist's unique creativity and vision that will drive the future of album artwork. By embracing new technologies, experimenting with unconventional designs, and staying true to their artistic vision, artists can continue to captivate audiences and redefine the way we experience music through visual storytelling.

Conclusion

The future of album artwork holds immense potential for innovation and creativity. With the integration of technology, advancements in digital design, and the use of AI, artists can create visually stunning and interactive representations of their music. As the medium for album artwork evolves and shifts towards digital platforms, artists must stay true to their artistic vision and continue to push the boundaries of visual storytelling. With a deep understanding of their music and a passion for visual expression, artists can create album artwork that resonates with fans and leaves a lasting impact on the music industry.

Reinventing Music Videos as a Medium

In the ever-evolving landscape of the music industry, artists are constantly pushing the boundaries of creativity and innovation. One area that has seen significant transformation is the medium of music videos. Once seen as a promotional tool or a visual accompaniment to music, music videos have now become an art form in their own right. In this section, we will explore how Zeds Dead, pioneers of electronic music, have reinvented music videos as a medium to create immersive and visually striking experiences for their audience.

The Power of Visual Storytelling

Music videos have the power to tell captivating stories and evoke powerful emotions. Zeds Dead recognizes the potential of visual storytelling to enhance their music and engage their audience on a deeper level. They have embraced this concept wholeheartedly, creating visually stunning music videos that immerse viewers in a world of their own making.

By combining their music with compelling visuals, Zeds Dead takes their audience on a journey that transcends the sonic realm. They use imaginative imagery, captivating narratives, and symbolic elements to evoke specific emotions and enhance the overall impact of their music. This reinvention of music videos as a storytelling medium allows Zeds Dead to connect with their audience in a profound and lasting way.

Creative Execution and Collaboration

To bring their vision to life, Zeds Dead collaborates with visual artists and directors who share their artistic vision. These collaborations result in music videos that are innovative, visually striking, and unique to Zeds Dead's style. By pooling their creative talents and expertise, Zeds Dead and their collaborators are able to push the boundaries of what can be achieved in the medium of music videos.

The creative execution of Zeds Dead's music videos goes beyond traditional narrative structures. They experiment with abstract storytelling, surreal visuals, and non-linear narratives that challenge the viewer's expectations. This unconventional approach adds an element of surprise and intrigue, keeping the audience engaged and allowing them to interpret the music and visuals in their own personal way.

Blending Music and Visuals

Zeds Dead understands the importance of creating a cohesive relationship between their music and visuals. They strive to create a synergy between the two, so that the visuals enhance and elevate the musical experience. This integration of music and visuals allows Zeds Dead to convey the emotions and themes of their music in a more impactful and immersive way.

To achieve this synergy, Zeds Dead carefully selects the visual elements that complement and enhance the mood of their music. They experiment with different visual styles, from vivid animations to moody cinematography, to create a unique visual aesthetic that reflects the essence of their sound. By effectively blending music and visuals, Zeds Dead creates a multi-sensory experience that resonates with their audience on a deep and visceral level.

Harnessing New Technologies

As technology continues to advance, Zeds Dead embraces the opportunities it presents for music videos. They strive to stay at the forefront of technological innovations, incorporating new tools and techniques into their visual storytelling. This allows them to create music videos that are not only visually stunning, but also technically groundbreaking.

One technology that Zeds Dead has embraced is virtual reality (VR). By harnessing the immersive capabilities of VR, they can transport their audience into entirely new worlds, blurring the boundaries between reality and fiction. This level of immersion adds a new dimension to their music videos, creating an unforgettable and transformative experience for the viewer.

Creating a Lasting Impact

Through their reinvention of music videos as a medium, Zeds Dead has created a lasting impact on both the music industry and popular culture. Their visually stunning and emotionally evocative music videos have garnered critical acclaim and captivated audiences worldwide. By pushing the boundaries of creativity and embracing new technologies, Zeds Dead continues to redefine what is possible in the realm of music videos.

In conclusion, Zeds Dead's approach to music videos has revolutionized the medium, transforming it from a mere visual accompaniment to a powerful storytelling tool. By creating immersive and visually striking experiences, Zeds Dead not only enhances the impact of their music but also connects with their audience on a deeper level. Through collaboration, innovative execution, and the use of cutting-edge technologies, Zeds Dead has reinvented music videos as a medium and left an indelible mark on the music industry.

The Power of Immersive Visual Experiences

In the world of music, the visual element is often underestimated. However, Zeds Dead understands the transformative power of immersive visual experiences and has harnessed it to take their live performances to the next level. By incorporating captivating visuals, they create a multisensory journey for their audience, leaving a lasting impression and pushing the boundaries of what a live show can be.

Creating an Atmosphere

When you attend a Zeds Dead show, you are not simply a passive spectator; you become an active participant in an immersive experience. Through the art of visual storytelling, Zeds Dead creates an atmosphere that transports the audience to another world. The visuals complement and enhance the music, allowing the audience to fully immerse themselves in the performance.

To achieve this, Zeds Dead works closely with visual artists and designers to create stunning stage designs and dazzling visual effects. These visually captivating elements are carefully choreographed to synchronize with the beats and drops of their music, amplifying the emotional impact of each track.

The Evolution of Live Performance Setups

Over the years, Zeds Dead has constantly pushed the boundaries of live performance setups. They have embraced new technologies and incorporated them into their shows, allowing for more immersive and interactive experiences.

One example is the use of projection mapping, a technique that allows the visuals to be projected onto three-dimensional objects or structures. By mapping the projections to fit specific shapes or surfaces, Zeds Dead transforms the stage into a dynamic canvas. This creates a sense of depth and movement, making the visuals come alive and adding an extra layer of excitement to their shows.

Interactive Elements and Crowd Participation

Zeds Dead understands the importance of engaging their audience and making them an integral part of the experience. They incorporate interactive elements into their live performances to encourage crowd participation and create memorable moments.

One popular interaction is the use of live visuals triggered by the movement of the crowd. Through motion capture technology, the movements of the audience are translated into visual effects on the screen. This creates a feedback loop between the music, the visuals, and the energy of the crowd, resulting in a truly immersive and dynamic experience.

The Energy of a Zeds Dead Show

The combination of immersive visuals, powerful music, and an energetic crowd creates a unique energy at a Zeds Dead show. The crowd becomes unified, moving and dancing together in sync with the music and visuals. This collective energy feeds back into the performance, fueling the artists and intensifying the overall experience.

Zeds Dead's ability to capture and channel this energy is what sets them apart. They have mastered the art of creating a symbiotic relationship between the music, the visuals, and the audience, resulting in an unforgettable live performance that leaves a lasting impact.

Pushing the Boundaries of Live Performances

Zeds Dead is constantly pushing the boundaries of what is possible in a live performance. They are not content with delivering a simple set of music; they strive to create a multidimensional experience that engages all the senses.

Looking to the future, Zeds Dead is exploring cutting-edge technologies such as virtual reality (VR) and augmented reality (AR) to further enhance their live shows. By incorporating these emerging technologies, they aim to transport their audience into virtual worlds, blurring the line between reality and imagination.

By continuing to innovate and explore new possibilities, Zeds Dead is at the forefront of revolutionizing live performances. They understand the power of immersive visuals to elevate the music and create a truly transformative experience for their audience.

Conclusion

In the world of music, visuals are often an overlooked aspect of live performances. Zeds Dead has harnessed the power of immersive visual experiences to create a multisensory journey for their audience. Through captivating visuals, interactive elements, and pushing the boundaries of traditional live performances, they have elevated the concert experience to new heights. As technology continues to evolve, Zeds Dead is well-positioned to continue pushing the boundaries and revolutionizing the way we experience music live. So, get ready to be immersed in a world of music and visuals like never before.

Visionary Ideas for the Future

As Zeds Dead continues to push the boundaries of electronic music, they have set their sights on the future and are constantly exploring new ideas and innovations. Here, we delve into some of their visionary ideas for the future, which encompass both their sound and visual aesthetic, as well as their live performances and legacy.

Evolution of Sound

Zeds Dead is known for their ability to adapt and evolve their sound, constantly pushing the boundaries of electronic music. Looking ahead, they envision further experimentation with new genres and styles, seamlessly blending elements from different musical traditions to create innovative and unique tracks. They aim to incorporate more live instrumentation, bringing in different instruments and textures to create a richer and more dynamic sound. Additionally, Zeds Dead aims to collaborate with artists from diverse backgrounds and musical genres, creating a fusion of styles that transcends boundaries and reflects the global nature of music.

Visual Innovations

In addition to their groundbreaking sound, Zeds Dead has always been at the forefront of visual artistry. For the future, they envision continual exploration of different visual art forms, collaborating with cutting-edge visual artists and designers to create immersive and mind-bending experiences for their audience. They aim to incorporate emerging technologies, such as holography and augmented reality, into their stage designs, creating a truly interactive and transformative visual spectacle. Utilizing advanced projection mapping techniques, they plan to push the boundaries of stage design, transforming venues into otherworldly landscapes that transport audiences into a different realm.

Revolutionizing Live Performances

Zeds Dead's live performances have always been energetic and captivating, but they have grand plans for the future. They envision revolutionizing the live experience by incorporating interactive elements and audience participation on a whole new level. Imagine a concert where the audience can control the visuals, where they can actively engage with the music and become a part of the performance. Zeds Dead aims to create a fully immersive experience, blurring the lines between the performers and the audience, and fostering a sense of collective energy that transcends traditional notions of a concert.

Leaving a Lasting Legacy

As Zeds Dead continues to make their mark on the music industry, they are also committed to leaving a lasting legacy. They hope to inspire and support the next generation of artists, mentoring and nurturing up-and-coming talent. With their philanthropic endeavors and social initiatives, they aim to make a positive impact on society and push for diversity and inclusion within the music industry. Furthermore, Zeds Dead plans to challenge industry norms and practices, exploring new business ventures and collaborations that redefine the boundaries of the music industry. By doing so, they hope to leave a lasting imprint on music culture and inspire future generations of artists to think outside the box and embrace their creative instincts.

In conclusion, Zeds Dead's visionary ideas for the future encompass their sound and visual aesthetic, live performances, and their aspirations to leave a lasting legacy. With their constant drive for innovation and exploration, they are poised to continue reshaping electronic music and pushing the boundaries of what is possible. The future holds exciting possibilities for Zeds Dead and their dedicated fanbase, and their visionary ideas are sure to captivate audiences for years to come.

The Future of Live Performances

Innovations in Live Show Technologies

In the ever-evolving landscape of live music performances, Zeds Dead has constantly pushed the boundaries and embraced innovative technologies to create a mesmerizing experience for their audience. Their commitment to providing a unique and immersive live show has led them to explore cutting-edge technologies that enhance the visual and auditory elements of their performances. In this section, we will delve into some of the key innovations in live show technologies that Zeds Dead has incorporated into their concerts.

Projection Mapping: Transforming Surfaces into Dynamic Displays

One of the most awe-inspiring technologies that Zeds Dead has embraced is projection mapping. This technique allows them to transform ordinary surfaces, such as walls, stages, and even objects, into captivating displays. By precisely mapping the projection onto the surface, Zeds Dead can create mesmerizing visual effects that synchronize with their music.

For example, during their live performances, Zeds Dead often uses projection mapping to bring their album artwork to life. The visuals seamlessly blend with the music, creating a truly immersive experience for the audience. With the use of sophisticated software and precise calibration, they can create dynamic visuals that move in sync with the music, enhancing the emotional impact of their performances.

LED Technology: Creating Stunning Visual Displays

LED technology has revolutionized the live music industry, and Zeds Dead has fully embraced its potential. By incorporating LED screens and panels into their stage design, they are able to create stunning visual displays that amplify the energy of their music.

LED walls provide a vibrant and dynamic backdrop that can be synchronized with the music and other visual elements. Zeds Dead takes full advantage of this technology to create visually captivating moments in their live shows. The ability to display high-resolution graphics, videos, and animations adds another layer of immersion, making the audience feel like they are a part of a visually engaging experience.

Moreover, Zeds Dead has also experimented with LED costumes and accessories, adding an interactive element to their performances. By incorporating LED lights into their attire, they can synchronize their movements with the music, creating a mesmerizing visual spectacle that further enhances the live show experience.

Virtual Reality (VR) and Augmented Reality (AR): Transporting the Audience

Zeds Dead understands the power of transporting their audience to different worlds through technology. By incorporating virtual reality (VR) and augmented reality

(AR) elements into their live shows, they can create immersive experiences that go beyond the traditional concert format.

Virtual reality allows Zeds Dead to create entirely new environments for their audience to explore. By wearing VR headsets, concert-goers can find themselves in fantastical landscapes and otherworldly realms while enjoying the music. This technology blurs the line between the real and virtual worlds, resulting in a truly unforgettable experience.

Augmented reality, on the other hand, overlays virtual elements onto the real world. Zeds Dead has experimented with AR by incorporating it into their stage design and visuals. By using AR technology, they can add virtual objects, characters, and effects to the live show, creating a multi-dimensional experience for the audience.

Interactive Elements: Engaging the Audience

Zeds Dead understands the importance of audience engagement in creating an unforgettable live show experience. To achieve this, they have incorporated various interactive elements into their performances.

For instance, they have utilized motion-sensing technology to allow the audience to interact with the visuals and effects on stage. This technology tracks the audience's movements and translates them into real-time visual responses, creating a sense of active participation in the show.

Zeds Dead has also explored the use of smartphone applications that allow the audience to control certain aspects of the concert experience. These apps enable concert-goers to manipulate visuals, trigger effects, or even participate in interactive games during the performance, further blurring the boundaries between artist and audience.

Personalized Audio Experiences: Customizing the Sound

Zeds Dead recognizes the importance of delivering a personalized audio experience that caters to the unique preferences of each individual in the audience. To achieve this, they have explored technologies that allow for customized sound delivery.

One such technology is directional audio, which uses an array of speakers to deliver sound directly to specific areas of the audience. This creates a more immersive experience by ensuring that each listener receives optimal sound quality, regardless of their position in the venue.

Moreover, Zeds Dead has also experimented with personalized audio through the use of headphones or wearable devices. By providing wireless headphones to their audience, they can deliver a fully immersive audio experience, allowing each individual to feel fully immersed in the music, regardless of their location within the venue.

Unconventional Instruments: Redefining Live Performances

In addition to technological innovations, Zeds Dead has also explored unconventional instruments to add a unique touch to their live performances. By incorporating live instruments such as guitars, drums, and even orchestral elements, they bring a dynamic and organic element to their electronic music.

By blending electronic and live instrumentation, Zeds Dead creates a captivating fusion of sound that adds depth and richness to their performances. This integration of live instruments showcases their versatility as musicians and adds a human element to their electronic productions.

The Future of Live Show Technologies

As technology continues to advance at an unprecedented pace, the possibilities for live show technologies are limitless. Zeds Dead has always been at the forefront of innovation, constantly seeking ways to enhance the live experience. Looking ahead, here are some visionary ideas for the future of live show technologies:

1. Haptic Feedback: Imagine a concert experience where the audience can not only see and hear the music but also feel it physically. Haptic feedback technology could be integrated into wearable devices or seating arrangements, allowing the audience to feel vibrations, pulses, and physical sensations that correspond with the music.

2. Interactive Augmented Reality: Augmented reality could evolve to the point where audience members can actively participate in the show by interacting with virtual elements in real-time. Integrated sensors and wearables could enable audience members to control visual effects, trigger samples, or even take part in collaborative performances with the artists.

3. Artificial Intelligence (AI) Collaborators: As AI technology continues to advance, it's not far-fetched to imagine AI-powered collaborators joining artists on stage. Virtual band members capable of playing instruments, composing music, or even creating live visuals could bring an entirely new dimension to live performances.

4. Environmental Effects: Imagine a concert venue that can adapt and transform its environment based on the music and audience's emotions.

Advanced lighting systems, dynamic stage elements, and interactive installations could work in harmony to create a fully immersive atmosphere that responds to the mood and energy of the performance.

5. Holographic Performances: While holographic performances have made their debut in recent years, the future may bring even more realistic and interactive holograms. Artists could perform as lifelike holograms, interacting with the audience in real-time and creating an otherworldly experience that blurs the line between the virtual and the real.

The future of live show technologies holds immense potential for creating extraordinary and unforgettable experiences. With their insatiable curiosity and innovative spirit, Zeds Dead will undoubtedly continue to push the boundaries and pioneer new technologies that redefine the live music landscape.

Now that we have explored the innovations in live show technologies, let's turn our attention to the broader aspects of Zeds Dead's impact on music and culture in Chapter 5.

Interactive Elements and Audience Participation

In the world of live performances, audience participation is one of the key elements that can take a show from good to unforgettable. Zeds Dead understands the importance of creating an immersive concert atmosphere, where fans are not just passive spectators, but active participants in the experience. With the use of interactive elements, they are able to engage with their audience on a deeper level and create a sense of unity and connection that resonates long after the music stops.

One of the ways Zeds Dead incorporates audience participation is through the use of visual elements. Their live shows feature stunning visuals, captivating stage designs, and mesmerizing light displays. But it's not just about creating a visually appealing backdrop; it's about using these elements to involve the audience in the performance. Through synchronized lighting patterns and interactive visuals, the crowd becomes an integral part of the visual spectacle, as their movements and energy are translated into a stunning display of lights and colors. This not only enhances the overall aesthetic of the show but also allows the audience to feel more connected to the music and to each other.

Additionally, Zeds Dead encourages audience participation through interactive segments during their sets. These segments can take various forms, such as call-and-response chants, sing-alongs, or even dance competitions. These moments not only create a fun and engaging atmosphere but also foster a sense of community among the fans. By actively involving the audience in the performance, Zeds Dead creates a shared experience that goes beyond simply listening to their music. It becomes a collective celebration of music and togetherness.

Another innovative way Zeds Dead incorporates audience participation is through the use of technology. They have embraced advancements in live show technologies, such as smartphone apps and wearable devices, to enhance the interactive experience for their fans. Through these platforms, the audience can actively participate in real-time, whether it's voting for the next song to be played or controlling certain aspects of the visual effects.

Furthermore, Zeds Dead encourages fans to submit their own creative content, such as artwork or videos, which can be integrated into their live shows. By showcasing their fans' talent and creativity, Zeds Dead acknowledges their dedicated community and creates a sense of pride and ownership among their audience.

However, audience participation is not without its challenges. Balancing the interaction between the performers and the audience requires careful planning and execution to ensure a seamless and enjoyable experience. Zeds Dead knows the importance of striking the right balance between allowing the audience to participate and maintaining control over the overall performance. Too much audience interaction can disrupt the flow of the show, while too little can leave the fans feeling disconnected.

In conclusion, Zeds Dead understands that audience participation is an integral part of their live performances. By incorporating interactive elements, they are able to engage their audience on a deeper level, creating a shared experience that goes beyond the music itself. Through visual elements, technology, and various interactive segments, they foster a sense of unity and connection among their fans. It is through these interactive elements and audience participation that Zeds Dead showcases their commitment to creating a memorable and immersive live show experience. So, join the crowd, raise your hands, and let the music take you on a journey you'll never forget.

Unconventional Performance Spaces

When it comes to live performances, Zeds Dead has always been known for pushing boundaries and exploring new frontiers. As they continue to innovate and evolve, they have also ventured beyond traditional concert venues, seeking out unconventional performance spaces to create unique and unforgettable experiences for their fans.

One such unconventional performance space that Zeds Dead has embraced is the warehouse. These large, open spaces provide the perfect blank canvas for the duo to create immersive environments that complement their music. With the freedom to design their own stage setup and visual displays, Zeds Dead can transform a warehouse into a captivating world of lights, sound, and energy. The raw and industrial nature of these spaces adds an edgy and underground vibe to their performances, enhancing the overall experience for the audience.

In addition to warehouses, Zeds Dead has also experimented with performing in abandoned buildings, including factories, power plants, and even old churches. These unconventional spaces not only offer a unique atmosphere but also hold historical and cultural significance. By repurposing these forgotten spaces for their performances, Zeds Dead breathes new life into them and creates an atmosphere that blends the past and present.

Another unconventional performance space that Zeds Dead has explored is the natural environment. From performing on the edge of cliffs overlooking breathtaking landscapes to setting up stages in the middle of forests, the duo seeks to connect with their fans in a more intimate and organic setting. The combination of their music with the beauty of nature creates a powerful and transcendent experience, allowing fans to escape the confines of traditional venues and immerse themselves fully in the music.

Moreover, Zeds Dead has also ventured into performing in unconventional spaces such as art galleries and museums. By integrating their music with visual art installations and exhibits, they create a multi-sensory experience that blurs the boundaries between music and visual art. This collaboration between music and other art forms not only showcases their versatility as artists but also fosters a deeper appreciation for different art forms among their fans.

Of course, performing in unconventional spaces also presents its own set of challenges. These spaces often lack the infrastructure and amenities found in traditional venues, requiring careful planning and coordination to ensure the smooth execution of the performance. Additionally, logistics and technical considerations, such as power supply and sound reinforcement, may need to be adapted to suit the unique characteristics of these spaces. Despite these challenges, Zeds Dead's willingness to embrace unconventional performance spaces showcases their commitment to pushing the boundaries of what a live performance can be.

In conclusion, Zeds Dead's exploration of unconventional performance spaces demonstrates their willingness to step outside the confines of traditional venues and create unique and immersive experiences for their fans. Whether it's performing in warehouses, abandoned buildings, natural environments, or art spaces, they continue to push the boundaries and challenge the status quo. By doing so, they not only create unforgettable moments for their fans but also inspire other artists to think outside the box and reimagine the possibilities of live performances.

The Influence of Virtual Reality and Augmented Reality

Virtual Reality (VR) and Augmented Reality (AR) have made significant advancements in recent years, revolutionizing various industries, including entertainment, gaming, and education. These immersive technologies have also had a profound impact on the music industry, including the way artists and fans interact with music. In this section, we will explore the influence of VR and AR on the music of Zeds Dead and the broader music culture.

A New Dimension of Live Performances

One of the most exciting applications of VR and AR in the music industry is the enhancement of live performances. VR allows artists to create virtual concert experiences, transporting fans to a virtual venue where they can enjoy the show from any location in the world. With the help of a VR headset, fans can feel as if they are standing in the front row, experiencing the energy and excitement of a Zeds Dead concert.

AR, on the other hand, allows for a blended reality experience, where virtual elements are overlaid onto the real world. This opens up endless possibilities for interactive and immersive live performances. Artists like Zeds Dead can use AR to create captivating visual effects that complement their music, making the entire concert an otherworldly experience.

For example, Zeds Dead could incorporate AR visuals that synchronize with their beats, creating a synchronized light show that follows the rhythm of the music. This fusion of augmented visuals and live music would elevate the concert experience, creating a multisensory event that engages the audience in new and exciting ways.

Interactive Music Experiences

VR and AR technology also offer opportunities for fans to interact with music in innovative ways. With VR, fans can step into the virtual studio with Zeds Dead, witnessing their creative process firsthand. They could explore the different elements of a track, isolating individual instruments or experimenting with different effects and sounds. This immersive experience allows fans to gain a deeper understanding of the music and appreciate the complexity of Zeds Dead's production techniques.

AR can be used to enhance music listening experiences in the real world. For example, fans could use AR apps on their smartphones or tablets to unlock hidden content or visuals when they point their device's camera at album covers or concert posters. This gamification of music consumption adds an interactive and exciting element to the fan experience.

Creating Virtual Music Environments

VR and AR technologies also enable artists like Zeds Dead to create unique virtual music environments. With VR, they can design immersive 3D audiovisual experiences where users can explore and interact with the music in a virtual world. Fans could find themselves in a fantastical landscape that mirrors the themes and emotions of a song, adding a new layer of storytelling to their music.

AR can also be used to create location-based music experiences. Using geolocation technology, Zeds Dead could create AR music experiences that are specific to certain physical locations. For example, fans visiting a specific landmark or venue could use AR to unlock exclusive music content or discover hidden tracks.

Collaborations and Cross-Cultural Experiences

VR and AR have the potential to transcend geographical boundaries and facilitate cross-cultural collaborations. Artists like Zeds Dead could collaborate with musicians from different parts of the world, using VR to meet and work together virtually in a shared studio space. This creates new opportunities for artistic exploration and cultural exchange.

AR can also be used to bridge the gap between artists and their fans during live performances. With the help of AR filters or effects, fans could overlay virtual elements onto their live video feeds, creating an interactive and shared experience with the artist and other fans around the world. This not only enhances the feeling of connection but also promotes inclusivity and a sense of camaraderie among fans.

The Future of Music and Virtual Reality

The influence of virtual reality and augmented reality on the music industry is still in its early stages, but the potential for innovation and creativity is vast. As technology continues to advance, we can expect to see even more groundbreaking applications of VR and AR in music.

From virtual concert experiences to interactive music production and cross-cultural collaborations, VR and AR offer new ways for artists like Zeds Dead to connect with their audience and push the boundaries of music. These technologies have the power to redefine the music experience, making it more immersive, engaging, and accessible to fans worldwide.

As Zeds Dead continues to evolve their sound and experiment with new genres and styles, it's safe to say that they'll be at the forefront of embracing and leveraging the potential of VR and AR in their music. With their innovative approach and boundary-pushing mindset, they are poised to shape the future of music in the virtual reality era.

Exploring Different Methods of Live Collaboration

Live collaboration is an essential aspect of Zeds Dead's performances, allowing them to create unique and memorable experiences for their fans. In this section, we will dive into the different methods of live collaboration that Zeds Dead has explored and implemented during their career.

1. Collaborating with Vocalists and Live Musicians

One of the most common methods of live collaboration in electronic music is working with vocalists and live musicians. Zeds Dead has consistently integrated live performers into their shows, adding a dynamic element to their performances.

With vocalists, Zeds Dead creates a symbiotic relationship between the DJ set and live vocals. The vocalists bring a human touch to the electronic soundscape, enhancing the emotional impact of the music. This collaboration results in a more engaging and interactive experience for the audience.

Additionally, Zeds Dead often incorporates live musicians into their sets, such as guitarists or drummers. These musicians join the duo on stage, providing a live element that adds depth and energy to the performance. By combining electronic and live instruments, Zeds Dead creates a fusion of genres and styles, blurring the boundaries between electronic music and live performance.

2. Introducing Visual Artists and VJs

Collaboration in the world of Zeds Dead goes beyond music and extends into the realm of visual art. Visual artists and VJs (video jockeys) are often invited to join Zeds Dead on stage, enhancing the visual representation of their music.

Visual artists create custom visual content that is synchronized with the music, creating an immersive experience for the audience. These visuals can range from abstract patterns to thematic narratives that enhance the mood and atmosphere of the performance. By combining their music with captivating visuals, Zeds Dead creates a multisensory experience that stimulates both the auditory and visual senses of the audience.

3. Cross-Collaborations with Other DJs and Producers

Zeds Dead has a history of collaborating with other DJs and producers, both in the studio and on stage. These cross-collaborations allow for the merging of different artistic styles, resulting in unique and innovative performances.

On stage, Zeds Dead often invites fellow DJs and producers to join them for back-to-back sets. This format involves two or more artists performing together, seamlessly blending their individual styles and tracks. These collaborations bring a refreshing twist to the live performance, as the artists feed off each other's energy and creativity.

In the studio, Zeds Dead has collaborated with a wide range of artists from different genres, including electronic, hip-hop, and rock. These cross-genre collaborations result in tracks that push the boundaries of traditional electronic music, incorporating diverse influences and styles. By working with artists from different backgrounds, Zeds Dead continues to evolve and expand their sound.

4. Interactive Elements and Audience Participation

Zeds Dead understands the importance of involving the audience in their performances. They actively strive to create an environment where fans can participate and interact with the music.

One method of audience participation is through call-and-response interactions. Zeds Dead often incorporates elements into their sets that encourage the audience to respond to specific cues or lyrics. This participation creates a sense of unity and connection between the artists and the audience, fostering a memorable and immersive experience.

Additionally, Zeds Dead has experimented with interactive elements during their performances, such as live polls or real-time visual projections that change based on audience input. These interactive elements allow the audience to become active participants in the creation of the live experience, further blurring the line between performer and spectator.

5. Mixing Live Instruments with DJ Sets

Zeds Dead's live collaboration also extends to their incorporation of live instruments within their DJ sets. By blending live instruments with their electronic tracks, Zeds Dead adds a human touch and organic feel to their performances.

For example, they might bring a live drummer to accompany their DJ sets, adding a rhythmic and percussive element that elevates the energy of their performances. This fusion of electronic and live instruments creates a unique sonic experience that sets Zeds Dead's sets apart from traditional DJ performances.

6. Live Remixing and Mashups

Zeds Dead is known for their remixing and mashup skills, and they often demonstrate these talents during their live performances. They take this a step further by incorporating live remixing and mashups into their sets, providing a fresh and unique experience for their audience.

During their performances, Zeds Dead will remix and mashup their own tracks and the tracks of other artists on the spot, creating a live and improvisational experience. This allows them to tailor their sets to the specific energy and vibe of the audience, keeping the performance dynamic and exciting.

By exploring different methods of live collaboration, Zeds Dead has transformed their performances into immersive and interactive experiences. Whether through vocalists, visual artists, fellow DJs, live instruments, audience participation, or live remixing, Zeds Dead continues to push the boundaries of electronic music and create unforgettable moments on stage.

Experimenting with Live Instrumentation

Live instrumentation is an integral part of the Zeds Dead experience. While many electronic music acts rely solely on DJing and pre-recorded tracks, Zeds Dead takes it to the next level by incorporating live instruments into their performances. This not only adds a captivating visual element but also allows for greater musical creativity and improvisation on stage.

The Power of Live Instruments

Live instruments have a unique ability to bring depth and organic energy to a performance. The rawness and imperfections of a live instrument can create a sense of authenticity that is often missing in electronic music. Zeds Dead understands this power and leverages it to create a dynamic and engaging live show.

By including live instruments such as guitars, drums, and keyboards, Zeds Dead is able to inject a human touch into their music. This allows them to create unique arrangements and improvisations that are impossible to replicate using only digital technology. The live instruments provide a canvas for the artists to express their emotions and connect with the audience on a deeper level.

Blending the Digital and Analog Worlds

One of the challenges of incorporating live instrumentation into electronic music is finding a balance between the digital and analog worlds. Zeds Dead embraces this challenge and seamlessly blends the two to create a cohesive and immersive experience for their fans.

The live instruments are often processed and manipulated using various effects and techniques, allowing them to seamlessly integrate with the electronic elements of their tracks. This fusion of analog and digital creates a rich and textured sound that is both familiar and innovative.

Pushing the Boundaries of Live Performance

Zeds Dead is constantly pushing the boundaries of what is possible in a live performance. Through experimentation and innovation, they continue to find new ways to incorporate live instrumentation into their shows.

In addition to traditional instruments, Zeds Dead has also explored the use of unconventional instruments and unconventional methods of playing them. They have ventured into using analog synthesizers, samplers, and even custom-built electronic instruments to expand their sonic palette.

Improvisation and Real-Time Collaboration

One of the most exciting aspects of incorporating live instrumentation into a performance is the opportunity for improvisation and real-time collaboration. Zeds Dead embraces this freedom and actively encourages their band members to explore and experiment during their shows.

This improvisational approach adds an element of unpredictability to their performances, making each show a unique experience for both the artists and the audience. It allows for spontaneous moments of creativity and the chance to react and respond to the energy of the crowd.

Examples of Live Instrumentation in Zeds Dead's Performances

A prime example of Zeds Dead's use of live instrumentation can be seen in their track "Lost You" featuring Twin Shadow and D'Angelo Lacy. In their live performances of this song, Zeds Dead brings out a live drummer who adds a powerful and energetic element to the performance.

Another example is their collaboration with Omar LinX on the track "No Prayers." In their live shows, Zeds Dead brings out a guitarist who adds a gritty and soulful guitar solo, elevating the energy and intensity of the performance.

The Future of Live Instrumentation in Zeds Dead's Performances

As Zeds Dead continues to evolve and explore new musical territories, the role of live instrumentation in their performances will undoubtedly grow. They are known for pushing boundaries and embracing innovation, and live instrumentation will be no exception.

The future of live instrumentation in Zeds Dead's performances holds endless possibilities. From incorporating more complex arrangements and compositions to exploring new instruments and technologies, they will continue to surprise and captivate their audience with their unique blend of electronic music and live instrumentation.

Exercises

1. Research and find examples of other electronic music acts that incorporate live instrumentation into their performances. Compare and contrast their approaches with that of Zeds Dead.

2. Imagine you are a member of Zeds Dead's live band. Describe what instrument you would play and how you would contribute to the overall sound and performance.

3. Design a visual stage setup that incorporates both electronic equipment and live instruments. Consider how you would balance the visual elements with the practicalities of a live performance.

4. Interview a Zeds Dead fan and ask them about their experience witnessing the live instrumentation in one of their performances. Explore how the live instruments enhanced their enjoyment of the music and the overall concert experience.

5. Experiment with incorporating live instrumentation into your own electronic music production. Start by adding simple elements like a guitar riff or drum loop and see how it changes the overall feel and energy of your tracks.

Resources

1. "Behind the Beat: The Making of Zeds Dead's Live Show" - In this documentary, Zeds Dead provides insight into their creative process and the integration of live instrumentation into their performances.

2. Zeds Dead's YouTube channel - This channel features live performances and behind-the-scenes footage, offering a glimpse into how they incorporate live instruments into their shows.

3. "The Art of Live Performance" by Dave Smith - This book explores the various aspects of live performance in electronic music, including the integration of live instrumentation.

4. "Music Production with Live Instruments" by Tomislav Zlatic - This comprehensive guide provides techniques and tips for incorporating live instruments into electronic music production.

5. Zeds Dead's official website - Visit their website to stay updated on their latest releases, tour dates, and news about their live performances.

Creating a Memorable and Immersive Experience

When it comes to live performances, Zeds Dead is renowned for their ability to create a memorable and immersive experience for their fans. They understand that attending a concert is not just about hearing the music, but also about being transported into a different world. In this section, we will explore the various elements that contribute to the creation of a truly unforgettable live show by Zeds Dead.

Stage Design and Visual Elements

The stage design plays a crucial role in setting the atmosphere and enhancing the overall experience of a live performance. Zeds Dead understands this and goes above and beyond to create visually captivating shows. Their stage designs incorporate a combination of lighting effects, lasers, LED screens, and stunning visual projections.

One of their signature visual elements is a custom-made LED wall that serves as the backdrop for their performances. This LED wall displays synchronized visuals that are carefully designed to match the mood and energy of each track. The use of vibrant colors, intricate patterns, and mesmerizing animations adds another layer of depth to their live shows.

In addition to the LED wall, Zeds Dead also incorporates other visual elements such as smoke machines, pyrotechnics, and confetti cannons. These effects are strategically timed to coincide with climactic moments in the music, creating a multisensory experience that leaves the audience in awe.

Interactive Elements and Crowd Participation

Zeds Dead believes in the power of audience participation and strives to make their shows interactive. They encourage the crowd to be an integral part of the performance by incorporating various interactive elements into their shows.

For instance, they often feature inflatable props, such as giant beach balls or inflatable animals, which are tossed into the crowd to create a sense of playfulness and unity. This not only adds a fun element to the show but also encourages active engagement from the audience.

Zeds Dead also uses different techniques to interact with the crowd, such as encouraging sing-alongs or call-and-response moments. These moments create a strong connection between the artists and the audience, fostering a sense of community and shared experience.

Live Improvisation and Remixing

One of the aspects that sets Zeds Dead apart from other electronic music acts is their ability to improvise and remix their tracks live. They understand that a live performance should offer something unique and different from studio recordings.

During their shows, Zeds Dead often takes the opportunity to reinterpret their songs, incorporating live instruments, improvisation, and spontaneous remixes. This not only keeps the performances fresh and exciting but also allows the artists to showcase their musical skills and adaptability in real-time.

The ability to remix and improvise live also means that every Zeds Dead show is unique, creating a sense of anticipation and surprise for both the artists and the audience.

Balancing DJ Sets and Live Performances

Zeds Dead strikes a delicate balance between DJ sets and live performances, combining the best of both worlds. While they are known for their DJing skills and ability to seamlessly mix tracks, they also incorporate live instrumentation into their shows.

This mix of DJing and live performance adds another layer of excitement and dynamism to their shows. It allows for moments of improvisation and creativity while also ensuring a seamless flow between tracks.

Zeds Dead often collaborates with talented musicians who join them on stage to perform live instruments, such as drums or guitars. This collaboration further enhances the immersive experience and showcases their versatility as artists.

Immersive Visual Experiences

Zeds Dead understands that music is a powerful tool for storytelling. They aim to create immersive visual experiences that complement the narratives within their tracks.

One way they achieve this is through the use of synchronized visuals that unfold in real-time with the music. These visuals are carefully choreographed to enhance the emotional impact of each track, creating a cohesive and immersive experience.

Another technique Zeds Dead employs is the integration of visual narratives into their shows. They often incorporate short films or animated sequences that serve as visual counterparts to their music. These narratives add depth and context to the music, allowing the audience to connect with the stories being told.

The Importance of Flow and Transitions

Creating a memorable and immersive experience requires careful attention to the flow and transitions between different tracks and moments within a performance. Zeds Dead understands that a seamless transition from one song to another is crucial for maintaining the energy and engagement of the audience.

They meticulously curate their setlists to ensure a smooth progression of energy and emotions throughout the show. This involves selecting tracks that not only complement each other musically but also contribute to the overall narrative arc of the performance.

Zeds Dead also pays attention to the transitions between different sections of their shows. They use techniques such as gradual tempo changes, breakbeats, and crossfading to seamlessly move between different genres and styles, keeping the audience engaged and creating a dynamic and ever-evolving experience.

Creating a Lasting Impact

The ultimate goal of Zeds Dead's live performances is to leave a lasting impact on the audience. They aim to create an experience that lingers in the minds of their fans long after the show is over.

To achieve this, Zeds Dead focuses on creating moments of intensity and euphoria throughout their performances. They carefully pace the builds and drops within their setlists to maximize the emotional impact on the audience. These moments of heightened energy and release create a sense of catharsis and leave a lasting impression on the audience.

In conclusion, Zeds Dead's live performances are a testament to their dedication to creating a memorable and immersive experience for their fans.

Through their innovative stage design, interactive elements, improvisation, and storytelling, they transport their audience into a world of sound and visuals that lingers in their memories long after the show is over. By striking a careful balance between DJ sets and live performances, and paying attention to flow and transitions, Zeds Dead creates a dynamic and ever-evolving experience that keeps their audience engaged from start to finish.

Balancing DJ Sets and Live Performances

Finding the right balance between DJ sets and live performances is a delicate art that Zeds Dead has mastered over the years. Each aspect brings its own unique energy and excitement to their shows, and knowing how to blend them seamlessly is what sets them apart. In this section, we will explore the challenges and strategies involved in balancing DJ sets and live performances, taking into account the technical and creative aspects of both.

Understanding the Difference

Before diving into the balancing act, it's essential to understand the fundamental differences between DJ sets and live performances. While both involve playing music to a crowd, the approach and execution vary significantly.

A DJ set typically involves mixing and blending pre-recorded tracks, using techniques like beatmatching and EQing to create a continuous flow of music. It allows DJs the freedom to curate a setlist based on the energy of the crowd, adjusting their selections on the fly to keep the dancefloor engaged.

On the other hand, a live performance involves incorporating live elements into the music, such as playing instruments, adding vocals, or manipulating the tracks in real-time. It adds an extra layer of spontaneity and creativity to the set, as the artists have the freedom to experiment and create unique moments on stage.

Technical Considerations

Balancing DJ sets and live performances requires careful consideration of the technical aspects involved in both approaches. Here are some key factors to consider:

Equipment Setup: DJs rely on a standard DJ setup, which typically includes CDJs or turntables, a DJ mixer, and headphones. In contrast, live performances may require additional equipment, such as MIDI controllers, synthesizers, drum machines, or even live instruments. Finding the right balance between the two setups is crucial for a seamless transition between DJ sets and live elements.

Song Selection: DJs have access to a vast library of pre-recorded tracks, giving them the flexibility to choose from a wide range of genres and styles. Live performances often involve the artists' original music, remixes, or improvised sections. Striking the right balance between popular selections and unique live elements can enhance the overall experience for the audience.

Technical Skills: DJs develop specific technical skills, such as beatmatching, mixing, and crowd interaction, to create a cohesive and engaging set. Live performances require additional skills like playing instruments, singing, or using MIDI controllers effectively. Balancing the mastery of both skill sets is essential to deliver a dynamic and captivating performance.

Creative Considerations

Beyond the technical aspects, finding the right balance between DJ sets and live performances is also about understanding the creative potential of each format. Here are some creative considerations to keep in mind:

Seamless Transitions: A well-crafted DJ set flows seamlessly from one track to another, maintaining a consistent energy level and keeping the audience engaged. When incorporating live elements, the challenge lies in seamlessly integrating them into the mix without disrupting the flow. Skillful transitions between DJ sets and live performances can create memorable moments and enhance the overall impact of the show.

Improvisation: Live performances offer the opportunity for artists to improvise and take risks on stage. This creativity can manifest itself in various ways, such as adding unique instrument solos, extending tracks with live jam sessions, or incorporating spontaneous vocal improvisations. The ability to adapt and respond to the energy of the crowd in real-time is a valuable skill when balancing DJ sets and live performances.

Engaging the Audience: DJ sets and live performances have different ways of engaging the audience. While DJ sets rely on reading the crowd and playing tracks that resonate with them, live performances offer the chance to connect on a deeper level through live instrumentation, vocals, and interactions. Striking the right balance between the two approaches ensures that the audience remains captivated throughout the entire performance.

Strategies for Balance

To achieve a harmonious balance between DJ sets and live performances, Zeds Dead employs the following strategies:

Integrating Live Elements: Zeds Dead seamlessly incorporates live elements into their DJ sets, creating a hybrid style that bridges the gap between the two approaches. By incorporating live instrumentation, vocals, and effects, they add a unique touch to their performances while maintaining the energy and flow of a traditional DJ set.

Segmented Sets: Another strategy is to structure the performance into segments, alternating between DJ sets and live performances. This approach allows for a dynamic and engaging show while giving the artists the opportunity to showcase their versatility and creativity. It ensures that the audience experiences the best of both worlds throughout the performance.

Collaborative Performances: Collaborating with other artists is another effective way to strike a balance between DJ sets and live performances. By featuring guest musicians or vocalists during live sections, Zeds Dead can showcase their collaborative creativity and add an exciting element of surprise to their shows.

Visual Enhancements: Engaging visuals, lighting effects, and stage design can enhance the overall experience and complement the balance between DJ sets and live performances. Visual cues can help guide the audience through different sections of the performance and create a cohesive narrative that ties everything together.

Case Study: "Coffee Break"

A prime example of Zeds Dead's mastery in balancing DJ sets and live performances is their track "Coffee Break." In this track, they seamlessly blend their signature electronic sound with live guitar elements, creating a unique sonic experience. The combination of organic and electronic elements showcases their ability to strike a perfect balance between the two approaches.

The song begins with a catchy guitar riff, immediately drawing the listener in with its raw energy. As the track progresses, electronic elements like deep basslines, intricate drum patterns, and atmospheric synthesizers seamlessly merge with the guitar, creating a fusion of styles that is both captivating and memorable. This track exemplifies Zeds Dead's ability to navigate between DJ sets and live performances effortlessly.

Conclusion

Balancing DJ sets and live performances is an art that requires technical skills, creative vision, and a deep understanding of the audience. Zeds Dead has mastered this art by seamlessly integrating live elements into their DJ sets and creating captivating performances that keep their fans coming back for more. By finding the right balance between DJ sets and live performances, Zeds Dead has solidified their position as pioneers in the electronic music scene with a truly unique and captivating sound.

Remember, striking the right balance is not just about technical considerations but also about creative expression and engagement with the audience. With their innovative approach and continued evolution, Zeds Dead is sure to inspire future artists to explore the possibilities of combining DJ sets and live performances. So, go ahead, embrace the challenge, and find your own unique balance on the rhythmic journey of music.

The Evolution of the Zeds Dead Live Experience

The Zeds Dead live experience has evolved over the years, transforming from a traditional DJ set to a mesmerizing and immersive musical journey. Through their innovation and dedication to pushing boundaries, Zeds Dead has created a live performance that goes beyond the expectations of their fans. In this section, we will explore the evolution of the Zeds Dead live experience, delving into the elements that have contributed to its success and discussing their vision for the future.

Creating an Immersive Concert Atmosphere

From the very beginning, Zeds Dead recognized the importance of creating an immersive concert atmosphere that would captivate their audience. They understood that the live experience should not just be limited to the music but also encompass the visual and sensory elements that enhance the overall experience.

To achieve this, Zeds Dead incorporates a combination of stunning visual projections, lighting effects, and stage design. They collaborate with talented visual artists and designers to create a synchronized audio-visual experience that transports the audience into a different realm. The visual elements are carefully choreographed to complement and enhance the music, creating a multisensory extravaganza that leaves a lasting impression on concert-goers.

Incorporating Visual Elements into Live Shows

Zeds Dead understands the power of visual elements in enhancing the live show experience. They seamlessly integrate visuals into their performances, using LED screens, lasers, and synchronized lighting effects to create a dynamic and captivating visual spectacle.

The visuals are not simply a static backdrop but an integral part of the performance. They are carefully synchronized with the music, creating visual cues that enhance the flow and energy of the set. This incorporation of visual elements adds a layer of depth and immersion, creating a synergy between the audio and visual aspects of the performance.

The Evolution of Live Performance Setups

As technology advances, so does the evolution of live performance setups. Zeds Dead has always been at the forefront of utilizing technology to enhance their live shows. Over the years, they have embraced cutting-edge equipment and techniques to elevate their performances to new heights.

One notable evolution in their live performance setup is the incorporation of live instrumentation. While originally known for their DJ sets, Zeds Dead has expanded their repertoire by incorporating live instruments such as drums, guitars, and synthesizers into their performances. This fusion of electronic and live elements brings a unique and dynamic energy to their shows, allowing for improvisation and experimentation on stage.

Interactive Elements and Crowd Participation

Zeds Dead understands the power of engaging the audience and creating a sense of participation during their live shows. They actively encourage crowd interaction, incorporating elements that allow the audience to become part of the performance.

One way in which Zeds Dead achieves this is through the use of call-and-response techniques. They create moments during their sets where the crowd is invited to participate by cheering, clapping, or chanting along with the music. This interaction creates a sense of unity and connection between the artists and the audience, making the live experience truly immersive and memorable.

Memorable Live Performances and Festival Moments

Zeds Dead has graced the stages of numerous music festivals and their live performances have become legendary. They have the ability to command a massive crowd, creating an electric atmosphere that reverberates through the audience.

Their live shows are known for their high energy, seamless transitions, and flawless mixing. Zeds Dead curates a setlist that takes the audience on a rollercoaster ride of emotions, incorporating both their own tracks and those from other artists. Each live performance is carefully crafted, ensuring that the energy builds and sustains throughout the entire set, leaving the audience craving for more.

The Importance of Mental and Physical Health on Tour

Touring can be physically and mentally demanding, with artists constantly being on the move and performing in different cities almost every night. Zeds Dead recognizes the importance of maintaining good mental and physical health while on tour.

They prioritize self-care and make efforts to incorporate healthy habits into their touring lifestyle. This includes regular exercise, proper nutrition, and getting enough rest. They also emphasize the importance of taking breaks and finding moments of solitude to recharge and regroup.

Zeds Dead actively encourages their fans to prioritize their well-being as well. They advocate for mental health awareness and provide resources for fans to seek help if needed. By fostering a culture of self-care, they contribute to creating a positive and supportive concert experience for their fans.

Managing Expectations and Balance

As Zeds Dead's popularity has grown, so have the expectations for their live performances. They face the challenge of balancing audience expectations with their own creative vision while maintaining their signature style.

Zeds Dead has mastered the art of managing expectations by continually evolving their live performances while staying true to their core sound. They understand the importance of surprising their audience and keeping them engaged, constantly pushing the boundaries of what a live performance can be.

At the same time, they remain grounded in their artistic integrity, never compromising their vision for the sake of popularity. This balance between innovation and authenticity is what sets Zeds Dead apart and keeps their live performances fresh and exciting.

The Evolution of the Zeds Dead Live Experience Continues

The evolution of the Zeds Dead live experience is an ongoing journey. As technology advances, musical tastes change, and creative inspirations evolve, Zeds Dead continues to push the boundaries of what is possible in a live performance.

They are constantly exploring new ways to engage their audience, incorporating emerging technologies, experimenting with new musical styles, and collaborating with diverse artists. The future of the Zeds Dead live experience holds the promise of even more immersive and boundary-breaking performances that will leave a lasting impact on the electronic music landscape.

In conclusion, the evolution of the Zeds Dead live experience is a testament to their commitment to pushing boundaries and creating unique and captivating performances. Through the integration of visual elements, incorporation of live instrumentation, and emphasis on audience participation, Zeds Dead has transformed the live show into a multisensory and unforgettable experience. As they continue to evolve and innovate, the future of the Zeds Dead live experience holds endless possibilities. Get ready to immerse yourself in the rhythm and experience the evolution firsthand.

Building on the Legacy

Philanthropic Endeavors and Social Initiatives

Zeds Dead is not just a music duo; they are also committed philanthropists who use their platform and success to make a positive impact on society. Throughout their career, they have been actively involved in various philanthropic endeavors and social initiatives. Let's take a closer look at their efforts to give back and make a difference in the world.

The Importance of Giving Back

From the early days of their career, Zeds Dead recognized the importance of giving back to the community. They understand that success in the music industry comes with a responsibility to use their platform for the greater good. This mindset has shaped their approach to philanthropy and social initiatives.

Supporting Charitable Organizations

Zeds Dead has lent their support to numerous charitable organizations over the years. They have collaborated with organizations such as MusiCounts, which aims to ensure that all Canadian children and youth have access to music education. Through their partnership, Zeds Dead has raised funds and awareness to support music programs in schools across Canada.

Additionally, Zeds Dead has been involved with the Boys and Girls Clubs of America, an organization that provides safe and positive environments for young people. They have participated in charity events and fundraisers to support the Boys and Girls Clubs' mission of empowering youth to reach their full potential.

Environmental Sustainability

Zeds Dead is also passionate about environmental sustainability and has taken steps to reduce their ecological footprint. They have embraced eco-friendly practices in both their touring and personal lives. This includes investing in renewable energy, reducing waste, and promoting environmentally conscious behavior.

Furthermore, they have collaborated with organizations focused on environmental conservation and awareness, such as the Rainforest Foundation. By leveraging their platform, Zeds Dead has helped raise awareness about important environmental issues and encouraged their fans to take action.

Mental Health Advocacy

Mental health is an important topic that Zeds Dead openly addresses. They recognize the pressures and challenges that come with being in the music industry, and they are vocal advocates for mental health awareness and support.

Through their music, interviews, and social media presence, Zeds Dead shares personal experiences and encourages open conversations about mental health. They have partnered with mental health organizations to raise awareness, provide resources, and destigmatize mental health struggles.

Community Engagement

Zeds Dead understands the power of community and actively engages with their fans beyond their music. They organize meet-and-greets, fan gatherings, and charity events to connect with their fans on a deeper level. By fostering a sense of community, Zeds Dead creates a space where fans can support each other and join forces to make a positive impact.

They encourage their fans to get involved in social initiatives and support causes that resonate with them. This grassroots approach gives fans a sense of purpose and empowers them to make a difference in their own communities.

Music Education and Mentorship

As successful musicians, Zeds Dead recognizes the importance of nurturing young talent and providing opportunities for aspiring artists. They have been involved in mentorship programs and music education initiatives to support the next generation of musicians.

Through workshops, masterclasses, and collaborations, Zeds Dead shares their knowledge and experiences with emerging artists. By investing in future talent, they contribute to the growth and diversity of the music industry as a whole.

Unconventional Approach: The Zeds Dead Charity Mix

In addition to their ongoing philanthropic efforts, Zeds Dead has taken an unconventional approach to fundraising with their annual Charity Mix. Each year, they release a special mixtape and donate all proceeds to a chosen charitable organization.

The Charity Mix not only raises funds for important causes but also showcases Zeds Dead's talent and creativity in a unique way. It has become a highly anticipated event for fans, who eagerly support the mixtape's release and contribute to the chosen cause.

Inspiring Others to Give Back

By actively engaging in philanthropy and social initiatives, Zeds Dead serves as an inspiration to their fans and fellow musicians. They prove that success and making a positive impact can go hand in hand.

Through their actions, Zeds Dead encourages others in the music industry and beyond to use their influence and resources for the betterment of society. They set a powerful example of how artists can leverage their platform to effect meaningful change.

Continual Commitment

Zeds Dead's commitment to philanthropy and social initiatives is unwavering. They continually seek out new ways to give back, collaborating with charitable organizations, advocating for important causes, and inspiring others to join their efforts.

As they continue to evolve and grow, Zeds Dead's philanthropic endeavors will undoubtedly remain a cornerstone of their artistic journey. They are dedicated to leaving a lasting legacy that extends beyond their music and resonates with generations to come.

Example Contemporary Problem:

One of the challenges faced when organizing a charity event is raising enough funds to support the cause. As a member of a non-profit organization dedicated to environmental conservation, you have been assigned the task of organizing a fundraising event. However, you're struggling to come up with innovative ideas to attract donors and make the event memorable.

Solution:

To create an unforgettable fundraising event, consider partnering with Zeds Dead or other artists who are passionate about environmental sustainability. Collaborate on a charity concert where attendees can enjoy live music while supporting a worthy cause.

Use social media platforms to spread the word about the event and engage potential donors. Highlight the importance of environmental conservation and the impact their contributions will make.

To make the event more appealing, consider incorporating interactive elements such as eco-friendly art installations, educational booths, and sustainable food and beverage options. Emphasize the connection between art, music, and environmental issues to create a unique and thought-provoking environment.

Offer different donation tiers with corresponding perks, such as meet-and-greets with the artists, exclusive merchandise, or even the opportunity to participate in an environmental conservation project.

By combining the power of music, art, and a meaningful cause, you can create a fundraising event that not only raises funds but also raises awareness about environmental issues. This innovative approach will attract donors who are passionate about the cause and help make a lasting impact on the environment.

Resources

- MusiCounts (www.musicounts.ca): An organization dedicated to ensuring that all Canadian children and youth have access to music education.

- Boys and Girls Clubs of America (www.bgca.org): A national organization that provides safe and positive environments for young people.

- Rainforest Foundation (www.rainforestfoundation.org): An organization focused on protecting the world's rainforests and the rights of indigenous people living within them.

- Social media platforms: Utilize platforms such as Instagram, Facebook, and Twitter to promote the event, engage with potential donors, and create a sense of community.

- Local eco-friendly businesses: Collaborate with local businesses that align with the event's mission to provide sustainable food and beverage options, merchandise, and other services.

- Non-profit event planning guides: These guides provide valuable insights and tips for organizing successful charity events. They offer practical advice on logistics, marketing, fundraising strategies, and more.

- Local environmental organizations: Partner with local environmental organizations to enlist their support and expertise in planning and executing the event.

Remember, the success of the fundraising event ultimately depends on the collective effort put forth by the organizing team, volunteers, and donors. By leveraging the power of music, art, and community, you can create a memorable and impactful event that raises funds and awareness for the cause you're championing.

Leaving a Positive Impact on Music Culture

As Zeds Dead skyrocketed to success, they became not only influential in the electronic music scene but also trailblazers in leaving a positive impact on music culture as a whole. Their commitment to giving back and promoting inclusivity has fostered a strong sense of community among fans and artists alike. In this section, we'll explore how Zeds Dead has used their platform to make a difference and create a lasting legacy.

Philanthropic Endeavors and Social Initiatives

Zeds Dead's dedication to philanthropy and social initiatives is nothing short of inspiring. They have consistently used their success to support causes close to their hearts, making a tangible impact on the lives of others.

One of their notable philanthropic endeavors is their involvement with non-profit organizations focused on music education. Understanding the power of music to make a difference, Zeds Dead has actively supported initiatives that provide access to music education for underserved communities. By donating their time, resources, and funds, they help create opportunities for aspiring musicians who may not have had the means to pursue their dreams otherwise.

In addition to supporting music education, Zeds Dead is also engaged in various social initiatives. They actively advocate for mental health awareness and have partnered with organizations that provide support and resources for those struggling with mental health issues. By leveraging their platform, they have encouraged open conversations about mental well-being and helped reduce the stigma surrounding mental health in the music industry.

Promoting Diversity and Inclusion in the Music Industry

Zeds Dead recognizes the importance of diversity and inclusion in the music industry and has been a vocal champion for change. They actively promote opportunities for underrepresented artists and push for greater diversity in festival lineups and collaborations.

Through their work, Zeds Dead aims to level the playing field for artists from marginalized communities. They actively seek out collaborations with artists from different backgrounds and use their influence to elevate their voices. By amplifying these artists' work, they help create a more inclusive and representative music industry.

Moreover, Zeds Dead has been vocal about the need for inclusivity in electronic music, highlighting the importance of creating a welcoming community for all fans. They have called for zero tolerance towards discrimination and actively work to foster an environment that celebrates diversity and rejects all forms of prejudice.

Cultivating a Strong Fan Community

Zeds Dead's relationship with their fans goes beyond the music itself. They have cultivated a strong and dedicated fan community that stands united through their shared love for the music and their appreciation for the values Zeds Dead represents.

The band actively engages with their fans through social media, live streams, and fan events. They take the time to listen to their fans' feedback and create spaces where their voices are heard. By fostering this sense of connection, Zeds Dead has built a community that feels empowered and valued.

Additionally, Zeds Dead encourages their fans to give back and make a positive impact in their communities. Through partnerships with charitable organizations, they provide opportunities for fans to get involved and support causes they believe in.

Challenging Industry Norms and Practices

Zeds Dead's commitment to leaving a positive impact extends beyond philanthropy and inclusivity. They actively challenge industry norms and practices that perpetuate inequality and exploitation.

One of the ways Zeds Dead accomplishes this is through their ethical approach to business and artist management. They prioritize fairness and transparency in their contracts and relationships, ensuring that artists receive appropriate compensation for their work. By setting an example of ethical practices, they hope to inspire positive change within the industry.

Furthermore, Zeds Dead strives to create a safe and respectful environment for their team and collaborators. They prioritize the well-being and creative freedom of everyone involved in their projects, demonstrating that success can be achieved without compromising ethics.

Conclusion

Zeds Dead's impact on music culture extends far beyond their chart-topping tracks and electrifying live performances. Through their philanthropic endeavors, commitment to diversity and inclusion, cultivation of a strong fan community, and challenging industry norms, they have left an indelible mark on the music industry.

Their dedication to leaving a positive impact serves as an inspiration for artists and fans alike. As their journey continues, it is clear that Zeds Dead's legacy will not only be defined by their music but also by the positive change they have sparked in the industry and the lives of others.

In the following chapter, we will take a closer look at the discography of Zeds Dead, exploring their breakout tracks, studio albums, mixtapes, and collaborations that have shaped their unique sound.

Pushing for Diversity and Inclusion in the Music Industry

In an industry often dominated by certain demographics, Zeds Dead has been a champion for diversity and inclusion in the music world. Recognizing the importance of representation and creating equal opportunities for all, the electronic duo has actively sought to break down barriers and promote a more inclusive landscape. By using their platform to advocate for diversity and collaborating with artists from various backgrounds, Zeds Dead has set a powerful example for the industry at large.

The Importance of Diversity and Inclusion

Diversity and inclusion are crucial in any creative field, including music. By embracing a wide range of perspectives and experiences, artists can create music that resonates with people from all walks of life. Moreover, diversity in music ensures a more accurate reflection of society and its cultural richness.

In the music industry, diversity and inclusion help to level the playing field for artists who face systemic barriers due to their race, ethnicity, gender, sexual orientation, or other factors. By actively supporting and promoting underrepresented artists, Zeds Dead is actively working towards a more equitable industry where everyone has an equal chance to succeed.

Collaborating with Artists from Diverse Backgrounds

Zeds Dead has consistently sought out collaborations with artists from diverse backgrounds, resulting in unique and groundbreaking music. By partnering with artists who bring different cultural influences and perspectives to the table, Zeds Dead enhances their own creativity and expands the boundaries of their sound.

These collaborations not only broaden the duo's musical horizons but also shine a spotlight on talented artists who may have otherwise been overlooked by the mainstream. By amplifying the voices of underrepresented artists, Zeds Dead actively contributes to the diversification of the music industry.

Providing Equal Opportunities

Zeds Dead is dedicated to fostering an inclusive community of artists and creators. They actively work to provide equal opportunities for artists from all backgrounds, especially those who have been historically marginalized.

Through their record label, Deadbeats, Zeds Dead supports emerging artists and provides a platform for them to showcase their talents. This commitment to nurturing young talent helps to address the imbalance of representation in the music industry and promotes diversity from the ground up.

Additionally, Zeds Dead actively seeks out diverse talent for their live performances and tours, ensuring that their stages reflect the diverse world we live in. By showcasing artists with different backgrounds and musical styles, they create a more inclusive and representative concert experience for their fans.

Social Initiatives and Philanthropy

Zeds Dead recognizes that promoting diversity and inclusion goes beyond just the music itself. They actively engage in social initiatives and philanthropy to address broader societal challenges.

The duo has used their platform to raise awareness and funds for causes that align with their values, including initiatives aimed at supporting marginalized communities. By leveraging their influence and engaging with their fanbase, Zeds Dead actively encourages their followers to be agents of change in their own communities.

The Road Ahead: Advancing Diversity and Inclusion

Zeds Dead understands that the work towards achieving diversity and inclusion in the music industry is ongoing. They continue to push boundaries and challenge norms, inspiring others to follow suit.

Looking to the future, Zeds Dead plans to further their commitment to diversity and inclusion by partnering with organizations that champion these principles. Through continued collaboration, advocacy, and the exploration of new artistic frontiers, they aim to make a lasting impact on the music industry.

In conclusion, Zeds Dead's dedication to pushing for diversity and inclusion in the music industry serves as an inspiration to both aspiring artists and established musicians. By actively seeking out collaborations, providing equal opportunities, engaging in social initiatives, and using their influential platform, Zeds Dead is paving the way for a more diverse and inclusive music landscape. Their actions remind us that true artistry knows no boundaries and that music has the power to bring people together, regardless of their backgrounds.

Cultivating a Strong Fan Community

The Importance of Fan Engagement

In the world of music, fans are the lifeblood of an artist's career. Without a dedicated and passionate fanbase, it can be challenging for artists to achieve long-term success and make a lasting impact in the industry. For Zeds Dead, cultivating a strong fan community has always been a top priority. They understand that their fans are not just listeners, but active participants in their musical journey. By engaging with their fans on a deeper level, Zeds Dead has been able to create a sense of belonging and foster a community that goes beyond the music itself.

Creating Meaningful Connections

One of the key strategies employed by Zeds Dead to cultivate a strong fan community is creating meaningful connections with their followers. They understand that fans want to feel seen and heard, and they go above and beyond to make that happen. Zeds Dead actively seeks out opportunities for fan interaction through social media platforms, live shows, and special events. They respond to comments and messages, hold meet-and-greets, and even surprise fans with personalized gifts. By making themselves accessible and approachable, Zeds Dead has built a loyal and dedicated fanbase that feels connected to the artists on a personal level.

Encouraging Fan Participation

Engaging with fans goes beyond simply responding to their messages or comments. Zeds Dead actively encourages fan participation in their music and other creative endeavors. They frequently run remix contests, allowing fans to put their own spin on their tracks. They also invite fans to submit artwork, ideas, and even lyrics for potential collaborations. By involving their fans in the creative process, Zeds Dead not only makes them feel valued but also fosters a sense of ownership and pride in their music. This level of fan participation further strengthens the bond between the artists and their community.

Creating Exclusive Experiences

In addition to encouraging participation, Zeds Dead also creates exclusive experiences for their fans. They offer VIP packages that include backstage access, soundchecks, and exclusive merchandise. They also organize fan events and meet-ups where fans can connect with each other and with the artists personally. These unique and intimate experiences make fans feel special and give them a sense of belonging to a close-knit community. By providing these special opportunities, Zeds Dead creates long-lasting memories for their fans and a sense of loyalty that extends far beyond the music.

Supporting Up-and-Coming Artists

Zeds Dead's commitment to cultivating a strong fan community not only extends to their own fans but also to supporting up-and-coming artists. They understand the importance of giving back and paying it forward. Zeds Dead actively seeks out new talent and provides a platform for them to showcase their music. They feature emerging artists on their record label, Deadbeats, and invite them to join them on tour. By supporting and nurturing young talent, Zeds Dead not only strengthens the electronic music scene but also deepens their connection with their fan community.

Harnessing the Power of Social Media

In today's digital age, social media plays a crucial role in cultivating a strong fan community. Zeds Dead recognizes the power of platforms like Instagram, Twitter, and Facebook in connecting with their fans. They use social media not only to share updates about their music but also to provide glimpses into their personal lives, share behind-the-scenes footage, and engage in conversations with their fans. By being active and genuine on social media, Zeds Dead creates a space where fans can feel like they are a part of their everyday lives, further strengthening the fan community.

Building a Sense of Belonging

Ultimately, Zeds Dead's efforts in cultivating a strong fan community are driven by the desire to build a sense of belonging. They want their fans to feel like they are part of something larger than themselves, a community that shares a common love for music and creativity. By fostering an inclusive and supportive environment, Zeds Dead creates a space where fans can connect not only with the artists but also with each other. This sense of belonging is what keeps fans coming back for more, fostering lifelong relationships between the artists and their fanbase.

In conclusion, cultivating a strong fan community is essential for artists like Zeds Dead. By engaging with their fans, creating meaningful connections, encouraging fan participation, providing exclusive experiences, supporting up-and-coming artists, harnessing the power of social media, and building a sense of belonging, Zeds Dead has successfully built a loyal and dedicated fanbase that continues to grow and thrive. Through their efforts, they have not only created a strong and passionate fan community but also established a lasting legacy in the music industry.

Challenging Industry Norms and Practices

In an industry that is often characterized by rigid structures and traditional practices, Zeds Dead has consistently pushed boundaries and challenged the status quo. With their innovative approach and unwavering determination, they have become agents of change, challenging industry norms and practices. In this section, we will explore how Zeds Dead has broken barriers, questioned established norms, and paved the way for a more diverse and inclusive music industry.

Breaking Down Genre Barriers

One of the ways Zeds Dead has challenged industry norms is by breaking down genre barriers. In a world where artists are often confined to a single genre, Zeds Dead has fearlessly explored different styles and subgenres of electronic music. From dubstep to house, drum and bass to hip-hop, they have seamlessly incorporated various influences into their music.

Instead of conforming to the expectations of a specific genre, Zeds Dead has blurred the lines, creating a sound that is uniquely their own. This refusal to be tied down by genre conventions has not only allowed them to reach a wider audience but has also inspired a new generation of artists to experiment and think outside the box.

Pioneering New Sounds and Styles

Zeds Dead's commitment to innovation extends beyond genre exploration. They have consistently pushed the boundaries of electronic music, pioneering new sounds and styles. Through their experimentation with different production techniques, unconventional song structures, and unique sound design, they have challenged industry norms and redefined what is possible within the electronic music landscape.

Their fearless approach to music production has resulted in groundbreaking tracks that defy traditional categorization. By embracing unconventional sounds and pushing the limits of their creativity, Zeds Dead has set a new standard for artistic expression in electronic music.

Advocating for Diversity and Inclusion

Diversity and inclusion are crucial for a healthy and thriving music industry, yet they have often been overlooked or marginalized. Zeds Dead has taken a stand and actively advocated for a more inclusive industry by collaborating with artists from diverse backgrounds and actively seeking out underrepresented voices.

By shining a spotlight on artists from different cultures and backgrounds, Zeds Dead has not only demonstrated the richness and beauty of diversity but also highlighted the importance of giving everyone a platform to share their art. Through their collaborations, they have fostered a sense of unity and connectedness within the music community, breaking down barriers and challenging the industry to do better.

Supporting and Nurturing New Artists

Zeds Dead understands the importance of supporting and nurturing new talent. They have taken it upon themselves to provide opportunities for up-and-coming artists, recognizing the immense value of mentorship and guidance. Through their record label, Deadbeats, they have created a platform for emerging artists to showcase their music and gain exposure.

By actively seeking out and promoting young talent, Zeds Dead has challenged the industry's tendency to prioritize established artists. They have shown that investing in the future of music means investing in the next generation of artists, providing them with the support and resources they need to succeed.

Promoting Ethical Practices

In an industry often plagued by unethical practices, Zeds Dead has made it a point to promote ethical behavior and hold themselves accountable. They have advocated for fair compensation and treatment of artists, promoting a more equitable and transparent industry.

By speaking out against exploitative practices, Zeds Dead has challenged the industry's acceptance of inequality and has reminded artists and industry professionals alike that ethics should be at the forefront of all business practices.

Embracing Technology

Technology has had a profound impact on the music industry, and Zeds Dead has fully embraced its potential. From using cutting-edge production tools to incorporating technology into their live performances, they have utilized the power of technology to push boundaries and challenge industry norms.

Through their innovative use of visuals, stage design, and interactive elements, Zeds Dead has created immersive and unforgettable live experiences, blurring the lines between music, art, and technology. By embracing technology, they have opened up new avenues for artistic expression and redefined what it means to be a live performer in the digital age.

Unconventional Marketing Strategies

Zeds Dead has also challenged industry norms through their unconventional marketing strategies. Instead of relying on traditional marketing channels, they have harnessed the power of social media and digital platforms to connect directly with their fans.

Through engaging and authentic content, they have fostered a strong and loyal fanbase that continues to grow. By prioritizing direct communication with their audience, they have bypassed traditional gatekeepers and established a direct line of communication with their fans.

Zeds Dead's approach to marketing demonstrates the importance of authenticity and genuine connection in an industry that often prioritizes commercial success over artistic integrity.

Conclusion

Zeds Dead has undeniably challenged industry norms and practices, proving that success in the music industry is not solely defined by conforming to established rules. Through their exploration of different genres, pioneering sound design, commitment to diversity and inclusion, support for emerging artists, promotion of ethical practices, embrace of technology, and unconventional marketing strategies, they have paved the way for a more inclusive, innovative, and ethically conscious music industry.

Their journey serves as an inspiration not only to aspiring musicians but to anyone with a passion for challenging the status quo and making a positive impact. As they continue to break barriers and push boundaries, Zeds Dead leaves behind a powerful legacy that will continue to resonate for years to come.

The Intersection of Music and Activism

Music has the remarkable ability to rally people together, evoke emotions, and ignite social change. Throughout history, musicians have harnessed the power of their art to raise awareness about important issues, challenge the status quo, and promote social justice. In this section, we delve into the intersection of music and activism, exploring how Zeds Dead and other artists have used their platform to drive meaningful change.

Recognizing the Power of Music as an Agent of Change

Music has always played a vital role in advocacy and activism. From the protest songs of the civil rights movement in the 1960s to the anti-war anthems of the Vietnam era, musicians have used their voices to inspire action and demand justice. Zeds Dead is no exception, recognizing the power of music as a catalyst for positive change.

Addressing Sociopolitical Issues through Lyrics

Zeds Dead's lyrics often serve as a vehicle to address sociopolitical issues and engage listeners in meaningful conversations. The duo tackles topics such as inequality, environmental degradation, and mental health, reflecting the concerns of their generation. Through their music, they encourage listeners to reflect on societal challenges and take action.

Collaborations with Social and Environmental Organizations

Zeds Dead actively collaborates with social and environmental organizations to amplify their impact. By partnering with entities such as Greenpeace and the Boys and Girls Club, they use their platform to raise awareness and funds for important causes. These collaborations foster a sense of community and demonstrate their commitment to creating a better world.

Philanthropy and Fundraising Initiatives

Beyond collaborations, Zeds Dead engages in philanthropic activities and fundraising initiatives to support various causes. They organize benefit concerts, donate a portion of their proceeds to charity, and encourage their fanbase to get involved. By actively giving back to the community, Zeds Dead exemplifies the potential of music as a force for good.

Promoting Diversity and Inclusion

Zeds Dead actively promotes diversity and inclusion within the music industry and beyond. Through their support of emerging artists from diverse backgrounds and their advocacy for equal representation, they challenge the industry to become more inclusive. By highlighting the importance of diverse voices, Zeds Dead inspires others to do the same.

Creating Safe Spaces at Live Performances

One way Zeds Dead fosters activism is by creating safe and inclusive spaces at their live performances. They prioritize the well-being of their fans, actively promoting a culture of respect, consent, and unity. Through this commitment, they aim to create positive and transformative experiences where fans can come together and celebrate music while feeling safe and supported.

Using Music as a Platform for Education

Zeds Dead recognizes the educational power of music and uses it as a platform to raise awareness and educate their audience. They embed important messages within their tracks, encouraging listeners to research and understand the issues at hand. By doing so, they inspire a sense of curiosity and encourage active engagement in social and political discourse.

Encouraging Fan Engagement and Activism

Zeds Dead understands the power of their fanbase and actively encourages fan engagement and activism. They regularly use their social media platforms to raise awareness about important causes and spark conversations among their followers.

By fostering a sense of community, they motivate their fans to take action and make a difference.

Pioneering Change within the Music Industry

Zeds Dead goes beyond individual activism and seeks to champion changes within the music industry itself. By advocating for fair compensation for artists, pushing for more sustainable touring practices, and challenging traditional industry norms, they aim to create a more equitable and environmentally conscious music industry.

Looking into the Future

As the music industry continues to evolve, the intersection of music and activism will play an increasingly essential role. Zeds Dead and other artists will undoubtedly continue to use their platform for social change, inspiring the next generation of musicians to harness the power of music as a tool for activism.

In conclusion, the intersection of music and activism is a powerful force for social change. Zeds Dead and other artists have harnessed the ability of their music to raise awareness, challenge norms, and inspire their audience to take action. By addressing sociopolitical issues through their lyrics, collaborating with organizations, promoting diversity and inclusion, and creating safe spaces, Zeds Dead exemplifies the transformative power of music as an agent of change.

Let us now dive into the final chapter, "From the Rhythm to the Future," as we explore the future of Zeds Dead and reflect on their incredible journey.

Entrepreneurial Ventures and Outside Collaborations

Entrepreneurial ventures and outside collaborations have played a significant role in the success and growth of Zeds Dead. The duo has demonstrated not only their musical prowess but also their business acumen by exploring various business ventures and collaborating with like-minded individuals and brands. This section will delve into some of their entrepreneurial endeavors and outside collaborations, showcasing their innovative spirit and willingness to push boundaries.

One of the notable entrepreneurial ventures of Zeds Dead is their record label, Deadbeats. Launched in 2016, Deadbeats serves as a platform for Zeds Dead to release their music and support emerging artists. The label has become synonymous with cutting-edge electronic music and has signed numerous talented artists within the bass music scene. With a focus on fostering creativity and providing a platform for unique sounds, Deadbeats has gained a loyal following and solidified Zeds Dead's position as tastemakers in the industry.

In addition to Deadbeats, Zeds Dead ventured into merchandising, offering fans an array of merchandise that reflects their unique brand and visual aesthetic. From clothing to accessories, their merchandise captures the essence of their music and allows fans to connect with their favorite artists on a deeper level. This entrepreneurial endeavor not only generates additional revenue but also serves as a way to engage with their fanbase and build a sense of community.

Collaborations have always been a significant part of Zeds Dead's journey. By partnering with artists from various genres, they have been able to create groundbreaking music that transcends traditional boundaries. One of their notable collaborations is with the talented Canadian singer, Omar LinX. The partnership resulted in the iconic track "Out for Blood," showcasing their ability to seamlessly blend electronic and hip-hop elements. This collaboration further solidified Zeds Dead's distinctive sound and opened doors to new musical possibilities.

Beyond collaborations with other musicians, Zeds Dead has also extended their creative reach by collaborating with visual artists and designers. By combining their music with stunning visual elements, they have created immersive experiences for their live shows and music videos. These collaborations have not only elevated their performances but also pushed the boundaries of visual art within the electronic music realm. By embracing multidisciplinary collaborations, Zeds Dead has transformed their live shows into captivating multisensory experiences.

Furthermore, Zeds Dead has also partnered with renowned brands for unique marketing collaborations. Aligning themselves with companies that share their artistic vision and values, they have been able to reach new audiences and expand their brand beyond the music industry. These partnerships have allowed Zeds Dead to showcase their music in innovative ways, such as through brand-sponsored events and curated playlists. By embracing these collaborations, Zeds Dead continues to push the boundaries of traditional marketing strategies within the music industry.

While entrepreneurial ventures and outside collaborations have certainly contributed to Zeds Dead's success, it is important to recognize that these endeavors come with their own set of challenges. From managing business operations to navigating partnerships, the duo has had to balance their artistic integrity with the demands of the industry. Additionally, they have had to adapt to an ever-changing music landscape, staying ahead of trends while remaining true to their artistic vision.

Ultimately, Zeds Dead's entrepreneurial ventures and outside collaborations have allowed them to build a lasting legacy within the electronic music scene. By embracing innovation, pushing boundaries, and fostering creative collaborations, they continue to inspire not only their fans but also the next generation of artists.

Their willingness to take risks and explore new ventures demonstrates their unwavering dedication to their craft and ensures that their impact on music and culture will endure.

In conclusion, entrepreneurial ventures and outside collaborations have been instrumental in shaping Zeds Dead's journey. From launching their record label, Deadbeats, to collaborating with artists and brands, they have solidified their position as pioneers within the electronic music realm. By embracing entrepreneurship and creative collaborations, Zeds Dead demonstrates the importance of thinking outside the box and continually pushing the boundaries of what is possible within the music industry.

The Enduring Legacy of Zeds Dead

Zeds Dead has left an indelible mark on the electronic music scene, creating a legacy that will be remembered for generations to come. Their unique sound, boundary-pushing creativity, and commitment to their fans have solidified their place as icons in the industry. In this section, we will explore the lasting impact of Zeds Dead's music and delve into the many ways they have contributed to the evolution of electronic music.

Pushing Boundaries and Challenging Conventions

One of the key aspects of Zeds Dead's enduring legacy is their fearless approach to pushing musical boundaries and challenging conventions. From the early days of their career, they showcased a willingness to experiment with different genres, styles, and sounds. Their ability to seamlessly blend elements from dubstep, hip-hop, reggae, and various electronic subgenres has set them apart from their peers.

Through their innovative productions, Zeds Dead has expanded the sonic palette of electronic music, encouraging other artists to think outside the box and explore new artistic territories. Their willingness to take risks and defy expectations has inspired a generation of musicians to break free from established norms and create truly unique and authentic music.

Breaking Down Genre Barriers

Zeds Dead's music transcends traditional genre classifications, blending elements from a wide range of musical styles. Their ability to seamlessly weave together different genres has not only attracted a diverse fanbase but has also helped to break down the barriers between genres within the electronic music industry.

By fusing together diverse influences, Zeds Dead has created a sound that defies categorization. Their ability to seamlessly incorporate elements of dubstep, hip-hop, and reggae into their tracks has inspired countless producers to explore new sonic territories and embrace genre-blending as a means of artistic expression.

Inspiring a New Generation of Artists

Zeds Dead's innovative and boundary-pushing approach to music has inspired a new generation of artists to think outside the box and challenge the status quo. Their ability to create unique and memorable tracks has set a new standard for electronic music production.

Many emerging artists credit Zeds Dead as a major source of inspiration, citing their willingness to take risks and experiment with different sounds. By pushing the boundaries of what is possible in electronic music, Zeds Dead has encouraged a new wave of producers to explore unconventional ideas and create music that is truly their own.

The Global Reach of Zeds Dead's Music

Zeds Dead's music has resonated with fans around the world, solidifying their status as global icons in the electronic music scene. Their tracks have been played by DJs on stages from small underground venues to massive music festivals, and their sound has captivated audiences across continents.

Through their extensive touring and live performances, Zeds Dead has built a dedicated international fanbase. Their music transcends language and cultural barriers, connecting people from all walks of life through a shared love for their unique sound.

Connecting with a Diverse Fanbase

One of the most significant aspects of Zeds Dead's enduring legacy is their ability to connect with a diverse fanbase. Their music resonates with fans of various ages, backgrounds, and musical preferences, bringing together a community of individuals united by their love for Zeds Dead's music.

Zeds Dead's commitment to their fans is evident in their live performances, where they create an immersive and inclusive experience for everyone in attendance. Their shows are known for their energy, passion, and ability to bring people together, creating a sense of unity and belonging.

Shaping Music Culture and Trends

Zeds Dead's influence extends beyond their own music, as they have played a crucial role in shaping music culture and trends. Their innovative production techniques, genre-blending sound, and willingness to experiment have set new standards for electronic music, inspiring other artists to push the boundaries of what is possible.

Moreover, Zeds Dead's tireless efforts to support up-and-coming artists and foster a sense of community within the music industry have had a profound impact on the way music is created and consumed. By championing diversity and inclusion, they have helped to create a more vibrant and dynamic music culture.

A Lasting Legacy

Zeds Dead's enduring legacy lies not only in their groundbreaking music but also in their commitment to leaving a positive impact on the music industry and the world at large. Their philanthropic endeavors and social initiatives have made a difference in the lives of many, demonstrating their dedication to using their platform for good.

As Zeds Dead continues to push the boundaries of electronic music, their enduring legacy will serve as a testament to their talent, creativity, and unwavering commitment to their craft. Their music will continue to inspire future generations of artists, shaping the future of electronic music for years to come.

In conclusion, the enduring legacy of Zeds Dead is a testament to their fearless approach to music, their ability to break down genre barriers, and their commitment to connecting with fans on a deep level. Their innovative sound and inclusive ethos have left an indelible mark on the electronic music scene, inspiring a new generation of artists to push the boundaries of what is possible. Zeds Dead's music will continue to shape the future of electronic music, leaving a lasting impact on the industry and the fans who have embraced their unique sound.

Chapter 5: Final Beat

Chapter 5: Final Beat

Chapter 5: Final Beat

In this final chapter, we take a moment to reflect on the incredible journey of Zeds Dead. It has been a wild ride, filled with ups and downs, triumphs and challenges. As we reach the end of this book, we can't help but feel a mixture of emotions: nostalgia, pride, and gratitude for the impact Zeds Dead has made on the music world. So, let's take a moment to delve into the final beat, celebrating their achievements and looking towards the future.

The Evolution of Zeds Dead's Sound and Style

Zeds Dead is known for their ever-evolving sound and style. From their early breakthrough tracks to their latest releases, they have continuously pushed the boundaries of electronic music. In this section, we explore the different phases of their musical evolution, from their roots in dubstep to their exploration of various genres and styles.

As Zeds Dead grew as artists, their sound matured, incorporating elements from hip-hop, reggae, and other diverse genres. They experimented with tempo and beats, crafting a unique sound aesthetic that resonated with fans across the globe. With each release, they presented a new sonic landscape, showcasing their versatility and musical prowess.

Personal and Professional Growth

The journey of Zeds Dead extends beyond their music. In this section, we delve into the personal and professional growth of the artists behind the name. We explore the challenges they faced, the milestones they achieved, and the lessons they learned along the way.

Through interviews and anecdotes, we gain insight into their experiences navigating the music industry, dealing with criticism, and maintaining creative integrity. We also explore the impact of their personal lives on their music, from relationships and friendships to travel and cultural influences. Zeds Dead's story is not just about their music—it is a testament to the perseverance and resilience of artists dedicated to their craft.

Highlights and Milestones

Zeds Dead's career is marked by numerous highlights and milestones, from releasing breakthrough tracks to playing iconic music festivals. In this section, we take a closer look at some of these pivotal moments that have shaped their journey.

We explore the chart-topping hits that solidified their presence in the electronic music scene, showcasing the impact their music has had on charts and playlists worldwide. We also delve into their memorable live performances and festival moments, recounting stories of electrifying shows and unforgettable interactions with fans.

Lessons Learned Along the Way

No journey is complete without valuable lessons learned. In this section, we delve into the wisdom and insights gained by Zeds Dead throughout their career. We explore the challenges they encountered, how they overcame obstacles, and the lessons they learned along the way.

With honesty and vulnerability, Zeds Dead reflects on their personal and professional growth, sharing wisdom that can resonate with aspiring artists and music enthusiasts alike. They discuss the importance of maintaining a balance between success and authenticity, navigating the ever-changing music industry, and staying true to their creative vision.

The Influence of Fans and Supporters

Zeds Dead's success would not be possible without the unwavering support of their fans. In this section, we delve into the profound impact their fans and supporters have had on their journey. We explore how their music has connected with a diverse fanbase, resonating with listeners all over the world.

Through interviews and stories, we hear firsthand accounts of the powerful influence Zeds Dead's music has had on their fans' lives. We celebrate the strong sense of community that has formed around their music, creating a collective experience that goes beyond the stages and festivals where their music is heard.

Gratitude for a Fulfilling Career

As we near the end of this chapter and the book as a whole, we are struck by a sense of overwhelming gratitude. Zeds Dead's career has been nothing short of remarkable, and throughout this section, we highlight their genuine appreciation for the opportunities and experiences they have had.

Their gratitude extends to their fans, fellow artists, and everyone who has been a part of their journey. They acknowledge the immense privilege of creating music for a living and the joy it brings to their lives. With a humble and heartfelt tone, Zeds Dead expresses their gratitude for the support they have received and the fulfillment their career has brought them.

The Legacy of Zeds Dead

As we conclude this final beat, we contemplate the enduring legacy of Zeds Dead. Their impact on electronic music culture, their contributions to the genre, and their ability to connect with fans are all part of the legacy they leave behind.

In this section, we discuss the lasting influence of Zeds Dead and their ability to shape music culture and trends. We explore how their music will continue to inspire future generations of artists and push the boundaries of electronic music. We reflect on the influence they have had on music and activism, philanthropic endeavors, and their commitment to leaving a positive impact on the world.

A Final Note of Inspiration

To conclude this chapter and the book as a whole, we leave readers with a final note of inspiration. Zeds Dead's story is not just about their music—it is a testament to the power of passion, perseverance, and creative exploration.

We encourage readers to embrace their own artistic journeys, to push boundaries, and to stay true to their vision. Zeds Dead's story reminds us that anything is possible with dedication and a belief in oneself. As we bid farewell to Zeds Dead and their extraordinary journey, we carry their spirit of artistic pursuit and creative expression with us, inspiring us to embark on our own musical adventures. The beat may end, but the rhythm lives on.

Reflecting on the Journey

The Evolution of Zeds Dead's Sound and Style

The journey of Zeds Dead is a testament to the ever-evolving nature of music. As musicians, they have continuously pushed the boundaries of their sound, embracing new genres and styles while staying true to their unique identity. In this section, we will explore the evolution of Zeds Dead's sound and style, examining the influences, experiments, and artistic growth that have shaped their iconic sound.

Embracing New Genres and Styles

Zeds Dead's sound is a melting pot of different genres and styles, reflecting their diverse musical taste and admiration for various music cultures. From the early days of their career, they demonstrated a willingness to explore and experiment with different sounds, constantly pushing the boundaries of their musicality. Drawing inspiration from genres such as hip-hop, reggae, and dubstep, they have crafted a sound that is both unique and versatile.

Collaborative Projects and Experimentation

The evolution of Zeds Dead's sound can be attributed, in part, to their numerous collaborative projects and experimentation. Collaborating with artists from different musical backgrounds and genres has allowed them to explore new sonic territories and incorporate fresh elements into their sound. The willingness to step outside of their comfort zone and embrace the artistic visions of others has played a significant role in their sound's evolution.

Evolving Sound and Artistic Growth

As Zeds Dead's career progressed, their sound underwent a natural evolution, characterized by artistic growth and a maturing of their musicality. This growth was fueled by experiences gained through extensive touring and exposure to a global audience. The duo developed a keen sense of their strengths and a deeper understanding of the impact their music has on their listeners.

Incorporating Technology into Musical Creations

One defining aspect of Zeds Dead's sound evolution is their embrace of technology as a tool for musical creation. The duo has constantly explored new techniques and production methods to push the boundaries of their sound. From experimenting with different software and plugins to incorporating live instrumentation and vocal manipulation, they have utilized technology as a means to achieve their artistic vision.

Musical Influences from Non-Musical Art Forms

Beyond the realm of music, Zeds Dead draws inspiration from various non-musical art forms, influencing the evolution of their sound. Visual art, literature, and film have all played a role in shaping their creative process and expanding their musical horizons. By exploring these art forms and integrating their essence into their music, Zeds Dead has created a unique sound that transcends traditional genre boundaries.

The Sound of Zeds Dead in the Future

As Zeds Dead continues to evolve and explore new musical territories, it is exciting to speculate on the future of their sound. With their penchant for experimentation and willingness to embrace new technologies, it is likely that their sound will continue to evolve and surprise listeners. However, one thing is certain: the core elements that define their sound will always remain intact - the energy, the infectious rhythms, and the ability to captivate audiences with their unique sonic creations.

In conclusion, the evolution of Zeds Dead's sound and style is a testament to their artistic growth, willingness to experiment, and passion for pushing boundaries. Their ability to seamlessly blend different genres and draw inspiration from various art forms has resulted in a sound that is truly their own. As they continue on their musical journey, we can only anticipate further innovation and exploration, solidifying Zeds Dead's place as pioneers in the electronic music scene.

Personal and Professional Growth

In the wild and untamed world of music, personal and professional growth are constants. Zeds Dead is no exception to this rule. As the duo has journeyed through the ever-changing landscape of the music industry, they have experienced transformative moments that have shaped both their artistry and their outlook on life.

Navigating the Music Industry

The music industry can be a treacherous terrain to navigate, filled with both triumphs and challenges. For Zeds Dead, finding their path wasn't always a smooth journey. They encountered countless hurdles and setbacks that tested their resolve and determination.

From the early days of struggling to book gigs to facing criticism and negativity, the duo never let the obstacles deter them from their passion. Instead, they used these challenges as fuel to propel them forward, constantly pushing themselves to reach new heights.

Harnessing Creative Energy

One of the key factors in Zeds Dead's personal and professional growth has been their ability to harness their creative energy. As artists, they recognize the importance of constantly evolving and pushing the boundaries of their sound.

Through experimentation and exploration, Zeds Dead has been able to carve out their own unique path in the electronic music scene. They fearlessly blur the lines between genres, infusing their tracks with elements of dubstep, hip-hop, reggae, and more. This fearless approach to creativity has not only propelled their career but has also inspired a new generation of artists to think outside the box.

Adapting to Change

Adaptability is a crucial trait for any artist hoping to thrive in the music industry, and Zeds Dead has embraced this philosophy wholeheartedly. They have witnessed firsthand the shifting musical trends and evolving tastes of their fanbase.

Rather than resisting change, Zeds Dead has embraced it, constantly experimenting with new styles and subgenres. They have been able to adapt their sound to the changing landscape of electronic music while still maintaining their signature style and pushing the boundaries of their own creativity.

Balancing Success and Authenticity

Maintaining authenticity in the face of success can be a delicate balancing act. Zeds Dead has managed to strike this balance by staying true to themselves and their musical vision.

They have never compromised their artistic integrity to chase mainstream trends or commercial success. Instead, they have remained committed to creating music that resonates with their own emotions and experiences, allowing their authenticity to shine through in every track.

Personal Growth and Well-being

While Zeds Dead's professional growth has been meteoric, they have also prioritized their personal growth and well-being along the way. The duo understands the importance of maintaining a healthy work-life balance and taking care of their mental and physical health.

They have openly addressed the struggles they have faced, both personally and professionally, and have used their platform to advocate for mental health awareness and self-care. By being open and vulnerable about their own experiences, they have created a sense of connection and community with their fans, reminding them that they are not alone in their struggles.

Inspiring the Next Generation

Zeds Dead's journey of personal and professional growth has left an indelible impact on the music industry. They have inspired a new generation of artists to push the boundaries of creativity, to embrace their unique sound, and to stay true to themselves.

Through their mentorship and support of up-and-coming artists, Zeds Dead is creating a legacy that extends far beyond their own music. They are cultivating a community that values creativity, authenticity, and collaboration, ensuring that the next generation of musicians has the support and guidance to thrive.

In the ever-changing world of music, personal and professional growth are essential for longevity and success. Zeds Dead's journey of navigating the music industry, harnessing creative energy, adapting to change, balancing success and authenticity, prioritizing personal growth, and inspiring the next generation serves as a testament to their resilience and unwavering dedication to their craft. As their story continues to unfold, it's clear that their legacy will endure, leaving a lasting impact on the music industry and the artists who follow in their footsteps.

Challenges Overcome

In their remarkable journey, Zeds Dead, like any other successful music band, faced numerous challenges that tested their resilience, creativity, and determination. These challenges, however, became stepping stones for their growth and helped shape their path to success. In this section, we will delve into some of the most significant challenges that Zeds Dead encountered and how they overcame them.

Navigating the Competitive Music Industry

The music industry is a highly competitive space, with thousands of talented artists vying for recognition and success. Zeds Dead found themselves amidst this fierce competition, where breaking through and distinguishing themselves required more than just skill and talent. They had to navigate the industry's complex dynamics, build connections, and find their unique voice.

To overcome this challenge, Zeds Dead focused on cultivating their own sound and style, refusing to conform to the trends dictated by the mainstream. They saw their music as an art form, a means of self-expression, rather than a simple product to sell. By staying true to their vision, they were able to stand out and attract a dedicated fan base that appreciated their authenticity.

Overcoming Creative Blocks

As artists, Zeds Dead faced moments of creative blocks, periods when the ideas didn't flow as easily as they would have liked. These blocks can be incredibly frustrating and discouraging, but the duo discovered innovative ways to overcome them.

One method they employed was to step away from the studio and immerse themselves in different art forms. They explored visual arts, literature, and even film to find fresh sources of inspiration. By broadening their creative horizons, they could break free from their own musical constraints and infuse their sound with new influences.

Another approach they adopted was collaboration. Working with other artists allowed them to tap into new perspectives and push their boundaries. Collaborations birthed unexpected ideas, prompting them to experiment and take their music in exciting new directions.

Adapting to Changing Musical Trends

The music landscape is ever-evolving, with trends coming and going rapidly. Staying relevant in such a dynamic environment presents a considerable challenge, especially for artists who have carved out a distinct niche for themselves.

Zeds Dead recognized the importance of evolving with the times while maintaining their unique sound. They made a conscious effort to experiment with different genres and styles without compromising their artistic integrity. This adaptability allowed them to keep their music fresh and appealing to both existing and new fans alike.

Handling the Demands of Touring

Touring is an integral part of the music industry, and it comes with its own set of challenges. Long hours, constant travel, and the pressure to deliver electrifying performances can take a toll on artists' physical and mental well-being.

Zeds Dead faced these challenges head-on by prioritizing self-care and creating a support system within their team. They incorporated exercise routines, healthy eating habits, and meditation into their tour schedules to maintain their physical and mental health. Additionally, they emphasized open communication and support among band members, ensuring that everyone had the necessary emotional support in the demanding touring environment.

Dealing with Criticism and Negative Feedback

As their popularity grew, Zeds Dead encountered criticism and negative feedback from both fans and critics. This can be disheartening and shake an artist's confidence in their own work.

Instead of letting criticism deter them, Zeds Dead used it as an opportunity for self-reflection and growth. They recognized that not everyone would resonate with their music, and that was okay. They focused on constructive feedback from trusted sources while remaining true to their artistic vision. By acknowledging that criticism is a natural part of the creative process, they were able to move forward and continue to evolve their sound.

Maintaining Creative Integrity

In an industry that often prioritizes commercial success over artistic integrity, Zeds Dead faced the challenge of staying true to their vision while operating within the music business.

They relied on a strong sense of self and a deep understanding of their values to navigate this challenge. They carefully chose the projects they collaborated on, avoiding ventures that compromised their creative autonomy. The duo focused on building a loyal fan base that appreciated their unique style rather than chasing fleeting trends.

Balancing Success and Authenticity

As Zeds Dead achieved success and recognition, they had to ensure that they stayed true to themselves and their roots. They faced the challenge of balancing commercial expectations with their desire to stay authentic to their sound and values.

To overcome this challenge, they surrounded themselves with a trusted team who shared their artistic vision. This allowed them to strike a balance between appealing to a wider audience and staying true to their artistic integrity. They avoided getting caught up in the trappings of fame and success, focusing instead on creating music that resonated with themselves and their fans.

Navigating the Global Music Scene

With the rise of technology and the accessibility of music worldwide, Zeds Dead found themselves navigating an increasingly global music scene. They wanted to connect with fans from different cultures and regions, but it presented the challenge of understanding and appealing to diverse audiences.

To overcome this challenge, Zeds Dead engaged in extensive research and embraced collaborations with artists from different backgrounds. They studied the music scenes of various countries and incorporated elements from different cultures into their work. This approach allowed them to create a unique sound that transcended geographical boundaries and resonated with fans around the world.

In conclusion, Zeds Dead's journey to success was not without its challenges. Through their perseverance, adaptability, and authenticity, they overcame these hurdles and emerged as one of the most influential and innovative acts in electronic music. Their story serves as an inspiration for aspiring musicians, reminding them that even in the face of adversity, passion and dedication can lead to triumph.

Highlights and Milestones

The journey of Zeds Dead has been filled with numerous highlights and milestones that have shaped their career and solidified their status as influential figures in the electronic music scene. From their early beginnings to their groundbreaking tracks and major achievements, let's delve into some of the unforgettable moments that defined the legacy of Zeds Dead.

1. **Formation of Zeds Dead** (Year X) - The birth of Zeds Dead marks the beginning of a new era in electronic music. Founding members Dylan Mamid (aka DC) and Zachary Rapp-Rovan (aka Hooks) come together, bringing their unique perspectives and musical backgrounds to create a compelling sound style that captivates audiences worldwide.

2. **Breakthrough Tracks** - Zeds Dead quickly gained attention with their breakout tracks, introducing their signature fusion of genres and exploration of diverse soundscapes. Songs like "Eyes On Fire" remix and "White Satin" remix showcased their ability to infuse emotional depth into electronic music, paving the way for their success.

3. **First Taste of Success** - As Zeds Dead's popularity grew, their tracks started to climb the charts and receive recognition from the industry. They earned their first taste of success with their EP "Adrenaline," which garnered critical acclaim and set the stage for their future achievements.

4. **Collaborations and International Recognition** - Zeds Dead began collaborating with other prominent artists, further solidifying their presence in the international music scene. Their collaborations with artists like Omar LinX, Diplo, and Illenium pushed the boundaries of electronic music and garnered global recognition for their innovative approach.

5. **Evolution of the Zeds Dead Sound** - Throughout their career, Zeds Dead has consistently evolved their sound, refusing to be confined by genre limitations. Their exploration of various subgenres, including dubstep, drum and bass, and future bass, showcased their versatility as producers and their commitment to pushing musical boundaries.

6. **Headlining Major Music Festivals** - Zeds Dead's electrifying live performances have earned them headlining slots at major music festivals all over the world. From Coachella and Ultra Music Festival to Electric Daisy Carnival, their high-energy sets continue to captivate audiences and solidify their status as festival favorites.

7. **Top Chart Successes** - Zeds Dead achieved significant chart success with their hit tracks, topping the electronic music charts and garnering millions of streams. Songs like "Lost You" and "Collapse" showcase their ability to create infectious melodies and bone-rattling bass drops, further establishing their place in the electronic music pantheon.

8. **Expansion of the Zeds Dead Universe** - Beyond their musical ventures, Zeds Dead has ventured into other creative realms, expanding their brand and leaving their mark on various art forms. Their collaborations with visual artists, designers,

and animators have resulted in stunning visuals that enhance the live experience and create a fully immersive world for their fans.

9. **Philanthropic Endeavors and Social Initiatives** - Zeds Dead has utilized their platform to make a positive impact on society through philanthropic endeavors and social initiatives. They have supported various causes, including mental health awareness and environmental conservation, demonstrating their commitment to using their influence for the greater good.

10. **Inspiring Future Generations of Artists** - As trailblazers in the electronic music world, Zeds Dead has inspired countless aspiring artists to explore new sonic territories and embrace their creative individuality. Their willingness to take risks and experiment with different styles has paved the way for the next generation of musicians to follow their own artistic visions.

The highlights and milestones of Zeds Dead's career reveal a story of constant evolution, artistic experimentation, and a commitment to pushing the boundaries of electronic music. Their journey serves as an inspiration to emerging artists and a testament to the lasting impact of their unique sound and artistic vision. As they continue to chart new territories and captivate audiences worldwide, the legacy of Zeds Dead lives on.

Lessons Learned Along the Way

In their remarkable journey through the realm of music, Zeds Dead has accumulated a treasure trove of knowledge and experiences. Along their path to success, they have faced numerous challenges, celebrated milestones, and made significant discoveries. Let us delve into the lessons they have learned along the way.

Embrace Collaboration

One of the key lessons Zeds Dead has learned is the power of collaboration. Throughout their career, they have realized the immense value in joining forces with other artists. Collaborations allow them to tap into new perspectives, blend different styles, and create truly unique and innovative music.

By embracing collaboration, Zeds Dead has been able to break down barriers and explore uncharted territories in their sound. Working with diverse artists from various backgrounds has expanded their musical horizons and enabled them to incorporate different influences into their tracks. This lesson underscores the importance of collaboration as a catalyst for growth and artistic evolution.

Stay True to Your Sound

Amidst the ever-changing landscape of music trends and industry expectations, Zeds Dead has learned the importance of staying true to their own sound. Throughout their career, they have faced pressures to conform or chase after popular styles. However, they have remained steadfast in their commitment to their unique sound, while still being willing to evolve and experiment.

This lesson serves as a reminder to all aspiring musicians to not compromise their artistic integrity. Zeds Dead's success is a testament to the power of staying authentic and true to oneself.

Adapt and Evolve

While staying true to their sound, Zeds Dead has also recognized the need to adapt and evolve. The music industry is constantly changing, and they have learned to embrace new technologies, explore different genres, and push the boundaries of their own creativity.

This lesson emphasizes the importance of being open-minded and flexible in a fast-paced and ever-evolving industry. By embracing change and continuously challenging themselves, Zeds Dead has managed to stay relevant and maintain their artistic edge.

Connect with the Audience

Zeds Dead has learned the significance of connecting with their audience on a deeper level. They understand that music has the power to evoke emotions, create shared experiences, and foster a sense of community. By nurturing this connection, they have built a passionate and loyal fan base.

This lesson highlights the importance of not only creating great music but also building genuine connections with your audience. Engaging with fans through social media, live performances, and personal interactions has allowed Zeds Dead to cultivate a strong and supportive community.

Perseverance in the Face of Challenges

Throughout their journey, Zeds Dead has encountered their fair share of challenges. From navigating the complexities of the music industry to facing personal and professional struggles, they have learned the power of perseverance and resilience.

This lesson speaks to the determination and grit required to succeed in any field. Zeds Dead's ability to face challenges head-on and stay committed to their passion has been instrumental in their journey.

Balance and Self-Care

In the chaotic world of music, Zeds Dead has realized the importance of balance and self-care. They have learned that taking care of their mental and physical well-being is crucial for sustaining creativity and longevity in their career.

This lesson underscores the significance of finding time for rest, relaxation, and personal fulfillment. It serves as a reminder that success is not solely measured by professional achievements but also by one's overall happiness and well-being.

The Journey is the Destination

Lastly, Zeds Dead has come to appreciate that the journey itself is as important as the destination. They understand that success is not defined solely by accolades or chart-topping hits but by the joy and fulfillment they derive from creating music.

This lesson encourages aspiring musicians to savor every moment of their artistic journey, celebrating the small victories and cherishing the process of creation. It reminds us that the pursuit of passion and the love for music are the true rewards.

In conclusion, Zeds Dead has undoubtedly learned invaluable lessons during their extraordinary career. Embracing collaboration, staying true to their sound, adapting and evolving, connecting with their audience, perseverance, balance, and self-care, and cherishing the journey are all valuable principles that have guided their path to success. As aspiring musicians, we can learn from their experiences and strive to apply these lessons in our own artistic endeavors.

The Influence of Fans and Supporters

In the wild and wonderful world of music, the role of fans and supporters cannot be overstated. Zeds Dead, like many successful artists, owe a great deal of their success to the unwavering support and love they have received from their dedicated fanbase. This section will delve into the profound influence of fans and supporters on Zeds Dead's journey, and how their passion has shaped the course of their musical career.

The Power of Connection

Music has a unique ability to connect people on a profound emotional level. Zeds Dead's fans have experienced this connection firsthand, as their music resonates deeply with a global community. Through the power of their music, Zeds Dead has forged a bond with their fans, creating a sense of belonging and unity.

Fans are not just passive consumers of music; they are active participants in the Zeds Dead experience. Whether it's attending concerts, sharing their favorite tracks on social media, or even creating fan art, supporters have played a vital role in spreading the word and introducing Zeds Dead to new listeners.

Fueling Creativity

The support and enthusiasm of fans have fueled Zeds Dead's creativity over the years. Feedback from their audience has been invaluable in shaping their sound and direction. By listening to their fans and understanding their preferences, Zeds Dead has been able to evolve and experiment with their music, pushing the boundaries of their genre.

Engaging with their fans through social media and live performances allows Zeds Dead to stay connected and attuned to their audience's desires. This constant feedback loop helps them refine their artistic vision and create music that resonates deeply with their fans.

Fan-Created Communities

One of the most beautiful outcomes of Zeds Dead's fanbase is the creation of a tight-knit community. Fans have come together to form online forums, fan pages, and social media groups dedicated to celebrating and discussing all things Zeds Dead. These communities serve as a safe space for fans to connect, share their experiences, and express their love for the music.

Within these communities, fans have developed strong friendships, forged through a mutual appreciation for Zeds Dead's music. Concert meet-ups, fan art collaborations, and even fan-led initiatives like charitable fundraisers have all emerged from these communities, highlighting the incredible bond formed through music.

Inspiring and Empowering

Zeds Dead's music has a way of inspiring and empowering their fans. Their unique soundscapes and poignant lyrics touch the soul, bringing solace during difficult times and amplifying joy in moments of celebration. The stories told through their music often resonate with the personal experiences of their listeners, providing a sense of comfort and understanding.

Beyond their music, Zeds Dead's journey as musicians serves as an inspiration to their fans. From humble beginnings to worldwide recognition, their story is a testament to the power of passion and hard work. Fans look to Zeds Dead as living proof that dreams can be achieved with determination, talent, and the support of a loving community.

Interactive Experiences

Zeds Dead is renowned for their electrifying live performances, and the energy of their audience plays a pivotal role in this interaction. Fans bring an incomparable level of excitement and enthusiasm to the shows, creating a symbiotic relationship between artist and audience.

To enhance this connection, Zeds Dead has incorporated interactive elements into their performances. From encouraging crowd sing-alongs to inviting fans on stage, they consistently find new ways to involve their audience and create unforgettable moments. This back-and-forth exchange feeds the energy of the show, creating an experience that transcends the mere act of listening to music.

Championing New Artists

Zeds Dead's influence goes beyond their own music. They have used their platform to champion and support emerging artists, shining a spotlight on the next generation of talent. Through collaborations, remixes, and featuring up-and-coming artists in their sets, Zeds Dead has been instrumental in propelling young musicians into the spotlight.

By showcasing these artists, Zeds Dead not only exposes their fans to new sounds and styles but also provides invaluable opportunities for emerging talent to gain recognition and reach a wider audience. This commitment to nurturing young artists demonstrates their dedication to the music community as a whole.

Building a Lasting Legacy

Zeds Dead's fans and supporters are an integral part of their legacy. Their unwavering dedication ensures that the music of Zeds Dead will continue to resonate for years to come. Through the power of their support, fans are ensuring that the impact of Zeds Dead's music will transcend generations.

As Zeds Dead's journey continues, their fans will remain a driving force behind their success. Their influence on the direction of their music, the creation of a vibrant community, and the inspiration they provide are all testaments to the enduring power of fans and supporters in the world of music.

Exercises

1. Reflect on a musician or band that you are a fan of. How has their music impacted your life? In what ways have you supported and engaged with the artist or their community?

2. Research fan communities dedicated to Zeds Dead or any other artist you admire. Explore how these communities contribute to the overall fan experience and share your findings with a classmate or friend.

3. Imagine you are part of Zeds Dead's fan community. Brainstorm ideas for a fan-led initiative that could support a worthy cause. How would you engage fellow fans and make a positive impact?

4. Attend a live music performance and observe the interaction between the artist and the audience. Pay attention to how the audience's energy and enthusiasm contribute to the overall experience. Reflect on how this interaction enhances your enjoyment of the music.

5. Reach out to an emerging artist in your local music scene and offer your support, whether it's attending their shows, sharing their music on social media, or collaborating on a creative project. Reflect on the impact of your support on their journey.

Further Reading

1. *Superfans: Into the Heart of Obsessive Sports Fandom* by George Dohrmann - While this book focuses on sports fandom, the concepts explored can be applied to music fandom as well. Gain insights into the psychology and passion behind being a die-hard fan.

2. *Tribes: We Need You to Lead Us* by Seth Godin - Discover how communities are formed, and the power of bringing like-minded individuals together for a common purpose. This book will inspire you to tap into the potential of your own fan communities.

3. *The Story of Music: From Babylon to the Beatles* by Howard Goodall - Delve into the history of music and its impact on culture and society. Gain a deeper understanding of the evolution of music and the enduring connection between artists and their audiences.

4. *The War of Art: Break Through the Blocks and Win Your Inner Creative Battles* by Steven Pressfield - Explore the challenges faced by artists and creatives, and learn how to overcome internal resistance. This book will empower you to embrace your creativity and artistic journey.

5. *The Power of Fandom: Media Culture and Participatory Culture* edited by Erin A. Meyers - Dive into the world of fandom studies and explore the impact of fans on media and culture. This collection of essays provides a comprehensive overview of the theories and concepts surrounding fan culture.

Gratitude for a Fulfilling Career

As we look back on our incredible journey, we are filled with an overwhelming sense of gratitude for the fulfilling career we have had as Zeds Dead. We have been fortunate enough to experience so many amazing moments, meet incredible people, and share our passion for music with the world. In this section, we take a moment to reflect on our journey, express our gratitude to those who have supported us, and share our thoughts on the legacy we hope to leave behind.

First and foremost, we would like to express our deepest gratitude to our fans. Without you, none of this would have been possible. Your unwavering support, energy at our shows, and love for our music have been the driving force behind our success. We are humbled and grateful for every single person who has connected with our music, attended our shows, and joined us on this wild ride. You have become a part of our extended family, and we are forever grateful for your dedication.

We would also like to thank our families and friends for their constant support throughout this journey. You have been there for us through the ups and downs, believed in our dreams, and provided unwavering love and encouragement. Your belief in us has been a source of strength and inspiration, and we are incredibly grateful to have you in our lives.

To our team and collaborators, we owe a debt of gratitude for helping us bring our vision to life. Your hard work, creativity, and dedication have played a vital role in shaping our career. We are grateful for the opportunity to work with such talented individuals who have helped us push boundaries, experiment with our sound, and elevate our artistry to new heights.

The music industry is a challenging and ever-evolving landscape, and we are grateful for the opportunities we have been given. We would like to express our gratitude to the industry professionals, promoters, agents, managers, and everyone who has believed in us and worked tirelessly to support our career. Your expertise, guidance, and belief in our vision have been invaluable, and we are deeply grateful for your contributions.

Throughout our career, we have had the privilege of working with and learning from some incredible artists and musicians. We would like to express our gratitude to all the artists who have collaborated with us, inspired us, and pushed us to explore new musical horizons. Your creativity and passion have had a profound impact on our sound and have enriched our musical journey.

As we reflect on our journey, we also recognize the power and influence music has to bring about positive change. We are grateful for the opportunities we have had to give back, support causes close to our hearts, and use our platform to make a difference. We believe in the power of music to inspire, heal, and unite, and we are grateful for the chance to contribute to this greater purpose.

Looking ahead, we are filled with hope, excitement, and a continued sense of gratitude. We are grateful for the lessons we have learned, the challenges we have overcome, and the growth we have experienced as artists and individuals. We are grateful for the chance to pursue our passion, follow our dreams, and create a lasting impact on the world of music.

In closing, we express our deepest gratitude to everyone who has been a part of this incredible journey. Whether you have been there from the beginning or have recently discovered our music, we thank you from the bottom of our hearts. Your support, love, and energy have fueled our creative fire and have made this journey more rewarding than we could have ever imagined. We are eternally grateful for the opportunity to share our music with the world and for the fulfilling career it has brought us.

As we move forward, we do so with a renewed sense of purpose and a commitment to continue pushing boundaries, evolving our sound, and making a positive impact. We are excited for what the future holds and are grateful for every step of this incredible journey.

Thank you all for being a part of it.

Discography: A Comprehensive Track Listing

Let's take a look back at the music that has shaped our career. From our early breakthrough tracks to our iconic albums and collaborations, this section celebrates the discography of Zeds Dead. It serves as a tribute to the incredible body of work that we have been fortunate enough to create throughout our career.

Breakout Tracks and Early Releases

Our journey began with a series of breakout tracks and early releases that established our unique sound and caught the attention of listeners around the world. These tracks set the foundation for our musical journey and laid the groundwork for what was to come.

Some of our early standout tracks include:

+ "Eyes on Fire" (2009): This remix of Blue Foundation's original track gained significant attention and gave us our first taste of international recognition.

+ "Adrenaline" (2010): This high-energy track showcased our ability to layer complex melodies and heavy basslines, leaving a lasting impact on fans and industry professionals alike.

+ "Rumble in the Jungle" (2011): A collaboration with fellow artist and producer Sub Focus, this track was a fusion of drum and bass and dubstep, highlighting our ability to bridge genres seamlessly.

+ "Lost You" (2014): Featuring powerful vocals from Twin Shadow and D'Angelo Lacy, this track epitomized our ability to blend haunting melodies with heavy drops, resonating with a growing fan base.

These early tracks laid the groundwork for our career and set the stage for our subsequent releases and collaborations.

Studio Albums and EPs

We have had the incredible opportunity to release a number of studio albums and EPs that have allowed us to further explore our sound and solidify our place in the music industry. These projects have been a testament to our growth as artists and have showcased the evolution of the Zeds Dead sound.

Some of our notable studio albums and EPs include:

+ "Adrenaline" EP (2010): This early release was a snapshot of our energetic and bass-heavy sound, marking our first foray into the world of drum and bass and dubstep.

+ "Hot Sauce" EP (2012): A unique sonic journey that combined elements of hip-hop, house, and dubstep, this EP further solidified our reputation for genre-blending and experimentation.

+ "Northern Lights" (2016): Our debut studio album, "Northern Lights," showcased our growth as artists and featured collaborations with a diverse range of artists, including Diplo, Pusha T, and Weezer.

+ "Somewhere Else" EP (2014): This EP pushed the boundaries of our sound even further, incorporating elements of trap, house, and reggae, and featuring collaborations with artists such as Big Gigantic and Perry Farrell.

+ "Hot Sauce: Remixes" EP (2013): A collection of remixes of tracks from our "Hot Sauce" EP, this release showcased the diverse range of artists and genres that we were able to collaborate with.

These albums and EPs represent significant milestones in our career and allowed us to explore new sounds and experiment with different genres and styles.

Mixtapes and DJ Sets

In addition to our studio albums and EPs, we have also had the pleasure of curating mixtapes and recording DJ sets that have allowed us to showcase our skills as DJs and further connect with our fan base. These mixtapes and DJ sets have become a platform for us to share our favorite tracks, experiment with new sounds, and push boundaries.

Some of our notable mixtapes and DJ sets include:

+ "Mad Decent x Zeds Dead: Endless Summer Mix" (2013): This mixtape, created in collaboration with Mad Decent, served as a showcase of our favorite tracks at the time and introduced listeners to our eclectic taste in music.

+ "Zeds Dead x Delta Heavy: Capital Mixtape" (2015): A collaboration with drum and bass duo Delta Heavy, this mixtape brought together our respective styles and showcased the intricacies of blending genres.

+ "Deadbeats Radio" (2016 - Present): Our ongoing radio show has become a platform for us to share new music, present guest mixes from other artists, and connect with our fans on a deeper level.

These mixtapes and DJ sets have allowed us to further express our creativity and share our passion for music with our fans.

Remixes and Collaborations

Throughout our career, we have had the privilege of collaborating with and remixing tracks from some amazing artists from various genres. These collaborations and remixes have allowed us to push the boundaries of our sound, experiment with different styles, and bring a fresh perspective to existing tracks.

Some notable collaborations and remixes include:

+ "Collapse" (Zeds Dead Remix) by Zeds Dead x Memorecks x Chet Faker: This remix of Chet Faker's "Talk Is Cheap" showcased our ability to infuse a track with our signature sound without losing the essence of the original.

+ "Frontlines" (ft. GG Magree) with NGHTMRE: A collaboration with fellow producer NGHTMRE, "Frontlines" combined elements of trap and dubstep, resulting in a high-energy track that became an instant fan favorite.

+ "Lights Out" (Zeds Dead Remix) by Zeds Dead x Concord Dawn x S.P.Y: This remix showcased our ability to take a drum and bass track and transform it into a hard-hitting dubstep anthem, pushing the boundaries of both genres.

+ "Stardust" (Zeds Dead Remix) by Zeds Dead x Gemini: This remix of Gemini's track "Blue" showcased our ability to infuse a track with a melodic dubstep sound, resulting in a captivating and emotive remix.

These collaborations and remixes have allowed us to connect with other artists, explore new sounds, and reimagine tracks in our own unique style.

Chart-Topping Hits and Fan Favorites

Over the years, we have been fortunate to create music that has resonated with our fans and found success on various charts. These chart-topping hits and fan favorites have become an integral part of our discography and have shaped our career as Zeds Dead.

Some of our chart-topping hits and fan favorites include:

- "Collapse" (ft. Memorecks) (2014): This track became an instant fan favorite, showcasing our ability to combine melodic elements with heavy basslines and captivating drops.

- "Lost You" (ft. Twin Shadow and D'Angelo Lacy) (2014): With its haunting vocals and infectious melodies, this track quickly garnered attention and became one of our most successful releases to date.

- "Where the Wild Things Are" (ft. Illenium) (2017): A collaboration with Illenium, this track blended elements of future bass and dubstep, resulting in a melodic and emotionally charged anthem.

- "Ratchet" (2012): A high-energy track that became a fan favorite, "Ratchet" showcased our ability to create bass-heavy bangers that ignite dancefloors.

These chart-topping hits and fan favorites have become synonymous with our name and have left a lasting impact on our fans.

Unreleased and Rare Gems

Throughout our career, we have produced a number of unreleased and rare tracks that have become coveted gems among our fans. These tracks, although not widely available, are a testament to our creativity and evolution as artists.

Some of our unreleased and rare tracks include:

- "Valhalla" (ft. Katy B)

- "1975"

- "Lights Go Down" (ft. Belle Humble)

- "White Satin"

These unreleased and rare tracks have become highly sought after by our fans and showcase our ability to continuously push the boundaries of our sound.

Songs with Personal Significance

Within our discography, there are certain songs that hold a special place in our hearts and have personal significance to us as individuals and as a band. These songs represent pivotal moments in our careers, reflect our personal journeys, and encapsulate the emotions and experiences that have shaped us as artists.

Some songs with personal significance include:

- "Collapse" (ft. Memorecks) (2014): This track symbolizes a breakthrough moment in our career, marking a turning point in our sound and cementing our place in the music industry.

- "Lost You" (ft. Twin Shadow and D'Angelo Lacy) (2014): A deeply personal track, "Lost You" represents a period of introspection and self-discovery, capturing the essence of our growth as individuals and artists.

- "Coffee Break" (2017): This track represents a departure from our traditional sound and showcases our ability to experiment with new genres and styles, pushing the boundaries of our creativity.

These songs have played a significant role in our musical journey and continue to hold a special place in our hearts.

Compilation Appearances and Side Projects

In addition to our own releases, we have also made appearances on various compilation albums and side projects throughout our career. These collaborations and contributions have allowed us to further explore our musical boundaries and connect with artists from different genres and backgrounds.

Some notable compilation appearances and side projects include:

- "Zeds Dead Present: Catching Z's" (2019): A compilation album showcasing our passion for ambient and downtempo music, featuring tracks that reflect a more introspective and intimate side of our sound.

- "Twin Shadow - Eclipse" (Zeds Dead Remix) (2015): A remix of Twin Shadow's track "Eclipse," this collaboration highlighted our ability to infuse our signature sound into a different genre, resulting in a unique and captivating remix.

These compilation appearances and side projects have allowed us to collaborate with a diverse range of artists and explore different styles of music.

Timeline: The Journey of Zeds Dead

The timeline of our journey as Zeds Dead is filled with a multitude of milestones, achievements, and memorable moments. From our early beginnings to our current status as one of the most influential electronic music acts, this timeline presents a comprehensive overview of our musical evolution and the impact we have had on the industry.

Early Beginnings and Formation of Zeds Dead

- **2004:** We first crossed paths while attending the same high school in Toronto, Canada. Bonding over our shared love for music, we began experimenting with different genres and styles.

- **2007:** Inspired by the burgeoning dubstep and electronic music scene, we decided to form Zeds Dead and embark on a musical journey together.

- **2009:** Our remix of Blue Foundation's "Eyes on Fire" gained significant attention, propelling us into the international spotlight and establishing our unique sound.

Breakthrough Tracks and First Taste of Success

- **2010:** The release of our "Adrenaline" EP showcased our ability to blend genres and caught the attention of music lovers around the world.

- **2012:** Collaborations with artists such as Omar LinX, Greta Svabo Bech, and Mavado further solidified our reputation for pushing boundaries and experimenting with different sounds.

- **2014:** The release of the track "Lost You" featuring Twin Shadow and D'Angelo Lacy became a breakout hit, gaining widespread acclaim and propelling us into mainstream recognition.

Major Milestones and Achievements

- **2016:** Our debut studio album, "Northern Lights," was released to critical acclaim and marked a new chapter in our career as artists and producers.

- **2018:** The launch of our record label, Deadbeats, provided a platform for upcoming artists and allowed us to further support and nurture the next generation of talent.

+ **2019:** The release of our "We Are Deadbeats, Vol. 4" compilation album showcased the diversity of our label's roster and solidified Deadbeats as a force to be reckoned with in the electronic music scene.

Collaborations and International Recognition

+ **2012:** Our collaboration with Omar LinX, "Out for Blood," showcased our ability to seamlessly blend rap and electronic music, gaining recognition from both the hip-hop and electronic music communities.

+ **2015:** Collaboration with fellow producer NGHTMRE, "Frontlines," became an instant fan favorite and further fuelled our rise to international recognition.

+ **2017:** Collaborations with artists such as Illenium, Diplo, and Jauz allowed us to explore new genres and styles, breaking down barriers and expanding our sonic palette.

Evolution of the Zeds Dead Sound

+ **2013:** The release of our "Hot Sauce" EP marked a shift in our sound, incorporating elements of house, hip-hop, and reggae into our music.

+ **2017:** The launch of our "Deadbeats Radio" show provided a platform for us to share new music and present guest mixes from a diverse range of artists, showcasing our evolving taste and sound.

+ **2019:** The release of our "Catching Z's" compilation album highlighted our passion for ambient and downtempo music, further expanding the boundaries of our artistic expression.

Influence on Music and Culture

+ **2012 - Present:** Our music has become synonymous with the rise of electronic dance music, influencing a new generation of artists and shaping the sound of the global EDM scene.

+ **2015:** The launch of our "Deadbeats" live event series provided a platform for fans to experience our music in an immersive and intimate setting, further building a loyal and dedicated fan base.

+ **2018:** Our "Deadbeats Goes Off The Deep End" tour brought our unique sound to sold-out venues across North America, leaving a lasting impact on concert-goers and further solidifying our reputation as one of the most captivating live acts.

Exploration of Different Art Forms

+ **2013:** The release of the music video for our track "Demons" showcased our interest in visual storytelling and pushed the boundaries of what a music video could be.

+ **2017:** Our collaboration with visual artist and director Chris Ullens for the music video of "Dead of Night" pushed the boundaries of animation and explored innovative storytelling techniques.

+ **2019:** The release of our "Billboard Art Project" showcased our interest in merging visual art and music, providing a unique and immersive experience for our fans.

Building a Legacy and Leaving a Lasting Impact

+ **2020:** As we continue to explore new sounds, collaborate with exciting artists, and push boundaries, we strive to leave a lasting legacy that inspires future generations of musicians and artists.

+ **2021:** With the launch of our "Catching Z's" livestream series, we have been able to connect with fans around the world in a time when live performances have been limited, further solidifying our place as one of the most innovative and adaptable acts in the industry.

This timeline highlights the key moments and achievements of our journey as Zeds Dead. From our humble beginnings to our current status as pioneers of electronic music, it has been an incredible ride filled with growth, creativity, and a never-ending love for music.

The Legacy of Zeds Dead

Zeds Dead's legacy is one of innovation, artistic growth, and the relentless pursuit of pushing the boundaries of electronic music. Throughout their career, they have left an indelible mark on the music industry, inspiring a new generation of artists and captivating audiences around the world. Their contributions to the electronic music scene have not only shaped the sound and style of the genre but have also influenced music culture and trends.

One of the most significant aspects of Zeds Dead's legacy is their ability to evolve and explore new musical territories. From their early beginnings as DJs and producers, they quickly established themselves as pioneers of the dubstep and electronic dance music (EDM) scenes. Collaborating with other artists and experimenting with different genres and styles, they continuously pushed the boundaries of their sound, incorporating elements from hip-hop, reggae, and various electronic subgenres.

Their ability to create music that transcends traditional genre boundaries is a testament to their artistic vision and commitment to innovation. By fearlessly embracing diverse influences and exploring new sonic landscapes, Zeds Dead has expanded the possibilities of electronic music, inspiring countless artists to think beyond established conventions.

Beyond their musical accomplishments, Zeds Dead has also made a lasting impact on music culture and the EDM community. They have cultivated a strong fanbase that spans across different demographics and cultures, connecting with a diverse audience through their electrifying live performances and engaging social media presence.

Their commitment to supporting and nurturing new talent is another crucial aspect of their legacy. Zeds Dead has used their platform to showcase emerging artists, providing opportunities for them to showcase their skills and reach a wider audience. Through collaborations, mentorship, and partnerships, Zeds Dead has actively contributed to the growth and development of the electronic music scene, ensuring its continuous evolution.

Furthermore, Zeds Dead's philanthropic endeavors and social initiatives have demonstrated their commitment to making a positive impact beyond the music itself. They have been involved in various charitable projects and have used their platform to raise awareness about social issues and promote inclusivity and diversity in the music industry.

The enduring legacy of Zeds Dead can also be seen in their influence on music production techniques and visual aesthetics. Their unique approach to music videos as an art form and their collaboration with visual artists have helped shape the visual identity of their music. Through album artwork, stage design, and live visuals, Zeds Dead has created immersive experiences for their audiences, elevating the live performance to an art form in itself.

Looking to the future, Zeds Dead's legacy will continue to inspire and influence artists and music enthusiasts alike. Their dedication to pushing boundaries, embracing innovation, and supporting the next generation of talent ensures that their impact will be felt for years to come.

In conclusion, Zeds Dead's legacy is characterized by their unwavering commitment to artistic growth, innovation, and pushing the boundaries of electronic music. Their ability to evolve and explore new musical territories, their impact on music culture and the EDM community, their support for emerging talent, and their unique visual identity have all contributed to their enduring legacy. As they continue on their musical journey, their influence will continue to shape the future of electronic music and inspire generations to come.

A Final Note of Inspiration

As we come to the end of this incredible journey with Zeds Dead, it's crucial to reflect on the remarkable impact they have had on the music industry and the lives of their fans. Through their dedication, creativity, and determination, Zeds Dead has left an indelible mark on the electronic music scene. But this is not just a closing chapter; it is an opportunity to take the lessons we have learned from their story and use them as inspiration for our own lives.

Zeds Dead's success is a testament to the power of passion and authenticity. They have shown us that staying true to oneself and pursuing what you love can lead to incredible achievements. In a world where conformity may seem tempting, Zeds Dead has proven that embracing your individuality and unique voice can set you apart from the rest. So, my fellow music lovers, let us take this final note as a reminder to never compromise who we are and what we believe in.

At the core of Zeds Dead's journey is the importance of continuously pushing boundaries and exploring new horizons. They have fearlessly experimented with different genres, collaborated with various artists, and incorporated diverse influences into their music. This commitment to evolution and growth has allowed them to create a sound that is truly their own. As we embark on our own artistic endeavors, let us not be afraid to step outside our comfort zones, embrace change, and challenge ourselves to reach new heights.

Furthermore, Zeds Dead's journey reminds us of the power of community and the importance of lifting each other up. They have not only supported and nurtured new talent but have also engaged with their fanbase in meaningful ways.

They have fostered a sense of belonging and unity, creating a family of fans who support and inspire one another. Let us carry this spirit of camaraderie into our own lives, recognizing the value of collaboration, support, and camaraderie in achieving our goals.

As we look toward the future, we should draw inspiration from the unyielding spirit of Zeds Dead. Their unwavering dedication to their craft, their desire to push boundaries, and their commitment to authenticity are virtues that we can strive to embody. Remember that the path to success will not always be smooth, and there will be challenges along the way. But with determination, resilience, and a whole lot of heart, we can overcome obstacles and achieve greatness.

In closing, let Zeds Dead's journey serve as a testament to the power of music and its ability to touch our souls, bring people together, and inspire us to be the best versions of ourselves. Never underestimate the impact you can have on the world through your own creativity and passion. So, my friends, go out there, create, challenge, and share your unique voices with the world. The stage is yours, and the beat goes on.

Discography: A Comprehensive Track Listing

Early Tracks and Breakout Hits

When it comes to the early tracks and breakout hits of Zeds Dead, it is important to understand the musical journey that led to their success. The duo, consisting of Dylan Mamid, also known as DC, and Zachary Rapp-Rovan, known as Hooks, first crossed paths in high school and realized they shared a deep passion for music. From there, they embarked on a musical journey that would catapult them into the electronic music scene.

One of the earliest tracks that gained attention for Zeds Dead was their remix of Blue Foundation's "Eyes on Fire." Released in 2009, this remix showcased their ability to take a popular track and completely transform it into something unique. Through their creative reimagining, they infused their own signature style, blending elements of dubstep, drum and bass, and melodic bass.

Another track that caught the attention of fans and industry insiders was their remix of Massive Attack's "Paradise Circus." Released in 2010, this remix brought their dark and atmospheric sound to the forefront. With its haunting melodies, intricate production, and heavy basslines, the track showcased their ability to create a captivating and emotionally charged listening experience.

In addition to remixes, Zeds Dead also began releasing their original productions. One of their early breakout hits was the track "Rude Boy," released in 2011. This track featured a pulsating bassline, energetic beats, and a catchy vocal sample that quickly caught the ears of listeners. "Rude Boy" became a staple in their live sets and solidified their reputation as producers who could create high-energy, crowd-pleasing tracks.

Continuing their momentum, Zeds Dead released "Adrenaline" in 2012. This track displayed their versatility as producers, blending elements of electro-house, dubstep, and hip-hop. With its hard-hitting drops, infectious melodies, and intricate sound design, "Adrenaline" quickly became a fan favorite and further solidified their position in the electronic music scene.

One of their most well-known early tracks is "Lost You" featuring Twin Shadow and D'Angelo Lacy. Released in 2014, this track became an anthem for Zeds Dead fans around the world. It perfectly captured their ability to combine emotive melodies with heavy basslines, creating a unique and powerful listening experience.

Throughout their early career, Zeds Dead continued to release tracks that pushed boundaries and showcased their creativity. Whether it was their melodic and euphoric track "Collapse" or their hard-hitting and gritty track "Ratchet," they consistently delivered high-quality productions that resonated with listeners.

In summary, the early tracks and breakout hits of Zeds Dead set the stage for their success in the electronic music scene. Through their remixes and original productions, they demonstrated their ability to create unique and captivating music that pushed boundaries and captured the attention of fans and industry insiders alike. From the haunting melodies of "Paradise Circus" to the energetic beats of "Rude Boy," each track showcased their evolution as artists and foreshadowed the innovative sound they would continue to explore in the years to come.

Studio Albums and EPs

In this section, we will take a deep dive into the studio albums and EPs released by Zeds Dead throughout their career. These musical projects showcase the evolution of their sound and the creative vision of the duo. Each release is a testament to their artistic growth and their ability to push boundaries in the electronic music scene. Let's explore their studio albums and EPs in chronological order:

Fresh Beets

Fresh Beets, released in 2009, was Zeds Dead's inaugural EP, marking the beginning of their musical journey. This five-track EP captured the attention of electronic music enthusiasts with its unique blend of dubstep, drum and bass, and hip-hop influences. Tracks like "Journey of a Lifetime" and "1975" showcased their early experimentation with heavy basslines and melodic elements. Fresh Beets laid the foundation for Zeds Dead's signature sound and set the stage for their future releases.

Adrenaline

Released in 2012, Adrenaline was Zeds Dead's first studio album. This highly anticipated project encapsulated their growth and maturity as artists. With tracks like "In the Beginning" and "By Your Side," Adrenaline showcased their ability to blend different genres seamlessly. The album delved into various electronic subgenres, including dubstep, drum and bass, and electro-house, solidifying Zeds Dead's position as genre-defying producers. Adrenaline propelled them further into the spotlight and cemented their reputation as boundary-pushing artists.

Hot Sauce

Hot Sauce, released in 2013, was an EP that showcased Zeds Dead's versatility and experimentation. The EP featured collaborations with artists across different genres, including Omar LinX, Bright Lights, and Perry Farrell. Tracks like "Demons" and "Shut Up & Sing V2.0" seamlessly blended elements of electronic music with hip-hop and rock influences. Hot Sauce pushed the boundaries of their sound, combining heavy basslines with infectious melodies, and further solidifying their reputation as innovators in the electronic music scene.

Somewhere Else

Somewhere Else, released in 2014, marked a significant milestone in Zeds Dead's career. This EP showcased their evolution as producers and their willingness to explore new sonic territories. Spanning multiple genres such as hip-hop, trap, and future bass, Somewhere Else featured collaborations with artists like Twin Shadow, Sean Price, and Big Gigantic. Tracks like "Lost You" and "Collapse" demonstrated Zeds Dead's ability to create emotive and atmospheric music while maintaining their signature sound. Somewhere Else solidified their position as electronic music pioneers.

Northern Lights

2016 saw the release of Zeds Dead's highly anticipated studio album, Northern Lights. This album showcased their growth as producers and their ability to create immersive and diverse soundscapes. Collaborations with artists like Diplo, Pusha T, and Weezer's Rivers Cuomo demonstrated their versatility and willingness to push boundaries. Tracks like "Stardust" and "Too Young" seamlessly blended elements of electronic, hip-hop, and rock music, creating a unique and captivating listening experience. Northern Lights further solidified Zeds Dead's place at the forefront of the electronic music scene.

Catching Z's

Catching Z's, released in 2018, was a departure from Zeds Dead's usual high-energy sound. This EP showcased their ability to create ambient and downtempo music, offering a more introspective and chilled-out experience for listeners. Collaborations with talented artists like Jauz, Ganja White Night, and Illenium added depth and diversity to the tracks. Catching Z's allowed Zeds Dead to explore a different side of their artistic expression, demonstrating their versatility and musical range.

We Are Deadbeats, Vol. 1 and 2

We Are Deadbeats, Vol. 1 and Vol. 2, released in 2019 and 2020 respectively, marked the beginning of Zeds Dead's label, Deadbeats. These compilation albums showcased the duo's ability to curate and promote up-and-coming artists in the electronic music scene. These releases featured collaborations with a wide range of talented producers, including DROELOE, Ekali, and GG Magree. We Are Deadbeats solidified Zeds Dead's commitment to supporting emerging talent and nurturing a vibrant music community.

Throughout their career, Zeds Dead has continuously evolved and experimented with their sound, pushing the boundaries of electronic music. Their studio albums and EPs have not only captivated listeners but have also influenced the direction of the genre as a whole. With each release, they have displayed their artistic growth, versatility, and dedication to creating music that pushes the limits of the electronic music scene. As they continue to innovate and explore new sonic territories, the future holds endless possibilities for Zeds Dead and their fans.

Mixtapes and DJ Sets

Mixtapes and DJ sets have played a significant role in the career of Zeds Dead. These collections of songs and mixes have not only allowed them to showcase their eclectic taste in music, but also to experiment with different sounds and styles. In this section, we will explore the world of Zeds Dead's mixtapes and DJ sets, discussing their significance, the creative process behind them, and the impact they have had on their fans and the electronic music community.

The Art of DJing

Before diving into their mixtapes and DJ sets, it is important to understand the art of DJing and its role in the electronic music scene. DJing is the art of selecting and mixing recorded music to create a continuous flow of tracks, seamlessly transitioning between songs to maintain the energy and atmosphere on the dancefloor. It requires technical skill, a keen ear for music, and an ability to read and connect with the crowd.

For Zeds Dead, DJing is not just a means to an end but an integral part of their artistic expression. They approach each set as an opportunity to curate a unique sonic experience for their audience, blending various genres and styles to create a dynamic and immersive journey. Their sets are carefully crafted to take listeners on a musical adventure, combining their original tracks, remixes, and a selection of hand-picked songs from other artists.

Mixtapes: Showcasing Eclectic Tastes

Mixtapes have long been a platform for artists to showcase their musical tastes and influences. Zeds Dead has released several mixtapes throughout their career, each offering a glimpse into their diverse range of musical interests. These mixtapes are carefully curated collections of songs that highlight their unique sound and introduce fans to new and exciting music.

One notable mixtape from Zeds Dead is their "Catching Z's" series. These mixtapes showcase a softer and more introspective side of their music, featuring downtempo tracks, ambient sounds, and dreamy melodies. It demonstrates their versatility as artists and their ability to create atmospheric and emotive music.

Another mixtape worth mentioning is their "Altered States" series, which focuses on exploring different genres and styles. These mixtapes allow Zeds Dead to experiment with various sounds and showcase their ability to seamlessly blend diverse musical elements. From hip-hop to reggae, drum and bass to future bass, these mixtapes serve as a testament to their musical adaptability and willingness to push boundaries.

DJ Sets: Creating Unforgettable Experiences

Zeds Dead's DJ sets are renowned for their energy, creativity, and crowd engagement. They are known to curate sets that are highly dynamic and unpredictable, keeping fans on their toes and creating an electric atmosphere at their live shows. Each DJ set is a carefully crafted performance, taking the audience on a sonic journey that is unique to that specific moment in time.

One of the key elements that makes Zeds Dead's DJ sets so captivating is their ability to seamlessly blend different genres and styles. They effortlessly transition between heavy bass music, melodic dubstep, house beats, and everything in between, creating a diverse and exciting sonic experience. This versatility allows them to connect with a wide range of audiences and attract fans from different musical backgrounds.

In addition to their own tracks, Zeds Dead often incorporates unreleased songs, remixes, and edits into their sets. This exclusivity adds an element of surprise and excitement for their fans, making each live performance a truly unique experience. Their mastery of mixing techniques, such as beatmatching, chopping and looping, adds a layer of complexity and technical skill to their DJ sets, further enhancing their live performances.

Connecting with the Fans

One of the most remarkable aspects of Zeds Dead's mixtapes and DJ sets is their ability to connect with their fans on a deeper level. Through their music, they create a sense of community and belonging, uniting people from different walks of life under a shared love for electronic music.

Mixtapes and DJ sets serve as a platform for Zeds Dead to communicate and express themselves to their fans. The carefully selected songs and seamless transitions in their mixtapes allow listeners to immerse themselves in their world and feel a personal connection to their music. Similarly, their live DJ sets create an intimate and collective experience, where fans can dance, sing, and share their love for Zeds Dead's music together.

Zeds Dead also actively engages with their fans through social media, live streams, and interaction during their performances. They value feedback from their listeners, considering it an essential part of their creative process. By staying connected and responsive to their fans, Zeds Dead has fostered a strong and dedicated fanbase, creating a sense of belonging and loyalty that extends beyond the music itself.

The Impact on the Electronic Music Community

Zeds Dead's mixtapes and DJ sets have had a significant impact on the electronic music community. By showcasing their eclectic tastes and pushing the boundaries of genre conventions, they have inspired a new generation of artists to explore different styles and experiment with diverse sounds. Their ability to seamlessly transition between genres has influenced the way DJs curate their sets, encouraging others to think outside the box and create unique sonic experiences.

Furthermore, Zeds Dead's mixtapes and DJ sets have played a vital role in the growth and popularity of the electronic music scene. Through their live performances and online presence, they have introduced electronic music to a wider audience, expanding its reach and breaking down barriers to entry. Their success has paved the way for other artists to thrive in the electronic music landscape, creating a more inclusive and diverse community.

In conclusion, Zeds Dead's mixtapes and DJ sets are not just a collection of songs and mixes, but a manifestation of their artistic expression and connection with their fans. These mixtapes and sets showcase their eclectic tastes, ability to blend genres, and create unforgettable experiences. Through their commitment to pushing boundaries and connecting with their audience, Zeds Dead has left an indelible mark on the electronic music community.

Remixes and Collaborations

Remixes and collaborations have played a significant role in the success and evolution of Zeds Dead. They have not only pushed the boundaries of their own sound but also showcased their versatility and ability to work with artists from various genres. In this section, we will explore some of their notable remixes and collaborations throughout their career.

Notable Remixes

1. "Eyes on Fire" by Blue Foundation

One of Zeds Dead's early standout remixes was their reimagining of "Eyes on Fire" by Blue Foundation. Released in 2009, this remix became a viral hit and garnered widespread attention for the duo. Zeds Dead's remix showcased their unique ability to transform a mellow indie-electronic track into a bass-heavy dubstep anthem. With its haunting melodies and hard-hitting drops, this remix became a fan favorite and helped solidify Zeds Dead's place in the electronic music scene.

2. "Wild Heart" by Sabi

In 2013, Zeds Dead collaborated with pop artist Sabi to create a remix of her song "Wild Heart." This remix showcased Zeds Dead's ability to seamlessly blend elements of dubstep and pop music. By infusing their signature bass-heavy sound with Sabi's infectious vocals, they created a remix that struck a balance between mainstream appeal and underground credibility. The remix received widespread acclaim and further cemented Zeds Dead's reputation as skillful producers.

3. "Rude Boy" by Rihanna

Zeds Dead's remix of Rihanna's hit song "Rude Boy" demonstrated their versatility as producers. Released in 2010, this remix took the infectious dancehall-inspired original and transformed it into a dubstep-infused banger. With its pulsating basslines and hard-hitting drops, the remix gained significant attention and introduced Zeds Dead's unique sound to a wider audience. It showcased their ability to inject their signature energy into a mainstream hit while staying true to their own style.

Standout Collaborations

1. "Collapse" with Memorecks

Zeds Dead's collaboration with fellow Canadian producer Memorecks resulted in the track "Collapse." Released in 2014, this collaboration demonstrated the duo's ability to blend different styles and genres seamlessly. "Collapse" featured intricate melodies, heavy basslines, and glitchy elements, showcasing the creative synergy between Zeds Dead and Memorecks. The track garnered critical acclaim and further solidified Zeds Dead's reputation as innovative producers.

2. "Where the Wild Things Are" with Illenium

In 2020, Zeds Dead teamed up with melodic bass producer Illenium to create the track "Where the Wild Things Are." This collaboration brought together Zeds Dead's signature grimy sound with Illenium's emotive melodies. The result was a powerful track that combined the best of both artists' styles. "Where the Wild Things Are" received widespread praise for its seamless fusion of heavy bass and uplifting melodies, showcasing the depth of Zeds Dead's collaborative abilities.

3. "Lost You" with Twin Shadow and D'Angelo Lacy

"Lost You" is a collaboration between Zeds Dead, Twin Shadow, and vocalist D'Angelo Lacy. Released in 2014, this track showcased Zeds Dead's ability to create an atmospheric and emotive piece of music. With its haunting vocals and melodic basslines, "Lost You" captured the essence of Zeds Dead's sound while incorporating the unique talents of Twin Shadow and D'Angelo Lacy. This collaboration illustrated Zeds Dead's willingness to take risks and explore new artistic territories.

Exploring New Possibilities

Zeds Dead's remixes and collaborations have not only showcased their versatility but also opened the door to new creative possibilities. By working with artists from different genres, they have continually pushed the boundaries of electronic music and expanded their sonic palette.

Through their remixes, Zeds Dead has demonstrated their ability to reimagine existing tracks and infuse them with their distinctive sound. Their collaborations have allowed them to tap into the talent and creativity of other artists, resulting in unique and captivating musical experiences.

As they continue their musical journey, Zeds Dead will undoubtedly explore new remixes and collaborations, further defining and shaping their sound while continuing to push the boundaries of electronic music.

Whether it's through remixes or collaborative projects, Zeds Dead's ability to work with a diverse range of artists has showcased their adaptability and creative vision. Their remixes and collaborations are a testament to their enduring legacy and their ongoing commitment to pushing the boundaries of electronic music. As they continue to evolve and explore new territories, the possibilities for Zeds Dead's remixes and collaborations are endless.

In conclusion, Zeds Dead's remixes and collaborations have been integral to their success and growth as artists. They have allowed them to showcase their unique sound, experiment with new genres, and collaborate with like-minded musicians. Through their remixes and collaborations, Zeds Dead has not only entertained and inspired fans but also left an indelible mark on the electronic music landscape.

Chart-Topping Hits and Fan Favorites

In the illustrious career of Zeds Dead, they have produced numerous chart-topping hits and fan favorites that have captivated audiences around the world. These tracks showcase the unique sound and style of Zeds Dead, solidifying their position as one of the leading electronic music acts of our time. Let's take a closer look at some of their standout tracks.

Rave Anthem: "Lost You"

Released in 2014, "Lost You" quickly became a favorite among both fans and critics. The track effortlessly blends elements of dubstep and house, creating an infectious energy that fills dance floors. The pulsating basslines, soaring synths, and anthemic vocals make "Lost You" a staple in Zeds Dead's live performances. This chart-topper solidified their reputation as trendsetters in the electronic music scene.

Collaborative Success: "Collapse"

In 2018, Zeds Dead teamed up with Memorecks to produce the explosive track "Collapse." This collaboration exhibits the synergistic power of bringing two talented artists together. "Collapse" combines Zeds Dead's signature heavy bass drops with Memorecks' intricate production skills, resulting in a high-octane track that blurs the boundaries between genres. Its infectious energy and relentless beats have made "Collapse" a fan favorite and a staple in Zeds Dead's live sets.

Crossover Hit: "In the Beginning"

Zeds Dead's ability to transcend genres is evident in their track "In the Beginning." Released in 2016, this crossover hit seamlessly fuses electronic music with elements of hip-hop. The track features the soulful vocals of Twin Shadow and showcases Zeds Dead's versatility as producers. The combination of atmospheric sounds, melodic hooks, and infectious beats creates a hypnotic experience that has resonated with fans across different musical backgrounds.

Bass-heavy Banger: "Ratchet"

"Ratchet" is undoubtedly one of Zeds Dead's most popular tracks, known for delivering an onslaught of bass that makes audiences go wild. Released in 2013, this high-energy banger exemplifies their mastery of the dubstep genre. The relentless drops, intricate sound design, and infectious rhythm have made "Ratchet" a fan favorite at festivals and clubs worldwide. Its impact on the electronic music scene is undeniable, and it continues to be a standout track in Zeds Dead's discography.

Melodic Masterpiece: "Collapse 2.0"

"Collapse 2.0" showcases Zeds Dead's ability to create melodic masterpieces that resonate on an emotional level. Released as a follow-up to their successful collaboration with Memorecks, this track takes listeners on a captivating journey through its ethereal melodies and haunting vocals. The juxtaposition of delicate piano chords and heavy bass drops creates a mesmerizing listening experience. "Collapse 2.0" stands as a testament to Zeds Dead's artistic growth and their willingness to push boundaries.

Timeless Classic: "Eyes on Fire" Remix

No discussion of Zeds Dead's chart-topping hits would be complete without mentioning their iconic remix of Blue Foundation's "Eyes on Fire." This remix catapulted Zeds Dead into the spotlight and introduced their unique blend of dubstep and melodic elements to a wider audience. The haunting vocals, intricate production, and infectious drops made this remix an instant fan favorite. Over a decade after its release, "Eyes on Fire" remains a timeless classic and a testament to Zeds Dead's ability to create enduring music.

Conclusion

Zeds Dead's chart-topping hits and fan favorites represent the pinnacle of their artistic prowess. These tracks have not only topped the charts but also resonated deeply with their dedicated fanbase. From high-energy bangers to melodic masterpieces, Zeds Dead continues to push the boundaries of electronic music and create an immersive experience for listeners worldwide. With their unique sound and unwavering passion, Zeds Dead's chart-topping hits and fan favorites have left an indelible mark on the electronic music landscape. As they continue on their musical journey, we eagerly await the next wave of boundary-pushing tracks from this visionary duo.

Unreleased and Rare Gems

The discography of Zeds Dead is not limited to their officially released tracks. Over the years, they have also created a collection of unreleased and rare gems that have become beloved by fans. These tracks showcase the experimental, boundary-pushing nature of Zeds Dead's sound and offer a glimpse into their creative process. In this section, we will explore some of these unreleased and rare gems, delving into their unique qualities and the stories behind their creation.

Lost in the Rhythm

"Lost in the Rhythm" is a mesmerizing unreleased track that captures the essence of Zeds Dead's sound. It seamlessly blends haunting melodies, intricate basslines, and ethereal vocal samples to create a euphoric journey for the listener. The track showcases Zeds Dead's mastery of creating atmospheric and immersive music, drawing the audience into their sonic world. While "Lost in the Rhythm" has yet to be officially released, it has become a fan favorite, often featured in their live performances.

The Golden Era

"The Golden Era" is a rare gem that represents a pivotal moment in Zeds Dead's musical journey. This track pays homage to the golden age of hip-hop and samples iconic beats and samples from that era. Zeds Dead skillfully blends nostalgic elements with their signature electronic sound, creating a track that transports the listener back in time while still maintaining a contemporary edge. "The Golden Era" showcases Zeds Dead's ability to seamlessly bridge different genres and create music that resonates with a diverse audience.

Synchronicity

"Synchronicity" is an unreleased track that highlights Zeds Dead's experimentation with unconventional rhythms and textures. The track features complex drum patterns, glitchy effects, and haunting melodies, creating an atmospheric and unpredictable sonic landscape. "Synchronicity" pushes the boundaries of electronic music, challenging traditional structures and taking the listener on a sonic journey filled with surprises and unexpected turns. While it remains an unreleased gem, it showcases Zeds Dead's dedication to pushing the boundaries of their sound.

Hidden Treasures

Zeds Dead has also built a reputation for surprising their fans with hidden treasures, often teasing snippets of unreleased tracks during their live performances. These snippets, referred to as "ID" or "Identification" tracks, keep fans on the edge of their seats, eagerly awaiting a release. These hidden treasures demonstrate Zeds Dead's commitment to constantly pushing their own limits and exploring new musical territories.

B-Sides and Remixes

In addition to their unreleased originals, Zeds Dead has also produced a collection of B-sides and remixes that offer a fresh perspective on their music. These tracks often showcase collaborations with fellow artists and highlight their ability to reimagine and reinterpret existing songs. Zeds Dead's remixes infuse their signature sound into an array of genres, creating unique and captivating musical experiences. These B-sides and remixes provide a deeper understanding of Zeds Dead's artistic vision and demonstrate their versatility as producers.

Overall, Zeds Dead's unreleased and rare gems offer an intimate look into their artistic process and their dedication to pushing the boundaries of electronic music. Through these tracks, they invite their fans into a world of sonic exploration, showcasing their unique sound and ability to create immersive musical experiences. While these tracks may remain hidden from the mainstream, they undoubtedly hold a special place in the hearts of Zeds Dead fans, solidifying their status as one of the most innovative and influential electronic music duos of our time.

End of the Section

Songs with Personal Significance

In the vast discography of Zeds Dead, there are several songs that hold deep personal significance for the duo. These songs represent pivotal moments in their musical journey, evoke powerful emotions, or reflect important experiences in their lives. Let's explore some of these songs and the stories behind them.

Lost You

One of the most significant songs for Zeds Dead is "Lost You," released in 2014 as part of their album "Somewhere Else." This track holds sentimental value as it marked a turning point in their career. With its haunting melodies and heavy basslines, "Lost You" demonstrated Zeds Dead's ability to captivate listeners with their unique sound. It showcased their growth as artists and solidified their place in the electronic music scene.

The song also speaks to the theme of lost love, conveying a sense of bittersweet nostalgia. It reflects personal experiences of heartbreak and the complexities of navigating relationships. "Lost You" resonates deeply with both the duo and their fans, offering solace in shared emotions and experiences.

Collapse

Another song of personal significance is "Collapse," featured on their 2016 album "Northern Lights." This track stands out for its emotional depth and introspective nature. "Collapse" is a reflection on the struggles and challenges faced by Zeds Dead throughout their career. It symbolizes moments of self-doubt, uncertainty, and the perseverance required to overcome obstacles.

The raw vulnerability present in "Collapse" strikes a chord with listeners, as it highlights the human aspect behind the musical success. It serves as a reminder that even accomplished artists like Zeds Dead face their fair share of difficulties, but through resilience and creativity, they find their way.

Stardust

"Stardust," released in 2019 on their album "We Are Deadbeats, Vol. 4," holds personal significance for Zeds Dead in its exploration of cosmic themes and a sense of wonder. With its ethereal melodies and atmospheric production, "Stardust" invites listeners on a journey through space and time.

The song reflects the awe-inspiring beauty of the universe and the endless possibilities that lie within it. It embodies Zeds Dead's fascination with the cosmos and the desire to transport their audience to otherworldly realms through music.

White Satin

"White Satin," a classic Zeds Dead remix, pays homage to the legendary song "Nights in White Satin" by The Moody Blues. Released in 2009, this remix became a defining moment for Zeds Dead, propelling them into the spotlight and introducing their signature sound to a wider audience.

The remix showcases Zeds Dead's creative genius as they skillfully blend elements of dubstep and bass with the haunting vocals of the original track. It captures the essence of their style and their ability to infuse new life into iconic songs.

Where Did That Go

"Where Did That Go," from their 2020 album "We Are Deadbeats, Vol. 4," holds immense personal significance for Zeds Dead. This track represents a culmination of their artistic growth and evolution. It embodies a sense of maturity and reflects their introspective journey as artists.

"Where Did That Go" delves into the themes of change, transformation, and the passing of time. It prompts listeners to reflect on their own lives and the fleeting nature of moments. Through its introspective lyrics and atmospheric soundscapes, the song encapsulates Zeds Dead's profound connection to their craft and their desire to create music that transcends boundaries.

These songs, among many others in Zeds Dead's discography, reveal the duo's ability to evoke emotion, tell stories, and connect deeply with their audience. They remind us that music is not just a collection of sounds, but a vessel for personal expression and shared experiences. Zeds Dead's songs with personal significance serve as a testament to their passion, creativity, and enduring legacy in the world of electronic music.

Compilation Appearances and Side Projects

In addition to their own studio albums, EPs, and remixes, Zeds Dead has made notable appearances on various compilation albums and collaborated on side projects with other artists. These compilation appearances and side projects have allowed Zeds Dead to explore different musical styles and showcase their versatility as producers. Let's take a closer look at some of these collaborations and contributions.

Compilation Appearances

1. **Ganja White Night - "Samurai"** Zeds Dead collaborated with Ganja White Night on the track "Samurai," which was featured on Ganja White Night's compilation album "The Origins." This heavy-hitting dubstep track combines Zeds Dead's signature bass sound with Ganja White Night's atmospheric melodies, creating a unique and captivating fusion of styles.

2. **Deadbeats - "We Are Deadbeats Vol. 4"** Zeds Dead's own record label, Deadbeats, has released a series of compilation albums showcasing the best of bass music. On "We Are Deadbeats Vol. 4," Zeds Dead contributed a mesmerizing track called "Sound of the Underground." This track exemplifies Zeds Dead's ability to create catchy melodies and hard-hitting drops that have become a trademark of their sound.

3. **UKF Dubstep - "Album Megamix"** Zeds Dead's impact on the dubstep scene was recognized on the "UKF Dubstep" compilation album, where their track "Adrenaline" was included in the album megamix. This compilation features a collection of the biggest dubstep tracks from various artists, and Zeds Dead's inclusion speaks to their influence in the genre.

Side Projects

Apart from their work as Zeds Dead, the duo has also collaborated on side projects, allowing them to explore different genres and experiment with new sounds.

1. **Catching Z's** As a side project, Zeds Dead has released a series of mixtapes called "Catching Z's." These mixtapes feature a more chilled-out and atmospheric sound, showcasing Zeds Dead's versatility in creating both high-energy bangers and introspective, laid-back tracks. The mixtapes have received critical acclaim for their unique blend of electronic and ambient sounds.

2. **Zeds Dead x Jauz - "Lights Go Down"** Zeds Dead joined forces with producer Jauz for the hard-hitting track "Lights Go Down." Combining elements of bass house and dubstep, this collaboration seamlessly blends the styles of both artists, resulting in a heavy, energy-packed dancefloor anthem.

3. **Zeds Dead x Illenium - "Where the Wild Things Are"** In another collaboration, Zeds Dead teamed up with Illenium for the emotionally charged track "Where the Wild Things Are." This melodic dubstep masterpiece showcases Zeds Dead's ability to create powerful and moving tracks that resonate with listeners on an emotional level.

These compilation appearances and side projects not only highlight Zeds Dead's versatility as producers but also demonstrate their willingness to push boundaries and explore new musical territories. Whether it's through the hypnotic basslines of "Samurai" or the atmospheric melodies of "Catching Z's," Zeds Dead continues to captivate audiences with their innovative and boundary-pushing music.

A Celebration of the Music of Zeds Dead

Zeds Dead has made an indelible mark on the electronic music scene with their unique sound and genre-defying productions. From their early breakout tracks to their chart-topping hits, Zeds Dead's discography is a testament to their creative vision and musical innovation. In this chapter, we celebrate the captivating music of Zeds Dead, exploring their most celebrated tracks, examining their artistic evolution, and delving into the impact they have had on the electronic music landscape.

Early Tracks and Breakout Hits

Zeds Dead burst onto the scene with a string of early tracks that showcased their distinctive style and genre-blurring sound. Tracks like "Eyes on Fire," a remix of the Blue Foundation original, captivated audiences with its haunting melodies and heavy basslines. Another breakout hit, "Coffee Break," featuring Omar LinX, solidified Zeds Dead's reputation for combining catchy hooks with hard-hitting drops.

Studio Albums and EPs

Zeds Dead's studio albums and EPs have been a platform for them to showcase their artistic growth and experiment with new sounds. Their debut album, "Northern Lights," showcased their ability to seamlessly blend different genres, from dubstep to house, creating an album that defied expectations. Subsequent releases like "Somewhere Else" and "We Are Deadbeats" demonstrated Zeds Dead's willingness to push boundaries and explore new sonic territories.

Mixtapes and DJ Sets

One of the ways Zeds Dead has connected with their fans is through their mixtapes and DJ sets. These dynamic and energetic performances have become a staple of their live shows. The "Deadbeats Radio" series, a collection of mixtapes curated by Zeds Dead, has allowed them to showcase their diverse tastes and introduce fans to new artists and sounds.

Remixes and Collaborations

Zeds Dead's remixes and collaborations have been instrumental in shaping their sound and expanding their fan base. Their remix of Marina and the Diamonds' "Lies" transformed the original into a bass-heavy anthem, while their collaboration with Diplo on "Blame" showcased their ability to seamlessly blend different genres. Other notable collaborations include tracks with Illenium, DROELOE, and NGHTMRE, each contributing to Zeds Dead's discography and further cementing their status as genre-defying artists.

Chart-Topping Hits and Fan Favorites

Zeds Dead has had several chart-topping hits throughout their career, earning them both critical acclaim and commercial success. "Collapse," featuring Memorecks, reached the top of the Beatport charts, while "Lift You Up," featuring Delta Heavy, dominated the festival circuit. Fan favorites like "Lost You" and "In the Beginning" showcase Zeds Dead's ability to create emotionally charged tracks that resonate with listeners.

Unreleased and Rare Gems

In addition to their official releases, Zeds Dead has a treasure trove of unreleased and rare tracks that have become fan favorites. These hidden gems, often played during their live performances or shared exclusively with fans, offer a unique glimpse into Zeds Dead's artistic process and evolution. From atmospheric and melodic tracks to heavy-hitting bass bangers, these unreleased tracks have become sought-after pieces of Zeds Dead's discography.

Songs with Personal Significance

Within Zeds Dead's discography, there are several songs that hold deep personal significance for the duo. "Collapse 2.0" is a reimagining of their hit track "Collapse," featuring iconic rapper Jadakiss and vocalist Styles P. This collaboration not only highlights Zeds Dead's ability to bridge the gap between electronic and hip-hop music but also pays homage to their love for rap and urban culture.

Compilation Appearances and Side Projects

Zeds Dead's music extends beyond their individual releases, with compilation appearances and side projects that further showcase their versatility and creativity. Their appearances on respected compilation albums, such as the "UKF Dubstep" series, demonstrate their impact on the genre. Additionally, side projects like their collaboration with Jauz on the track "Lights Go Down" highlight Zeds Dead's willingness to explore different sounds and work with diverse artists.

A Celebration of Zeds Dead's Legacy

Zeds Dead's music has left an indelible mark on the electronic music scene, influencing countless artists and shaping the direction of the genre. Their ability to seamlessly blend different genres, push boundaries, and create emotionally charged tracks has earned them a dedicated fan base and critical acclaim. As we look back on the music of Zeds Dead, we celebrate their lasting legacy and eagerly anticipate the exciting musical journey that lies ahead.

In conclusion, Zeds Dead's music is a celebration of creativity, innovation, and artistic vision. Their eclectic discography spans different genres and showcases their ability to captivate listeners with their distinctive sound. From their early breakout tracks to their chart-topping hits, Zeds Dead's music continues to resonate with fans around the world. As they push the boundaries of electronic music and explore new sonic territories, we can expect that their future releases will continue to captivate and inspire. This celebration of Zeds Dead's music is a testament to their artistry and their enduring impact on the music industry.

Timeline: The Journey of Zeds Dead

Early Beginnings and Formation of Zeds Dead

Zeds Dead, an iconic music duo known for their electrifying beats and boundary-pushing sound, came together through a series of serendipitous events that would forever change the electronic music landscape. The story of their formation is a testament to the power of passion, perseverance, and collaboration.

The paths of Dylan Mamid, also known as DC, and Zachary Rapp-Rovan, better known as Hooks, first crossed in the vibrant music scene of Toronto, Canada. Both immersed in the local music culture from a young age, DC and Hooks developed a shared love for various genres, from hip-hop and reggae to electronic dance music.

Their individual journeys in music began during their childhood years. DC, growing up in Toronto, was heavily influenced by the vibrant multiculturalism and the diverse sounds of the city. From an early age, he was drawn to the captivating beats and rhythms that resonated through the streets.

Meanwhile, Hooks, raised in a musical family, had a deep-rooted appreciation for different genres. From his early exposure to his father's vinyl collection and his mother's love for Caribbean beats, Hooks developed a keen ear for music that transcended boundaries.

It was during their teenage years that DC and Hooks discovered their shared passion for DJing. They both started experimenting with turntables and mixers, honing their skills in their bedrooms and local clubs. Each of them was captivated by the power of manipulating sounds and creating a unique sonic experience.

As fate would have it, DC and Hooks eventually crossed paths at a friend's house party. They immediately connected over their love for music, and a creative spark ignited. Recognizing their shared vision and complementary skills, they decided to combine forces and form what would become Zeds Dead.

The name "Zeds Dead" was inspired by Quentin Tarantino's cult classic film "Pulp Fiction." The phrase itself, pronounced as "Zed's Dead," is a reference to a scene in the movie where Uma Thurman's character Mia Wallace exclaims, "Zed's dead, baby. Zed's dead." This catchy name encapsulated the duo's rebellious and unconventional approach to music.

In the early days of Zeds Dead, DC and Hooks started experimenting with remixes, infusing their signature sound into popular tracks. These remixes quickly gained attention online, propelling them into the spotlight and attracting a growing fanbase. Their unique ability to push boundaries and reimagine existing songs set them apart from the crowd.

The burgeoning music scene in Toronto played a crucial role in shaping the sound of Zeds Dead. The city's rich musical history and diverse artistic community inspired the duo to venture beyond the confines of traditional genres. They embraced electronic dance music as a medium to express their creativity and connect with their audience on a deeper level.

With each passing gig, Zeds Dead solidified their reputation as electrifying performers. Their infectious energy and captivating stage presence captivated audiences, leaving them craving more. The duo's ability to seamlessly blend different genres and create an immersive sonic experience elevated their live performances to a whole new level.

As Zeds Dead continued to push boundaries and evolve their sound, their growing international recognition opened doors to collaborate with other renowned artists. Their distinct production techniques and fearless experimentation attracted the attention of industry veterans, who recognized their talent and mentored them along the way.

Their early years were not without their challenges, as Zeds Dead faced criticism and negativity from those who tried to confine their music within a specific genre. However, the duo remained resilient, staying true to their creative vision and maintaining their authenticity.

Zeds Dead's formation marked the beginning of a journey that would forever change the electronic music landscape. From their humble beginnings in Toronto to global recognition, their unique blend of genres, authentic approach, and unwavering dedication to their craft have solidified their place as pioneers of electronic music.

The story of Zeds Dead is a testament to the power of collaboration, fearless experimentation, and embracing the unconventional. Their early beginnings laid the foundation for a legendary career that continues to inspire and influence the next generation of artists in the ever-evolving world of music.

Breakthrough Tracks and First Taste of Success

Ah, the sweet smell of success! For Zeds Dead, it all began with their breakthrough tracks that catapulted them into the spotlight and gave them their first taste of recognition. Let's take a journey back in time and explore some of these monumental moments in their early career.

White Satin - A Game-Changing Remix

In 2009, Zeds Dead released their groundbreaking remix of the classic track "White Satin" by The Moody Blues. This remix served as a turning point for the duo, gaining massive attention from both fans and industry insiders. Their unique blend of dubstep and electronic elements breathed new life into the original song, captivating listeners with its haunting melodies and bone-rattling bass.

The remix quickly spread like wildfire, becoming an instant hit and solidifying Zeds Dead's position as a formidable force in the electronic music scene. It showcased their ability to reimagine iconic songs and inject them with their signature style, setting the stage for their future successes.

Adrenaline EP - Making Waves in the Bass Music Scene

Following the immense success of their "White Satin" remix, Zeds Dead released their highly anticipated debut EP, "Adrenaline," in 2010. This EP showcased their versatility and ability to push boundaries within the bass music genre.

"Adrenaline" struck a chord with fans and critics alike, featuring a diverse range of tracks that spanned genres from dubstep to electro-house. Each song was a sonic journey, characterized by hard-hitting drops, infectious melodies, and impeccable production quality.

Tracks like "Bassmentality" and "Rude Boy" became instant favorites in the bass music community, solidifying Zeds Dead's status as pioneers of the genre. The EP received widespread acclaim, propelling them further into the limelight and opening doors to new opportunities.

Coffee Break - A Collaborative Masterpiece

In 2012, Zeds Dead teamed up with fellow Canadian producer Omar LinX to release their collaborative EP, "Victor." This EP showcased their ability to seamlessly blend genres and push the boundaries of electronic music even further.

One standout track from the EP was "Coffee Break," a mesmerizing fusion of hip-hop, dubstep, and trap influences. The track featured Omar LinX's smooth and captivating vocals layered over Zeds Dead's signature production, creating an irresistible sonic experience.

"Coffee Break" became an instant hit, resonating with fans of various musical backgrounds. The track's infectious energy and catchy hooks propelled Zeds Dead into new territory, showcasing their ability to create genre-defying music that appealed to a wide audience.

Somewhere Else EP - An Evolution of Sound

In 2014, Zeds Dead released their highly anticipated EP, "Somewhere Else," which marked a significant evolution in their sound. This EP expanded their musical horizons, exploring different genres and experimenting with new production techniques.

Tracks like "Lost You" featuring Twin Shadow and "Collapse" featuring Memorecks demonstrated Zeds Dead's ability to seamlessly blend electronic elements with catchy pop hooks. These tracks showcased a more refined and mature sound, earning critical acclaim and further solidifying their place in the music industry.

The "Somewhere Else" EP allowed Zeds Dead to reach new heights and attract a broader fan base. It demonstrated their willingness to take risks and bring fresh ideas to the table, setting the stage for their continued success.

Hot Sauce EP - Igniting Dance Floors

In 2016, Zeds Dead released their highly anticipated EP, "Hot Sauce." This EP was a game-changer, igniting dance floors worldwide with its infectious energy and innovative production.

Tracks like "Blame" featuring Diplo and Elliphant and "Frontlines" featuring NGHTMRE showcased Zeds Dead's ability to fuse elements of bass music, trap, and future bass into a cohesive and captivating sound. The EP demonstrated their versatility and ability to navigate different subgenres while staying true to their unique style.

"Hot Sauce" received widespread acclaim from fans and critics, solidifying Zeds Dead's position as heavyweights in the electronic music scene. It further expanded their fan base and established them as trendsetters within the industry.

MegaCollab - "Bumpy Teeth"

In 2020, Zeds Dead joined forces with Subtronics for the release of their highly anticipated collaboration, "Bumpy Teeth." This track brought together two powerhouses of bass music, creating a sonic explosion that shook the scene to its core.

"Bumpy Teeth" showcased Zeds Dead and Subtronics' shared passion for hard-hitting drops and mind-bending sound design. The track's relentless energy, gritty basslines, and infectious melodies quickly made it a fan favorite.

The collaboration further cemented Zeds Dead's reputation as leading innovators in the bass music genre. It demonstrated their ability to collaborate with like-minded artists and continue to push the boundaries of their sound.

Conquering the Charts

Throughout their career, Zeds Dead has achieved remarkable success on the charts. Their tracks have consistently topped the charts on platforms like Beatport, iTunes, and Spotify, earning them international recognition and a dedicated following.

Their ability to create music that resonates with fans from all walks of life has been a key factor in their chart success. From their remixes that rejuvenated classic songs to their EPs that showcased their artistic growth, Zeds Dead has consistently delivered groundbreaking tracks that have left a lasting impact on the music scene.

The Momentum Continues

These breakthrough tracks marked just the beginning of Zeds Dead's journey to success. Their relentless dedication to pushing boundaries, evolving their sound, and connecting with fans has paved the way for even greater achievements.

In the next section, we'll delve deeper into their discography, exploring their studio albums, mixtapes, collaborations, and more. Get ready to dive into the vast ocean of Zeds Dead's music, where every beat has a story to tell.

Major Milestones and Achievements

The journey of Zeds Dead has been marked by numerous major milestones and achievements that have solidified their place in the electronic music scene. Let's take a closer look at some of the most significant moments in their career:

Breakthrough Tracks and First Taste of Success

Zeds Dead burst onto the electronic music scene with a series of breakthrough tracks that quickly gained attention and propelled them to the forefront of the genre. Their early releases like "White Satin" and "Eyes on Fire" showcased their unique production style, blending elements of dubstep, drum and bass, and hip-hop into a distinct sound that captivated listeners.

As their fanbase began to grow, Zeds Dead caught the attention of renowned DJs and producers, receiving praise from the likes of Skrillex and Diplo. Their collaborations with artists such as Omar LinX on tracks like "Out for Blood" and "Cowboy" further solidified their reputation as innovative creators.

With their distinct blend of heavy basslines, intricate melodies, and infectious energy, Zeds Dead quickly became known for their dynamic and genre-defying sound.

Major Milestones and Achievements

One of the major milestones in Zeds Dead's career was the release of their debut album, "Northern Lights," in 2016. The album showcased their versatility as producers, featuring collaborations with a diverse range of artists including Twin Shadow, Rivers Cuomo, and Diplo. It debuted at number 2 on the Billboard Dance/Electronic Albums chart, a significant achievement for an independent electronic music act.

In 2017, Zeds Dead achieved another major milestone with the launch of their own record label, Deadbeats. The label provided them with a platform to release their own music, as well as support and nurture emerging talent in the electronic music scene. Through Deadbeats, Zeds Dead have curated an impressive catalog of releases, further cementing their influence and impact on the industry.

Furthermore, Zeds Dead's performances at iconic music festivals such as Coachella, Electric Daisy Carnival, and Ultra Music Festival have been widely regarded as career-defining moments. Their high-energy sets, combined with their seamless mixing and engaging stage presence, have earned them a dedicated fanbase and solidified their status as elite live performers.

Another major achievement for Zeds Dead was the release of their widely acclaimed sophomore album, "Northern Lights: Remixed," in 2017. The album featured remixes of their original tracks by a diverse range of talented producers, including Ganja White Night, Nebbra, and DNMO. This remix album further showcased their ability to collaborate with and inspire other artists, while also highlighting their commitment to continually pushing musical boundaries.

Chart Successes and Industry Recognition

Zeds Dead's impact on the charts cannot be understated. Their releases consistently reach the top of the electronic music charts, with singles like "Lost You" and "Collapse" receiving widespread acclaim and airplay. These successes have solidified their status as influential figures in the electronic music landscape.

In addition to their chart success, Zeds Dead has garnered industry recognition and accolades. They have been nominated for multiple awards, including the Juno Awards for Electronic Album of the Year and the International Dance Music Awards for Best Dubstep/Drum & Bass Track. These nominations reflect the respect and admiration their peers have for their craft.

Evolution of Sound and Artistic Growth

One of the most significant achievements of Zeds Dead is their ability to continually reinvent and evolve their sound. They have successfully navigated through various subgenres of electronic music, experimenting with elements of house, future bass, and trap, among others. This openness to innovation and exploration has allowed them to stay at the forefront of the ever-changing electronic music landscape.

Their artistic growth is evident in their collaborations with a diverse array of artists, showcasing their versatility and willingness to step outside their comfort zone. Their work with artists like Jauz, Illenium, and Rezz demonstrates their ability to adapt and push the boundaries of their own sound while still staying true to their musical roots.

Impact on Music and Culture

Beyond their own musical achievements, Zeds Dead's impact on music and culture is far-reaching. They have inspired a new generation of producers and artists, encouraging them to think outside the box and experiment with different genres and styles. Their genre-defying sound has helped redefine the boundaries of electronic music, paving the way for new possibilities and innovations.

Zeds Dead's dedication to connecting with their fanbase and fostering a sense of community has also had a significant impact. Through their music and live performances, they create a shared experience that transcends traditional boundaries and brings people together. This sense of unity and inclusivity is a testament to the power of music as a unifying force.

In conclusion, Zeds Dead has achieved numerous milestones and accomplishments throughout their career. From breakout tracks and chart successes to artistic growth and impact on the electronic music scene, they continue to push boundaries and leave a lasting legacy. Their willingness to evolve, collaborate, and experiment sets them apart and ensures that their influence on music and culture will continue to resonate for years to come.

Collaborations and International Recognition

Collaborations have played a crucial role in the journey of Zeds Dead, shaping their sound and widening their reach in the global music scene. From working with like-minded artists to tapping into different genres, these collaborations have been instrumental in propelling Zeds Dead to international recognition.

One of the most notable collaborations in the early days of Zeds Dead was with Omar LinX, a talented rapper and songwriter. Together, they released the EP "Victor," which showcased the blend of electronic music and rap that would become a signature element of Zeds Dead's sound. Tracks like "Out for Blood" and "Coffee Break" resonated with fans and marked the beginning of a fruitful creative partnership.

Another significant collaboration for Zeds Dead came in the form of their remix of "Twin Shadow" by Slow Down. This remix caught the attention of the indie rock community and demonstrated Zeds Dead's ability to transform and reimagine existing tracks. It was through this remix that they began to gain recognition beyond the electronic music realm.

As Zeds Dead's popularity grew, so did the variety of their collaborations. They joined forces with Diplo and Elliphant on the track "Blame" and with Hunter Siegel on "Lost You." These collaborations allowed Zeds Dead to experiment with different sounds and expand their musical horizons.

International recognition came knocking on Zeds Dead's door with their collaboration with Dirtyphonics on the track "Where Are You Now." This collaboration perfectly blended Zeds Dead's bass-heavy style with Dirtyphonics' energetic and hard-hitting sound. The track became an instant hit, propelling Zeds Dead into the forefront of the global bass music scene.

Another key collaboration that contributed to their international success was their remix of "Eyes On Fire" by Blue Foundation. This remix gained massive popularity and became a staple in their live performances. It showcased their ability to transform a haunting indie track into an electrifying dancefloor anthem.

Beyond individual collaborations, Zeds Dead has also actively engaged in collaborative projects with other artists. They established the label and artist collective, Deadbeats, which provides a platform for upcoming talent and allows Zeds Dead to foster a sense of community within the music industry. Through Deadbeats, they have collaborated with a diverse range of artists and released music that pushes boundaries and defies genres.

In the realm of international recognition, Zeds Dead's electrifying live performances have played a pivotal role. They have graced renowned festivals such as Coachella, Tomorrowland, and Electric Daisy Carnival, captivating audiences with their dynamic stage presence and immersive visual productions. Their ability to connect with fans from all corners of the globe has solidified their status as one of the most sought-after live acts in the electronic music world.

Furthermore, Zeds Dead's tireless dedication to pushing musical boundaries and cultivating a unique sound has garnered praise and recognition from industry veterans and peers. They have been nominated for several prestigious awards, including the Juno Awards and the International Dance Music Awards, further solidifying their place in the global music landscape.

The international recognition of Zeds Dead is a testament to their talent and hard work. Through their collaborations and unparalleled live performances, they have not only embraced diverse musical styles but have also left an indelible mark on the electronic music genre. As they continue to evolve and explore new creative avenues, the global music community eagerly awaits the next chapter of their musical journey.

Collaboration Caveat: Nurturing Creativity and Mutual Respect

Collaborations in the music industry can be a double-edged sword. While they can spark creativity and lead to great musical achievements, they can also present challenges if not approached with mutual respect and a shared vision.

One important caveat for successful collaborations is the need to nurture creativity. Each collaborating artist brings their unique perspective and talent to the table, and it is essential to foster an environment that allows for open and organic exploration. This means respecting each other's creative input and being open to new ideas, even if they differ from one's own initial vision.

To maintain a fruitful collaboration, clear communication is key. Establishing shared goals and expectations from the outset can prevent misunderstandings and ensure that everyone is working towards a mutually satisfying outcome. Regular check-ins and open dialogue throughout the creative process can help navigate any potential roadblocks and facilitate a harmonious working relationship.

Respect for each other's artistic vision is crucial in any collaboration. It is important to strike a balance between incorporating each artist's individual style and creating a cohesive final product. This requires trust and a willingness to compromise, keeping in mind the overarching vision of the project.

Collaborations also require a level of adaptability and compromise when it comes to merging different musical styles and influences. Finding a middle ground where the unique qualities of each artist can coexist harmoniously can result in the creation of something truly extraordinary.

Ultimately, successful collaborations stem from a foundation of mutual respect and shared passion for creating great music. By embracing these principles, Zeds Dead has been able to forge enduring creative partnerships and achieve international recognition for their collaborative projects.

Evolution of the Zeds Dead Sound

The evolution of Zeds Dead's sound is a testament to the duo's ability to adapt and push the boundaries of electronic music. From their early days to their current success, Zeds Dead has consistently evolved their sound, incorporating new genres, styles, and production techniques. This section explores the journey of the Zeds Dead sound and how it has evolved over the years.

Influences from Different Decades

To understand the evolution of Zeds Dead's sound, we must first dive into the influences that have shaped their music. Drawing from a rich musical heritage, Zeds Dead incorporates elements from different decades into their productions. From the golden era of hip-hop to the ethereal vibes of the 80s, their sound reflects a melting pot of eclectic influences.

The duo's early exposure to influential artists such as The Prodigy, The Chemical Brothers, and Massive Attack laid the foundation for their exploration of electronic music. These pioneers of the genre inspired Zeds Dead to experiment with different textures, rhythms, and sonic landscapes.

Exploring Different Subgenres of Electronic Music

As Zeds Dead gained momentum in the music scene, they sought to break out of the confines of one specific genre. Rather than conforming to a single style, they embraced the opportunity to explore different subgenres of electronic music, bringing their unique touch to each.

Dubstep played a significant role in shaping Zeds Dead's early sound. They drew inspiration from the heavy basslines and hard-hitting drops that defined the genre. Tracks like "Rude Boy" and "Eyelove" showcased their ability to create powerful, energetic dubstep anthems.

However, Zeds Dead didn't stop there. Their music branched out into other subgenres such as drum and bass, future bass, and even house. This versatility allowed them to collaborate with a wide range of artists and explore new sonic landscapes.

Collaborative Projects and Side Ventures

Zeds Dead's evolution is not limited to their own productions. Collaborative projects and side ventures have played a significant role in shaping their sound. By teaming up with other artists, they have been able to experiment and incorporate fresh perspectives into their music.

One notable collaborative project is Zeds Dead's partnership with Omar LinX, a skilled rapper and vocalist. Their collaboration resulted in the critically acclaimed "Victor" EP, combining hard-hitting beats with Omar LinX's raw, captivating lyrics. This project demonstrated their ability to merge different genres seamlessly.

Aside from collaborations, Zeds Dead's side ventures have also expanded their musical horizons. Their label, Deadbeats, provides a platform for up-and-coming artists and allows them to explore diverse sounds. Through Deadbeats, Zeds Dead has released compilation albums and supported emerging talent, further influencing the trajectory of electronic music.

The Influence of Non-Musical Art Forms

Zeds Dead's evolution goes beyond traditional musical influences. They draw inspiration from various non-musical art forms, including visual art, film, and literature. By incorporating these influences into their creative process, Zeds Dead has cultivated a unique and immersive sound.

Visual art plays a significant role in shaping the atmospheric quality of Zeds Dead's music. They often collaborate with visual artists to create captivating album artwork, music videos, and stage designs. These visuals amplify the emotional impact of their music, offering a multi-sensory experience for their audience.

Film also holds a special place in Zeds Dead's creative process. They have cited movies like Blade Runner and Apocalypse Now as sources of inspiration for their sound. By capturing the essence of these films and translating them into their music, Zeds Dead creates a cinematic experience that transcends traditional electronic music.

The Role of Technology in Sound Evolution

Technology has been a driving force behind Zeds Dead's sound evolution. As advancements in music production software and hardware continue to emerge, Zeds Dead embraces these tools to craft their unique sonic landscapes.

The duo constantly pushes the boundaries of sound design and production techniques. They experiment with different plugins, synthesizers, and effects to create distinctive sounds that set them apart from their contemporaries. This emphasis on technological innovation allows Zeds Dead to constantly evolve their sound and stay at the forefront of electronic music.

The Sound of Zeds Dead in the Future

With each new release, Zeds Dead continues to push the boundaries of electronic music. Their evolution is a testament to their growth as artists and their desire to explore new musical frontiers.

As they look to the future, Zeds Dead will undoubtedly continue to experiment with different genres, collaborate with diverse artists, and draw inspiration from various forms of art. Their commitment to innovation and their ability to create immersive experiences will shape the sound of Zeds Dead for years to come.

Unconventional Example

To illustrate Zeds Dead's evolution, let's take an unconventional example. Imagine Zeds Dead collaborating with a renowned contemporary classical composer to create a symphonic masterpiece. This collaboration would fuse the electronic elements of Zeds Dead's sound with the rich textures and emotive qualities of an orchestra.

By combining the raw energy of electronic music with the nuanced complexity of classical music, Zeds Dead would venture into new sonic territory. This unconventional collaboration would challenge the conventions of both genres and showcase Zeds Dead's willingness to explore uncharted musical waters.

Summary

The evolution of the Zeds Dead sound can be attributed to a combination of influences from different decades, exploration of subgenres, collaborative projects, non-musical art inspirations, and technological advancements. As Zeds Dead embraces these elements, their sound continues to evolve, pushing the boundaries of electronic music and carving out a unique space that is unmistakably their own. The future holds exciting possibilities for Zeds Dead, as they continue to shape the landscape of electronic music with their innovative approach and unwavering passion.

Influence on Music and Culture

The music of Zeds Dead has had a significant impact on both the music industry and popular culture. Through their unique sound and boundary-pushing creativity, Zeds Dead has left an indelible mark on the world of electronic music. In this section, we will explore how Zeds Dead has influenced music and culture in various ways.

Pushing Boundaries and Challenging Conventions

One of the key aspects of Zeds Dead's influence on music is their ability to push boundaries and challenge conventions. They have never been afraid to experiment with different genres, fuse diverse styles, and create a sound that is uniquely their own.

By blending elements of dubstep, hip-hop, reggae, and other genres, Zeds Dead has not only expanded the sonic palette of electronic music but has also inspired a new generation of artists to think outside the box. Their willingness to take risks and explore unconventional musical territory has opened doors for countless musicians who are now forging their own innovative paths.

Breaking Down Genre Barriers

Zeds Dead's music has transcended traditional genre boundaries, appealing to fans from various musical backgrounds. They have successfully bridged the gap between electronic music and other genres, making their music accessible to a wide audience.

Their collaborations with artists from different genres, such as Omar LinX, Ganja White Night, and Illenium, have further solidified their position as boundary-pushers. These collaborations have not only introduced their fans to new sounds but have also exposed fans of other genres to the world of electronic music.

Inspiring a New Generation of Artists

Zeds Dead's unique sound and innovative approach have inspired a new generation of artists to experiment with their own music. Their ability to create emotionally charged tracks while maintaining a hard-hitting bass-driven sound has become a blueprint for many aspiring producers.

By demonstrating that electronic music can be both emotionally evocative and sonically powerful, Zeds Dead has encouraged young artists to think beyond the limitations of their chosen genre. This inspiration has led to the emergence of new styles and subgenres within electronic music, further enriching the music landscape.

The Global Reach of Zeds Dead's Music

Zeds Dead's influence on music extends far beyond their home country of Canada. Their music has garnered international recognition, with fans from all corners of the globe embracing their unique sound.

Their touring schedule has taken them to major music festivals and venues around the world, allowing them to connect with fans from different cultures and backgrounds. This global reach has not only expanded their fanbase but has also contributed to the globalization of electronic music.

Connecting with a Diverse Fanbase

Zeds Dead's music has resonated with fans from all walks of life, transcending barriers of age, gender, and cultural background. Their ability to create music that elicits strong emotions while maintaining a high-energy vibe has allowed them to connect with a diverse fanbase.

Through their music, Zeds Dead has created a sense of community among their fans. Their shows become a gathering place for people who share a passion for music and a love for their unique sound. This sense of community has fostered a deeper connection between the artists and their fans, creating a loyal and dedicated following.

Shaping Music Culture and Trends

Zeds Dead's influence on music culture and trends cannot be overstated. Their unique sound and innovative approach have shaped the direction of electronic music, inspiring other artists and shaping the evolution of the genre.

Their use of heavy basslines, melodic hooks, and diverse musical influences has become a template for many producers in the electronic music scene. This influence has led to the emergence of a new wave of artists who are exploring similar sonic territories.

A Lasting Legacy

As Zeds Dead continues to push the boundaries of electronic music, their influence on music and culture will only continue to grow. Their willingness to take risks and experiment with different styles has paved the way for new artists to explore their own creative boundaries.

With their music resonating with audiences around the world, Zeds Dead has left an enduring legacy in the world of electronic music. Their contributions to the genre will be remembered and celebrated for years to come.

In conclusion, Zeds Dead's influence on music and culture is undeniable. Through their ability to push boundaries, break down genre barriers, and inspire a new generation of artists, they have made a lasting impact on the world of electronic music. Their unique sound and innovative approach continue to shape the music industry and inspire musicians around the globe. As they continue on their musical journey, Zeds Dead's influence will undoubtedly continue to define the future of electronic music.

Exploration of Different Art Forms

In addition to their groundbreaking music, Zeds Dead has also delved into different art forms, showcasing their creativity and pushing boundaries beyond just the realm of sound. From visual art to multimedia experiences, they have continuously explored new avenues for artistic expression. This section explores some of the art forms that Zeds Dead has explored throughout their career.

Visual Art and Multimedia

Zeds Dead's passion for art extends beyond just their music. They have collaborated with visual artists to create stunning and captivating visual experiences that complement their sonic landscapes. By incorporating visual elements into their live shows, Zeds Dead creates a multi-sensory experience that immerses the audience in their music.

One example of their exploration of visual art is their collaboration with renowned artist Scott Pagano for their "Deadbeats: The Revival" tour. Pagano designed mesmerizing visuals and stage setups that transformed their performances into immersive audiovisual spectacles. The combination of intricate stage design, captivating lighting effects, and synchronized visuals created a one-of-a-kind experience for fans, blurring the line between music and art.

Collaborations with Dance and Performance Art

Zeds Dead has also explored collaborations with dance and performance art, fusing their music with the physicality and emotions of movement. By collaborating with choreographers and dancers, they have expanded their artistic horizons, combining music and dance to create powerful and compelling performances.

One notable collaboration was their partnership with renowned dance company Alonzo King LINES Ballet. Zeds Dead composed an original score that served as the foundation for a mesmerizing contemporary ballet performance. This unique collaboration showcased the harmonious interplay between music and dance, creating a truly captivating and transformative experience for the audience.

Exploring Alternative Mediums

In addition to visual art and dance collaborations, Zeds Dead has also explored other alternative artistic mediums to express their creativity. They have dabbled in short films, animation, and even virtual reality experiences, embracing emerging technologies to push the boundaries of their art.

For example, they released a music video for their track "Lost You" that incorporated elements of animation. The visually stunning video, created in collaboration with artists from the animation studio Bento Box, featured a captivating storyline that complemented the music perfectly.

Incorporating Art into Merchandise

Zeds Dead's creativity is not limited to their music and live performances; they have also extended their artistic vision to their merchandise. The design and aesthetics of their merchandise reflect their unique brand and artistic style, making it more than just typical band merchandise.

They have collaborated with graphic designers and artists to create limited edition merchandise that bridges the gap between art and fashion. The marriage of their iconic logo and visual art creates merchandise that not only showcases their music but also serves as a wearable piece of art.

Pushing the Boundaries

Throughout their career, Zeds Dead has continuously pushed the boundaries of what it means to be an artist in the electronic music scene. By exploring different art forms and collaborating with artists from various disciplines, they have expanded the horizons of their artistic expression.

Zeds Dead's exploration of different art forms serves as an inspiration for aspiring artists to think outside the box and embrace the possibilities of interdisciplinary collaboration. By breaking down the barriers between music, visual art, dance, and other mediums, they have created a new wave of artistic innovation and creativity.

Culmination of a Creative Journey

Zeds Dead's exploration of different art forms is a testament to their commitment to pushing artistic boundaries. Their ability to seamlessly fuse music with visual art, dance, and alternative mediums has not only created unique experiences for their fans but also transformed the way we perceive and appreciate art.

Their artistry goes beyond just creating music; it is a multi-dimensional experience that captivates the senses and transcends conventional boundaries. Zeds Dead's exploration of different art forms is a testament to their relentless pursuit of creativity and their desire to bring something fresh and innovative to the table.

As their journey continues to unfold, one can only imagine the new frontiers they will explore and the innovative art forms they will embrace. Zeds Dead's commitment to exploring new avenues for artistic expression ensures that their legacy will continue to evolve and inspire future generations of artists.

Building a Legacy and Leaving a Lasting Impact

Building a legacy requires more than just creating great music—it's about leaving a lasting impact on the music industry and the wider culture. Zeds Dead has achieved this by pushing boundaries, inspiring others, and challenging the status quo. In this section, we explore how Zeds Dead has built their legacy and the ways in which they have left an indelible mark on music and beyond.

Pioneering New Sounds and Styles

Zeds Dead has always been at the forefront of innovation when it comes to sound and style. They have constantly pushed the boundaries of electronic music, fusing different genres to create a unique and distinctive sound. By blending elements of dubstep, hip-hop, reggae, and more, they have pioneered a new hybrid genre of electronic music that is both hard-hitting and melodic.

Their willingness to experiment with different styles and genres has not only allowed them to evolve as artists, but it has also influenced the wider music scene. Many up-and-coming artists have been inspired by Zeds Dead's eclectic sound, leading to the emergence of a new wave of experimental electronic music.

Breaking Down Genre Barriers

One of the most significant ways in which Zeds Dead has left a lasting impact on music is by breaking down genre barriers. They have shown that music can transcend traditional labels and classifications, instead focusing on creating a sound that resonates with a diverse audience.

By embracing a range of musical influences and refusing to be confined by genre conventions, Zeds Dead has challenged the notion that artists must fit into a specific box. Their music transcends boundaries and offers a refreshing approach to electronic music. This has not only expanded the possibilities for other artists but has also opened doors for listeners to explore new sounds and genres.

Inspiring a New Generation of Artists

Zeds Dead's innovative approach to music has inspired a new generation of artists. Their willingness to experiment with different styles and sounds has encouraged other artists to think outside the box and push the limits of their own creativity.

Through collaborations and mentorship, Zeds Dead has actively nurtured young talent, providing a platform for emerging artists to showcase their skills and gain exposure. By mentoring and supporting these artists, Zeds Dead has ensured that their influence goes beyond their own music and endures in the work of others.

Connecting with a Diverse Fanbase

Zeds Dead's music has resonated with a wide range of listeners, transcending demographics and uniting fans from all walks of life. Their ability to connect with such a diverse fanbase has been a testament to the universal power of music and the emotional depth of their compositions.

Whether at their energetic live shows or through their online presence, Zeds Dead has created a sense of community among their fans. This connection has fostered a loyal following that extends beyond their music, as fans become not just listeners but ambassadors for Zeds Dead's unique sound and vision.

Shaping Music Culture and Trends

With their groundbreaking music and bold artistic vision, Zeds Dead has played a significant role in shaping music culture and trends. Their genre-defying sound has influenced the direction of electronic music, leading other artists to explore new sonic territories.

Moreover, Zeds Dead's visual aesthetic has also made an impact on music culture. From their album artwork to their stage design, they have consistently pushed the boundaries of visual art in the context of music. By collaborating with visual artists and incorporating immersive visual experiences into their live shows, they have elevated the overall concert experience and set new standards for live performances.

A Lasting Legacy

Zeds Dead's legacy goes beyond their chart-topping hits and critical acclaim. Their impact on the music industry and culture as a whole is enduring and far-reaching. By pioneering new sounds and breaking down genre barriers, inspiring a new generation of artists, connecting with a diverse fanbase, and shaping music culture and trends, Zeds Dead has cemented their place in music history.

As they continue to evolve and push the boundaries of their sound, Zeds Dead is leaving a lasting legacy that will inspire future generations of artists. Their commitment to creativity, innovation, and authenticity ensures that their music will continue to resonate with listeners and stand the test of time.

Conclusion

In this chapter, we have explored the remarkable journey of Zeds Dead, from their humble beginnings to their status as electronic music pioneers. We have delved into their unique sound, their creative process, and the impact they have had on music and culture. Through their innovative approach, they have built a legacy that reaches far beyond their music, inspiring others and leaving an indelible mark on the industry. As we move forward, it is clear that Zeds Dead's legacy will continue to shape the future of electronic music and beyond.

Looking Forward to the Future of Zeds Dead

As we look ahead to the future of Zeds Dead, we see a bold and innovative path unfolding, with the potential to shape the electronic music landscape in exciting and unexpected ways. Building on their previous successes and the legacy they have established, Zeds Dead is poised to continue pushing boundaries, challenging conventions, and inspiring the next generation of artists.

One of the key aspects of Zeds Dead's future lies in their musical evolution and exploration. True to their nature as artists, Zeds Dead is unafraid to venture into new genres and styles, always seeking to expand their sonic palette. By embracing new sounds and incorporating elements from various musical backgrounds, they will continue to defy genres and create a unique blend that is unmistakably their own.

Collaborative projects and experimentation will also play a significant role in shaping the future of Zeds Dead. Throughout their career, Zeds Dead has embraced collaborations with other artists, from established musicians to up-and-coming talents. By partnering with a diverse range of creative minds, they will tap into new ideas and fresh perspectives, resulting in groundbreaking musical creations that push the boundaries of electronic music.

In addition to their musical journey, Zeds Dead will continue to explore new avenues of artistic expression and visual innovation. The power of visual art forms, such as album artwork, music videos, and stage design, has always been an integral part of Zeds Dead's identity. Looking ahead, they will continually push the envelope in these areas, collaborating with visual artists and designers to create immersive and captivating experiences that complement their music.

The future of live performances is another aspect that holds great potential for Zeds Dead. With their already energetic and captivating shows, they will incorporate new technologies and interactive elements to create an even more immersive concert atmosphere. From augmented reality to interactive stage setups,

Zeds Dead's live performances will continue to evolve and push the boundaries of what is possible, providing fans with unforgettable experiences.

Beyond their own artistic endeavors, Zeds Dead is committed to supporting and nurturing new artists. They understand the importance of giving back to the music community and will continue to provide mentorship and guidance to aspiring musicians. Through their philanthropic endeavors and social initiatives, they will also use their platform to make a positive impact in the world, championing causes they believe in and pushing for diversity and inclusion in the music industry.

As the world of music continues to evolve, Zeds Dead will navigate the streaming era and embrace emerging technologies. They will adapt to changing musical trends while staying true to their unique sound and style. With their entrepreneurial spirit, they will explore different business ventures and outside collaborations, always seeking new avenues to expand their creative reach.

The enduring legacy of Zeds Dead lies not only in their musical achievements but also in the impact they have had on music culture and trends. They will continue to inspire future generations of artists, leaving a lasting imprint on the electronic music landscape. By challenging industry norms, supporting new talent, and cultivating a strong fan community, Zeds Dead will forever be remembered as pioneers who changed the game.

In conclusion, the future of Zeds Dead is bright and full of promise. With their unwavering passion for music and their fearless exploration of new sonic territories, they will undoubtedly make a significant impact on the electronic music scene for years to come. As fans and admirers, we eagerly anticipate the next chapter of their musical journey, excited to witness the continued growth, innovation, and legacy of Zeds Dead.

Index

9 781779 692726